COLONIAL CUBA

EPISODES FROM FOUR HUNDRED YEARS OF SPANISH DOMINATION

COLECCIÓN CUBA Y SUS JUECES

From the Same Author:

Historia de la Química Industrial
Total Quality and Productivity Management
Performance Management
Strategic Planning
Management Development
Process Improvement Teams
Quality Strategies
Gestión de Futuro
Once Upon a Time (co-author)
Contramaestre
Baraguá
Poetas y Memorias de Cuba
Jimaguayú
Freedom Embattled (co-author)
Republican Cuba
Exiled Cuba
Three Days in March
Guáimaro
Colonial Cuba

EDICIONES UNIVERSAL, Miami, Florida, 2014

The Cathedral of Havana
(The Baroque Roman Catholic Cathedral of the
Virgen María de la Concepción Inmaculada de La Habana)

Its construction was started during Cuban Colonial times in 1748 and finished in 1777. It is set in the former *Plaza de La Ciénaga* (Swamp Plaza), the site where water overflow from the city was allowed to run.
It was designed with asymmetrical features (one of the towers is wider than the other), as most other great Cathedrals in Europe, to signify that perfection is only an attribute of God.

To **Nicolás Samuel**
the youngest in our family
and the most likely to
witness the end of the
XXI century.
May God and Destiny
make you proud to be
an American and
bless you for your
Cuban Ancestry

In Memoriam:
Dr. Samuel Nodarse

RAÚL EDUARDO CHAO

COLONIAL CUBA

Episodes from Four Hundred Years of Spanish Domination

Copyright © 20014 by Raúl Eduardo Chao

Primera edición, 2014
EDICIONES UNIVERSAL
P.O. Box 450353 (Shenandoah Station)
Miami, FL 33245-0353. USA
Tel: (305) 642-3234 Fax: (305) 642-7978
e-mail: ediciones@ediciones.com
http://www.ediciones.com
Library of Congress Catalog Card No.: 2014937057
ISBN-10: 1-59388-260-2
ISBN-13: 978-1-59388-260-0

Front Cover:
The Lighthouse at the entrance of the Harbor of Havana. The 82-foot tower was built by the Spanish Colonial Government in 1845. Behind it, is the historic fort called *Castillo de los Tres Reyes del Morro*, built in 1589 in response to raids on Havana Harbor.

Back Cover:
The *Catedral de la Virgen María de la Concepción Inmaculada de La Habana* (Cathedral of The Virgin Mary of the Immaculate Conception); 1853 hand-colored wood engraving from the collection of the author.

Todos los derechos
son reservados. Ninguna parte de
este libro puede ser reproducida o transmitida
en ninguna forma o por ningún medio electrónico o mecánico,
incluyendo fotocopiadoras, grabadoras o sistemas computarizados,
sin el permiso por escrito del autor, excepto en el caso de
breves citas incorporadas en artículos críticos o en
revistas. Para obtener información diríjase a
Ediciones Universal.

Table of Contents

Prologue — 9

I Pre-Colombian Cuba

1 The First "Discoverers" of the Caribbean — 13
2 Some Essential Facts about the Taino Culture — 20
3 Meanwhile, in the Iberian Peninsula... — 27

II From 1492 to 1506

4 Chirstopher Columbus Chases after a Dream — 37
5 The Future Admiral on the Way to America — 43

III From 1506 to 1600

6 Expansions and Troubles in the Caribbean — 55
7 The Story of Fray Bartolomé de Las Casas — 63
8 Cuba and the Four Great Conquistadores — 73
9 First Successes and Perils for Colonial Cuba — 89
10 A European Perspective of the Conquista — 103
11 Cuba Becomes a Formal Spanish Colony — 116
12 A Chaotic Start for the Colony of Cuba — 128
13 A Shrinking Population Under Chaos — 141

IV From 1600 to 1700

14 A Stable Population with Diminishing Chaos — 159
15 Spain Considers the Worth of Cuba — 168
16 Cuba's Growth Began to Show Up — 179

V From 1700 to 1800

17 The XVIII Century Opens a New Era in Cuba — 197
18 The Effervescense of the XVIII Century in Cuba — 210
19 The British and Sugar Created a New Cuba — 222

VI From 1800 to 1895

20 The Decade when Spain Lost its Empire — 237
21 A Constitution Enlivened Things in Cuba — 250

22 Peaceful Normality Briefly Reurned to Cuba	264
23 Peace and Prosperity Finally Arrive in Cuba	278
24 Cuba Got a Fresh Look but no Independence	294
25 The First Pro-Independence Movements in Cuba	315
26 A Precarious Tranquility in the Late 1800s	330
27 The War Against Spain Exploded in 1868	353
28 The War of 1868 Warms Up	369
29 Madrid Realizes Cuba was Out of Control	387
30 The War of 1868 Comes to an End	405

VII From 1895 until 1898

31 For Cubans, Peace Was Only a Timely Pause	425
32 A New War of Independence Became Inevitable	445
33 Cuban Independence War was Renewed with Brio	462
34 Lots of Progress in the War Front at the Start	484
35 A Strong Succession of Victories for the Cubans	504
36 The Impasse in the War Cannot be Resolved	519
37 At the End, Credit to Win the War Went to the US	536

Epilogue 554

Appendices 556

I	Governors of Colonial Cuba, 1535-1898	557
II	Dupuy de Lôme Letter to Canalejas	561
III	Weyler's Reconcentration Policy	562
IV	Chronolgy of the Slave Trade in the Americas	563
V	October 10, 1868: The Ten Year War Manifesto	564

Alphabetical Index 566

Prologue

THIS BOOK IS THE THIRD in a series of treatises on the history of Cuba; it joins **Republican Cuba** and **Exiled Cuba** to complete a historical perspective extending from a few years before the encounter of Christopher Columbus with the island in 1492 to the end of Spanish domination of Cuba in 1898.

During the 400 years of Spanish presence in Cuba, paraphrasing Fernando Ortiz, Cuba's eminent social anthropologist, Spain's relationship with the island consisted of successive stages of discovery, neglect, rediscovery, colonization, development, exploitation, imposition, late accommodation and final grieving. Cuba's relationship with Spain, on the other hand, also had successive stages of identification, adaptation, reform, autonomy, annexation, independence and, finally, belittlement. Immersed in these two currents of unshared interests, Cubans and Spaniards had to deal with important issues of mutual concerns such as slavery, economic needs and the form of government that could please both sides. We hope this book provides enough substance to unravel and understand the excluding ambitions of these two nwtions over four centuries.

In the end, Cubans had to find for themselves how to carve a new nationality out of an exploitative colonial status. They never suspected that at the end of the Spanish colonial stage, a possible neocolonial status could emerge by the proximity to the United States, as well as a desilusion with their own untested political leaders.

Cuba won its release from Spanish control after bloody and dreadful wars, yet it faced an uncomfortable and unwelcomed tutelage from its neighbor to the north. Regardless of whether it was benign or oppressive, Cuba was never able to force it out of its body politic. It ended up consuming its energies and its political initiatives. In many minds it led to a constant deprecation of both Spain's *de jure* control and American *de facto* control for years before its independence. Among many others, it left unresolved three issues that have never been elucidated: Would the US have lost the 1898 War without the Cuban armies? Could Cuba have won independence without American intervention? Why did Cuba disconnect from the rest of Hispanic America to the extent that throughout its five centuries of life (Colonial, Republican and Exile Cuba) not one Latin American country has helped in its struggle for freedom?

It has not been easy to reduce the history of 400 years of *Colonial Cuba* into 550 pages. Many good friends and colleagues have contributed to these volumes with their comments, their insights and prized images. This author is eternally grateful for their interest, their generosity and their wisdom. He also hopes the reader will get to know Cuba a little better.

RAÚL EDUARDO CHAO
CORAL GABLES, FLORIDA
MAY 2014

Pre-Colombian Cuba

A Taino gathering along the Mayabeque river, early 1400s

1
The First "Discoverers" of the Caribbean

WHEN COLUMBUS LANDED in the Bahamas on October 12, 1492, his first encounter was with simple communities populating the entire Caribbean; we know them today as the Tainos. They were pacific and gentle seafaring indigenous people under constant raids and siege by rather large tribes of Caribes, who were ferocious rivals from southern continental areas. [1] In spite of this tenacious threat, the Tainos had developed a distinct language and culture. Columbus described them as "physically tall, handsome, pacific, helpful and with a gentle personality." He once explained, on a letter to Fernando I of Spain:

«They traded with us and, with good will, gave us everything they had... they took great delight in pleasing us... They are very gentle and without any evil traits; they never murder or steal... I can assure Your Highness that in all the world there can be no better people... They love their neighbors as themselves, and they have a much more sweet and musical talk than us; they are always gentle and always laughing.»

In 1492, Tainos were found in every one of Columbus' stops around the Caribbean region. But the Tainos were not there by themselves. In the western tip of Cuba, the Tainos shared the lands of the Guanahatabeyes. In the Lesser Antilles, there were numerous Caribes, from Guadeloupe to Grenada, and in Florida there were Timacua and Ais tribes peacefully sharing their territories with the Tainos.

---

[1] The *Taínos* were historically enemies of the neighboring *Caribe* tribes, another group with origins in South America who lived mainly in the eastern Antilles. For much of the 15th century, the *Taíno* tribes were being driven to the western islands in the Caribbean (north of South America) because of raids by the *Caribes*. The *Caribes* were ferocious warmongers, sadistic, and adept at using poison-tipped arrows. They took women as captives, resulting in many *Taino* women speaking *Caribe* languages. Men were frequently captured and sacrificed, made slaves, or prized as bodies for the rites of cannibalism of the *Caribes*.

The Taíno called *Guanahaní* the first island where Columbus landed; Columbus renamed it *San Salvador*. [2] Columbus called the Taíno "Indians", a reference to his well known goal of finding a path to Asia. With time, this designation grew up to encompass all the native peoples of the Western Hemisphere. Columbus also developed a fondness for the Taino. A group of Taíno guests, men and women, accompanied him on his return voyage back to an expected fabulous reception in the court of Spain.

The Tainos, simple men and women as they were, had a well defined social structure. [3] The island of Cuba was divided into large dominions held by great rulers who evidently exerted substantial power; they were at the tip of an elaborate complex social pyramid. Under these great rulers there were several smaller chiefs and leaders, an intermediate middle class of free landholders, and a bottom rung of indentured servants, vassals and slaves. Most likely, the individual positions in the social scale were hereditary; only an individual's valiant defense of the tribe provided access to a higher rank.

In 1516 Fray Bartolomé de Las Casas sent Cardinal Cisneros a relation of peoples residing in the island of Cuba. It included five sorts of tribes:

The **Lucayans**; they were imported slaves from the Bahamas.

The fisher-folk of the many small keys around Cuba, who were not given a specific name or origin. They were occasional residents without roots.

---

[2] Spanish for Holy Savior, a reflection on Columbus' desperation to find an end to his own discomfort and his gratitude for God's timely prevention of a possible mutiny by his men.

[3] Contrary to what was believed until the 1950s, modern developments in ethnology, paleontology, anthropology, linguistics and DNA caracterization processes have shown the *Taino* to be a much more complex and enduring civilization than originally thought.

The *Guanahatabeyes*, also known as Guanatabeyes; a rude and anti-social, non-agricultural group living in the western end of the Island. [4]

The *Siboneyes* (or Ciboneyes),[5] similar to the fisher-folk, but permanent residents; too tame and largely held in bondage by the Tainos.

The *Tainos*, [6] the more advanced and dominant group, many of them former residents of the island of *Hispaniola*.

The Tainos were one of several Arawak peoples of South America and the Taíno language was a branch of the Arawakan language family of northern South America. Linguistically, the more advanced tribes spoke Lokono, the native Arawak language of Guyana. Scholars nowadays agree that Taino, or at least its Xaragua form, was the general speech of *Hispaniola* and parts of Cuba when the Spaniards arrived.

At the time of Columbus' arrival in 1492, there were five settlements or autonomous jurisdictions of Tainos on Hispaniola (today's Haiti and Dominican Republic), each led by a principal Cacique (chieftain), to whom significant tributes were paid. In Cuba, the largest island on the Antilles, 29 separate such jurisdictions existed; some of these native inhabited locations that later became Spanish cities retaining the original Taino names: Havana, Batabanó, Camagüey, Baracoa and Bayamo.

Of all the natives from the Caribbean islands, the Caribes were the ones who fought most effectively against the Spaniards; their behavior led Colón and other Spanish Conquista-

---

[4] It would not be far fetched to think of *Guanahatabeyes* as the "barbarians" in *Taino* times. They lived side by side with the *Tainos* in western Cuba but left behind no record whatsoever of their culture.

[5] The name *Siboney* means "cave dweller" in *Taino* language. Most *Siboney* people lived in caves. To this day it is not known how the *Siboneyes* arrived to the Caribbean.

[6] The word *Taino* means "good" in the Xaragua language predominantly spoken by the natives peoples of Cuba, Puerto Rico and *Hispaniola*.

dores to unfairly attribute warlike tendencies to all of the island's tribes, including the Tainos.

Two hypotheses have emerged as to the region from South America from where the Tainos came from,:

Some ethnologists contend that the ancestors of the Taíno came from the center of the Amazon Basin, went north of the Orinoco valley and reached the West Indies by way of Guyana and Venezuela. From there they migrated to the Lesser Antilles, then Cuba and finally the Bahamas. This hypothesis is supported by numerous similarities found in the Taino area with the ancestral cultures and language of the Orinoco Valley and the Amazon Basin.

A second hypothesis contends that the ancestors of the Taíno originated in the Colombian Andes and migrated from the Andes to the West Indies and Central America, the Guyana, Venezuela, and the Amazon Basin of South America. The Taíno traditions (their creation story, for instance) postulates that they emerged from caves in a sacred mountain on present-day Hispaniola.

Over the course of one century, the Tainos became almost extinct in Cuba and the rest of the Caribbean. The main culprit were diseases rather than enslavement, warfare and cruelty on the part of the Spanish colonists.[7] By the end of the XVI century, fewer that 500 full-bloded Tainos were left in Cuba.

Guanahatabeyes in Pray, an engraving by Theodore De Bry

The Guanahatabey was Cuba's first culture. They were described as a shell culture living mostly in caves and living off mollusks, fish, and fruits. At the time of the discovery and the conquest, the guanahatabeyes were in the process of extinction in their caverns on the western end of Cuba.

---

[7] In December 1518, an outbreak of *smallpox* was recorded in Cuba. It reportedly killed 80% of the native population.

Images above: left to right, top to bottom:

A ceremonial **Taino dance**;

a **Taino Cacique** or Chieftain;

two houses, on the left for a family, on the right for the settlement's Cacique;

a **Taino Dujo** or ritual seat (made from a hard wood called *Guayacán*) currently in the British Museum. Sitting on this type of stools, Caciques and Shamans exerted their power over the *Taino* universe and monitored and controlled the occult forces that regulated all human affairs.

Images above: left to right, top to bottom:
Caverna de los Petroglifos Guanahatabeyes, discovered in 1954 by members of the *Sociedad Espeleológica de Cuba*;
a group of **Guanahatabey fishermen** following their tribal chieftain;
a 1937 Cuban Postal Stamp honoring the **Siboneyes** and their *Habano* Cigars;
a map indicating the **distribution** of *Tainos* and *Siboneyes* across Cuba.

Images above: top to bottom:
1562 drawing of **Taino** workers panning for gold on a river margin;
internal structure of a **Taino** noble house;
a **ceremonial playground** of Tainos in Cuba.

2
Some Essential Facts about the Taino Culture

THE TAINO CULTURE was the result of 7,000 years of adaptation to the environment found in the Caribbean islands. Tainos believed in powerful spiritual forces that controlled nature. Their spirits could choose to reveal themselves as sculptures, and that was the inspiration and the rationale needed by many Taino artisans. Many *Cemis*,[8] as these wood or stone sculptures were named, were found in caves, hidden from the destructive threats of *Caribes* or from the religious activism of Christian conquistadores. Caves, in their rituals, were the places where humans first came to this world, as well as places where they would rest after death.

In broader terms, Taino society was composed of two distinct clases: the *Naboríes* (equivalent to European commoners) and the *Nitaínos* (similar to the noble European class). The *Naboríes* included three classes of commoners: at the very bottom there were *Tamemes* or laborers, wholly dependent on the local rulers, who could request their labor at will and instantly. Next above them were the *Middle Naboríes*,[9] probably the larg-

---

[8] *Taíno* religion was centered on the worship of two main deities. *Yúcahu* was the god of cassava and maintenance, and *Atabey* was the goddess of rain, rivers and the sea. They and other lesser gods (for instance, *Uragán*, god of tempests and destruction) were materialized as *Cemíes*. The spirits of the ancestors were often also represented as *Cemíes*, Some *Cemíes* were housed in sanctuaries but most were kept close to home, and received food regularly for their sustenance. *Cemíes* were invoked in case of sickness and were exhibited during rituals *adivinatorios* (public seances). Caciques and Shamans were frequently tattooed with images of their ancestor-*Cemíes*, at ceremonies called *Buhuithus*, during which strong mixtures of hallucinogenic snuffs called *Cohoba* (prepared by shamans from the beams of a species of Piptadenia trees) were inhaled.

[9] In many *Taino* settlements, the Spaniards found that most *Naboríes* were *Siboneyes*, a fact that initially confused many Conquistadores that tried to understand the *Taino* culture.

est category of people, who were also serfs but were tied to the land and would do farming, household chores and any local tasks that did not require travelling. The highest category were the *Guaoxerfs* [10] or free landholders, which commanded a level of respect similar to Knights in European culture. The lower rung of the aristocratic class were the *Behiques*,[11] which were either nobles with territorial rights, medicine-men, shamans or certain individuals with exalted hereditary positions in society. Nobles ruling small numbers of *Naboríes* were still called *Nitainos*, a position similar to European low level noblemen. A higher noble class had power over all local Nitainos and were called the *Baharis* in Hispaniola and *Caciques* in Cuba. Both terms included men as well as women.[12] Both terms signify "lord of the land." Caciques in Cuba had the priviledge to wear golden pendants called *Guanins*, lived in square larger *Bohíos* than the rest of the population and sat in *Dujos* (wooden stools) rather than the ground in special ceremonies and when receiving visitors.

Taino household artifacts can be characterized as Neolithic tools: pottery plates, bowls, water jars, cooking pots, shell and stone knives, needles, spatulas, scrapers. Personal toys and gadgets were made out of clay: whistles, rings, collars, beads,

---

[10] Their name probably originated the term *Guajiro*, which in Cuba was given to white farmers of humble origin.

[11] Keepers of the *Cemís*.

[12] *Tainos* had a matriarchal family system. Women had the right of inheritance, both of goods and titles. A male would only inherit anything if he had no sisters. Newlyweds would live in the households of the mother of the bride since she was considered more important than the father of the groom. In general, men as well as women, could have more than one spouse. *Baharis* usually had over a dozen mates. The only sexual differences were that -by and large- women did the agriculture and men fished and hunted. Women's responsibilities included preparing food staples for children and men (agriculturals as well as rodents known as *Hutias* and other wild mammals and birds). Men's responsibilities were to make fishing nets and ropes (out of palm fibers), make *Macanas* (wooden war bludgeons), dug out *Kanoas* (canoes for 25 to 150 people), construct their own bows and arrows and build *Bohios* (made out of wooden poles, woven straw and palm leaves) with help from both men and women living in their *Yucayeques* (settlements).

pendants. Utilities were made out of wood or grasses: baskets, textiles, house roofs. There were also cotton-woven objects and -rarely- wood carvings inlaid with gold, bone, shells and precious stones.

Most often Tainos fished, hunted and gathered together without clothing. On ceremonial occasions all men wore short skirts around their waist; single women were generally naked but after marriage they were expected to wear *Naguas*, a similar garment that only covered their front side.

Tainos loved to play a ritual ball game called *Batey*. Two opposing teams of 10 to 30 men competed in the central plazas of their settlements or in rectangular fields also called *Bateyes*. The games had the purpose of resolving community conflicts. Caciques usually made wagers on the outcome of the games. The mechanics of the *Batey* games were to get a solid rubber ball on the opponents territory without dropping it in the ground, in which case the ball was transfered to the opposing team.

The Taino spiritual life centered around their *Cemís*. As mentioned before, their major god was *Yúcahu* (which literarily means "spirit of the *Cassava*"). The second most important god was *Atabey*, Yúcahu's mother and the supreme power of waters and fertility. There were several minor gods, mostly related to *Cassava*; [13] the most important of which was *Baibrama*, a helpful

---

[13] *Cassava (Manihot esculenta)*, also called manioc, yuca and tapioca, is a woody shrub of the Euphorbiaceous family native to South America; it is extensively cultivated as an annual crop in tropical and subtropical regions for its edible starchy tuberous root, a gluten free major source of carbohydrates. *Cassava* is the third-largest source of food in the tropics, after rice and maize, and is a major staple food in the developing world, providing a basic diet for over half a billion people. It is one of the most drought-tolerant crops, capable of growing on marginal soils. *Cassava* root is a fall-back resource, i.e., a "food security crop" in times of famine across the world; it is, however, a poor source of protein. A diet consisting predominantly of *Cassava* root can cause protein-energy malnutrition. Like other roots and tubers, *Cassava* contains anti-nutritional factors and toxins and must be properly prepared before consumption, otherwise it can leave enough residual cyanide to cause acute cyanide intoxication, goiters and ataxia or partial paralysis.

assistant in the successful cultivation and growth of *Cassava*. *Baoinavel* and his twin brother *Márohu* were the gods of rain and good weather. As bad or evil gods the Tainos had *Coatrisquie*, the divinity that ruled over floods and *Guataubá*, a wicked assistant to *Huragán*, the god of storms.

In the Taino cosmology and oral tradition the sun and the moon came out of caverns at night, the sun to wait at the cavern entrance until morning and the moon to ascend right away to the skies. Men and women were created by the union of *Deminaán*, a caracol, and a female turtle. The oceans were created by a flood, after a father murdered his vicious and disobedient son. The father placed the son's bones into a *Calabash* or large gourd and burried it. Once the gourd was under ground, it broke, the bones turned into fish and water began to pour out until the entire earth was covered. With the protection of their Cemís, Tainos had nothing to fear except the curses of *Maboya*, a nocturnal deity who destroyed crops and was much feared; it was only placated by elaborate sacrifices, which never involved human beings.

Many Taino terms were included in the Castilian vocabulary of Cuba such as Bohío, Hamaca, Maní, Ñame, Maraca, Ají, Yuca, Mamey, Guayaba, Cupey, Ceiba, Iguana, Carey, Jicotea, Manatí, Buey, Güiro, Batey, Nasa, Petate, Barbacoa, Batea, Cabuya, Casabe, Cacique, Canibal, Caoba, Guacamayo, Jamaica, Papagayo, Piragua, Papaya, Sabana, Tiburón, Canoa, Huracán, Conuco, to mention but a few.

Several Taino inventions were adopted by Europeans, among which the most popular (aside from smoking) was the use of the hamaca. During sea travel, sailors used to sleep and rest on hard woden surfaces until they began to install *hamacas* on board and the underdecks to rest suspended in mid-air.

Images above: left to right, top to bottom:
Flowers of the **Manioc** (*Manihot esculenta*), a plant with edible tuber-roots;

the tuber roots of the Manioc. The plant was also called *yuca*;

Cassava bread, a very popular staple in Cuba even 500 years after the decline of the *Taino* culture;

Tainos engaged in a **Batey game**;

a typical **Taino family** in the 1500s.

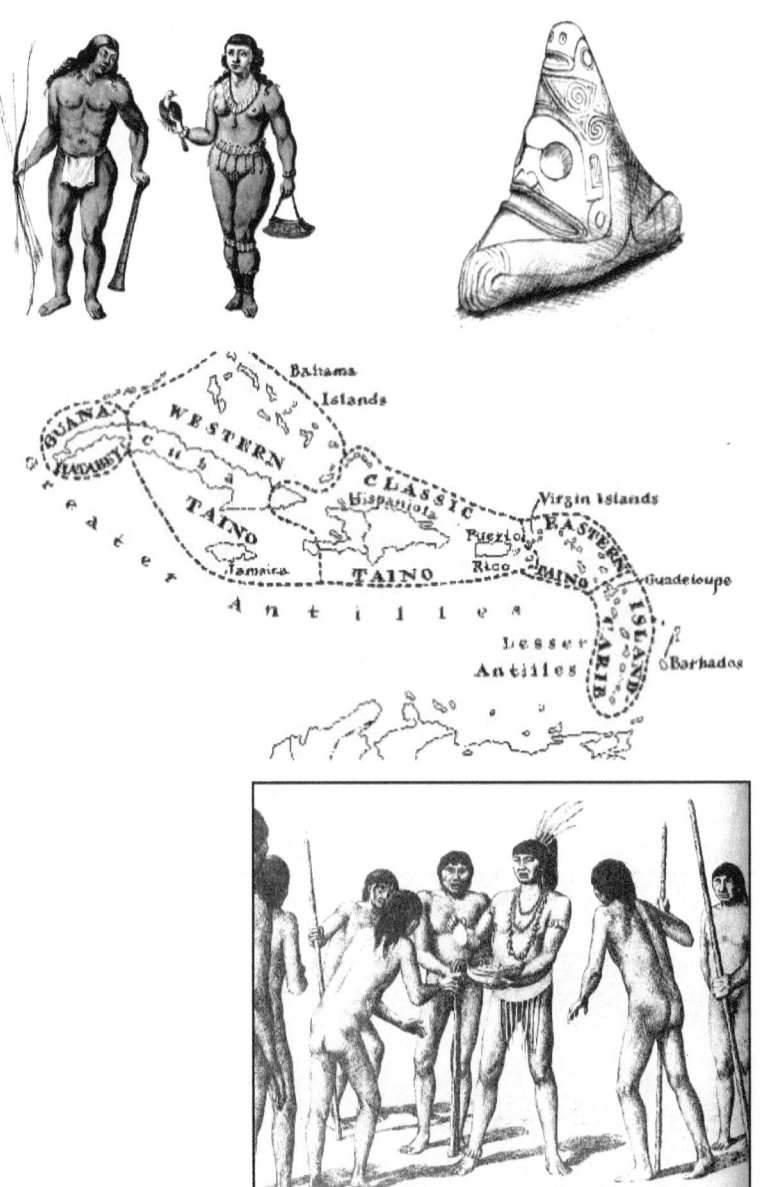

Images above: left to right, top to bottom:

A couple of **Caribe natives**;

a **Taino Cemí**, a sculptural object housing a deity or an ancestral spirit, of which dozens have been found in Cuba;

a map of the Caribbean sea showing areas habitated by the different **Taino groups**;

a **Behique** (medicine-man) tending to his clients.

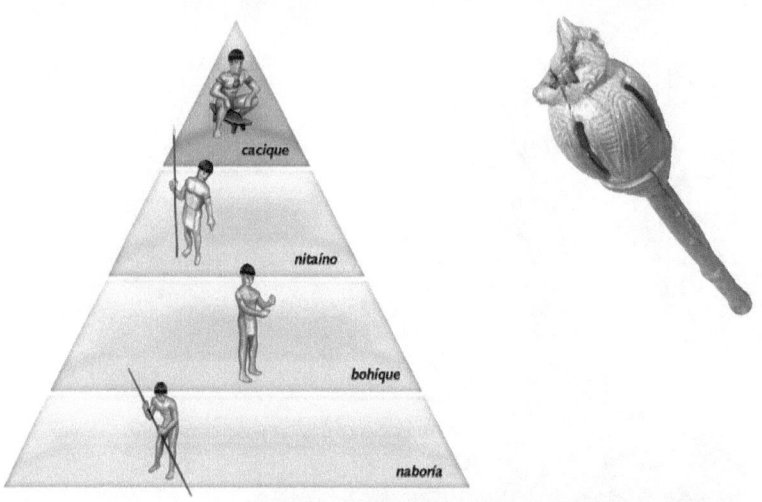

Images above: left to right, top to bottom:
The **social scale** of different subjects in Taino society;
a **Taino Maraca**, a favorite musical instrument made with a gourd;
a **Taino Areito** *or* ceremonial feast;
Tainos using a **Barbacoa** (barbecue) to roast fish.

3
Meanwhile, in the Iberian Penninsula...

THE SPAIN THAT WAS to find the *Tainos* in Cuba and the rest of the Caribbean sea, was the result of numerous contributions from ethnic groups that moved into the Iberian peninsula from Africa in the south, from the Mediterranean in the east and across the Pyrenees from the north, over the course of several centuries. That formidable blend of cultures settled as *Iberians* along the Mediterranean coast, *Celts* in the interior and north-west, *Lusitanians* in the west and *Tartesians* (the only indigenous people) in the south-west.

Trade settlements were successively established by seafaring Greeks, Carthaginians and Phoenicians in the south and east coast since the IX century AD. The Greeks eventually became the greatest influence in the buildup of the Spanish nation and were responsible for the name *Iberia*, taken from their name for the *Iber* (Ebro) river. In time, the *Celtiberians* (the fuse of all these peoples) faced a Roman conquest that submitted the entire peninsula in IX AD.

Under Roman control the peninsula was called *Hispania* and its inhabitants and culture were Romanized, including admission of the powerful and wealthy into the Roman aristocracy. Emperors Trajan, Hadrian, and Theodosius I, the philosopher Seneca, and the poets Martial, Quintilian, and Lucan were born in Hispania.

One of the most commonly recognized Roman impacts in Spain was the acceptance of slavery as a fact of daily life. Most Spanish towns had a significant slave population; slaves had no rights, could not own property or choose their trade. Some built the churches, monuments, aqueducts and roads of Roman Spain; others worked as domestics at the wealthier homes; a few were well educated and served their masters as doctors, teachers, accountants and messengers.

After the collapse of the Roman Empire, unlike what occurred in Britain, Gaul and Germania, the Roman influence and the interest in Roman classical culture was not discarded. Spain retained its Romanic language, its religion and its laws. The centuries of uninterrupted Roman rule and settlement left a deep and enduring imprint upon the culture of Spain, and it has lasted to this day.

In the V century the first Germanic tribes (many had been enlisted to serve in Roman armies) began to invade *Hispania*: Visigoths, [14] Vandals, and Alans. After their conversion to Christianity, the Iberian peninsula became Catholic. As in the rest of the Roman empire, there was never a date after which the empire was no more; it was a progressive de-Romanization and a weakening of Rome as the central authority.

The largest impact on Spain's development was made by the Visigoths, yet it was more than anything a soft occupation. Visigoths were uninterested in everyday political events in the peninsula. They did not blend with the Spaniards; they did not produce a strong literature; their language did not provide many words to the languages of Iberia. When the Moors arrived in the 8th century, the Visigoths had no claim on the loyalty of the Hispanic people.

South of Spain, in North Africa, Arab tribes dominated large territories starting in 640 AD (present day Morocco, Algeria, Western Sahara, Mauritania). Taking advantage of a Visigoth civil war in 711 AD, a large number of Moors [15] crossed the Strait of Gibraltar and defeated and killed King Roderic of His-

---

[14] The Visigoths were one of the branches of the Goths, the other being the Ostrogoths. Before settling in Iberia, the Visigoths, under Alaric I, invaded and sacked Rome in 410 AD. They took pride in comparing themselves to the Biblical Jews, and being as much a wandering chosen people as the Jews were.

[15] The term *Moors* refers to Muslims of Arab or African descent. It is not a well defined referent, has never been used by Muslims and has no real ethnological significance.

pania at the Battle of Guadalete.[16] They soon occupied the southern part of Spain, all of Portugal and part of France, calling their Iberian territory *Al-Andalus*. Their advance into all of Europe was only stopped in France by Germanic Franks under Charles Martel at the Battle of Tours in 732. The complete occupation of the Iberian peninsula was prevented in the North, at Covadonga, Asturias, by Pelayo, a Visigoth nobleman who founded the Kingdom of Asturias.

The rulers of *Al-Andalus* (with the rank of Emirs) became subordinate to the *Caliphs* in Damascus. After a few years, a second independent Emirate was established in Cordoba, on the southern part of Iberia, by Arabs from the Arabian peninsula. Soon *Al-Andalus* was rife with conflicts with this second Emirate as well as with Christian Visigoth leaders within the population. Medieval Iberia suffered from constant warfare between Christians and Muslims and by 1150 many Christians and Jews began to abandon their homes and lands under the threat of death, conversion of emigration. By 1250, Muslim power was consolidated and only one Kingdom ruled Iberia, the Emirate of Granada.

In 1250 many Latin based Romance languages were spoken in the Christian kingdoms of Iberia: Castilian, Aragonese, Catalan, Galician, Asturian and Leonese, as well as the ancient Basque language. Although Castile was not the wealthiest or the most developed region of Iberia, songs and official documents were often written in Castilian (rather than Latin); it eventually prevailed and turned into modern Spanish. Other languages did not disappear, however, and have lasted until today.

---

[16] The location of the Battle of Guadalete (or Battle of Jerez de la Frontera) has never been established. It resulted in the Muslim occupation of Toledo. Most accounts of this battle are untrustworthy and full of legend and fantasy. One part of the legend states that Roderic's army consisted of 100,000 troops facing 187,000 Muslims under arms. Another part of the legend is that Roderic was easily killed because he had come to the field in a chariot drawn by eight white mules and the mules refused to move, making him a sitting target.

By the time the XV century started, Castile, in the northern and central areas, was the most important Christian Kingdom in the Iberian peninsula. The second most important was the Kingdom of Aragon, in the northeastern part of the peninsula. When Henry IV of Castile died in 1474, the War of the Castilian Succession (1475-1479) broke. [17] In 1469 Isabel I of Castile had married Ferdinand II of Aragón; she ended up winning the throne, uniting both Kingdoms (Castile and Aragon) [18] and setting the stage for the expulsion of the Muslims from the Iberian peninsula and the "discovery of America."

Pope Alexander VI bestowed on Isabel and Ferdinand the title of "Catholic Monarchs," and officially baptized the Spanish territory as the Kingdom of Spain. [19] The first order of business for Isabel and Ferdinand was to complete the expulsion of Muslims from the peninsula. For seven hundred years, after the Battle of Covadonga was won by Visigoth King Pelayo of Asturias, the Christian territories of the peninsula had grown in size at the expense of *Al-Andalus*. Isabel and Ferdinand completed the job by encircling and taken the city of Granada, the last stronghold of the Muslims.[20]

On January 2, 1492, *Boabdil* surrendered complete control of the Emirate of Granada to Isabel and Ferdinand of Spain. It ended the recapture of the Iberian peninsula and the end of *Al-*

---

[17] Juana la Beltraneja, supported by Portugal and France, competed for the throne of Spain with Isabel I of Castile, sister of the deceased Henry IV, who was supported by the Kingdom of Aragon and the Castilian nobility.

[18] By an agreement signed by Isabel I and Ferdinand II on January 15, 1474, Isabel held more authority than Ferdinand over the joined Kingdom of Spain, although their power was shared. To remind misogynists of that fact, a common saying became popular in Spain: "Tanto monta, monta tanto, Isabel como Fernando." (roughly translated [sic] in the English world of the times as "Isabel and Fernando, six from one and half a dozen from the other").

[19] The Kingdom of Spain included at that point Aragón, Sicily, Castile and Naples. Immediately after the *Reconquista* it incorporated the Canary Islands.

[20] Granada was founded by Muslims in the XI century after the civil war that ended the Caliphate of Cordoba. It became a reluctant tributary to the Kingdom of Castile and with its help became a Muslim Emirate in 1238.

Andalus. The surrender terms included an agreement called the *Mudéjar*, by virtue of which the city's Muslim inhabitants could continue unmolested in the practice of their faith and customs. Mudéjar Muslims, however, were soon forced to convert to Christianity by Cardinal Francisco Jiménez de Cisneros. Their Mosques were turned into Churches. They ended up following the steps of the Jews, which had been forced to convert or be expelled or executed a few years before. [21]

The fall of Granada and the end of 800 years of Muslim domination allowed the new Kingdom of Spain to enter a great phase of exploration and colonization in the Americas. The resources from the New World enriched Spain and gave rise to a vast Empire, at the time the largest in the world. The Spaniards brought to Cuba and the rest of the Americas the good and the bad of seven hundred years of triying to rescue their peninsula from the Musims.

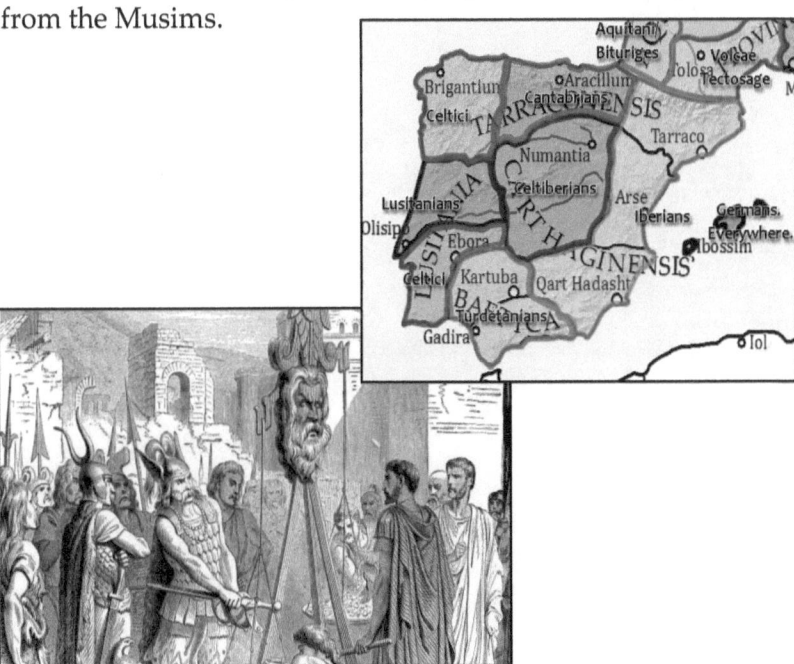

The ***ethnical composition*** of Spaniards in a map and engraving from the XVIII century.

---

[21] Converted Jews were called *Marranos*. Converted Muslims were called *Moriscos*.

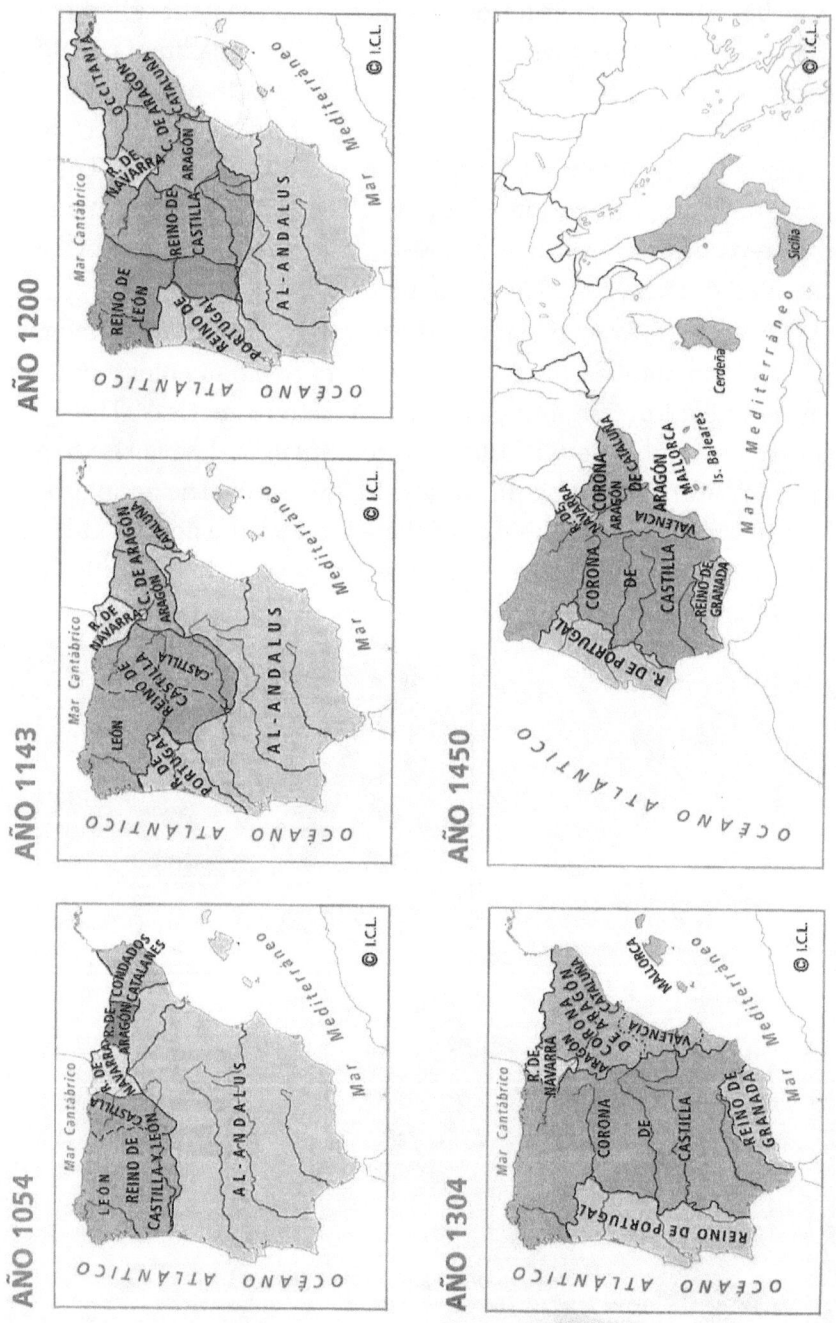

*The evolution of **Al-Andalus** over time*

Main Characters of Roman, Muslin and Christian Spain (711-1492):

First Row: Romans **Hannibal** and **Seneca**, both born in Iberia; Visigoth leader **Alarico I**, the man who took and sacked Rome in 410 AD.

Second Row: **Roderico** or *Rodrigo*, the Visigoth King who lost Spain to the Muslims in 711 AD; **Boabdil**, the last Emir of Granada, defeated by the Catholic Monarchs in 1492; **Don Pelayo**, the Asturian King who won the Battle of Covadonga and prevented the Muslims from totally occupying Iberia.

Third Row: **Isabel I** and **Ferdinand II**, the Catholic Monarchs who completed the expulsion of Muslims from Iberia; Don Rodrigo Diaz de Vivar, **el Cid Campeador**, the Spanish hero of the *Reconquista*, never bested on the battlefield.

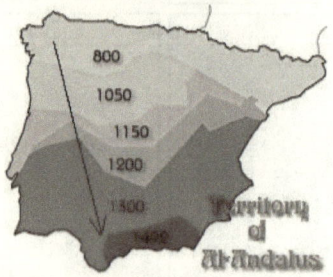

From left to right, top to bottom:

The **Battle of Guadalete** (711 AD), where Visigoth King Roderico lost to the Muslims and gave rise to *Al-Andalus*;

the **Battle of Covadonga** (722 AD), where future King Pelayo of Asturias prevented the Muslims to conquer the North of the Iberian peninsula;

a map showing the **retreat of the Al-Andalus** frontiers during 700 years of *Reconquista*;

The **surrender of Granada's** Muslim Emir *Boabdil* to the Catholic Monarchs, signaling the end of the Granada Caliphate in 1492.

From 1492 to 1506

Christopher Columbus (1451 ?-1506)

4
Christopher Columbus Chases after a Dream

THE YEAR WAS 1485. *Hernán Cortés*, the man who as a Spanish Conquistador would lead the expedition that caused the fall of the Aztec Empire in Mexico, was born in Medellin, Castile to a family of lesser nobility. Another explorer, *Giovanni da Verrazano*, a Florentine that would become famous as the first man to travel up and down the Eastern coast of North America (working for Francis I of France), was born in Val di Greve, south of Florence. In due course he would have a large bridge named after him. In the Iberian peninsula, the Spanish Inquisition was going full blast under the direction of *Tomás de Torquemada*. Also in Spain, in 1485, Young Isabel I of Castile and Ferdinand II of Aragon had a child, *Catalina de Aragón*, born in Alcalá de Henares, near Madrid. The newborn girl would be betrothed at age 3 to Arthur, the King of Wales, heir to the Throne of England. After becoming his wife at 16, he died and Catalina would become the first wife of Henry VIII and be, after all, Queen of England in 1509. It all collapsed by 1525 when England King Henry VIII became infatuated with his mistress Anne Boleyn.

More pertaining to our story, however, was a young mariner, Christopher Columbus, who accompanied by his son Diego, took passage in 1485 on a ship from Lisbon to Palos de Moguer, Spain. There Columbus left his son at a Monastery named *La Rábida*, where he met a learned monk called Antonio de Marchena.[22] Together, they shared their dreams to explore the Western Atlantic in search of a path to China and Japan.

---

[22] Marchena, years later, would write a letter of recommendation for Columbus, addressed to Hernando de Talavera, Isabel I's confessor. It opened doors for Columbus.

Columbus had been on that quest for over eighteen years. He had sent his brother Bartolomé to the courts of Henry VII of England and Charles VIII of France in a futile search for financial support. Only in *La Rábida* he had found sympathetic and helpful ears; everywhere else he found apathy and little interest.

In 1486, after living in Lisbon for a year and failing to interest the Portuguese Crown in his project,[23] Columbus made a trip to Spain to entice King Ferdinand and Queen Isabel to support his plans. At the time, the itinerant Spanish court was meeting in the city of Cordoba. The monarchs referred his proposal to Hernando de Talavera,[24] a prominent political and religious figure of the times and eventual Bishop of Avila and Archbishop of Granada. The Talavera Commission [25] met in Salamanca for two weeks and, after a cursory review, declared the idea "vain and worthy of rejection".

Not prone to give up that easy, Columbus obtained help from Don Luis de la Cerda, Duke of Medinaceli in 1487; he had serviced and lived at the Duke's house for two years, and had received 3000 Maravedis for his work. He made many attempts to interest Don Luis in his explorations across the seas west of Europe, but his attempts to secure the help of the Duke failed. So he was, again, on to Cordoba and the Royal Courts.

---

[23] It has been speculated that King John II of Portugal had entered an agreement with a Flemish man living in the Azores called *Dualmo*, who had discovered, in 1487, a land barrier to the west of Europe. King John presumably had ordered everyone in the Lisbon court to maintain this as a matter of extreme secrecy, while he kept telling the Spaniards that the only route to Asia was round the southern cape of Africa. There has never been confirmation of this tale.

[24] Hernando de Talavera was a converted Jew and fell victim to the Spanish Inquisition following Isabel's death in 1507. He suffered prison until the Pope ordered his release.

[25] The Talavera Commission was composed, according to Ferdinand Columbus, son of Christopher, of astronomers, cosmographers, sea-farers and philosophers. Most Commission members agreed that the earth was spherical but questioned Columbus stated distance from Europe to Asia.

In Cordoba Columbus fell in love and married Beatriz Enriquez de Arana, the orphan child of a farming family. She soon became pregnant with Ferdinand; Columbus continued his quest for exploration funds with more zest and desire than before. He appreared many times at Royal Councils before learned Commissioners and devoured many scholarly volumes from the Royal libraries. [26]

In 1488 Columbus revisited Lisbon. King Juan II had less interest in his projects than before, since a mariner called Bartolomé Díaz had just returned from India on a trip that took him around the Cape of Good Hope, south of Africa. His brother Bartolomé, once more, was sent to London, seeking the support of Henry VII. He returned, once more, empty-handed. Colombus then decided to travel to Granada, to witness the surrender ceremony by which *Boabdil*, the last Emir of Granada, renounced to all Muslims possessions in the peninsula. Sensing that the energies of the Crown could be now redirected towards his Atlantic venture, he contacted the monks in *La Rábida*; they got him a meeting with the Catholic Monarchs. Following a canon that many years later would be followed by businesses interviewing potential candidates for hire, Isabel I sent Columbus 20,000 Maravedies for expenses to visit the Courts, including proper attire (US$ 700 in 2014 money)

This time the meeting went quite well. He asked for the hereditary position of Admiral of the Ocean Sea, as well as Viceroy and Governor of all the lands he might find; in addition, he asked for ten percent of all revenues from the entire venture. His plan was initially rejected by the Treasurer of the Crown, reconsidered by Isabel I, and finally approved by the Courts, the Queen and the King, under what was called the Capitulations of Santa Fe. On April 17, 1492, he signed a contract with the Royal house. Within five months three ships were sailing downriver on their way to the Canary Islands and beyond.

---

[26] Many of these books are currently at the *Biblioteca Colombina* in Seville. They are full of marginal notes handwritten by Columbus, as well as sketches and diagrams from his hand.

Fishermen from *Palos de Moguer* (also called *Palos de la Frontera*, in Andalusia) almost unanimously thought Columbus was a fool engaging in a worthless and dangerous adventure.

Images, top to bottom, left to right:

Christopher Columbus, in a drawing from a Spanish Medieval book; a schematic diagram of a **Nao** similar to Columbus' ships; Columbus showing **Ferdinand II of Spain** his proposed route to China and Japan. Photo of a panel from the bronze doors installed in the US Capitol in 1922.

Images, top to bottom, left to right:

The **Moors** as they were expelled from the Iberian peninsula;

a US postage stamp showing the meeting of Columbus with the cloistered priests of the Monastery of **La Rábida**;

Columbus departing from **Palos de Moguer**, August 3, 1492.

Images, top to bottom, left to right:

Henry VII, King of England, first monarch of the House of Tudor, the "Greedy King," father of Henry VIII; he married his son Arthur to *Catalina de Aragón;*

Charles VIII, King of France, was known as the "Friendly King." He was the last of the *Valois*. Died of a subdural hematoma after hitting his head on a door lintel on his way to a tennis match.

Juan II, King of Portugal; he was baptized by Nicolás Maquiavelo as the "Perfect Prince." He championed the exploration of the coasts of Africa and came too late to sponsor expansions in the Americas. He obtained from the Pope a piece of the action with the *Treaty of Tordesillas* in 1494.

All these three Kings were **unconvinced** by the presentations of Bartolomé Columbus, on behalf of his brother Christopher, and missed the opportunity to lay claim to the entire New World in 1492.

On the bottom, **Chistopher Columbus** presenting his plans to Isabel I in the Courts of Salamanca. Ferdinand is not present in this painting by Verziog.

5

The Future Admiral on the Way to America

EIGHTY SEVEN MEN were aboard the three ships hired by Columbus to accompany him in his Western Atlantic adventure. Two of the ships were *caravels* (light sailing vessels, about 45 ft long, displacing 60 tons at the most, each carrying 25 men): the *Pinta* (owned by the Pinto family) and the *Niña* (property of a man called Juan Niño). The third was the flagship, a larger and heavier *Nao* (a carrack, [27] 60 ft long and displacing 150 tons, with 37 men on board), owned by a man called Juan de la Cosa, who went on the trip as ship master. All three ships were old and of modest size compared with the vessels of the times; they were definitely not intended for exploration. The Nao, where Columbus traveled, was called *Marigalante*, Spanish for "Gallant María." It had a single deck and three masts, and traveled much slower than the two caravels. It was later rebaptized as the *Santa María*.

Contrary to the tales told by enemies of Spain, the crews of the three ships were not criminals or drunkards but experienced seamen from the port of Palos de la Frontera and from the region of Galicia in northern Spain. Bartholomew and Christopher Columbus had interviewed each one of them and found out their experiences and expectations. Only four men with delinquent records showed up [28] during the recruiting and

---

[27] *Carracs* were three-masted sailing ships developed by the Portuguese for Atlantic exploration. They had high rounded sterns and a large aftcastle and were usually square-rigged on the two forward masts. They were large enough to be very stable in heavy seas and roomy enough to carry provisions during long trips. They were used, for instance, by Vasco da Gama when he circumnavigated Africa, by Verrazano when he explored the north coast of North America and by Magallanes and Elcano when they circumnavigated the globe.

[28] One had killed a man during a fight; the other three had helped him escape from jail.

Columbus got them an amnesty after they signed for the trip. Also contrary to legends, Queen Isabel I did not have to pawn her jewelry; the trip was financed by a syndicate of seven noble men, friends of Columbus, all from Genoa but residents in Seville; the group included Lorenzo di Pierfrancesco de Medici, whom Columbus called *il Popolano*. He belonged to a junior branch of the House of Medici. Lorenzo was a very wealthy retired man who had once been Florentine ambassador to Paris.

Daily life abord the three ships consisted of prayers several times during the day, singing all the time, and specific tasks assigned to every man. In four hour turns, half the crew would work while the other half rested. Only the ship captain had a cabin, everyone else slept and rested on deck. A *grumete* (cabin boy) kept track of the time with a sand clock, which had to be turned every half hour. Meals were served once a day, each man at a designated place on deck. On the stern of each ship there was a hutch for urination and excretion; they called it "going to the garden." Once a week each man was asked to jump overboard to take a bath. Contrary to popular myth, in order to prevent sunstrokes, no man was allowed to remove his shirt during the journey.

Columbus had a well planned plan to explore the Atlantic ocean. He knew of the Trade Winds (a brisk westward wind from the coast of Europe towards the southern Atlantic ocean) and the Gulf Stream (a strong sea current from the west Atlantic, reaching all the way to the British islands). His great contribution to the maritime sciences was to set a clockwise path for the outbound and the return trip. Starting from Spain, the right direction was to go south taking advantage of the Trade Winds. The next step would be to leave the favorable wind and head west to reach land, returning home co-currently with the Gulf Stream. It was a strategy that never ocurred to the Portuguese, who always remained near the west coast of Africa, taking advantage of the Trade Winds all the way to the southern tip of the continent.

During his first trip Columbus sailed on August 3rd (helped by the southward Trade Winds) from Palos de Moguer to the Canary Islands. There he took provisions in *La Gomera*, made some repairs to the *Pinta* and re-rigged the *Niña's* sails, leaving westward (out of the Trade Winds) on September 6th. [29]

After 29 days out at sea, on October 7th, 1492, an "inmense flock of birds was spotted." On October 12th, at 2:00 AM, land was sighted by a sailor named Rodrigo de Triana.[30] Columbus called it *San Salvador*; to the indigenous residents it was *Guanahaní*, and it was probably today's Grand Turk island in the Bahamas. Continuing his trip, Columbus found Cuba on October 28th and la Hispaniola on December 25th. There the *Marigalante* ran aground at today's Caracol Bay, Haiti, and had to be abandoned. A fort was constructed with its wooden planks and given the name *La Navidad*. Columbus made an agreement to protect the fort with the lord of those territories, the Cacique *Guacanagarix*. [31] By January 15th, 1493, the *Pinta* and the *Niña* set sail for the Azores, on the way to Barcelona. A strong storm forced him to deviate to Lisbon [32] on March 4th, but on March 15th he anchored his ships in the Catalonian port that today features a monumental column in his honor.

---

[29] As the trip progressed West, Columbus observed that the needle of his compass was no longer pointing to the North star. He concluded that the magnetic field of the earth was such that the needle pointed to an invisible point on the earth and not to the absolute North; the crew was told of that phenomenon and was impressed by the man's knowledge of astronomy.

[30] Rodrigo de Triana (AKA Juan Rodríguez Bermejo) won the 10,000 Maravedís promised to the first man to spot land. In today's dollar values, Rodrigo's prize would amount to US $335.

[31] *Guacanagarix* was one of the five caciques of Hispaniola and, unknown to Columbus, a man not to be trusted. All the men who stayed at *La Navidad* were massacred before Columbus returned on his second trip. *Guacanagarix* himself was later dispossed of his Taino titles by his own people and abandoned in the woods.

[32] It has been speculated that Columbus intentionally went to Lisbon to make and after-the-fact pact with Juan II of Portugal and get a better deal that he had from the Spanish crown. Modern scholars consider it very unlikely. It was enigmatic, however, that he had to spend a week there.

Columbus was received as a hero in Barcelona and the rest of Spain and Europe. He had brought with him several natives and some gold, as well as a couple of tobacco plants, several pinefruits, four ot five ajís, a turkey and a hammock, but none of the coveted species like black pepper, ginger or cloves. His report indicated he had reached Asia and the coast of China. [33] His account was very fictional:

«... harbors and rivers are exceptionally wide... many rivers are loaded with gold... there are many species to be had, like in the Orient...»

Pope Alexander VI, in 1494, granted Spain all lands mentioned by Columbus but reserved for Portugal anything East of a North-South meridian, 370 leagues west of Cape Verde, according to the *Tratado de Tordesillas*.[34]

On September 24, 1493, Columbus set sail for the Americas again. Now he had two *Naos* and fifteen Caravels. On November 3rd he arrived to the Caribbean and began to visit and name the islands of Dominica, Guadalupe, Monserrate, Antigua, Santa Cruz, Once Mil Vírgenes, Puerto Rico, ending his trip in Hispaniola, where he found a new Cacique (*Caonabo*) who had defenestrated *Guacanagari*. After Hispaniola he visited *Juana* (Cuba, which he thought was a peninsula of China) and Jamaica, returning then to Spain.

On this second trip Columbus recommended to the Kings of Spain to bring into servitude the Caribe natives, because they were abusing the good-natured Tainos.[35] The Crown refused;

---

[33] He actually mentioned *Cipango* and *Antilia*; in any case, he mistook Cuba for Asia and Hispaniola for China.

[34] Tordesillas was a town in Valladolid, Spain. The Portuguese had reclaimed that, by virtue of the Treaty of Alcacovas (1479) and the Papal Bull *Aeterni Regis* (1481), all islands west and south of the Canary Islands belonged to them. *Tordesillas* was a diplomatic solution for both countries.
A note of interest: Chile claimed a sector of Antartica in 1950, and Argentina claimed the Falkland islands in 1960, in both cases invoking the Treaty of Tordesillas.

[35] It has been alledged that his real motivation was to sell the slaves in Portugal to pay for his travel expenses and have enough left for investor's dividends; the gold his explorers and crew encountered in the Americas was not even remotely sufficient.

Columbus disobeyed Queen Isabel and forcibly took and enslaved 1,200 Tainos by mistake. They were shipped to the peninsula but half of them died on the ships. Upon arriving in Spain, Isabel I ordered all survivors to be freed. A great number of explorers from the second trip, not finding enough gold to justify their hard work, returned to Spain by the end of 1495. Some had started families with native women and were allowed to take them to Spain. In the meantime, John II of Portugal began to spread the rumor that he had found his own territories in the Americas.

Hastened by those rumors, on May 30th 1498, Columbus undertook his third trip, this time leaving port with only six ships. From August 4th to the 12th, he explored the north of what is now Venezuela, including the Orinoco River, Margarita, Tobago and Granada, returning to Hispaniola on August 19th. He was physically and mentally exhausted, was suffering from gout (recurrent attacks of acute inflammatory arthritis and swollen joints), had developed rheumatic arthritis and ophtalmia. He asked Queen Isabel to appoint an assistant to help him govern. The crown appointed Francisco de Bobadilla, a member of the Castilian Order of Calatrava. As soon as Bobadilla arrived in Hispaniola he began to receive complaints about Columbus.[36] Bodadilla, in an attempt to make himself popular and secure Columbus position for himself, arrested his master and his brothers on October 1st 1500, supplanted him in his post, confiscated all their wealth, and sent all three to Spain in chains. They remained in jail until King Ferdinand found time to order their release.

Upon hearing Columbus defense, Fernando and Isabel restituted their possessions but did not restore their titles; they authorized, however, a fourth and last trip to America by the Co-

---

[36] More than anything, the explorers were mad at Columbus exaggerations about the opportunities to find gold in Hispaniola. They considered themselves betrayed and hoodwinked.

lumbus brothers and appointed a new man, Nicolás de Ovando, as governor of the Indies.

On his fourth trip Colombus was accompanied by his 13 year old son Fernando. He left Cádiz on May 12th 1502 and had planned to land on Hispaniola on June 29th. The new governor refused to open the port for his expedition. He went on to Jamaica, Isla de Pinos (Cuba), and present day Honduras, Nicaragua, Costa Rica and Panamá. His ships were damaged by a storm and he was stranded in Jamaica for a full year, during which time Ovando refused to provide any help. On February 29th 1504, he secured the help of the natives by accurately predicting a lunar eclipse. Help was provided and he sailed to Spain, arriving in San Lucar de Barramedaa, Castile, on November 7th 1504.

The Columbus that returned to Castille in 1504 was probably only 52 years old. Several times he had had influenza and his body was riddled with arthritis from prolonged, recurrent and severe attacks of food poisoning as the result of poor sanitation and improper food preparation during his trips. He died in Valladolid on May 20th 1506. In 1542 his remains were transfered to Colonial Santo Domingo (present day República Dominicana) and in 1795, when France took the island of Hispaniola, the corpse was transfered to the Cathedral of Havana. In 1898, when Spain lost the island of Cuba, they took Columbus remains with them and placed them in an elaborate catafalque in the Cathedral of Seville, where it is today.

A rare 1905 Cuban
Columbus Stamp

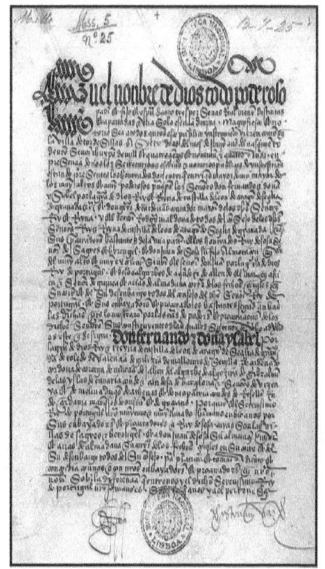

Images, top to bottom, left to right:

Columbus presenting his plan to the Spanish Courts in *Sevilla*. In this 1843 painting by Emanuel Gottlieb Leutze, Ferdinand I is present (see page 42);

The **Capitulaciones de Santa Fé** (Columbus protocolary and financial agreements with Ferdinand and Isabel);

The *Tratado de Tordesillas*, dividing the New World areas of exploration between Spain (West) and Portugal (East).

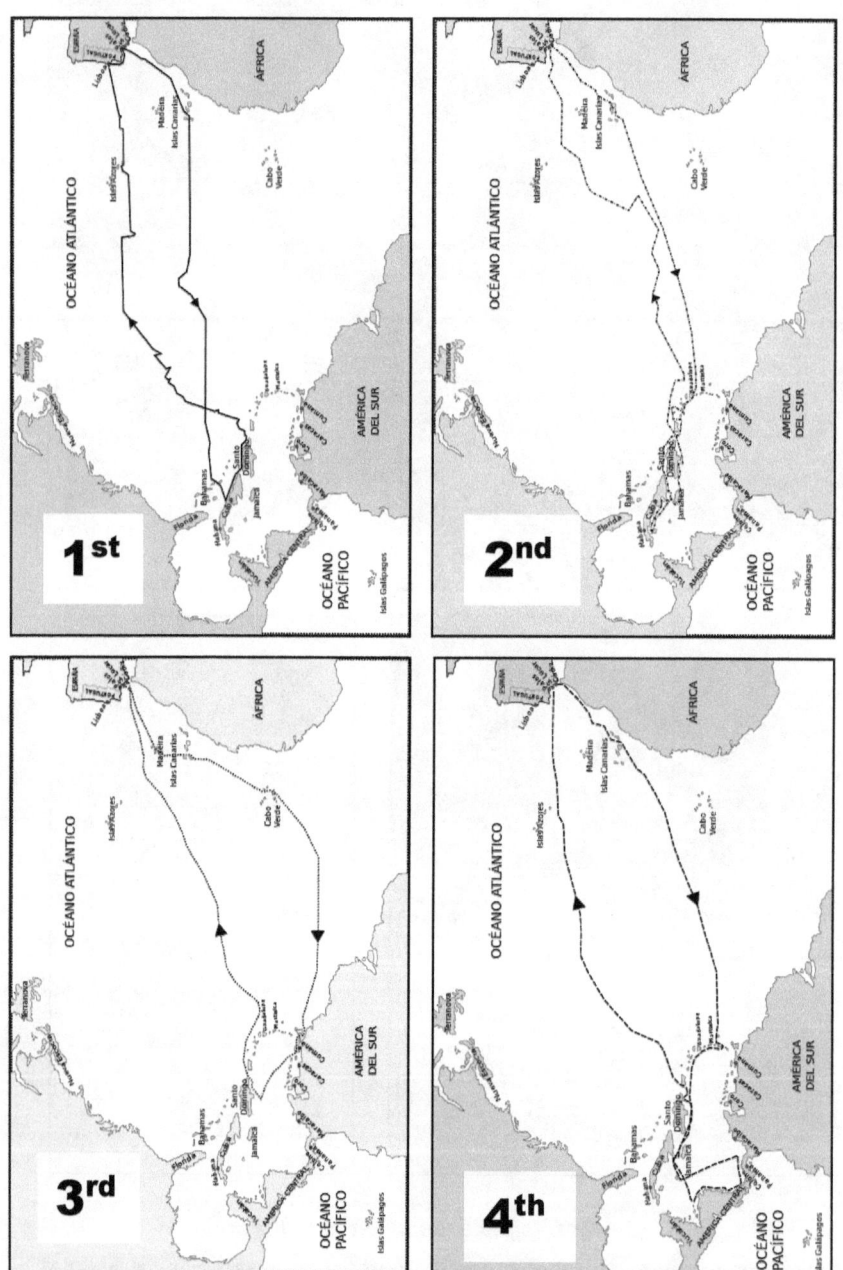

Maps:
The four trips of Columbus to America, 1492, 1493, 1498 and 1502.

Images, top to bottom:

Columbus **arriving in Cuba**, October, 1492;

Columbus **presenting his findings** to the Kings of Spain, March, 1493;

Columbus **in Chains**, back to Spain from his third trip, October, 1500.

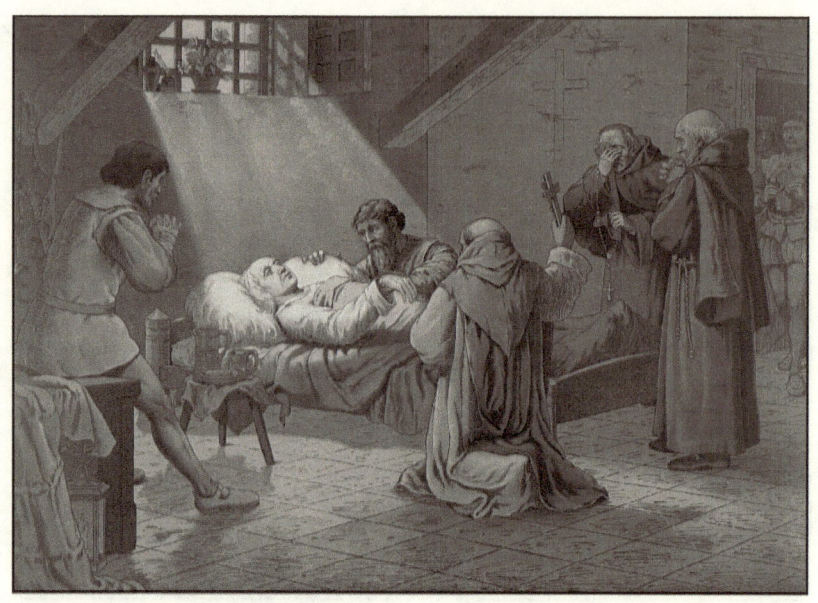

Images, top to bottom, left to right:

Columbus on his **death bed** in Valladolid, May, 1506;

two postage stamps **honoring Columbus**, from Cuba (1942) and the US (1892);

Columbus tomb in the Cathedral of Seville.

From 1506 to 1600

6
Expansions and Troubles in the Caribbean

IN 1509, CHRISTOPHER COLUMBUS son, Diego, was appointed Governor of the Indies. He replaced Nicolás de Ovando y Cáceres, [37] who in turn had replaced Francisco de Bobadilla in 1502. Ovando's turn in the highest position in the Americas had been marked by bloody campaigns, brutalities, massacres and cruelty. He was notorious for having introduced into the American continent the cultivation of sugar and for having imported the first African slaves.

Among the few positive things that Ovando made in Cuba was to recruit Sebastian de Ocampo to explore the coasts of the territory and elucidate if it was an island or a peninsula, as Colombus had believed.

Ocampo left Santo Domingo in two ships manned only by sailors. He headed north through the strait that separated Cuba from the Hispaniola (the Old Bahama Channel) and headed west. The first land sighted were Maisí and Baracoa. Continuing northwest the expedition spotted Gibara, discovered by Columbus sixteen years before, Puerto Padre, Matanzas bay, and the port of Carenas (Havana) where he stopped to inspect and repair his ships.

West of Carenas port he could see that to follow the coast he had to change course slightly towards the south; he felt he was about to start the easterly return trip. Indeed, after arriving at

---

[37] Nicolás de Ovando, a noble and pious member of the Anti-Muslim fighting *Orden de Alcántara*, was a good friend of Isabel I and a distant relative of Hernán Cortés. She appointed him to replace Bobadilla after a very serious recommendation from Columbus. Columbus, of course, had become a mortal enemy of Bobadilla after the later had sent him back to Spain in chains in 1500. When Ovando travelled to America, he carried with him 10,000 colonists in 30 ships. Among the passengers were Juan Ponce de León, the Florida explorer, Francisco Pizarro, the conqueror of the Inca Empire, and Bartolomé de las Casas, a protector-to-be of all American natives.

San Antonio he took a track due south and soon he found himself navigating waters that Columbus had seen in 1494, when he sailed along the south of Cuba trying to find out whether it was an island or the mainland.

Continuing along the south of the island he discovered the bay of Jagua (today's Cienfuegos) where he camped at an indigenous key which now bears the name of Ocampo. The expedition continued their circumnavigation, recognizing the coast by the maps that other mariners had drawn, verifying that the territory was indeed an island. After eight months, they traveled back to Hispaniola. Within the next ten years the Spaniards founded seven villages in Cuba.[38]

Having recognized these good deeds by Ovando, Diego Columbus started his Governorship with a more informed view of the territories under his command. He had been a page at the Spanish Courts in 1492, when his father departed in his first trip to the New World. Now it was his turn to manage and defend, on behalf of the Spanish crown, the lands his father had obtained for Spain.

After becoming Governor of the Indies Diego took residence at *El Alcázar* in Santo Domingo, capital of today's Dominican Republic. Two years into this position, he was promoted to Viceroy of the Indies, a title he held until 1518. Most of his time was devoted to regain the titles and privileges granted to his father but denied to him in 1500. He married into nobility, however, as he made María de Toledo Rojas his wife; she was the niece of the 2nd Duke of Alba, who in turn was a cousin of King Ferdinand II of Spain. Through these contacts, Diego was able to move the remains of Christopher Columbus to the Cathedral of Santo Domingo. The privileges denied to Diego were bestowed on his son Luis in 1536: the title of Admiral of the

---

[38] It was an amazing adventure for the times. Not only Ocampo had travelled all the time against the Gulf current but he also had discovered the Gulf of Mexico and the waters of the southern Caribbean, opening the seas for future explorations by De Soto (Florida), Cortés (Mexico), Pizarro (South America), and Nuñez de Balboa (Pacific Ocean).

Indies, a lifetime annuity of 10,000 ducats, [39] the fiefdom of Jamaica (with considerable lands and revenue-producing property), a 25 square leagues estate in Panamá and the titles of Duke of Veragua and Marquis of Jamaica.

One of the issues left unresolved by Nicolás de Ovando fell on the hands of Diego Columbus: the repercussions after the horrible murder of Cacique Hatuey. Ovando had complained to King Ferdinand...

«The enslaved Africans I had brought to Hispaniola are fleeing into Taino territory, teaching them bad customs. The Tainos are providing asylum and it makes very difficult to capture the slave defectors. I could deal with disobedient servants but can hardly retrieve runaways from the rainforests in Hispaniola.»

Ovando understood well that Cacique Hatuey and his followers were greeting and embracing the runaway Africans as allies. He decided to fight him at all costs. Not able to protect his 400 men from the weapons of Spain, Hatuey decided to head for the island of *Caobana* (Cuba), to mobilize the Tainos there for an more balanced campaign. [40] According to Bartolomé de las Casas, these were the words of Hatuey (while showing him a basket full of gold and jewels):

«The bearded intruders worship gold and spread slavery, misery and death at their pass. They fight and kill, usurp our lands and crops, persecute us, seduce our women and violate our daughters. They have to be returned to the sea.»

Once in Cuba, Hatuey faced the forces of Diego Velázquez and Hernán Cortés. For three months the Tainos kept a posse of Spaniards pinned down around the settlement of Baracoa (a town founded earlier by Velázquez). Hatuey was finally ap-

---

[39] A *ducat* (from the Medieval *ducatus* or the Duke's Coin) was worth about $ 2.00 in today's money. In the past it was the name of a popular currency in Venice, Sicily, many countries and kingdoms in Germany, Holland, Flanders and Eastern Europe. It lost its mercantile value after World War I.

[40] Hatuey could only offer his followers macanas, stone axes and wooden lances; the Spaniards, of course, had firearms, steel lances and swords. They were protected by shields, helmets and metalic meshes, aside from horses and tracking dogs.

prehended with 25 of his men [41] on February 2nd 1512; they all died at a stake. The scene was described by Las Casas as follows:

«"When tied to the stake, the cacique Hatuey was told by a Franciscan friar who was present... something about the God of the Christians and of the articles of Faith. He was told what he could be saved and go to heaven. The Cacique was also told he would go to Hell where, if he did not adopt the Christian faith, he would suffer eternal fire. Hatuey asked the Franciscan friar if Christians all went to Heaven. When told that they did, he said he would prefer to go to Hell.»

Once the Hatuey rebellion was over, Diego Velázquez began the exploration and colonization of the rest of the island. He divided the men he had in Baracoa in two groups, asigning each a large number of Tainos as servants (in practice the difference with slavery was minimal), to build roads, open the forests, carry weapons and tools and hunt for food. One of the groups went northwest, to the region of *Maniabón* (today's Holguín). The other went straight west to the region of *Bayamo*. By 1515 his men had founded seven villages (having started with Baracoa in 1511): Bayamo in 1513; Trinidad, Sancti Spíritus and San Cristobal de La Habana in 1514; Puerto Príncipe and Santiago de Cuba in 1515. Santiago was designated as the government headquarters. Once the villages were stable and functioning, large plots of land in the countryside were granted to the colonists, with their economic viability assured through the mechanism of the *Encomiendas*. [42]

---

[41] Very few men in Cuba believed Hatuey's message or followed his plea; few joined him to fight. Velázquez, on the other hand, knew that when Tainos lost their Cacique they became disorganized and escaped from danger.

[42] The word derives from the Spanish *Encomendar*, which means "to entrust". The term was first used during the *Reconquista*, when the *adelantados* (advanced troops) in the peninsula were given the right to extract tribute from Muslims in areas reclaimed from the control of the Emirate. Unlike in the peninsula, however, the *Encomenderos* in Cuba were given help in acquiring the lands where the natives were "entrusted" to them, but were not granted property of the lands. The *Encomiendas* were abolished in 1720, but in places like Mexico (where a somewhat similar system existed among members of certain tribes), the *Encomenderos* were made ilegal only after the Mexican Revolution of 1911.

The *Encomienda* was a revocable and non-transferable legal construct by which a colonist committed to dress, feed, instruct and Chistianize a number of aborigines in exchange for the right of profiting from their work. An *Encomendero* had to give priority to government works, particularly mining, gold searching (mostly raking and skiming river sands) and road and building construction (building forts, bridges and public infrastructure). On a private level, *Encomenderos* could use their assigned indians for cattle raising, food gathering and preparation, leather tanning and other domestic chores. Many natives were forced to work beyond their physical limits, however, and were harshly punished if they resisted. From 1911 on, the phrase "*sin indios no hay Indias*," (without indians there are no Indies) reflected the importance of the indenture labor for the *Colonizadores*; it became the top argument to justify the abuses of the *Encomienda* system. [43] It is worth noticing that giving tribute in the form of work was not something new to the Tainos. They had been doing that for centuries after the Siboneyes began to enter their territories. It was easy for the Spaniards to capitalize on an already established Indian tradition.

A Cuban old Stamp showing a **Taino Cemi** from the *Montané Museum*, founded at the *University of Havana* in the 1920s.

---

[43] Only full-blooded Tainos were entered into the Encomienda system. A mixed-race indian, the product of intermarriage with Spaniards or Blacks, was never subjected to servitude.

Images above, left to right, top to bottom:

Diego Columbus, first Governor of the Indies in 1509;

Cacique Hatuey burning at the stake in 1512;

Diego Velazquez de Cuellar, friend of Columbus, member of the crew of Columbus on the second trip, first *Adelantado* of Cuba in 1518, founder of the first towns in Cuba;

a **1540 map of Havana**, showing projected fortifications and developments;

a **1942 postage stamp of Cuba**, celebrating the discovery of Tobacco.

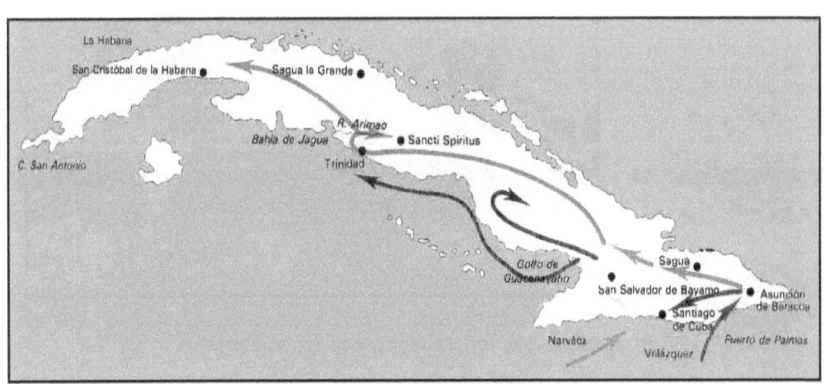

Images above, left to right, top to bottom:

A plaque commemorating the circumnavigation and survey of Cuba by **Sebastian de Ocampo** in 1507;

a portrait of **Ocampo**;

a cartoon showing the **founding of Santiago de Cuba** by Velázquez in 1515;

the routes exploring Cuba taken by **Pánfilo de Narvaez** in 1513 and Velázquez in 1514. Narvaez became a resident of Cuba and explorer of Florida while Velázquez, governor of Cuba, organized the first expeditions to explore Mexico.

Images above, left to right, top to bottom:

A drawing showing an **Encomendero** watching over Indians in the fields;

a drawing showing the **cruelty of Encomenderos** in Cuba;

two drawings by a Quechua nobleman, **Guamán Poma** (1535-1616), showing the protective duties and the cruelty of *Encomenderos*. The drawing on the right also shows an abusive priest;

ruins of **El Alcázar de Santo Domingo**, residence of Diego Columbus. It was there that Cortés, Pizarro, Balboa and Velázquez planned their conquests of Mexico, Perú, Panamá and Cuba. It was built in 1514 with 22 bedrooms and 72 doors and windows, without using a single nail.
It was restored to its greatness in 1955.

7

The Story of Fray Bartolomé de las Casas

BARTOLOME DE LAS CASAS (1484-1566) was a man of immense contradictions. On one hand he is considered a great humanitarian, the protector of the disappearing Taino indians, who could not physically tolerate the hard labor expected of them by the Spaniards. On the other hand, he was importantly instrumental in one of the greatest evils in human history: the importation of African slaves into the American continent to do the hard labor the Tainos could not perform.

Las Casas was born and grew up in Seville, where he witnessed the triumphant return of Columbus in 1493. His father (*Pedro Las Casas*, a merchant, descendant from one of the families that migrated from France and founded Seville) [44] and three uncles had joined the crew of Columbus on its second voyage to the Americas. In 1498 his father returned to the Caribbean, this time aboard a ship carrying two hundred slaves, one of which he brought with him back to Spain and gave it to Bartolomé as a present while he was a student at Salamanca.[45] In 1502 Bartolomé accompanied his father to Hispaniola, on the same expedition carrying Nicolás de Ovando. Bartolomé became an *hacendado* and slave owner of a dozen or so Tainos in the province of *Cibao*. In 1510 he became the first Catholic priest to be ordained in the Americas and joined the Dominican friars. As a priest he joined other Dominicans defending the institution of the *Encomiendas*. The entire Order of Santo Domingo

---

[44] Las Casas original family spelled their name *Casaus* They were probably *conversos*. Most Spanish last names that describe things (Casas, Rios, Puente, Lago, Tapia, Pozo, Puertas, etc.), are of *converso* heritage.

[45] After a 1500 royal order, *Adiutor*, Bartolomé's slave, had to be returned to Hispaniola.

de Guzmán (O.P.s) was asked by the crown to leave Hispaniola because of their support for the *Encomiendas*.

In 1513 Las Casas was the Spanish army chaplain during Velázquez' conquest of Cuba; he was a witness to the burning of *Hatuey* in Baracoa. A few months later he was awarded an *Encomienda* rich in gold and Taino slaves on the *Arimao* river near the town of *Fernandina de Jagua* (today's Cienfuegos). It was there that he had a dream in which he recalled an impassionate 1511 sermon by a Dominican preacher, Fray Antonio de Montesinos. Las Casas would later paraphrased the sermon in one of his writings:

«Tell me by what right of justice do you hold these Indians in such a cruel and horrible servitude? On what authority have you waged such detestable wars against these people who dealt quietly and peacefully on their own lands? Wars in which you have destroyed such an infinite number of them by homicides and slaughters never heard of before. Why do you keep them so oppressed and exhausted, without giving them enough to eat or curing them of the sicknesses they incur from the excessive labor you give them, and they die, or rather you kill them, in order to extract and acquire gold every day.»

That sermon had outraged Diego Columbus, who was present, and prompted King Ferdinand II's decision to ship the Dominican friars back to Spain. Later on the King was persuaded of the truthfulness of the Montesinos' positions and promulgated the Laws of Burgos, [46] the first code of ordinances that protected the indigenous people of the Americas.

Las Casas was so distressed by the situation of the indians that he gave up his slaves and his *Encomienda* and parted for Spain. There, on December 24, 1515, he met King Ferdinand II

---

[46] While preserving the institution of the *Encomiendas* and the mission of converting natives to Catholicism, the Laws of Burgos limited the number of natives under each *Encomendero* to less than 150, and rigurously regulated the regime of work, pay, provisions, living quarters, hygiene and family care. Women four months pregnant were exempted from work. No punishments were allowed for any natives under any circumstances. These orders created a momentum for reform but they were so poorly applied and adhered to that there were viewed simply as a way to legalize the tragic indian situation.

briefly and was promised a later, more detailed meeting. Unfortunately Ferdinand died on January 25, 1516, (Isabel I had died on November 26th 1504) and his temporary successor, while Ferdinand's son Prince Charles [47] was not of age, was Cardenal Ximénez de Cisneros, a reformer of the Franciscan friars, [48] Gran Inquisitor, founder of the *Universidad Complutense de Madrid* and probably the most influencial figure during the reign of Ferdinand II and Isabel I. Las Casas never got to present his denunciations of abuses at the Courts of Spain and Ximénez Cisneros was no help since he could no longer tolerate the unrelenting insistance of Las Casas. [49]

The only man who helped Las Casas in Spain was young Carlos I (Diego Columbus was his allied in the Americas). By then, however, there was a widespread opposition to Las Casas' ideas. He tried to provide a solution to the lack of labor if the *Encomiendas* were outlawed and suggested importing more slaves from Africa, an idea he was later to recant. At the time his fostering slavery increased the number of his enemies. Tainos, in the meantime, began to revolt in Hispaniola. [50]

His detractors used these events as proof that the only way to pacify the indians was to use military force. Las Casas entered a monastery in Hispaniola and became a Dominican itin-

---

[47] Charles assumed the trone in June of 1519 as Carlos I of Spain and Carlos V of the Holy Roman Empire. He had been born in Ghent, in the Flemish region of Belgium. His grandfathers were Ferdinand II of Spain and Maximilian I, Holy Roman Emperor. His aunt was Catherine of Aragón, first wife of Henry VIII of England. He spoke several languages and one of his favorite sayings was: «I speak Spanish to God, Italian to women, French to soldiers and German to my horse.»

[48] Under the Ximénes de Cisneros reform, all ordained friars (Franciscans or not) had to give up their mistresses, reside in the parish in which they practiced, hear confessions on Saturdays and preach every Sunday. The resistance was so intense that in the 1530s hundreds of monks fled to Africa with their concubines and converted to Islam.

[49] At the time, and for most of the next two centuries, there were irreconciliable differences between Franciscans and Dominicans.

[50] The Dominican convent in *Chiribichi* (Venezuela) was sacked by indians. Settlements of Dominican friars were raided in *Cubagua* (an island south of Margarita in Venezuela). The Caribes attacked settlements in *Cumaná* (east of Caracas).

erant priest. He began to travel strenously (Mexico, Panamá, Nicaragua, Guatemala, Cuba, Jamaica and Spain) and began to write his *Historia de las Indias*, (History of the Indies), soon to be followed by *Brevísima Relación de la Destrucción de las Indias* (A Short Account of the Destruction of the Indies). He accused *Encomenderos* of mortal sins from the pulpit, excommunicated them and refused absolution to slave owners, even on their death bed, unless their indians were freed and their property returned to them. In 1555, after Las Casas had sent his two books to Felipe II, [51] son of Charles V and Isabel de Portugal (and King of Spain starting in 1554), he found a formidable enemy in Toribio de Benavente, a Franciscan friar and scholar. To the accounts of Las Casas that Spaniards had committed abuses against native indians, Benavente argued that;

«Las Casas is an ignorant and arrogant troublemaker. He once denied baptism to an aging Indian who had walked many leagues to receive it, only on the grounds that prudish father Las Casas did not believe that the man had received sufficient doctrinal instruction.»

This type of rejection tormented Las Casas until his death in 1567; his ideas were rejected by Spanish society and he was widely considered a heretical extremist. The British often used Las Casas writings in their opposition and wars against Spain.[52] Las Casas has been openly accused by historians of exaggerating the presumed atrocities described. His figures on the initial populations of the Americas have proven to be too high, hence his claims of decimated natives were too large. He knew he was completly ignoring the deadly effect of diseases brought to the New World by the Spaniards.

The author that most widely disseminated the ideas of Bartolomé de Las Casas during the 1500s in Europe was

---

[51] They were only published, according to Las Casas wishes, forty years after his death. It was perplexing why Las Casas had made that determination, which ran against his urgency to resolve the indian problem.

[52] For the British, Las Casas' writings became the basis for the *Leyenda Negra* (the Black Legend), the continuous accusation and slanders that denounce Spain's imperial past as a stain in the history of humanity.

Theodorus de Bry (1528-1598), a jeweler, plate engraver and book editor from the city of Liege, in Belgium. De Bry created and published a large number of engraved illustrations to accompany his book *"Historical and True Account of the Cruel Massacres and Slaughters of above Twenty Millions of Innocent People Committed by the Spaniards, written in Spanish by Casaus (Las Casas), an Eye-witness of those Things."* He included in the first edition (1598) of this book[53] a series of horrifying illustrations of Spanish torture, none of which were drawn from life. These images, for 500 years, have been considered the embodiment of the Spanish encounter with the New World. The vast and grotesque amount of illustrations in De Bry's book had a remarkable influence on the European perception of the New World, particularly the presumed agressiveness and contempt of Spain for human life. It was an integral part of the *Leyenda Negra*. The verisimilitude of these drawings was as suspect as the stories of Las Casas, particularly since de Bry never crossed the Atlantic.

The *Leyenda Negra*[54] embodies an anti-Spanish propaganda created in the 1600s by writers from rival European powers, mostly from England and the Netherlands, to counter Spain's strength and influence in the world's political and economic theater. This propaganda characterized Spain as a heartless, intolerant, hypocritical, pharisaic and explotative country. The origin of the Black Legend was probably in medieval Italy, which from the 1300s to the end of the 1500s was very hostile to Spain. It was a normal reaction for a country (Italy) dominated by a foreign power (Spain). Documents from the times of the Spanish Inquisition, for instance, show that torture was used, but not more often or with a higher degree of cruelty than in other regions of Europe. To focus and isolate Spain as

---

[53] It would be worthwhile to explore why a Flemish speaking Protestant engraver, who lived almost his entire life in Huguenot strongholds in northeastern France, spent so much time illustrating an old book written in vernacular Spanish by a Catholic priest.

[54] The term was coined by Julián Juderías, a Spanish historian, sociologist and journalist, in his 1914 book *La Leyenda Negra y la Verdad Histórica* (The Black Legend and Historical Truth).

an extreme case of inhumanity with little regard for historical context, is precisely the myth propagated by the Black Legend.

Images above, left to right, top to bottom:

Fray **Bartolomé de las Casas** (1484-1566);

Theodor De Bry (1528-1598), the excellent engraver and poor historian who contributed to propagate Las Casas' exaggerations regarding the cruelty of Spain towards the Indians of America);

a **Cuban and Spanish postal stamps** commemorating the presence and work of Las Casas during the colonization of Cuba.

Images from De Bry's book, top to bottom:

Multiple hangings. Note the Spaniards are much larger and clothed than the naked natives. The etching brings an element of power and erotic licentiousness to the scene (the hanging woman on the right);

Burning of troublemakers. The scene on the left seems inspired by Catholic paintings of the descending of Christ from the cross. On the right, cruelty is depicted in the image of a man's arm being chopped off.

Images from De Bry's book, top to bottom:

Cannibalism among the Indians. On the right, a human body is roasted on a grill. On the left a native woman exchanges her jewels for a piece of human flesh, while a man offers an anchor for trade. Other natives do the same on the right, while several Spaniards try to keep order;

Nude body of a nubile woman. An erotic image of a hanged woman exits from a dark tabernacle, probably a reference to saints' niches in Catholic churches. Spanish cruelty is depicted as two dogs eat the sliced body of a child while a priest (left) does not object to the butchery.

«The Spaniards with their horses, their spears and lances, began to commit murders and other strange cruelties. They entered into towns and villages, sparing neither children nor old men and women. They ripped their bellies and cut them to pieces as if they had been slaughtering lambs in a field. They made bets with each other over who could thrust a sword into the middle of a man or who could cut off his head with one stroke. They took little ones by their heels and crushed their heads against the cliffs. Others they threw into the rivers laughing and mocking them as they tumbled into the water. They put everyone they met to the edge of the sword.»

«One time I saw four or five important native nobles roasted and broiled upon makeshift grills. The cried out pitifully. This troubled our Captain; he commanded that from there on they be strangled.»

«They are slaughterers and enemies of mankind; they even taught their hounds, to tear natives to pieces at first sight. And, when, although rare, the Indians put to death some Spaniards upon good right and law of justice, the Spaniards decided that for every one Spaniard killed they had to slay one hundred Indians.»

«One time the Indians received us with food and good cheer! The Spaniards, put them all to the edge of the sword in my presence, more than three thousand souls. In three or four months (myself being present) there died more than six thousand children.»

Images above: some of the many books based on Las Casas accounts (with etchings by De Bry) that became part of the **Black Legend against Spain**. On the frame, the exaggerated and damaging words of Las Casas, so many times quoted as truthful by enemies of Spain.

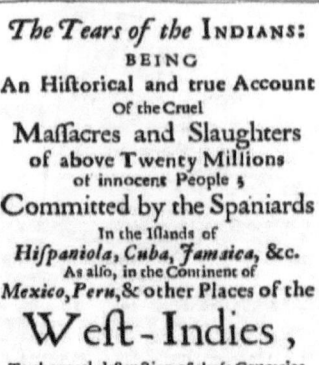

Images above, left to right, top to bottom:

Franciscan priest **Fray Francisco Ximénez de Cisneros, O.F.**, pro-tempore Spanish monarch after the death of Ferdinand II;

the **announcement** of De Bry's book;

the **first page** of De Bry's book (1598);

Cover of *La Historia General de las Indias*, by Dominican priest **Fray Bartolomé de las Casas, O.P.**

8
Cuba and the Four Great Conquistadores

ONE OF THE CLUMSY CLAIMS of father Las Casas was that the Americas were one the most populous areas of the world; this exaggeration allowed him to increase the horror associated with the alleged atrocities committed by the *Conquistadores*.

In the XV century, the population of an area depended on the fertility of its lands and the agricultural technology that the inhabitants had reached to work the soil, produce food and secure life's staples such as wood, fiber and water. Upon arrival of the Spaniards, most American territories were unprofitable forests and mountainous regions. Las Casas, however, presented the forests of the Caribbean and its few rivers as one of the world's most populous land, a busy workplace like no other in Europe. Nicaragua, for instance, was described as a rich region, full of overflowing towns, that extended for more than three or four leagues in diameter. Its towns, according to him, were literally much larger than any European cities. Modern archeology, of course, has not found a trace of such dense human populations. Logically, most of those regions had a human density no greater than those of today's Amazon jungles; the technical tools they had were very rudimentary, incapable of feeding large numbers of families. [55]

The exception would be developed empires, particularly the Maya, the Inca and the Aztec. The Inca, at the top of their development, had an area of about two million square kilometers.

---

[55] The population consisted mostly of small wandering tribes who practiced cannibalism -anthropophagy in more elegant terms. In fact, cannibalism derived from *Caníbales*, the term used by Spaniards for the Caribe people. Human flesh was probably the only unlimited protein source for many peoples of the Americas.

In some areas they had fertile agricultural lands where good yields could be obtained; the empire, however, was mostly steep and barren land with uncultivable forests. Their agricultural techniques were rudimentary, years or rather a millennium behind what was practiced in the Mediterranean region, particularly France and Italy. The Incas had almost no trade; some cities had monumental structures, but they were few. It is doubtful that the population of the Inca empire, could be higher than that of Spain at the time. [56]

The Aztec empire was of similar area than the Iberian Peninsula. [57] Soil fertility in the areas under Aztec control was rather poor and the agricultural development of the Aztecs was just as poor. Production of foodstuffs required enormous amount of work without the benefit of the wheel,[58] and commerce was still at the level of barter.[59] It is unlikely that the population of the Aztec empire would exceed more than one third to one half that of contemporary Spain. The Maya civilization was similar in size, but ist inhabited lands were too dense in non-edible vegetation. It was unlikely that the Mayan population, at its peak, would be more that one tenth of Spain's.

The exagerations of Las Casas reached too far to be believable. He claimed, for instance, that the Spanish massacred most Aztecs, «in four or five hundred leagues around Tenochtitlán, at the center of the empire. This comprised more people that the populations of Toledo, Sevilla, Valladolid, Zaragoza and Barcelona, all together...» In the words of Menéndez y Pidal: [60]

---

[56] At the end of the XV century, during the times of the discovery of America, Spain had a population of perhaps 5 million people.

[57] Not to be confused with current Mexico, which is, after all, a Spanish and North American creation. The Aztecs occupied an area four times smaller than today's Republic of Mexico.

[58] The Incas had not discovered the wheel either.

[59] The Aztecs had not developed the concept of money and gold had no monetary value.

[60] Ramón Menéndez y Pidal (1869-1968), an extraordinary Spanish philologist and historian, born in Galicia, member of the Spanish Academy for 67 years, exiled in 1939 to France, Cuba and the US, where he taught at Columbia University in New York.

«*Las Casas presenta la colonización de America como un inmenso desierto de fatigosa monotonía, donde no hay otra cosa que infernales crímenes inculpados cien y cien veces a todos los Cristianos... un discurso de escándalo, un libelo infamante, donde se enormiza de tal forma la realidad que invalida el insólito valor moral de su generosa denuncia.*» (Las Casas presents the colonization of America as a vast desert of tiresome monotony, where there is nothing but infernal crimes attributed hundreds of times to all Christians... a scandalous speech, a defamatory libel, where such overstated reality invalidates the moral value of his generous denunciation.)

Bartolomé de Las Casas, nevertheless, had an extraordinary influence over future perceptions about the Spanish exploration and occupation of the Americas. The men who sailed beyond Europe after the "reconquest" of the Iberian peninsula, departed from Cuba to conquer new territories, Christianize native Americans and open trade routes on behalf of Spain. History has designated them as the *Conquistadores*. They were simple soldiers, explorers, priests and adventurers at the service of the Spanish crown. They departed from Cuba because there were no riches to be had there and because Cuba was turning into the springboard for all fantasies and illusions of a New World where fortunes, positions and power could be acquired fast.

By and large the *Conquistadores* were amateur warriors brandishing European strategies, weapons and cavalry, searching for territories they could own and utilize for their own purposes, whether religious, political or economic. Many men served on infantry groups; most of them had no military experience. Priests helped with administrative duties since they were the only ones who could write and read. The core of each campaign was always manned by professional soldiers or mercenaries that had had warfare experience during the *reconquista* or the wars in northern Africa. Native Americans were also part of the *Conquista* throngs. They served as interpreters, guides, physicians, scribes, nurses and servants. Many non-Castillian speaking Europeans joined the Spanish forces, usually hispanizing their names; a notable one was *Amerigo Vespucci*, aka Americo Vespucio.

There were four very famous *Conquistadores* that captivated the imagination of people in Europe: *Hernán Cortés*, the conqueror of the Aztec Empire; *Francisco Pizarro*, the man who led the conquest of the Inca Empire; *Vasco Nuñez de Balboa*, the European that for the first time saw the Pacific Ocean, and *Juan Ponce de León*, the explorer of Florida and the first European to enter what is now the United States. Several Catholic religious orders sent ministers to support the explorations, care for the *Conquistadores* souls, evangelize the natives and pacify the occupation efforts. They were mostly Dominican, Franciscan, Carmelite and Jesuit priests.

The *Conquistadores* did not reserve their fighting energies and maltreatment only for the natives. They frequently fought among themselves with the same ferociousness, harshness and inhumanity. As we shall see later, Diego Velázquez, governor of Cuba, and Diego Colombus, the Vicerroy, for instance, were mortal enemies of Hernan Cortés and tried to boycot his mission; Franciscio Pizarro and Diego de Almagro, his *Adelantado*,[61] became enemies and Almagro was eventually executed by Pizarro's men.

The first *Conquistadores* were organized and launched from Cuba by Diego Velázquez de Cuellar, Cuba's first *Adelantado* and governor.[62] His first two missions out of Cuba were of no significance: on the first, in 1517, Francisco Hernández de Córdoba was sent to the coast of Yucatán, where Velázquez had news of strong natives that could serve as slaves. Hernández de Córdoba returned with news of his landing but no slaves. On the second, his nephew Juan de Grijalba was sent to Yucatán with four ships in 1518, landed in the Tabasco region of current Mexico, reported to Velázquez that he had seen gold in

---

[61] In the Middle ages, *Adelantado* was a title given to Spanish nobles for service to their kings; in the Americas, they were nobles, their titles granted by the monarchs with the right to become governors of the areas where they worked as *Conquistadores*.

[62] By 1511, Diego Velázquez had colonized and pacified Hispaniola and Cuba, under orders from Diego Columbus.

the area, stayed in the region for nine years and died there in 1527, without bringing gold or riches back to Velázquez.

The third expedition brought different results. Enticed by the gold findings in Tabasco, Velázquez sent Hernán Cortés (Chief Magistrate of the Court of Santiago de Cuba) to Mexico in 1519, with the result that the entire Aztec Empire, as well as all its gold, fell under Spanish control. Unfortunately Velázquez and Cortés had never gotten along and a year later Velázquez ended up sending Pánfilo de Narváez [63] to arrest Cortés, who took advantage of his knowledge of the terrain and was waiting for Narváez, defeated him and made him prisoner.

The vanquisher of the Aztecs, Hernán Cortés (1485-1547), first set sail for America in 1504, joining an expedition to Cuba. Four years later he was in Mexico, commanding an expedition of 600 men and a few horses. There, he would strategically align some natives against others and be victorious above all of them. In 1522, King Charles I of Spain, aka Charles V of Germany, rewarded him with the title of governor of New Spain (today's Mexico).

Cortés fought his way into Tenochtitlán, the capital city of the Aztec Empire, by fighting natives in Tlaxacan and Cholula. At the time, the Aztec Empire was under the command of Emperor Montezuma II. Cortés took the Mexican Emperor hostage and his troops plundered and despoiled Tenochtitlán. Cortés demanded and obtained a sizable gold and jewelry ramson for Montezuma II, but his troops were defeated and Tenochtitlán was recovered by the Aztecs in June of 1520, in what is now

---

[63] Pánfilo de Narváez (1478-1528) was a Castilian related to Velázquez by marriage. He had conquered Jaimaica in 1509 and explored eastern Cuba with Bartolomé de las Casas in 1511. He was responsible of *the Masacre de Caonao*, near present day Camagüey, where in a bloodthirsty frenzy, Narváez troops anihilated an entire village of Tainos that had come forward to greet them. This occurred in the presence of Las Casas and became the main reason for his many campaigns in favor of humane treatment of Cuba's native population. Narváez eventually died on an expedition to North America after a storm wrecked his ships. Only four of his men survived and began a land trek from the Florida panhandle to the Spanish posessions in Mexico. Eight years later they arrived safely at Culiacán, Sinaloa, Mexico, where they founded a Spanish settlement.

called the *Noche Triste*.[64] Cortés full domination of the Aztec Empire did not come about until 1521. It was, to that point, the largest and wealthiest posession Spain had acquired in the New World. Cortés was forcibly retired to Spain in 1540 and spent the last years of his life trying to be recognized for his achievements. He died in Spain in 1547, leaving some of his fortune to a girl named simply María, believed to be a daughter that *la Malinche* had with him.

While this was happening in Mexico, a *Conquistador* named Francisco Pizarro, departing from Cuba, was ready to advance the Spanish cause by taking over the Inca Empire of Perú.

One of the most important campaigns of Spain in the Americas was the conquest and colonization of Perú. Less that 200 men captured the *Sapa Inca Atahualpa* in the 1532 Battle of Cajamarca in Perú. The Empire included not only Perú but also regions like present day Chile, Colombia and the Amazon jun-

---

[64] The *Noche Triste* (The Night of Sorrows) occurred on June 30, 1520. Following the death of Montezuma II (pelted by stones, accused by the Aztecs of cowardice in the presence of a new King, Cuitláhuac), Cortés troops, under severe attack by the Aztecs and very short of food and water, tried to retreat away from Tenochtitlán, not knowing the Aztecs had damaged four of the bridges in the causeways leading out of the city.

Cortés attempted to escape using the Tlacopan road, which was apparently unguarded. The fighting at the bridge was furious after hundreds of canoes with Mexicans showed up in the middle of the retreat. Many soldiers drowned because the weight of the gold they were carrying for and by themselves. Cortés returned several times to the bridge after reaching dry land. On one of these occasions he rescued Pedro de Alvarado, his own second in command, unhorsed and wounded.

Alvarado had been his friend in Cuba and had been part of the Cortés expedition to Mexico, leading one of his ships. He had been left in charge of Tenochtitlán while Cortés fought Pánfilo de Narvaez when he was sent to Mexico to arrest Cortés. As he saw Alvarado collapsing and crumbling, Cortés cried inconsolably as he realized the extent of his humiliating defeat, hence the naming of the event as *la Noche Triste*. It has been estimated that 450 Spanish Conquistadores and 4,000 of their native allies died, while probably 350 Aztecs perished in the effort.

Once Cortés found safe refuge in Tlaxcala, he began to plot a new siege of Tenochtitlán, which he accomplished with predominantly native people in 1521. His common wife, *la Malinche*, also survived *la Noche Triste*. She had been his interpreter Nahuatl-to-Mayan, which required a priest, Gerónimo de Aguilar to complete the process with Mayan-to-Castilian translation.

gles; it all fell into Spanish hands. It was one of the greatest military victories in world's history.

In 1528, when the Spanish *Conquistadores* arrived at the borders of the Inca Empire, the territory under Inca jurisdiction extended from present southern Colombia to the Maule River in Chile, across the jungles of the Amazon River; it was one of the more mountainous and impenetrable areas in the world. Its extension was probably close to 2 million square kilometers in area, with a total population of 16 million people. The Empire was past its glorious zenith but the *Tahuantisuyu*,[65] as the Incas called it, was the largest territory under a single ruler on all known regions of the word known to the Incas. The Empire was run by descendants of its founder, a man called *Huayna Capac*; his sons were named *Huáscar* and *Atahualpa*. The sons [66] had a war of succession going at the time of Pizarro arrival. *Atahualpa* had been his father's right hand assistant in his conquest of what is now Ecuador and was closer to *Huayna Capac* than his legitimate son *Huáscar*. In fact, *Huáscar* was in Cusco at the time *Huayna Capac* died [67] and proclaimed himself the new *Sapa Inca* (only Emperor). The army, however, backed *Atahualpa*; the resulting war of succesion debilitated and distracted the empire and provided an easier burden to Francisco Pizarro. The Spanish brought horses, metal armor, cannons, swords and firearms to Perú. Atahualpa was able to recruit an army of 30,000 warriors, captured *Huáscar* in Cusco and sent messengers all over the empire. The very same day this occurred, Pizarro, with his three brothers Gonzalo, Juan and Hernando,

---

[65] *Tahuantisuyu* literally meant land of the four quarters, the regions of the Empire in which the territory was divided.

[66] *Atahualpa* was an illegitimate son of *Huayna Capac*. *Huáscar* was the legitimate son of *Coya Mama Raua Occllo*, the sister-wife of *Huayna Capac*.

[67] Possibly from smallpox, a disease that had been brought to Perú by the Spaniards.

were descending from the Andes into the Inca town of Cajamarca. [68]

Atahualpa, victorious over his brother, received the *Conquistadores* with gifts and good will. He agreed to meet De Soto, and later Pizarro himself. On the date agreed for a meeting with Pizarro, *Atahualpa* showed up with 7,000 unarmed soldiers. A friar accompanying Pizarro showed *Atahualpa* a Bible and told him that they were there by virtue of a mandate from God. *Atahualpa* took the bible in his hands and placed it by his ear, declaring he could not hear anything from the Spaniard's God. [69] Indignant by the Inca's contempt for the Bible the Spaniards attacked the Emperor, brought him into submission and made him prisoner, all before the surprised eyes of his followers. Eventually Pizarro executed *Atahualpa* and his 12-man honor guard, but not before *Atahualpa's* men tried to rescue the Emperor by filling a room to the ceiling with gold and silver.

Pizarro and De Soto were opposed to *Atahualpa's* death but the opinions and wishes of their troops prevailed. He was accused of polygamy, incestuous marriage, idolatry and other sins that were not outlawed by the Inca culture. He was garroted and died in 1533, after converting to Chistianism.

After *Atahualpa's* death, the *Tahuantisuyu* (the Inca Empire) was considered ended, but numerous revolts ensued. The last Inca was *Túpac Amaru*, who was murdered by the Spaniards in 1572, closing a conquest that took 40 years to be completed. The end of the story is that Pizarro had Almagro killed in 1538; he had been his former companion, conqueror of Chile and in time his mortal enemy. Almagro's descendants later avenged his death by killing Pizarro in 1541.

---

[68] Reports had it that he counted with 168 men, 106 on foot and 62 on horses. One of the men on horse was Hernando de Soto, who would become famous during his incursions in Florida starting in 1527.

[69] Atahualpa had never seen a book in his life. It is said he threw the Bible on the ground.

The man who fought side by side with Francisco Pizarro during the conquest of Perú was an old hand among the Spanish *Conquistadores*: Hernando de Soto.

De Soto had been born into a noble but poor family in 1497in Jerez, Spain. Unlike many other *Conquistadores*, he received a solid education at the University of Salamanca, where he almost graduated as a lawyer. In 1533 he became the main organizer of the conquest of the Inca Empire and was the top strategist for the successful battle to capture Cusco. He returned to Cuba and Spain as a wealthy man, with no less than 18 thousand ounces of pure Inca gold.

He settled in Seville and married; he became restless, however, when he heard about the exploration of Florida. In 1539, barely six years after the death of *Atahualpa* and once more eager for conquests, he set out from Cuba towards North America, where he discovered the Mississippi river.[70] In the midle of his successes he was struck with fever and died on May 21, 1542 in Louisiana. His body was buried at sea, at the mouth of the Mississippi river.

The fourth important Conquistador that sailed from Cuba was Vasco Nuñez de Balboa (1475-1519). He was of aristocratic blood, his father an *hidalgo*, lord mason of the Castle of Balboa, his mother had the title of Lady of Badajoz.[71] Their son originally settled in Hispaniola and later in Cuba. His first trip to America had been with Juan de la Cosa and he faithfully followed the Law of the *Quinto Real*.[72] He became a wealthy man. In 1501, however, at the age of 25, he was almost ruined and in 1509, wishing to escape his creditors, he set sail as a stowaway.

---

[70] He personally financed an expedition of 10 ships, 700 selected men and a crew of poligraphers, interpreters and professional explorers. On May 18, 1539 he landed at Tampa Bay, moving later to present day Georgia and Alabama.

[71] It was said at the times that people like him were "men of good family who were nor reared behind a plow."

[72] One fifth of all the gold findings were for the crown of Spain, four fifths were for the finder.

With time, due to his experience, inteligence and personality, he became governor of the territory of Veragua in today's Venezuela. It was there that he first heard of a "New Sea" on the other side of Panamá, which was then a new kingdom, rich in gold and men who were easy to conquer. He organized an expedition to find what is now the Pacific Ocean. With 190 men and a pack of tracking dogs, he began to cross the dense jungles of the istmus of Panamá on September 1, 1513. He described it as...

"going across jungles, rivers and swamps, ascending cordilleras and descending into hot valleys where enormous grasses were taller than big men."

On September 25 he reached the summit of a mountain range along the *Chucunaque* river, a tributary of the Tuira river in today's province of Darien, Panama. From there he saw an immense new ocean. He immediately had a fleet of small ships built and transported in pieces across the mountains to the western side of the istmus, to the sea shore at what is today the Gulf of San Miguel. A few days after he arrived, on September 29, raising his arms, his sword in one, a standard with the image of the Virgen Mary in the other, Balboa walked knee-deep into the new ocean, claimed posession of it and all surrounding lands on behalf of the Monarchs of Spain and drank a glass of its waters. He had defeated several Caciques on his way, had collected gold and pearls and had sent the corresponding fifth part to Spain.

Due to the customary, inevitable and inescapable disputes, Balboa was accused of stealing and taking merits from others by a powerful elderly nobleman, Pedro Arias Dávila (aka Pedrarias), the Spanish governor of Darien. Under his orders, Balboa was made prisoner by Francisco Pizarro in 1519. An executioner beheaded him with an axe, in front of his friends, at age 44.

The death of Cortés, Pizarro, De Soto and Balboa did not end the story of the *Conquistadores*. They dominated the news during the Renaissance and the Elizabethan Age. Their success in acquiring monopolies on much of the world's trade and their control of the New World, brought untold gold and silver riches, great prosperity, power and influence to Spain. The Spaniards had successfully taken the Iberian peninsula, after nearly eight hundred years of dominance by Muslim Moors, to the peak of wellbeing and national prosperity in a world formely dominated by the British and other European powers.[73]

Two views of **La Malinche**, the native woman who assisted Hernán Cortés during the conquest of Mexico after he left Cuba. On top, a XIX century drawing by an unknown artist; on the bottom, the famous mural *by Diego* Rivera.

---

[73] Many other *Conquistadores* served Spain during the XVI century: Francisco Vázquez de Coronado, Juan Ponce de León, Juan de Oñate, Alvar Núñez Cabeza de Vaca, Pedro Méndez de Avilés, Martín de Ursua, Francisco de Orellana and Gonzalo Jiménez de Quesada, to mention a few.

Images above, top to bottom, left to right:

Hernán Cortés (1485-1587), conqueror of the Aztecs;

the image of Cortés by **Diego Rivera** on the National Palace in Mexico city. Knowing that noble men were proud of their legs, Rivera painted Cortés with large, deformed looking knees;

Montezuma II, Emperor of the Aztecs;

a view of the Aztec city of **Tenochtitlán**.

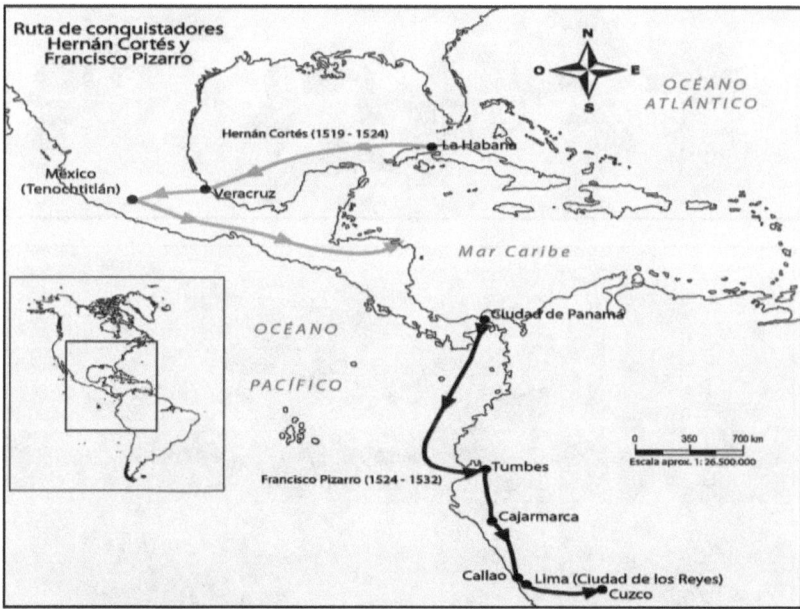

Images, top to bottom:

The retreat of Cortés from Tenochtitlán on **Noche Triste**, the Night of Sorrows, June 30, 1520;

the trajectories of **Cortés** through Aztec lands of Mexico and **Pizarro's** on his way to the capital of the Inca Empire in Perú;

a portrait of *Pánfilo de Narváez*, the *Conquistador* sent to Mexico to arrest Hernán Cortés in 1520.

Images above, top to bottom, left to right:

Francisco Pizarro (1476-1541), conqueror of the Incas;

Atahualpa, Emperor of the Incas;

the **arrest of Atahualpa** on November 16, 1532 at Cajamarca, where he had been invited by Pizarro;

the **death of Atahualpa** on August 29, 1533.
He was strangled with a garrote and later burned at the stake.

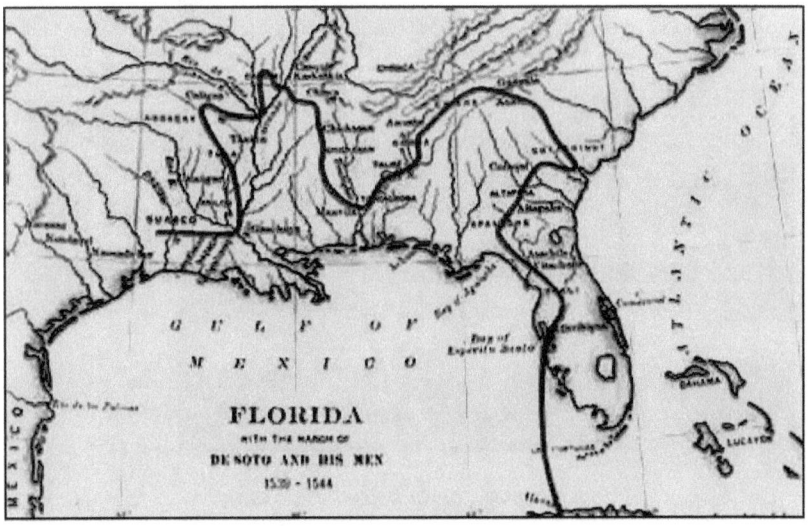

Images above, top to bottom, left to right:

Hernando de Soto (1497-1542), first European to enter territory that is now the United States;

Ponce de León (1460-1521), leader of the first Spanish expedition into Florida (which he named) in search of the Fountain of Youth;

a map showing the **trajectory of De Soto** in Florida, Georgia and Alabama in 1544.

Images above, top to bottom, left to right:

Vasco Nuñez de Balboa (1475-1519), the first European to have seen and reached the Pacific Ocean;

a US Postage Stamp commemorating the **discovery of the Pacific Ocean**;

the many **expeditionary routes taken by Balboa** during his lifetime, covering five continents;

Balboa **taking possession** of and submerging himself in the Pacific Ocean on September 29, 1513.

9

First Successes and Perils for Colonial Cuba

AS THE ADVENTURESOME SPANISH *Conquistadores* spread from Cuba to the rest of America, a profound mistake was taking place in the gold-deprived island. A town that in time would become the capital of the island, was founded in the wrong place. On July 25, 1515, the day the Catholic Church was celebrating the sainthood of San Cristóbal, the standard of Castile was planted at the mouth of the *rio Güines*, or *Mayabeque*, in the southern coast of what the Spaniards identified as the *Cacicazgo de la Habana*. [74] It was the seventh Spanish settlement founded in the island and was baptized by Pánfilo de Narváez as the *Villa de San Cristobal de la Habana*. [75]

A few months of experience showed that the place selected to create the town was not appropriate because of its humidity; the settlement was moved north, to the banks of the river *Casiguaguas* (also known as *Almendares*, or *Chorrera*); this location also proved inconvenient, this time due to difficult access to a secured body of water. Finally, four years later, the decision was made to move the small population [76] to its final des-

---

[74] The reason the original place of Havana was in the southern coast was probably that it would be in the path of many expeditions of the times that were headed to the north and eastern side of South America; having a town in southern Cuba could facilitate trade and replenishment of provisions.

[75] The location of the original Havana was near today's Batabanó, an enclave already inhabited by a small number of Tainos. It resembled a tiny and spartan military garrison. The name honored both Columbus (whose first name was *Cristobal* in Spanish) and *Habaguanex*, the Cacique who commanded the seas from Cuba to he north of South America.

[76] It was reported that the first settlers were 38 permanent residents and 13 temporaries. At the time, these figures did not usually include women, children, black slaves or native indians.

tination, a beautiful port that had been named *Carenas*. [77] It had been discovered by Sebastián de Ocampo during his circumnavigation of the island in 1507 (November 16th). Under a *ceiba* tree, [78] the founding fathers met and young Cuban clerics celebrated a first Mass; church and state officials later paraded the new town flag three times around the *ceiba* tree trunk. [79] Centuries later, in 1828, a small neo-classical church, el *Templete*, was erected at the place of this first Mass to mark the spot.

Columbus never visited any of the three Havanas. For quite a while, interestingly, the name of the town was spelled in different ways since an official spelling was never established. Las Casas (in Cuba 1514-1520) wrote the name of the town as *la Aana, la Vana, Sant Havana* and *La Habana*. From there on it has been *Havana* in Italian, *La Habana* in Spanish, while the British write *Havana*, the Germans *Havanna* and the French La *Havane*.

Not five years had passed since Havana began to grow on the western side of the bay formely called *Carenas*, the town began to suffer the sudden and quick attacks of pirates sponsored by the Kings of France. In 1520, a group of Spanish ships

---

[77] The name *Carenas* came about because Ocampo had "careened" there (sealed) his ship's bottoms using some tar (asphalt) found in the area. The only remains left today at the old Almendares river location is the small fort of *La Chorrera*, designed by military architects from the Antonelli Roman family, who were at the service of the Spanish crown.

[78] *Ceiba* is the generic name of many species of huge tress (up to 70 ft tall) found in the jungles of Central America, the Caribbean, West Africa and some islands in Southeast Asia. *Ceiba pentandra* is its botanical name.

[79] All *Ceibas* were attributed magical powers and became highly revered trees in Taino Cuba. In the 1600s they became sacred trees for the *Yorubas* who were arriving in Cuba as slaves from their kingdoms in Nigeria and Senegal; it was no doubt due to the similarity of the *ceiba* with the magic African *baobab* tree. *Ceibas* are considered homes of the *Orishas* or deities, who are thought to perch on their branches, particularly *Aggayu Sola*, the protector of travelers. Nowadays, on November 16*th*, many *Habaneros* attend the "Mass of the Mute" at Havana Cathedral and solemnly walk a few blocks to the *ceiba* tree by the *Templete* (a 1960 specimen that has replaced the original tree). They walk three times around the tree, touching the bark with their left hand and holding the right hand over their hearts. They are supposed to have a wish come true. There are many *ceiba* trees all over Cuba, in town squares and cemeteries, as well as along the main roads.

leaving Havana for Spain were attacked by Giovanni da Verrazzano, an Italian mercenary at the service of France, who robbed all treasures carried by the convoy. Other French corsaries came in the 1520s to plunder the small village of Havana. It was then that the Spanish crown began to build fortifications to protect the city. *La Fuerza* castle [80] was built across the sacred *ceiba* where the city had been founded; French privateers, however, continued to plunder the city until the mid 1500s. The isolated and unprotected trading port suffered numerous attacks by buccaneers, pirates and corsairs. [81]

The first serious attack to Havana by a corsair was made by Jacques de Sores in 1555; he took Havana easily, plundering the city and burning it to the ground. He could not find much of value in the city and left highly frustrated. He was instrumental, however, in the Spanish decision to fortify the city. From there on, the traffic from Havana to the peninsula (upon the recommendation of Pedro Menéndez de Avilés, an adviser to King Felipe II), began to be made in convoys, large annual fleets where numerous ships made possible the mutual protection of their cargo. [82] Recent archeological studies have shown

---

[80] When Havana was settled in 1515 in the place it is today, the main square of the new town was not where the *Plaza de Armas* is today. It was next to a *La Fuerza* Castle, which was not the fortress that we know today either; the first fortress called *La Fuerza* was a wooden structure near to but not exactly where the *Castillo de la Fuerza* is today.

[81] *Bucaneers* were adventurers with fairly large ships who attacked coastal cities and towns for their personal benefit. They were originally based on Hispaniola but eventually established a large base of operations in Tortuga island. *Pirates were* similar to bucaneers but their acts of criminal violence were committed preferably on the high seas; they also profited directly from their stolen cargo. *Corsairs* (aka privateers) were individuals authorized by the French government to conduct raids on a nation at war with France. Their seized goods were sold at auction, with *Corsair* crews receiving a portion of the proceeds.

[82] In Spain these fleets were called the *Flotas de las Indias*. Eastbound, they sailed to Seville or Cadiz transporting agricultural goods, lumber, raw industrial metals, silver, gold, gems, pearls, spices, sugar, tobacco and silk. Passengers, civil servants, textiles, books and tools were transported on the westbound return trips. Pirates resorted to only shadow the fleets and attack the stragglers.

that the treasures carried out by the convoys were much larger than those registered in the cargo records; Spanish merchants and individual front men resorted to contraband to avoid paying their 20% taxes to the *Casa de Contratación de Sevilla*, the Spanish Empire taxing and commerce agency. By he end of the 1500s, Spain had become the richest country in Europe. Her wealth, however, was dilapidated by the Habsburgs [83] fighting wars against the Ottoman Empire and all other major European powers. Eventhough the Spanish Empire lasted until the early 1800s, Spain's wealth lost its luster by the end of the 1600s.

What the Spanish throne had accomplished with its explorations and colonizations, suffered a severe setback in the following centuries from two fronts: buccaneers, pirates and corsairs in the XVI to XIX centuries attacked and plundered their ships; Colonial rivals (England, France, the Dutch, Portugal) invaded Spanish territories and established their own settlements throughout the XVII century.

Piracy in the islands of the Caribbean were only overcome in the 1800s when the navies of countries with posessions in the area began fighting the marauders. Their peak of activity were the years between mid-1600s to mid-1700s.

Typically, pirates, bucaneers and corsaries were castaway former sailors looking for lucrative opportunities either by seizing the cargo of ships sailing to Europe or by attacking the coastal cities that received the wealth in transit. Piracy, at times, was given a legal status (privateers or corsaires) by colonial powers, particularly under King Francis I (1515-1547) of France. The towns most favored for attacks were Cartagena, Panama City, Santiago de Cuba and Santo Domingo. The pil-

---

[83] The House of Habsburg occupied the throne of the Holy Roman Empire between 1438 and 1740; at different points the family had members in the thrones of England, Germany, Hungary, Spain, Portugal and Dutch and Italian kingdoms. The family took its name from a fortress in Switzerland, where a nobleman called Otto II gave himself, for the first time, the title of Count of Habsburg in the XI century.

laged ships, attacked both in the Caribbean and all the way across the Atlantic, were almost always from Spain. [84]

Among the British privateers, the best known was Sir Francis Drake (1540-1596), vice admiral, navigator and politician in the Elizabethan era. [85] His exploits were acclaimed in England while the Spaniards considered him a bastard and referred to him by the derogatory name of *El Draque*. King Felipe II offered a reward of 20,000 ducats for his capture. [86] Drake's main field of action was the Caribbean, particularly Cuba, and Panama, [87] which was the place at which the gold and silver from Peru was transferred overland to the Caribbean. It was said that Drake was so successful taking gold from Spain (some batches weighted more than 20 tons of gold) that on many ocassions he had to bury it since he had no way to carry it out with him.

While Drake was proving he was unstoppable, the Dutch, the French and, obviously the British, began seeking to expand their colonial holdings in America now that Spain had proven them to be so profitable. As early as 1538, for instance, French Huguenots established settlements in the West Indies, particularly the island of St Kitts. Within two decades the British displaced them; they were in turn expelled by Spain. In 1624, the

---

[84] Although *Corsaires* were not part of the French navy, they were considered legitimate combatants in France, providing the ship's captain had a valid *Lettre de Marque* or *Lettre de Course* (hence the name *Corsaires*). If captured by Spain, they could claim the status of prisoners of war and escape being hanged. These prerogatives gave them a flamboyant and swashbuckling reputation. Corsair activities were known in the Middle Ages but achieved their zenith when there were new opportunities to take the huge wealth that Spain was transfering from America to Spain.

[85] Elizabeth I of England awarded Drake his knighthood in 1581. Drake's motto was *Sic Parvis Magna* (Great things come from small things).

[86] About US $7 million in today's money. It was said that frustrated for not being able to capture Drake (after his raids in Cartagena, Colombia, San Agustín in Florida, and Santo Domingo (all within 12 months), Felipe II of Spain decided to invade England and ordered plans for an attack by *La Armada Invencible* (the Spanish Armada).

[87] The *Istmus of Panama* was known to Spain as *Tierra Firme*; the British called it the *Spanish Main*. It has been the venue of many novels and films.

British took again from Spain the island of St Kitts, and reached an agreement with the French to jointly own the land. St Kitts became the base for British and French expansion into Antigua, Monserrate, Tortola, Anguila (by the British), and Martinique, the Guadalupe archipielago and St Barts (by the French). At the end, the British fought the French and kept St Kitts (as well as Nevis) for themselves. The French also established one of their colonies in Fort Caroline, near what later became Jacksonville, Florida. Spain, the most powerful Christian kingdom of the times, could not provide enough military presence to sustain exclusive ownership of the Americas. Those were times of frequent wars among Europeans; every time a war exploded in Europe, privateering and large scale incursions resulted in the Caribbean. On ricochet, trade and territory disputes in the Caribbean resulted in European powers fighting each other in the Old Continent.

In the meantime, Spain was making a succession of long term mistakes. Spanish capital was almost uniquely dedicated to extracting mineral and agricultural wealth from the colonies. Exports to the peninsula were preferred to building productive, self-sustaining settlements in the New World. Massive shipments of silver and gold to Western Europe began to fuel inflationary stresses. Wars in Europe began to consume enormous amount of wealth. Spain's inefficient system of tolls and tariffs hampered commerce. Spain's aristocracy disparaged investing in industrial opportunities as beneath their class, hence few industrial enterprises were promoted or supported in the New World if they required capital. Profitable trade continued between Spain and its colonies but the level of wealth it created began to decline and, with it, the power and influence of Spain. It was all going to dramatically collapse at the time of the French Revolution in 1789.

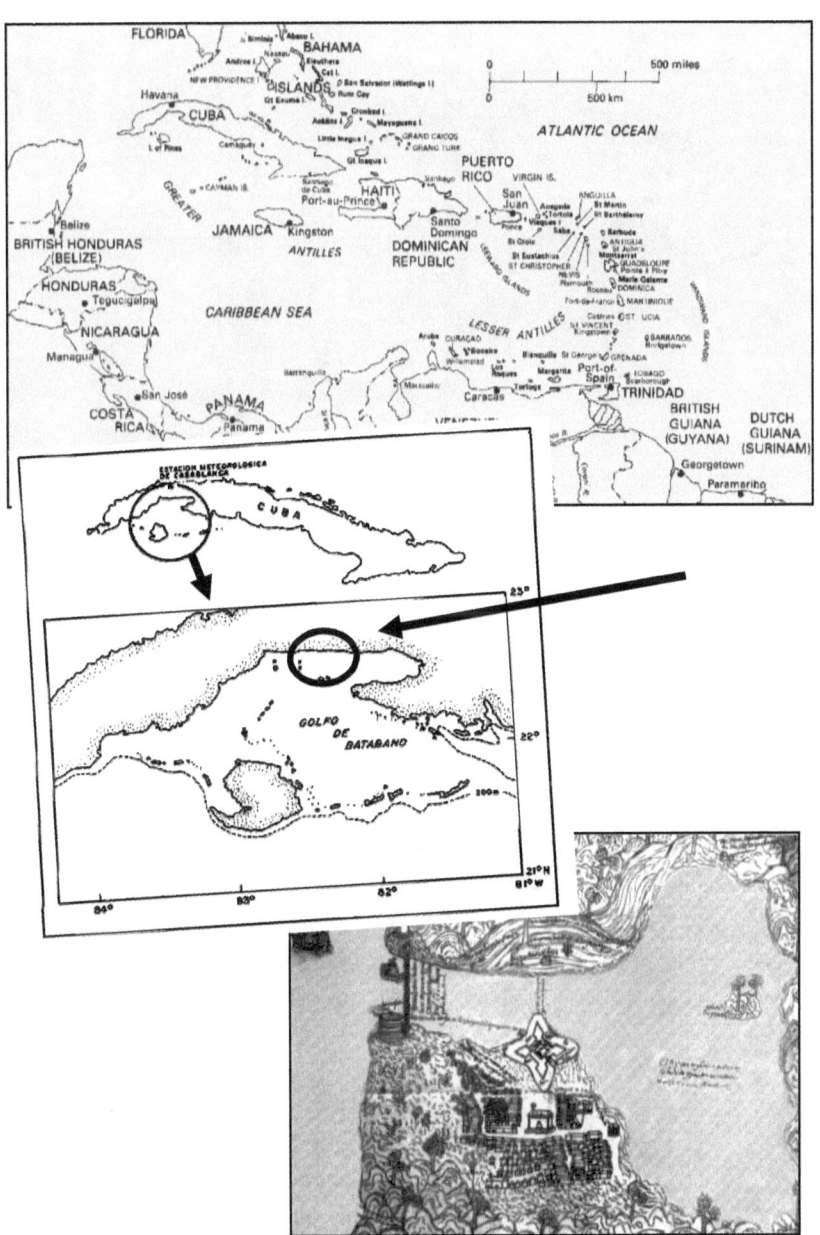

Images above, top to bottom:

A map of the **Caribbean area**;

the location of the **original settlement** of San Cristobal de la Habana, near today's town of Batabanó;

a map of the **settlement on Carenas** bay, the location of present day Havana.

Images above, left to right, top to bottom:

An **Old map of Santiago** de Cuba, favorite prey for pirates;
old painting of the **city of Havana**, taken from one of its southern hills;

the area where the second intent to establish the city of Havana took place, near the estuary of the *Almendares* river. All that remains today is **La Chorrera** fort (on the circle);

the **Templete**, where the first Mass and *Cabildo* were celebrated during the founding of Havana in its present location.

El Templete and the *Ceiba*

These are your instructions:

Your wish is written, preferably in a piece of coarse wrapping paper. A roll is made, inside of which you place a clove of garlic and a nail to which the tip has been cut off. Add several fish scales and tie down the bulk with three green and three yellow ribbons. Climb on a horse or walk and reach the area in front of the house of government. Walk across the *Plaza de Armas*; it has been a long time since people strolled on these streets or walked them without boozing. Watch out for puddles on the streets; watch out for gangs or bands of thieves. Get safely in front of the *Templete*. Check out the surroundings, the people, the smells. Touch the *Ceiba* and wait until midnite.

Get your wrapping paper bundle with your right hand, touch the Ceiba with your left hand, go around the tree exactly thirteen laps, make a wish, watch out, only one wish, and plant your now dead bundle, containing your wish, on the side of the tree where the sun animates it every morning. The tree will mew like a cat, will strut and snort, will shake, cry and clean itself shedding tears. Labor begins in the midst of blood and light: mangoes and guavas, oranges, star apples, maracas, melons and a *drúmete nengrito* (go to sleep, my negro child). The templo will give birth to fireworks —tightening, trembling— and white and black *güijes* (spirits) and Chinese children will move towards the harbor, boating and throwing spooky ghosts. Meanwhile the Ceiba will continue to give away fruit, words, guitars, orchestra shouts, cornucopias, carnival and rituals, good wine, hope, fishermen, fish, and warm chunks of bread.

The yearly ceremonies of every November 16th around the *Ceiba del Templete* in Havana

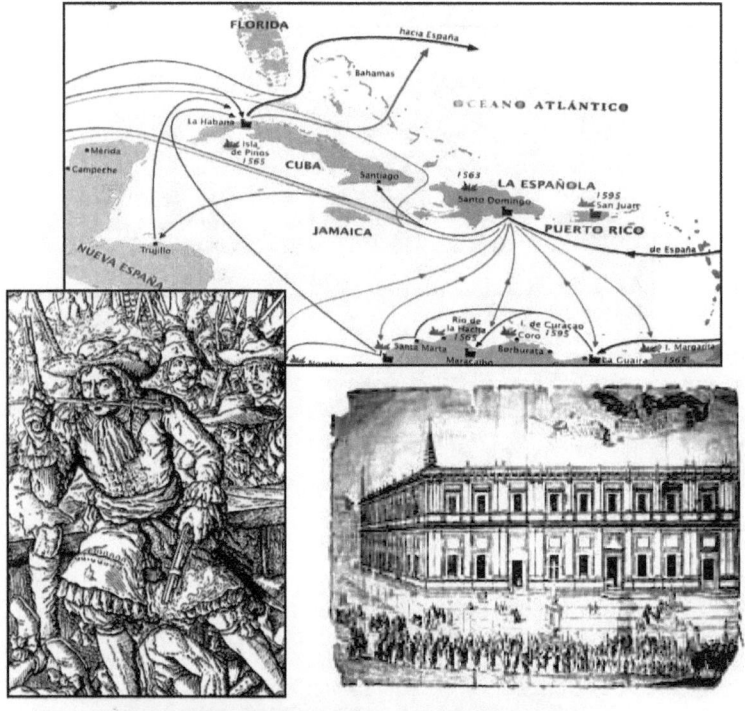

Images above, left to right, top to bottom:

The movement of **Spanish cargo ships around the Caribbean** as they brought their precious cargo of gold and silver to Havana harbor, sailing to Spain every year in reinforced convoys (*La Flota de las Indias*);

Admiral Sir Henry Morgan, of the English Royal Navy, a privateer and pirate who made a name for himself raiding settlements in the Caribbean;

la Casa de Contratación de Sevilla, Spain's agency having the monopoly of commerce with the Americas;

Elizabeth I of England and **Felipe II** of Spain.

Images above, left to right, top to bottom:

Sir Francis Drake (1540-1596), British vice Admiral, privateer, navigator, politician and slaver under the orders of Elizabeth I of England;

the Queen awarding Drake a **knighthood** in 1581;

Sir Francis and his friends playing bowls. He was informed of the approach of the **Spanish Armada** during a game and continued playing after asking his friends not to quit in the middle of the match;

Drake buried at sea. The last two images are relief plaques from the base of Drake's statue in Tavistock, Devon, England.

Images above, left to right, top to bottom:

A series of portraits of **French Huguenots** during times of their conflicts with Spain and their encroachments on her territories in the Caribbean;

the most successful French *corsaire*, **Jacques de Sores** (1520-1571);

French **corsaires taking over a Spanish cargo ship** on its way to the peninsula before the organization of the convoys in the first decade of the 1500s.

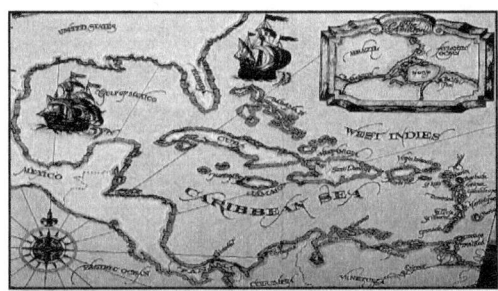

For most of the XVI century Cuba and Hispaniola were abandoned as the initial residents began to deliriously explore continental America in search of larger and more productive sources of gold and silver. Both islands returned to wilderness. Forests grew back, the underbrush went uncontrollably wild and made the islands difficult to penetrate, cattle left behind multiplied rapidly.

This attracted British and French indentured servants trying to escape their masters. Here were immense territories without good protection where they could run at leisure, hunt for good cattle and be totally free. They made friends with natives and learned their survival skills. The natives welcomed them as they did not act as overseers or look down on them as inferior.

Using native techniques, the new residents of Cuba and Hispaniola began to preserve and smoke meat and cure hides to sell to passing Spanish, British and French ships. The fires they used to dry meat were called *boucanes* by the natives (damp sticks of wood kept the fires low as fat and bones were added to produce smoke). Soon a vigorous market developed; the ship mates would sell the processed meat bought in Cuba and Hispaniola to towns in the area and other ship crews, hence the descriptive label of *buccaneers*. At this point in history there was no piracy involved and no shame to be called a *buccaneer*. Soon the Spanish crown decided to stop these deserters and fugitives from profiting from the bounty of their lands and began to seize all ships approaching Cuba and Hispaniola to buy food supplies.

Aside from meats, the buccaneers bought in Cuba and Hispaniola large quantities of fresh produce: *maisi* (maize/corn), white potatoes, sweet potatoes, manioc (yuca/cassava), *mani* (peanuts), tomatoes, okra, squash (including pumpkin), *yayama* (pineapples), *bija* or achiote (Bixa orellan), papaya, avocado (aguacate), wild rice, pecans, cacao (chocolate) and sage. It is estimated that Cuban, Dominican and other Caribbean natives developed 25% of the world's food crops. Most of the medicinal plants and food crops that are now staples in Europe, Africa and Asia, were first encountered in the 15th century Caribbean.

Buccaneers in Cuba

Images above, left to right, top to bottom:

Pedro Menéndez de Avilés (1519-1574), the Spanish admiral remembered for planning the annual trans-oceanic eastern bound convoys carrying the gold of America from Havana to Cadiz.
He was the founder of St Agustin;

pirates buying their booty on the sands;

a French **Lettre de Marque** (license to seize enemy merchant vessels);

a common scene in the XVI century, a **pirate counting his plunder** aboard his ship.

10

A European Perspective of the Conquista

IT WOULD BE AN UNDERSTATEMENT to say that when European explorers began to show up in America they found civilizations that were centuries behind theirs in all measures of development. While the Guanahatabey inhabitants of western Cuba were painting crude images on the walls of caverns, Sandro Botticelli was painting the *Birth of Venus* in 1485; Andrea del Verrochio had produced his *Baptism of Christ* in 1475 and Michelangelo Buonarotti was about to finish the standing *David* statue now present at the Museum of the Academy in Florence. In other areas of accomplishment, the European culture had produced classical scholars like Desiderius Erasmus (1466-1536), [88] extraordinary rulers like Maximilian I (1459-1519), Holy Roman Emperor, [89] and mathematicians like Nicolas Copernicus (1473-1543), [90] the astronomer that first placed the sun, rather than the earth, at the center of the known universe.

---

[88] Erasmus of Rotterdam, was a Dutch Renaissance humanist, Catholic priest, social critic, teacher, and theologian. He was the first proponent of religious toleration, and enjoyed the sobriquet "Prince of the Humanists"; he has been called "the crowning glory of the Christian humanists."

[89] Maximilian I was a Holy Roman Emperor, King of Germany, of Hungary, Dalmatia and Croatia, Archduke of Austria, Duke of Burgundy, Brabant, Lorraine, Styria, Carinthia, Carniola, Limburg, Luxembourg, Gelderland, Landgrave of Alsace, Prince of Swabia, Count Palatine of Burgundy, Princely Count of Habsburg, Hainaut, Flanders, Tyrol, Gorizia, Artois, Holland, Seeland, Ferrette, Kyburg, Namur, Zutphen, Margrave of the Holy Roman Empire, the Enns, Burgau, Lord of Frisia, the Wendish March, Pordenone, Salins and Mechelen.

[90] Nicolas Copernicus had a doctorate in Canon Law and was a polyglot physician, a classics scholar, translator, governor, diplomat, and the economist who in 1517 set down a quantity theory of money, which is to this day a fundamental concept in economics.

At the time of their encounters with Europeans, the native inhabitants of all of America lacked a non-symbolic means of preserving their records on a portable storage medium. [91] Their communications were limited to codified carvings inscribed or engraved in stone or paper, much like the ancient Egyptians logographic hieroglyphs [92] dating as far back as 3400 BC. [93] Cave paintings and petroglyphs were common in continental native America; they are not considered writing because they did not represent language directly. After meeting the Europeans, those means of recording events, ideas and feelings, faced not only the completeness of Spanish, Portuguese, English and Dutch writing but the means of enormous divulgation offered by Gutenberg's (1395-1468) invention of the printing press. [94]

Prominent beyond art, religion, music, knowledge and language, the three most important necessities of mankind have always been food, clothing and lodging. Shelters, in particular, were significantly underdeveloped in native America. At the time when caves and rudimentary huts were all the protection that Caribbean peoples enjoyed against bad weather, danger and pests, Europeans had already developed habitats fulfilling

---

[91] The many tools and writing materials used throughout history include stone tablets, clay tablets, bamboo slats, wax tablets, vellum, parchment, paper, copperplate, styluses, quills, ink brushes, pencils and pens. As a possible exception, it is speculated that the Incas might have employed knotted cords known as *quipu* (or *khipu*) as a writing system.

[92] The Egyptians, however, had logographic (a visual symbol representing an idea) as well as alphabetic hieroglyphs (a symbol that stands for a letter or sound). The alphabetic hieroglyphs, infinitely more precise than the logographics, were deciphered in Napoleonic times when the Rosetta Stone was discovered in 1799. None of the American native peoples, anywhere in the continent, had developed an alphabetic script system capable of keeping records and accounts; none was able to write everyday letters and communications. Even older than the Egyptian system, the Mesopotamians are believed to be the first writers, using triangular shaped stylus pressed into soft clay, i.e., cuneiforms that stood for phonetic elements or syllables.

[93] Hieroglyphs faded from popular use after the Roman Empire began its rule of the Egyptian nation with the arrival of Augustus in 30 BC.

[94] A pair of workers, one a plate printer, the other a plate inker, working in a Gutenberg press in 1450 could produce 3,600 printed pages in a day.

and exceeding those purposes; they ranged from single and multiple stone and wood houses for the general population to palatial buildings, castles and mansions for their nobility, the church ministers and the upper clases. [95] In continental America, before the European encounter, natives were living, at best, in clay-floored, one-room-houses made of resources found in nature, typically strips of large dry branches tied together with flexible tree barks. These "houses" were dark and stuffy and people only kept their things inside and would nap there on hot afternoons; the rest of the time they remained outside the enclosures. Only the Incas and the Aztecs had built multistory stone houses with stone stairways connecting floor levels, as well as primitive aqueducts where people bathed and drank. Native houses in the Americas were dwellings that provided shelter to tribe members but had no primary connection to child rearing or single family togetherness; they were not an economic unit of production, consumption, and inheritance.

Given those facts, it is difficult to understand why any sensible European would wish to change the comfort of his or her abode in the Old World to move to a land with minimal amenities and accomodations.

Contrary to common understanding, the men who came to America in the first trip of Columbus were probably the most socially advanced and genteel group of people that visited the New World in the first fifty years of explorations. They had been interviewed and vetted personally by Columbus or the Pinzon brothers. All bandits, brigands, outlaws, robbers and

---

[95] Ancient Egyptians began building flat topped houses made of sun-dried bricks at around 3,100 BC. The Asyrians built even better dwellings after discovering that buildings made with fire-baked and glazed bricks would last almost forever. The ancient Greeks lived in stone houses with slanted roofs. The Romans added central heating to their living accomodations around central atriums or courts. The "barbarians" that invaded the Roman Empire supported their roofs with frameworks of heavy timber and filled the spaces in between with clay. Afterwards came castles with thick stonewalls, water filled moats and drawbridges for the nobles and rich and stone structures with high roofs above ground to house the clerics. By the 1400s, even the most humble of peoples in Europe had built half timbered houses with brick foundations, crossbeams and slanting braces, plastered with clay and straw.

anti-socials were screened out. According to Columbus, the trip was reserved to curious explorers, trailblazers, men who had an adventuresome bent and wished to undertake a serious and risky escapade in search of glory, fame and wealth. The men that followed after the trip of October 1492, on the other hand, were mostly gamblers, chance takers, fortune seekers without scruples, daredevils, mercenaries, philanderers, swindlers and cheats. They were commanded by men of ideals that were legitimately lusting for wealth and fame; these leaders turned out to be incapable of restraining the uncontrollable cruelty and ambition of the men they brought with them. There is no doubt that both leaders and adventurers under their direction were partly responsible for the devastation and extinction of entire nations and tribes across the continent.

It is well known that many native peoples in the Americas were practically extinguished 200 years after the *Conquista*. The main culprit, however, was not the excessive and merciless cruelty of the *Conquistadores* but chiken pox, the highly contagious viral disease for which native Americans had not developed inmunity anywhere in the continent. [96] Over the years, however, a false and sinister genocidal rhetoric has pushed a narrative that the Spaniards, profiting from the expected elimination of all native peoples, distributed among native Americans blankets infested with dried chiken pox pustules taken from those diseased. There is not any historical or convincing evidence in that regard.

The men leading the throngs of explorers and adventurers that invaded the lands found by Columbus in 1492 were ambitious and fearless daredevils like Diego Velázquez de Cuellar, Hernán Cortés and Francisco Pizarro, in Cuba, Mexico and

---

[96] Chicken pox, although common and rarely fatal among Europeans, proved deadly to indigenous Americans; explorations by Spaniards were often immediately followed by massive epidemics, sometimes destroying the entire population of many villages and even large cities. It has been estimated that more than 80% of native Americans died due to this European disease. In fact, it is difficult to find an American tribe, from Alaska to Tierra de Fuego, that was untouched by this ravaging epidemic.

Perú, together with minor figures such as Pedro de Alvarado in Guatemala, Francisco de Montejo in Yucatán, Álvar Núñez Cabeza de Vaca in today's Texas and later in Uruguay, Pedro de Mendoza in Argentina and Pedro de Valdivia in Chile; they were the leaders of the Spanish conquest of central and meridional America. A closer look at the top three will characterize the dilemas of all *bona fide* Spanish *Conquistadores*.

Diego Velázquez de Cuellar (1465-1524), a crew member on Columbus' second trip and future governor of Cuba, was a well intentioned man that resented the personal authority of Diego Columbus, Christopher's son; he tried to sidestep Diego and report directly to Madrid. He also despised his subordinate Hernán Cortés and tried to sabotage his trip to Mexico; he even ordered Pánfilo de Narváez to take Cortés prisoner. [97] He had no will or patience to control men under his authority and died a bitter and ruined man, resenting that he had not shared in the pilfered bounty from Mexico.

Hernán Cortés (1485-1547), a "pale faced man" Velázquez always called "Cortesillo," was a distant relative of Nicolás de Ovando; in 1501 he almost went to Italy to fight in the Spanish Wars under Gonzalo Hernández de Córdoba, el "Gran Capitán." He decided to go to America at the last minute, hoping to join the 32 ships Ovando had hired for his trip to America. [98] Due to an accident he did not get to America until 1506; at the time he was 22 years old and declared himself to be a man «who prizes the beauty of honor, the delights of fame and the deviousness of loving all available women.» He had told his friends he would «either dine to the sound of trumpets or die on the scaffold.» Eventually he would be present at the burning of chief Hatuey, would accumulate some wealth, sire several children from native girls and seduced and breached a mar-

---

[97] Pánfilo de Narváez ended up fighting Cortés when he followed Velázquez' orders to aprehend him. It cost him 2 years of imprisonment in Veracruz.

[98] The expedition included 100 pigs, 300 chickens, 35 cows, 120 horses and mares and 13 Franciscan Friars.

riage promise to Catalina de Cuellar, a relative of Velázquez. [99] Cortés never commanded men in battle yet, not anticipating any resistance from the Aztecs, Velázquez commissioned him to lead the expedition to Mexico. After a disillusioned Velázquez dismissed Cortés as the man in charge of the Mexican expedition, Cortés stole all available animals and foodstuffs in Santiago de Cuba and fled to Mexico on November 18, 1518. [100]

It is unknown how the town citizens fed themselves after Cortés' escape. In his conquests, Cortés proved to be merciless; he had no time or interest in restraining his followers.

Francisco Pizarro (1471-1541), a distant cousin of Hernán Cortés, was the illegitimate son of a Spanish infantry colonel and a woman of poor means. He grew up illiterate and was part of Balboa's 1513 expedition to find the Pacific Ocean. He was tantalized about reports of great wealth in Peru, could not get permission for an expedition from Panamá's governor and travelled to Spain to appeal to King Charles I. After finally landing in Perú [101] his plans failed and he never reached the Inca capital; he struck out again on his second trip and finally confronted Inca Atahualpa on a third trip, at the Battle of Ca-

---

[99] He ended up marrying Catalina, with the forgiving Velázquez acting as his wedding witness. Cortés' new wife turned out to be a sickly and lazy lady. After his wedding, according to his friends, Cortés devoted himself to "collecting women." Contemporaries also told the world that "Cortés could scarcely speak without swearing."

[100] Aside from all the animals, Cortés carried to Mexico 5,000 rations of bread, 2,000 sides of unsliced bacon, 15 bags of beans and chickpeas, 60 barrels of wine and 10 of vinegar, and 6,000 loafs of Cassava bread. Cassava was one of the native foods of Cuba that the Spaniards consented to eat; luckily it lasted, without deterioration, much longer than wheat bread. The entire expedition cost Cortés less than 20,000 pesos (US $ 30,000 in today's money). The adventure, like most exploratory journeys of the times, was a classical private enterprise. It followed medieval practices: the crown gave permission, the commander fitted things at his own expense and he and the volunteers shared in the profits, if any.

[101] On his first attempt to find and colonize Perú, Pizarro had 80 men and 40 horses but very few provisions; his initial failed attempts were evident by the names he gave to some of his encounters in Peruvian territory: *Puerto deseado* (desired port), *Puerto del hambre* (port of hunger), and *Puerto quemado* (burned port).

jamarca on November 16, 1532. Pizarro made him prisoner and eventually executed him.[102] Diego de Almagro, his second in command, thought Pizarro had overstepped his authority and complained to the crown of Spain. For that *faux pas* Almagro was punished and executed. Pizarro died at the hands of Almagro's son, who killed him on June 26, 1541. He had taken the Inca Atahualpa's sister as his mistress, had married several Spanish women and fathered several illegitimate children with native women; most of all, he entered in the history of warfare with the most improbable record of a single and fascinating military victory. In his conquests, however, Pizarro proved to be responsive to authorities and fearful of not staining his memorable reputation, but did nothing to protect the indigenous people from the greed and prejudice of his followers.

The men who served under these and other leaders of the *Conquista de America* were in all likelihood the children of those who had participated in the recapture of Granada; they were the embodiment of those Spaniards that recovered Spain from Muslim hands. They believed themselves to be heroes; they acted with passion, moving forward without scruples to achive their goals of fortunes and fame. They did not care about the personal consequences of their actions and did not have Spain's prestige among their concerns. Cortés and Pizarro were certain they had breathtaking accomplishments and compared themselves to Alexander and Cesar; during their time in office they knew of no other alternative than to rule as absolute monarchs.

In Peru, Francisco Pizarro, who shared the grunt and sweat with his own brothers, consented to the barbarity of his troops

---

[102] On his second trip Pizarro had two ships, 160 men and 75 horses. Before he reached land, one of his men intercepted an Inca raft carrying a load of textiles, ceramic objects, and several much-desired pieces of gold, silver, and emeralds. That was all the enticement Pizarro needed. After receiving reinforcements, he returned to Panamá, organized a new expedition and undertook his third attempt to reach the Inca capital. It was not until 1532 that, with Hernando de Soto by his side, he directed 200 of his men to face Atahualpa's 80,000 soldiers. Pizarro captured the Inca leader and executed him, even after his subdits had paid a sizeable ransom by filling a room (22 ft by 17 ft in area, to a height of 8 ft) with gold objects.

because he felt their fear, isolation, doubts and uncertainties; he also accepted as normal the frequent fights and betrayals among the Spaniards. It does not justify but explains the disgraceful behavior of his troops. Not all Spaniards who went to America mesmerized by the gold rush, ended healthy and enriched. Many perished in unequal skirmishes before huge numbers of indigenous defenders. Among the troops there were no lack of prominent royal advisors, nobles and priests who argued incessantly for justice and good treatment of the natives. Likewise, there can be no doubt about the concern and moral debate that existed among many *Conquistadores* over the soul of the Indians; it was a peculiar inconsistency, fueled intellectually by Dominican friars, who defended the humanity of the natives despite a bitter contemporary history as leaders and supporters of the Inquisition in Spain.

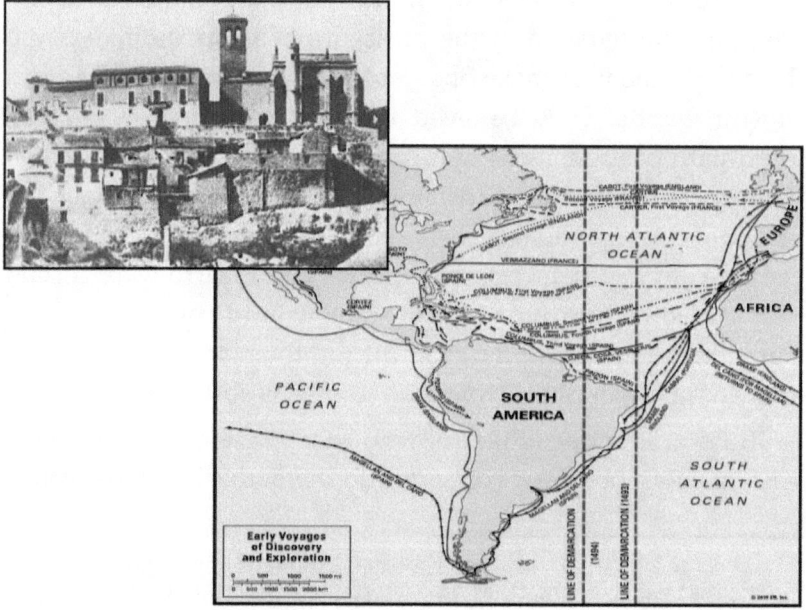

Images, top to bottom:

The house (left to the tower) in the town of *Tordesillas* (Castille) where the **Treaty of Tordesillas** was signed between Juan II of Portugal and Spain's Catholic Monarchs on June 7, 1494;

The map **delimitating the territories** where Spain and Portugal could colonize in the New World according to the Treaty.

Arts in the XV and XVI centuries, *top to bottom, left to right:*
The **Baptism of Christ** by Verrocchio, 1475
the **David** by Michelangelo, 1503;
the **Birth of Venus** by Botticelli, 1485;
Taino, Aztec and **Inca** artworks

Images, top to bottom, left to right:

Maximilian I, Emperor of the Holy Roman Empire;

Desiderius Erasmus of Rotterdam;

Nicolas Copernicus;

The first **paper currency** known in history, 1611.

Images, top to bottom, left to right:
The **Gutenberg** (1395-1468) printing workshop in 1432;
two men **producing a book** on a Gutenberg press;
Spanish playing cards, a favorite pastime of the *Conquistadores*;
Hieroglyphs from the Aztecs, the Tainos and the Incas.

Tlaloc   Huitzilopochtli

A Pantheon of Gods and Goddesses of Native Americans.
Images, top to bottom, left to right:

Kukulcán, the Feathered Serpent of the Mayas;
Aztec gods **Tlaloc**, god of the rain and **Huitzilopochtli**, god of the war;
Xochipilli, Aztec goddess of arts, flowers, dance and beauty;
a wall bas-relief of **Viracocha**, the great creator in Inca mythology;
a group of unidentified **Taino deities** carved on primitive stelae.

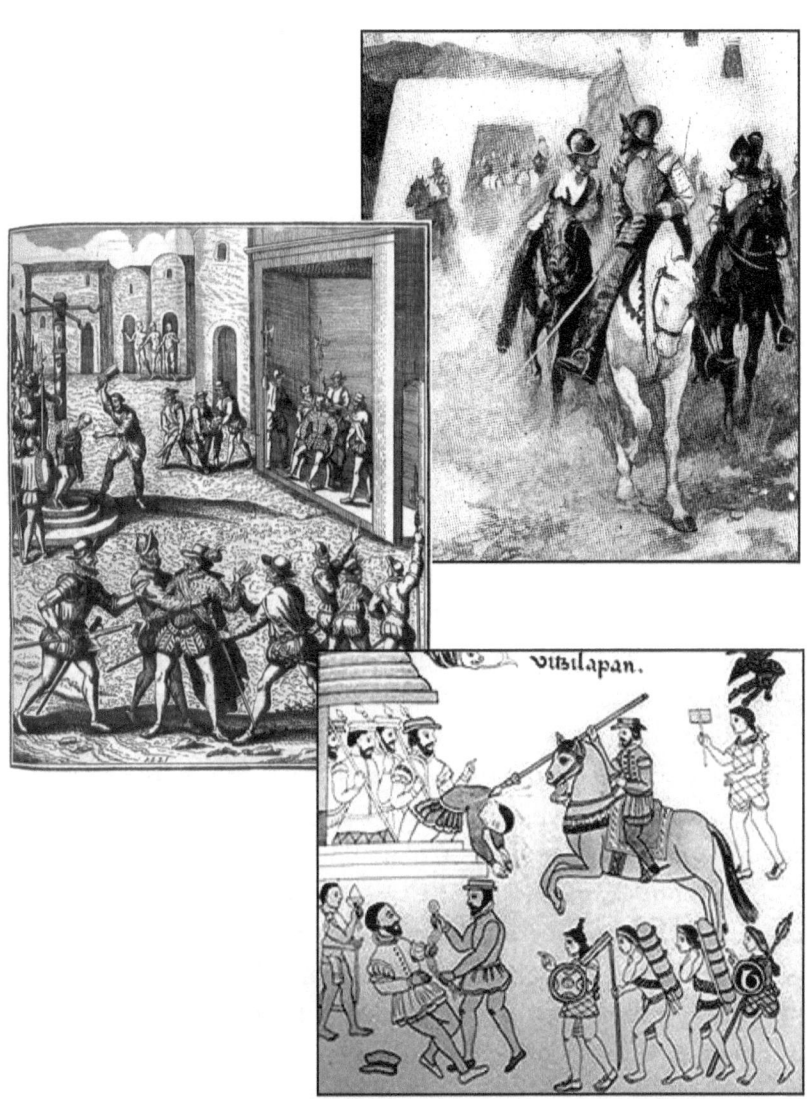

Some of the Numerous Fights of Conquistadores against each other.

Images, top to bottom, left to right:

The **three Pizarro brothers**: *Francisco* was murdered in his home by a band of Almagro supporters, *Juan* was killed during an uprising in Cuzco, *Gonzalo* was beheaded for treachery after his army deserted him;

Capture and execution of **Diego de Almagro**, decapitated or garroted on July 8, 1538 by the Pizarros;

On June 4, 1520, **Hernán Cortés defeats the troops of Pánfilo de Narvaez** at Cempoala, Veracruz; he had been ordered by Diego Velázquez to apprehend Cortés.

11
Cuba Becomes a Formal Spanish Colony

THE INDUCTION OF CUBA as a Spanish colony took place in 1510, when Diego Columbus, as Viceroy of the American territories appointed Diego Velázquez as governor and *Adelantado* in Cuba. Within four months he departed the town of Salvatierra de la Sabana, [103] a seaport in southwestern Hispaniola, and went ashore near the eastern tip of Cuba, in the Maisi region of Oriente. There he founded the village of *Nuestra Señora de la Asunción de Baracoa* [104] on August 15, 1511; it was the first settlement and the first capital of Cuba.

Barely a year after the founding of Baracoa, Diego Velázquez had to confront the uprising of the Taino cacique *Yahatuey* or *Hatuey*, who had fled Hispaniola and took refuge in Cuba with a party of 400 men, women and children when his territory was overwhelmed by Spanish presence. Hatuey tried unsuccessfully to warn natives in Cuba about the Christians about to land in their shores but he was mostly ignored. He resorted to quick attacks against Spanish property and, in a move replicated by Máximo Gómez in the 1895 Cuban War of Independence, he confined the Spanish *Conquistadores* to their fort in the town of Baracoa.

---

[103] Salvatierra de la Sabana was a settlement founded by Diego Velázquez in 1504 and later abandoned by the Spaniards in 1540. The French revived the town under the name of *Les Cayes* in 1785, the year when John James Audubon was born there; in 1818 the town was visited by Simón Bolivar seeking support for the independence movement across South America. Since 1936 *Les Cayes* has been the largest producer of *Vetiver* in the world, with a production of some 200 tons per year. *Vetiver* bas been in high demand since the 1800s for the fragrant essential oil contained in its roots. It is used as a fixative in 90% of French perfumes.

[104] Baracoa's name originates from the indigenous Taino or Arauaca voice *Barauca*, meaning "a place near the sea."

Late in January of 1512 he was captured, tied to a stake and burned alive.[105] Some of Hatuey's Taino friends and loyal warriors joined him in a frontal rejection of Spanish rule: **Ameyro**, *Cacique* of Jamaica; **Anacaona**, *Cacica* of Quisqueya; **Aramaná**, *Cacique* of north *Borikén* (today's Puerto Rico); **Aymaco**, *Cacique* of southern *Borikén* and leader of the 1511 Taino rebellion in the island; **Cacicaná** *Cacique* of central Cuba, who became friend of Alonso de Ojeda and Pánfilo de Narváez; **Camagüebax**, *Cacique* of Camagüey, executed by Pánfilo de Narváez; **Canimao**, *Cacique* of *Guanima* (today's Matanzas); **Guababo**, *Cacique* of *Maguá* (today's Haiti); **Guarionex**, *Cacique* of *Quisqueya* and *Borikén*; **Guayacayex**, *Cacique* of Havana and Matanzas, a leader of the 1510 Indian revolt that resulted in the death of 30 Spanish men and women as they crossed the San Juan river; [106] **Mabey**, Hatuey's best friend. After fighting the Spanish in central Cuba he was killed after he was cornered at the edge of a cliff fighting a *mano-a-mano* with a Spanish soldier; **Tínima**, Cacique Princess of Camagüey, daughter of Camagüeybax, and married to Captain Vasco Porcallo de Figueroa [107], an assistant to Ovando and founder of Puerto Príncipe, Sancti Spíritus, San Juan de los Remedios, and Trinidad; **Macaca**, *Cacique* of Bayamo, friend and assistant of Sebastian de Ocampo, Cuba's first circumnavigator; **Maniabón**, *Cacique* of southern and northern Oriente.

Retaliations for the empathy and support to Hatuey by the the Taino *Caciques* in the eastern part of Cuba was swift and hard. It was reported that more than 3,000 Tainos were violent-

---

[105] Hatuey famously rejected Bartolomé de las Casas' offer to embrace Christianity before death. He asked Las Casas if Spaniards went to heaven. The answered was yes... Hatuey then said, according to Las Casas: «I do not want to go there but to hell; I do not wish to be where there would be Spaniards. I do not wish to see such cruel people again.»

[106] Such event prompted Diego Velázquez to change the name of the village from *Guanima* to *Matanzas* (Spanish for slaughter).

[107] Vasco Porcayo was the wealthiest *Encomendero* in Cuba and, according to contemporary accounts, «the most aggressive in the pursue of beautiful Taino girls, many of whom bore his children.»

ly treated by Francisco de Morales and Pánfilo de Narváez in the areas ruled by Caciques *Macaca* and *Maniabón*. Francisco de Morales was excessively heartless and cruel and Velázquez had to call him to task, sending him back to Hispaniola. [108]

The conquest of Cuban territory was one of many asymmetrical collisions between two cultures [109] that took place in America after the arrival of the European *Conquistadores*. It was a prelude of what was to happen in Mexico, Perú, North America and everywhere else in the New Word.

The conflicts and combats between Tainos and *Conquistadores* in Cuba lasted for 30 years, until submission and diseases ended the control of the island by its native population. All throughout the conflicts, the Taino *Caciques* never accepted the Spanish domination and were not resigned to slavery or servitude, preferring to be annihilated. The Spaniards, on the other hand, believed there was gold in Cuba [110] and were determined to find and grab it, satisfy the crown and wallow in wealth.

At the outset, Velázquez knew of the gentle disposition of Taino natives. On a letter to his cousins in Spain he wrote:

«these natives are very meek and fearful people, not bad, all naked as their mothers bore them, without good weapons and without law. We know the weakness of the weaponry opposing us: just frail

---

[108] Francisco de Morales, second in command to Velázquez, arrived in Cuba determined to defeat the natives at any cost. He had warned Diego Colombus that «the Tainos from Cuba have been in touch with those of Hispaniola and they will not receive us with music and flowers.»

[109] Many historians have theorized that the development gap between native Americans and Europeans was in the order of 4,500 years. This places the level of technology and maturation of the Taino culture as similar to those of Stonehenge in England, the start of the Minoan civilization in Crete and the settlement of Sumerians in southern Mesopotamia; at that time, the entire world population was probably below 30 million inhabitants.

[110] Gold from Hispaniola (estimated as 5,000 Kg between 1503 and 1510, equivalent in today's currency as US $ 6 Billion), far from satisfying the Spanish monarchs, increased their urging Velázquez to strive for more. The Spanish King was pressured to seek gold by Miguel Pasamonte, crown treasurer, and Lope Conchillos, the King's secretary; Velázquez was compelled to the same search by Juan Francisco Grimando and Gaspar Centir, representatives of Genoese banks in Seville.

cane arrows tipped with stone, bone or tooth fish, thrown with small bows with little power to drive, with a range of no more than forty or fifty paces, all dispersed and unable to pierce our shields and metal breastplates; the best warriors have wooden spears with fire-hardened tips and, occasionally, hardwood batons and stone axes handled with both hands. Their tactics are limited to short-term incursions since they are limited by the food reserves they could collect, which assured them at the most five to seven days.»[111]

Physically, the Tainos were of medium height and build, tan-skinned, with straight black hair. They were distinguished from other groups by their habit of deforming the skull. According to Las Casas they were,

«skilled swimmers and magnificent boaters aboard their oar-fitted canoes capable to carry from fifty to seventy men; they have high resistance to undertake long marches, but not great strength.»

Velázquez' strategy during the occupation of Cuba was to take time before moving into the countryside. Two factors were important: he needed to explore the mood of the natives; if he found it hostile, he had to neutralize them to prevent actions against his lines of communications and military supplies. Second, he had to secure food for his troops. He had not forgotten the terrible famine endured in the early years of Hispaniola's conquest, when in their zest for gold no one bothered or had time to cultivate the land and raise cattle. To his advantage was the fact that natives had never seen a horse and came to think that horse and man were one invulnerable self.[112]

Hatuey had monitored the arrival of Spanish troops from the coasts of Cuba. He tried to convince the natives to throw their gold into rivers and evacuate women and children to the

---

[111] There were appproximately 200,000 natives in Cuba. They knew how to make fire and could carve wood, stone and bones to make very rudimentary penetration weapons, suitable for small hunting rather than fighting.

[112] The Spaniards not only adapted their weapons to the territory conditions (long European swords were replaced by curved single-edged short blades more suitable for hand combat in dense forests), but also introduced tracking dogs in Cuba, as well as horses. In the words of Velázquez, «...after God, we owe our victories to dogs and horses.» One of the laments of Bernal Díaz del Castillo when he described the *Noche Triste* was «the amount of horses that were lost.»

mountains, yet he could not even get the chiefs to organize the defense of the beaches. Eventually he had to face a formidable enemy who was equipped with Castilian muskets, crossbows, spears, pikes, swords and daggers of steel, protected by helmets, heavy armor, shields, and *Cotas de Malla* [113] of heavy metal; they were also helped by bloodhounds and workhorses.

In addition to the superiority of their tactics, combat experience and military organization, the Spaniards under Velázquez had the cooperation of numerous aboriginal Dominicans, Jamaicans, and even native Cubans. It was not difficult to face the few natives that supported Hatuey, with "bare bellies and weak arms," which lacked the solidarity from other indigenous communities in the region; it evidently could not yield any other result than the defeat of the rebels.

Additionally, the Spanish army was in the early 1500s at the peak of their performance. Many on their ranks had fought Muslim soldiers in Spain. Over the years preceding the *Conquista*, they had prevailed over the Muslim horsemen's cutlasses, as well as the spears of the French knights and the pikes of the Swiss mercenaries. [114] Once the Arabs had conquered North Africa in 711 AD, they had crossed to the Spanish peninsula across the legendary Pillars of Hercules.[115] Christian Visigoth King Don Rodrigo fought them, fell prisoner, tried to open negotiations for his freedom, fell into a trap when the Muslims feigned agreement with him, was betrayed, had his head sawed up and placed on a pole; the severed cranium was then

---

[113] *Maille Cotte* in French, a breastplate metal guard made of cast iron or steel rings, arranged in such a way that each one is threaded to at least four others, forming a fabric. In Castilian, a *Cota de Malla* is also commonly known as a *loriga*.

[114] A cutlass was a short curved sword with a blade sharpened on the cutting edge and a solid cupped guard. French knight spears were typically used in jousting or tilting tournaments. Pikes were pole weapons, very long spears (at times 25 ft, weighting 10 Kg) used by infantry. They were used to defensively stop the advance of an enemy rather than to be thrown.

[115] In Arabic they were called *Jebel-ut-Tarik*, a term that was hispanized to Gibraltar.

paraded before his army and sent to Damascus to amuse the Caliph.

The repulsive sight of Don Rodrigo's severed head became fixed in the minds of the Spanish army for many centuries; so was the image of the unruly retreat and slaughter of Rodrigo's army. The men that came to Cuba and America for the *Conquista*, after 700 years of submission to the Arabs, were mentally prepared to do unto others what had been done to them. They were ready to use any foul means to secure victories. They would not tolerate any cult other that Christianity. They would beat any enemy at their own game, with subterfuge if necessary, with no pity taking precedence over their prejudice and no reasoning obstructing their intolerance. Such were the men that faced the natives of Cuba and America and forged a colonial status that would last four hundred years.

During the *Reconquista*, the Spanish army was successfully transformed into a formidable fighting force. Muskets were introduced in the picket lines; discipline was improved; the Spanish infantry and military administration was streamlined; large funds were invested in artillery; hospitals were created and military health given top priority; ammunition was systematized to eliminate multiple classes of gauges; in-time payments to soldiers became a sacred practice.[116]

Once the troops of Hatuey were subdued, Velázquez began the second stage of his operations: the complete pacification of the island. Pánfilo de Narváez was sent to the Bayamo region with 30 *arqueros*, a contingent of native collaborationists and a large pack of dogs, which he characterized as

«*mastines de guerra, perros de pelea, rancheadores y mallorquines, verdaderos perrazos de más de 150 libras de peso, cabezas grandes, ágiles y fieros...*» (war hounds, fighting, rancher dogs, true large dogs weighting over 150 pounds, with big heads, both agile and fierce).

---

[116] Prior to Isabel and Ferdinand it was not unusual for the army to be twenty months in arrears for the salaries of the soldiers.

Francisco de Morales, with a similar force, was sent to the Holguín area. Both Narváez and Morales were given as a second but important priority to gather foodstuffs, scouts and men and women that knew how to raise domestic animals and to cook. Velázquez, in the meantime, became the champion of the *Encomiendas*. The only *Caciques* that were persecuted were those who continued to rebel; they were replaced by submissive ones. The official policy became to peacefully and profitably search for gold and precious stones.

Caribbean sea in 1560 by Diego Gutiérrez

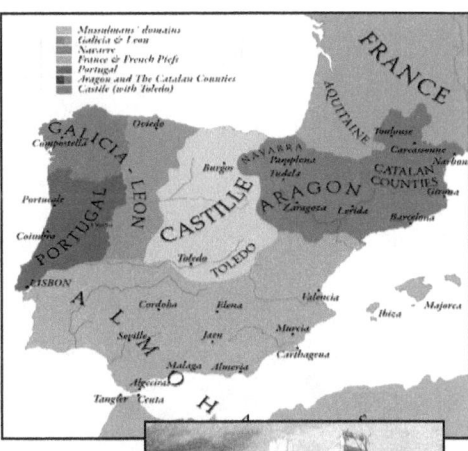

Images, left to right, top to bottom:

Don Rodrigo, last Christian Visigoth King of Spain;
Spain before the **Reconquista**;
The Siege of Granada;
The **expulsion of the Muslims** from Spain.

Images, left to right, top to bottom:

Cannibalism in the New World, from *Vespucci Mundus Novis*, 1505;
Capture of Atahualpa in Cajamarca, 1533;
Aztec Emperor Montezuma, dressed as a Spanish noble;
Canimao, Cacique of Guanima (Matanzas, Cuba), **Anacaona** Cacica of Hispaniola and Taino Princess *Tínima*, from Eastern Cuba.

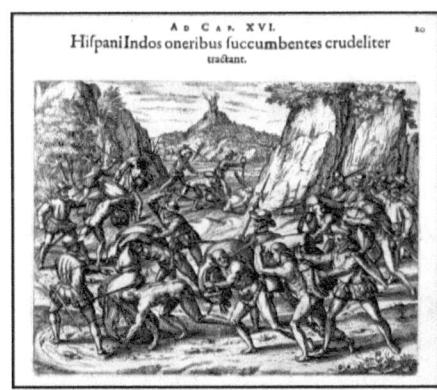

Images, left to right, top to bottom:

Pánfilo de Narváez *(1470-1528), leader of failed expeditions;*

German engraving showing the **cruelty of the Conquistadores**;

graphic illustrations of **chicken pox** *disease* as it became epidemic in America, as per *Codice Florentino XII, 53v;*

a group of **Peruvian natives** fighting the Spaniards in Cuzco;

an engraving showing **Pánfilo de Narváez** falling prisoner to *Hernán Cortés* in Veracruz, at a time when Velázquez had asked him to incarcerate Cortés for defiance.

Images, left to right, top to bottom:
The **asymmetrical skirmishes** between Natives and Conquistadores;
Francisco Pizarro loading his booty in Lima;
Conquistadores, from left, swordsman, arquebusier, pikeman.

The Asymmetrical wars to death between Natives and Conquistadores across the Americas

12

A Chaotic Start for the Colony of Cuba

NO SOONER HAD VELAZQUEZ sent Pánfilo de Narváez to Veracruz to arrest Hernán Cortés in March of 1520, Diego Columbus, Velázquez boss, sent Alonso de Zuazo, [117] to Cuba in February of 1521 to investigate and open a cause against Velázquez; Zuazo found Velázquez guilty of *abuso de poder* and deposed him as Governor of Cuba. Six months later, on September of 1521, Diego's boss, Emperor Charles V of Spain, overruled Diego Columbus and restored Velázquez to his post. Other than those maneuvers, [118] things proceeded normally in Cuba: Santiago de Cuba replaced Baracoa as the capital of the island and as the bishopric or seat of the Catholic Church in the

---

[117] Zuazo (1466-1539) was a Spanish lawyer (guaduate of Salamanca) and colonial judge. Like Velázquez he was against Indian slavery and favored the importation of Blacks to work the land, particularly if they were "younger than 20 and married." In 1524 Cortés, rehabilitated and appointed Governor of Mexico, left for Central America and designated Zuazo as *Justicia Mayor* (Chief Justice) of Mexico. He was ousted on April 1525 by a self-proclaimed Mexican government that confiscated all of Cortés properties and tortured some of Zuazo's friends to force them to reveal the location of Cortés' treasures. Zuazo moved to and died in Hispaniola, again serving as a civil judge.

[118] Diego Velázquez died on June 12 1524, bitter and poor, having been denied any profits from the immensly successful colonization of Mexico. He was replaced as governor by Manuel de Rojas, the mayor of Santiago de Cuba. Rojas was a nobleman, born in Segovia, who had married Velázquez' niece. In 1525 Rojas was accused of misappropriation of funds and having received inappropriate favors from Velázquez. He eventually lost his fortune and moved to Perú with his brother Gabriel, not before bargaining and crafting the appointment of his son Juan as Cuba's master treasurer. Rojas was replaced in Cuba by Juan de Altamirano, who in turn was replaced by royal decree with Gonzalo de Guzmán as third governor of Cuba on April of 1526. One of the first decisions of Gonzalo de Guzmán once he took posession of his mandate was to indict Altamirano for embezzlement and larceny, as well as, in his words, «his surliness, vapidness and levity.»

island. Also, after Velázquez death,[119] the Tainos began to revolt frequently and with more intensity than ever; it lead to a period of increased cruelty which lasted for almost ten years. Trying to bring things to normal, Madrid promulgated a gentle pacification policy that included a restructuring of the *Encomiendas* and the first safety rules for labor in the mines. Fray Pedro Mexía de Trillo, Franciscan provincial from Hispaniola, was sent to Cuba to see to it that the new regulations were followed. As he tried to organize agricultural colonies where natives would be taught how to cultivate and would pay a share of their income to the crown, Governor Gonzalo de Guzmán, then current governor of Cuba, objected and disavowed the effort.[120]

Gonzalo de Guzmán, together with Pánfilo de Narváez, were well connected to the Spanish crown. In 1518 they secured from the King a decree giving them life terms of office as *Concejales o Regidores* (Councilors or Regents), Guzmán in Santiago de Cuba and Narváez in Bayamo. Most other public officials were appointed for limited terms. Narváez, in particular, was charged by his contemporaries as having a selfish intention to entrench himself and his friends in perpetuity under the facade of a high-minded and statesmanly plan to secure the continuity of local governments. When word got to the King that there were protests for his favoritisms in the lifetime appointments of Guzmán and Narváez, the King's solution was to

---

[119] Velázquez had so many enemies that after his death a proclamation was issued inviting everybody, assured of immunity, to come forward with details of his malfeasance. A flood of insinuations, accusations and calumnies resulted, his archives were ransacked and he was convicted by public opinion of gambling, stealing supplies for the Mexican expedition, having levied taxes and pilfering the funds, uttering blasphemous utterances and even «stealing a horse and a mule.»

[120] By most accounts Governor Guzmán was not a fair man. He had been a steadfast friend and advocate for Velázquez before the courts in Madrid during the Velázquez disputes with Cortés and Diego Columbus. When he replaced Altamirano in the governorship, he was also appointed *Repartidor de Indios*, and had the same level of authority that Velázquez had enjoyed. He was ruthless in his investigations and was largely moved by personal vindictiveness.

appoint enough other lifelong Councilors to balance the powers invested in Guzmán and Narváez. One of the consequences of this proliferation of local Councilors -at least in Cuba- was to weaken the value of lifetime tenures for friends of the crown. A regulation requiring all appointees to be *bona fide* residents of the island was passed in 1529 by 5 of the Councils in Cuba's six towns; such move was specifically intended to unseat Narváez and it was unmistakably not liked by the King's advisors.

Pánfilo de Narváez, after taking part in the conquest of Jamaica in 1509 and in the failed expedition to Mexico to "take Cortés dead or alive" in 1521, was appointed *Adelantado* of Florida by Charles V. He sailed from the shores of the Guadalquivir river in Sanlúcar de Barrameda,[121] north of Cadiz, in Andalucía, on June 17, 1527 with 300 men and landed in today's St. Petersburg, Florida, among hostile *Apalachee* natives. Trying to return on an overland trek to Cuba via Mexico (his vessels had been destroyed by a storm), he perished with all his men except four, one of which was Alvar Núñez Cabeza de Vaca.[122]

It is interesting to note that in 1529, after the regulations approved by the town Councils in Cuba were accepted by the King, the principle of "Cuba for the Cubans," or at least "for the residents of Cuba," was firmly -if only temporarily- established.

---

[121] Sanlúcar was a town founded by the Greeks beyond the Strait of Gibraltar in 1000 BC, at a place frequented by Phoenician traders since the 8th century BC. It is mentioned by Aristotle, Pliny and Herodotus in their writings. It was seized by the Muslims in 815 AD and recovered by King Alfonso X of Castile in 1264. After 1492 it was home to Columbus and Magallanes.

[122] Cabeza de Vaca traveled for 8 years on foot from the point Narváez and his crew died in the Florida panhandle to Mexican territory, where he connected with a Spanish settlement. During this incredible journey he was made a slave, became a trader, served as a shaman to various tribes and begat several children with native women. Back to Spain he wrote his memoires in a book called *La Relación* (The Account), considered today a valuable proto-anthropologist treatise. In a well established pattern in Spanish America, as soon as he was appointed *Adelantado* in *Rio de la Plata*, present day Argentina in 1540, he was arrested by Domingo Martínez de Irala, a political enemy, and exiled to Spain where he was sentenced for illegal appropriation and poor administration of crown moneys. Although his sentence was commuted he never returned to America and died a wretched and miserably poor man in Seville.

The Governor and all Councilors and royal officers were Cuban residents; townspeople were invested with the authority to select advocates that represented them in the local courts as well as in the Royal Councils of Madrid and Seville; oftentimes the residents were empowered in practice -if not *de jure*- to proceed against or in favor of the Governor.

Eventhough the King agreed to these regulations in the spirit of removing the burden of Cuba's political in fights from his agenda, he repeatedly had to intervene in Cuban affairs to settle disputes. When Gonzalo de Guzmán's brother-in-law Pedro Nuñez de Guzmán died leaving a sizable fortune, the Governor transferred his wealth to his widow, who happened to be his new wife. At least six members of the family protested, including the mother of the deceased who had never left Spain. The courts had to get involved, a series of scandalous lawsuits ensued and the issues were not resolved for years, until the King had to intervene. By then, the entire population of the island had taken sides, a mass in the Cathedral of Santiago was interrupted by a melee led on one side by Gonzalo de Guzmán and on the other by the Mayor of Santiago; it had to be controlled by the local police. After years in which the King vacillated and did not intervene, the case ran its course and lawyers were enriched; the King finally dictated sentence in favor of Guzmán and his wife. Not two years had passed, and Guzman was replaced in the Governorship of Cuba by the island's debt collector, Juan Vadillo, who lasted 30 days as Governor of Cuba. He apparently resigned because the meager salary[123] he was receiving and moved to Hispaniola. His resignation was not accepted by the King and he had to show up in Santiago de Cuba. There he found Guzmán guilty of election fraud, unapproved taxes collected and not remitted to Spain, unauthorized and illegal appointments, illicit slave trade, misrepresentations in reports to the crown, assignment of natives as serfs of his

---

[123] A salary of 600 silver Maravedises per diem had been approved, payable from Cuba's budget. In today's money it would have been US$ 200 daily.

family members and inequitable distribution of native labor. He was forced to pay a large fine and in 1532 showed up in Spain with boxes full of documents and a Bishop as his advocate.[124] As soon as Governor Guzmán and Bishop Ramirez departed for Spain, Vadillo returned to Hispaniola after designating Manuel de Rojas to be Governor in his stead.

In the meantime, discontent and resentment grew among Tainos that had been "distributed" as serfs among the Spaniards. Many of them began to escape and take refuge in the numerous keys surrounding the Cuban territory. Ocasionally they would go to the main island in groups and make depredatory raids. When the vigilance and hostilities began to make life difficult in the keys, many Tainos took refuge in the mountains surrounding Santiago. They became known as the *Cimarrones*.[125]

Taino *Cimarrones* preceded escaped Black slaves (also called *Cimarrones* or *Maroons*) and, like the slaves would do later, built their own independent towns.[126] In certain parts of Cuba, be-

---

[124] Santiago de Cuba's Bishop Miguel Ramírez, OP was a close friend and associate of Governor Guzmán, as well as an insistant meddler in political affairs; in 1531 he had issued a writ of excommunication to anyone who would testify against Governor Guzmán during Vadillo's inquire. Vadillo himself was not free of transgressions; he was accused in Cuba of seizing a hoard of gold that had been mined by the husband of the Bishop's niece. The Bishop denounced him at a homily in the Cathedral; Vadillo walked out before the Bishop could conclude his sermon and complained to the King. Bishop Ramírez retaliated by excommunicating Vadillo. The King finally ruled in favor of Vadillo and compelled the Bishop to withdraw his excommunicaation.

[125] Cimarrón was a term used for runaway Tainos escaping to the countryside to live as outlaws, as well as for domestic animals escaping their houses. The word comes from the Taino term *Si'marran,* meaning "flight of an arrow." In Cuba the walkaway Tainos usually build their own independent habitats known as *Palenques*, where men, women and children lived away from the mines, the encomiendas and the formal agricultural plantations to which they had been assigned. After the importation of slaves into Cuba, there were also *Palenques* with Black populations; they existed in the island until the times of the independence wars.

[126] It was not unusual to find large settlements (30 or more families) of Taino *Cimarrones* living in hideouts concealed in the inhospitable mountains of the Oriente region.

cause they knew the territory very well, they formed alliances with pirates, corsairs, hoodlums and thugs to outsmart the Spanish bounty hunters that were trying to find them. They became expert path finders for kidnapers, ambushers and raiders of mule trains carrying treasures to the port cities. They cared little about their share of gold, silver or jewels but were interested in iron, which they used to make the tips of their rudimentary weapons. Over the years, a strange informal coalition developed between the British and the native and Black slave Cimarrones. While Indians in Hispaniola were treated poorly by their Spanish masters, the English falsely prided themselves as "emancipators" who allied with natives and Blacks to "liberate" them from the evil Spaniards. Everybody knew, however, than more than anybody else, the British were actively involved in the slave trade from Africa.

Everywhere in Cuba the initial years of the Spanish conquest were characterized by chaos, particularly after the death of Velázquez and the succession of Guzmán, Vadillo, Rojas and a second period of Guzmán in the governorship. There were daily charges and counter-charges against governors, bishops, council officials and private individuals. The order of the day was corruption, bitter personal quarrels, slanders, misappropriations, arrests, excommunications and even murders. Things seemed to settle after May 4, 1537 when Hernando de Soto was appointed by the King[127] as *Adelantado* of Florida and Governor of Cuba.

It is worth remembering that Charles V was a "foreign" King to the Spaniards. He was the eldest son of *Felipe el Hermoso* and *Juana la Loca*, the daughter of Ferdinand and Isabel I, the Catholic Monarchs. He was born in Flanders, a territory within the Holy Roman Empire that paid tribute to France until 1528. During his reign (1519-1556) Spain conquered Mexico and Peru and extended the Spanish Empire throughout Central and

---

[127] De Soto was the first to be appointed to hold these titles and offices by Charles V himself. All others had been nominated and served at the will of Velázquez or the Councils.

South America; he sponsored the trip of Magellan to circumnavigate the earth, which laid the foundation for the Spanish colonization of the Philippines. Charles V, however, was not well liked by the Spaniards, not only because he had not been born in the peninsula and spoke Castilian with difficulty but also because he spent Spanish funds to fight wars were Spain had nothing to win except glory for its King. His lack of attention to what was happening in Cuba [128] resulted in numerous disputes between civil and ecclesiastical authorities; add to that the over importance of city Councils, where the majority of members were appointed by the King and oftentimes prevailed over Governors and Bishops. Falling between the cracks were the destinies of Cuba's native population, whose interest was not to work the mines or the land but to stroll, dance in the *Areitos*, make love, smoke and stay in the shade. [129]

In the meantime, the little gold Cuba had began to be more and more difficult to be found. The tragedy of De Soto's explorations of lands north of Cuba diminished the enthusiasm for traveling to unknown territories.[130] What moved many Span-

---

[128] The records of the time show that Charles V was concerned about the miserable conditions native populations had to endure. He was too busy, however, to know of the determination of their *Conquistadores* to extract work and services from the indians at any and all costs.

[129] Charles V of the Holy Roman Empire (Germany) aka Carlos I of Spain, was the heir of the three most important royal dynasties in Europe: the Habsburgs, the Valois and the Spanish House of Castille, León and Aragón. Most of his reign was devoted to the enormously expensive Italian Wars against France. He was also the King who halted the Ottoman advances in Europe by defeating Suleiman in Vienna in 1529. He was a rabid opponent of Protestantism and the main mentor of the *Council of Trento* and the Society of Jesus. He was known in Europe as a man of peace and serenity, more European than Spanish, who most of the time spoke in French or German rather than Castilian.

[130] De Soto landed in today's Bradenton, Florida in May 1539. He traveled through Georgia, the Carolinas, Tennessee, Alabama, Mississippi, Arkansas, Oklahoma, Louisiana and Texas, encountering native ambushes and conflicts all along the way. He finally died in 1542 near present day McArthur, Texas, of a semitropical fever. He never found the spectacular treasures he anticipated, nor did he find reasonably hospitable places where to rest. At the end his men had been reduced in half, most of them were sick or injured and were wearing animal skins for clothing.

iards in Cuba was the lure of participating in the draining of Mexico and Perú's wealth. Many adventuresome residents of the island began to enroll in the risky ventures of exploration of the continent. Few things happened across the Cuban territory, with the exception of Havana. The trade routes were being established. The French *corsairs* were making travelling across the Atlantic an intolerable hazard. The solution was to establish a meeting point of gold carrying ships to cross the ocean together under escort. Although Trinidad was considered because of its proximity to the north coast of South America, Havana became the top choice because of its splendid and well protected anchoring facilities. It would transform the island of Cuba for the rest of its history.[131]

Images above, left to right:
a **Black Cimarron** trying to escape from his master's dogs.
Slaves **mining gold** in Cuba;

---

[131] The first incident of the French attacking Spanish *galeones* in Havana took place in the summer of 1537, when two corsario vessels disembarked, took all the gold from two Spanish ships anchored inside the bay, ransacked the city and stole sacred ornaments from Havana's Cathedral.

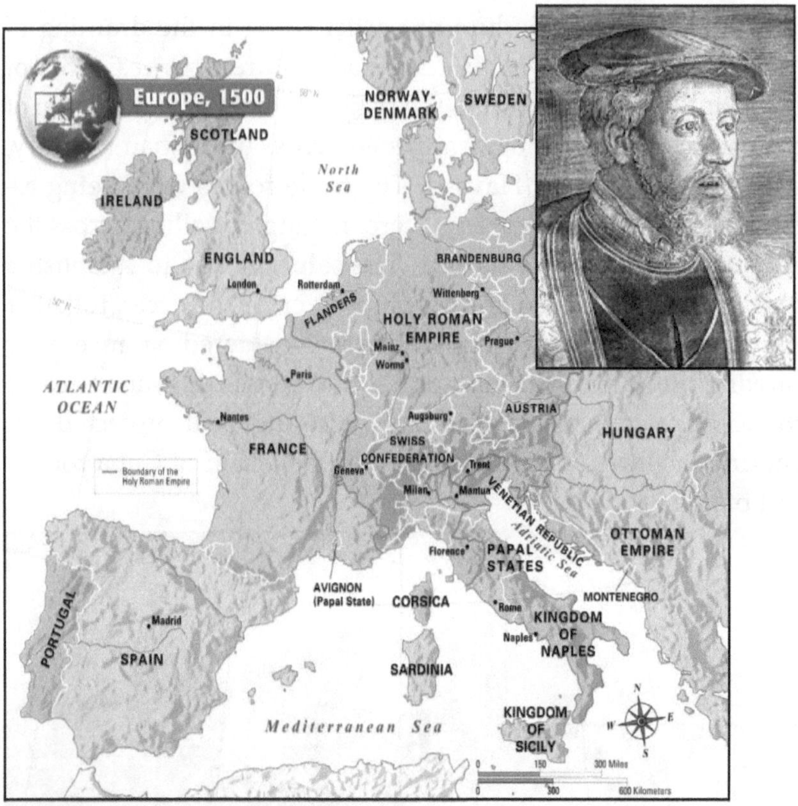

Images, left to right, top to bottom:
Charles V, Emperor of the Holy Roman Empire;
a **Map of the Holy Roman Empire** in the 1500s;
a contemporary woodblock of the **Emperor**;
the **emblem** of the Holy Roman Empire.

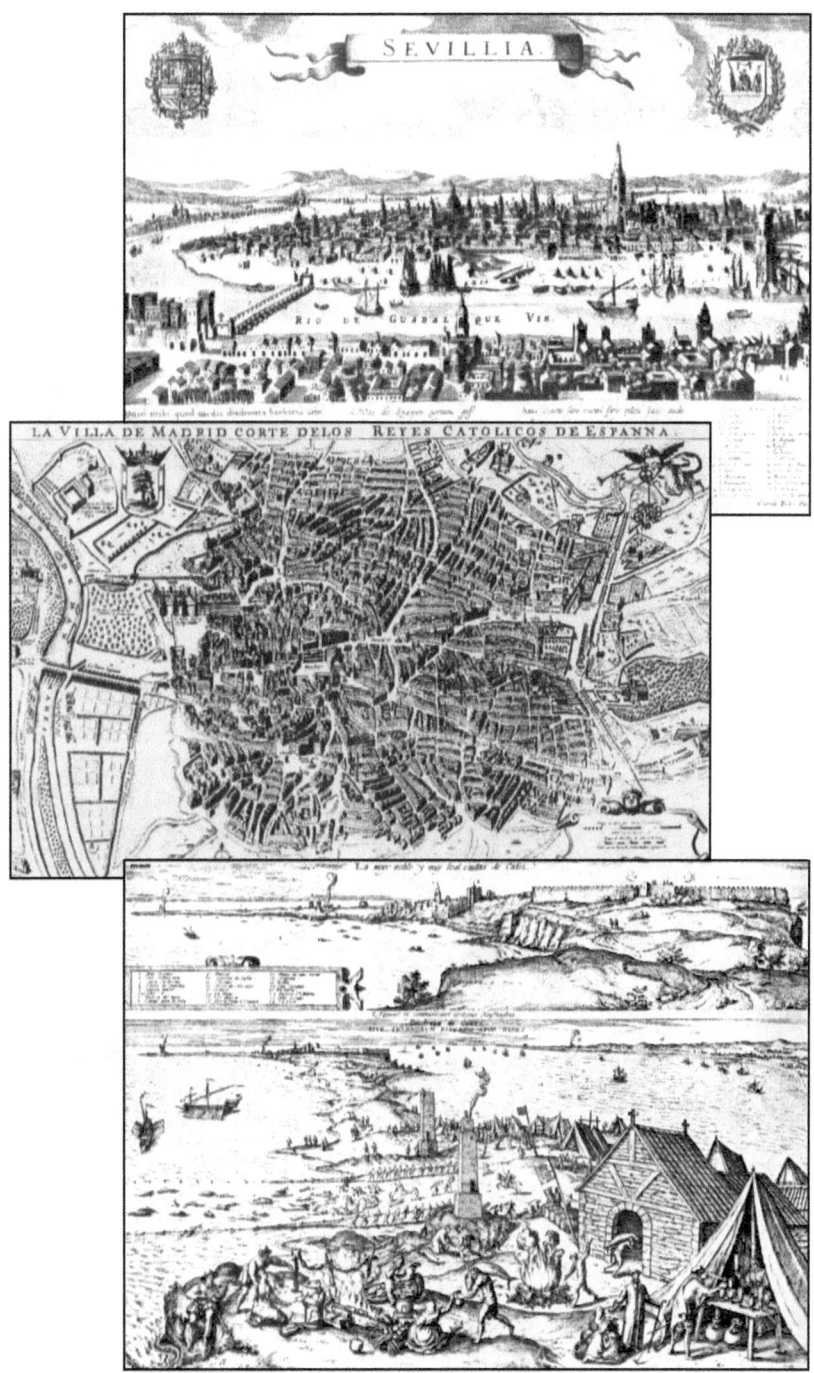

Three important XVI Century Spanish cities during the Colonization of Cuba. From top to bottom:

Sevilla, Madrid, Cádiz.

Images, left to right, top to bottom:

Two Spanish **Doublon coins** from 1507;

an eight **Maravedis** coin;

Hernando de Soto, presumably drinking from the **Fountain of Youth** in Florida;

Cabeza de Vaca, the conquistador who did not give up after a defeat and walked for eight years across the jungles, from the Florida panhandle to the Mexican territory.

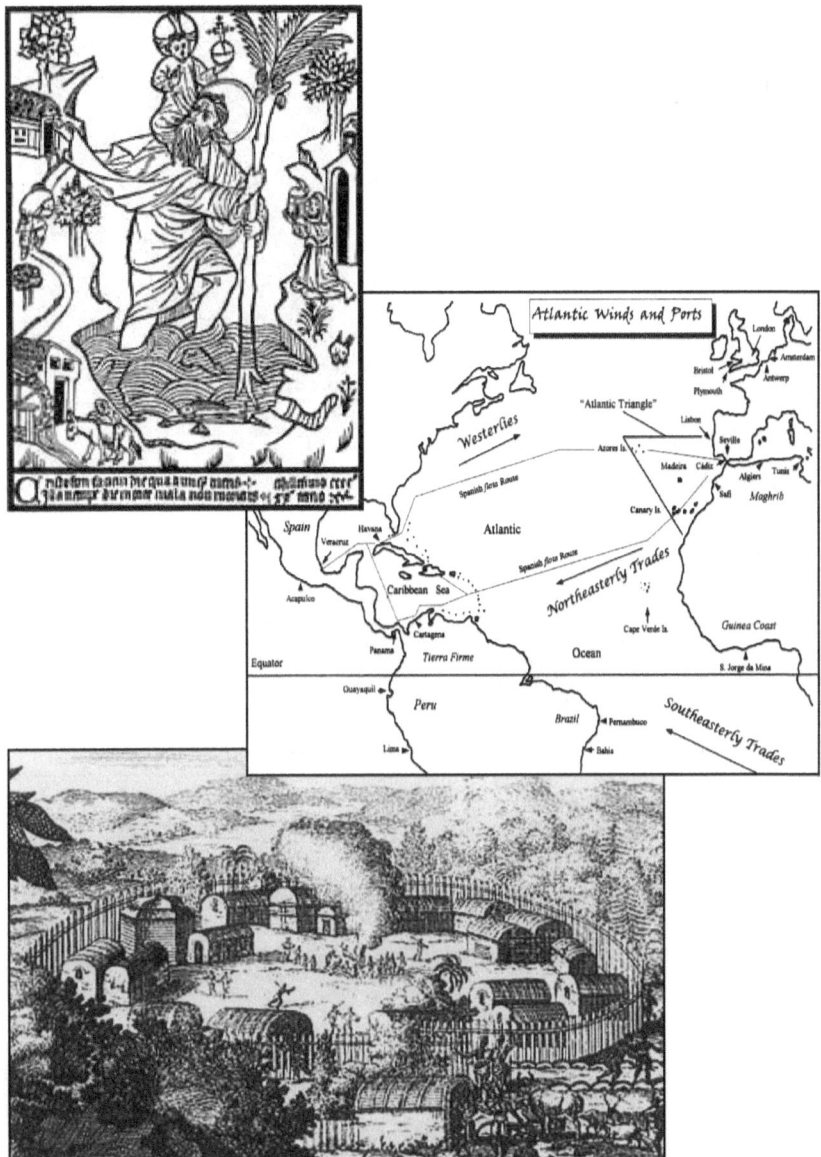

Images, top to bottom:

San Cristobal de la Habana, a name for the Cuban Capital that blended an homage to Christopher Columbus and the name that the Tainos gave the region;

a map with the **prevailing winds** in the Atlantic. It justified the choice of Havana as the meeting point for the Gold Fleet;

a contemporary representation of a **Palenque**, the type of "town" built by Tainos in the XVI century and later copied by Black slaves when they ran away.

Images, left to right, top to bottom:

An etching showing some common typical **fruit trees in Cuba** that were unknown to Europeans;

the zone in Eastern Cuba **populated by Tainos** and their descendants into the XXI century;

a housing unit of **Taino descendants** in the Oriente region of Cuba. Photo taken in 1935.

13
A Shrinking Population Under Chaos

AS ALL ISLANDS in the Caribbean were losing residents to the allure of wealth, affluence and grandeur in the continent, French corsairs continued to harass and torment the Spanish conquered lands in the Caribbean, particularly Cuba. In 1537 several Spanish ships anchored in Havana harbor were easily sacked by two well armed French ships. Not contented with the loot they found aboard, they proceeded to plunder Havana's churches and take all gold instruments of worship and, surprisingly, several religious icons sent from the Bishop of Seville to Bishop Miguel Ramírez of Santiago de Cuba, who had presented them to the future Episcopal see in Havana. The chalices and effigies were two years later replaced by Inés de Bobadilla, wife of Hernando de Soto who, in the now traditional process of political nepotism,[132] had been appointed by De Soto as acting governess of Cuba during his exploration of Florida.

This successful 1537 raid of Havana was followed in 1543 by Jean-Françoise de la Roche, Lord of Roberval,[133] a French adventurer who briefly took Santiago de Cuba and Havana. De la Roche was a distant relative of François I, King of France, who

---

[132] It is not easy to identify when the leaders in Cuba started the practice of bestowing patronage –particularly jobs and titles- in consideration of personal relationships rather than on merits or legal claims. It probably began with Velázquez and has continued to these days by the Castro clan. The word comes from the Latin *nepos*, meaning nephew; during the Middle Ages, Catholic popes and bishops, having no offspring of their own, started the custom of appointing their nephews to positions of priviledge.

[133] In 1541, a repentant de la Roche sailed up the St. Lawrence River with 200 settlers -many of them released prisoners- and founded a settlement on the margins of the river. Their first winter in Canada was so harsh that most of the settlers died; those who survived returned to France in 1543.

could not have been more displeased with Spain's growing empire in America. Since becoming king in 1515, he had been struggling against the power of Spain's king Carlos I.[134] Carlos was the most promising heir of the Habsburgs, the most powerful ruling house of Europe and the major obstacle to the power of the French monarchs in Europe.

François I never stopped doing things that would annoy Carlos I. Starting in 1520 he allied France with Carlos' enemies –including the Muslim Turks and the German Lutheran princes- to fight against Spain. He was the first European monarch to commission privateers and pirates to prey on Spanish ships bearing gold from the Americas to Spain. He commissioned corsairs to attack Spanish settlements all throughout the New World. In 1524, he finally hired a Florentine sailor, Giovanni da Verrazzano (aka Jean Florin), to do against Carlos I whatever suited his purposes, under the guise of finding a western sea route to the real Indies.[135]

Facing continuous attacks by French corsairs, Carlos I granted permission to construct stone fortifications to protect the

---

[134] Carlos had inherited the throne of the Holy Roman Empire from his grandfather Maximilian, had succeeded *Felipe el Hermoso*, his father, to the wealthy principality of Flandes and his mother Juana *la Loca*, daughter of the Catholic Monarchs Ferdinand and Isabel, to the throne of Castille, León and Aragón. Carlos V's lands surrounded France on the northeast, the east and the south, and his wealth was far superior to François I's.

[135] At the time there was a belief in European circles that there was a passage to India called the *Straits of Anian;* the rights to exploit it was up for grabs to whatever country would find it. The only certainty was that it must be in the northern hemisphere since the Spaniards had exhausted all possible locations in the southern hemisphere. That was what moved Verrazzano to go north and enter –for the first time- what is now the harbor of New York. After exploring for two months Narragansett Bay, the coast of Maine and Newfoundland, Verrazzano returned to France empty handed, to the great annoyance of François I, who refused to pay him. Busy with his tricks against Carlos I, François I did not sponsor other explorations to North America until 1534, when he commissioned Jacques Cartier, a native of Saint-Malo, to return to Newfoundland. Cartier was the first European to see, kill, slaughter and serve a polar bear for dinner, which he identified as «*a brave animal, as big as a calf and white as a swan.*» Cartier returned to France after a well deserved vacation in Havana, where he decided to baptize with the name *Canada* the lands he had discovered (from the native word *Kanata*, meaning village).

new port of Havana. In 1544 the *Castillo de la Fuerza* was inaugurated, as well as *San Felipe y Santiago*, the first hospital to serve the growing population of Havana.[136] The French corsairs avoided the Havana area and attacked Baracoa the following year, taking all worldly possessions of the settlers, including, once again, all icons, sculptured images, chalices, wax candles, and even musical instruments from the church. Chaos continued in the top administrative positions in the island of Cuba. In the 40 years from 1535 to 1575,[137] twelve governors had the maximum authority –both *de facto* and *de jure*- in Cuba:

Gonzalo de Guzmán (1535-1538), was deposed due to conflicts with fray Pedro Mexía de Trillo and accusations of favoritism by the *Cabildo de Santiago*;

Hernando de Soto (1538-1542), was appointed also as *Adelantado de la Florida*; he ordered the construction of *La Fuerza* fort and left Cuba on April 5, 1539, to initiate the conquest of *la Florida* with Vasco Porcallo de Figueroa; he died in 1542 on the banks of the Mississippi in Arkansas or Louisiana. He was an excellent horseman, fighter, and tactician;

Inés de Bobadilla (1539-1544); when her husband Hernando left Cuba for Florida, she became *de facto* governess of Cuba. She installed a woman statue (*La Giraldilla*, by Gerónimo Martín Pinzó, a Cuban-born sculptor) on top of the *La Fuerza* castle. The statue symbolizes Isabel waiting for Hernando, her husband. It is reported she hoped for the return of Hernando every single day;

Juan de Avila (1544-1546), was appointed once the death of De Soto was confirmed. He was known for his tyranny and corruption. His home in Havana, built with materials extorted from the people, was baptized the "House of Fear." He started

---

[136] Havana was declared the seat of government in Cuba in 1553 by the *Audiencia de Santo Domingo.* In 1603 the *San Felipe y Santiago Hospital* was turned over to the Order of the Brothers of San Juan de Dios.

[137] The average population of the entire island of Cuba was estimated to be no more than 5,000 people between 1535 and 1570.

the *Zanja Real*, the aqueduct carrying water from the Chorrera River to what was later Cathedral Square in Havana;

Antonio de Chávez (1546-1548), assumed the government of Cuba in 1546 and finished the works of the aqueduct. His reputation was as bad as Juan de Avila's. Baracoa was sacked during his tenure, which ended in 1548;

Gonzalo Pérez de Angulo (1548-1555), was the last civilian governor during the XVI century. He was commended for the suppression of the *Encomiendas*,[138] yet was considered as a coward by his contemporaries. He was made responsible for the lack of defense during the attack of Havana by Jacques de Sores in 1555 (Angulo sought refuge in Guanabacoa); afterwards he was jailed and sent to Spain to be indicted for cowardice;

Diego de Mazariegos (1556-1565), took possession of the governorship of Cuba just before becoming *Conquistador* of Chiapas and governor of Venezuela. He was a cousin of Alonso de Estrada, a natural son that King Ferdinand had with a Jewish lady. To atone for his relationship to the Jews, Mazariegos was forced to wear a *Sanbenito* [139] for the rest of his life. He started the fortification later known as *El Morro*;

Francisco García Osorio (1565-1567); he succeeded his close friend Mazariegos in 1565. When Mazariegos retired to Spain, his galleon was captured by French corsairs Fornoux and Lacroix near Mariel; they demanded a hefty ransom from García Osorio. Rather than pay it Osorio sent a rescue ship which took the corsairs by surprise, killing 15, taking 50 prisoners to Havana and rescuing Mazariegos;

---

[138] Pérez de Angulo liberated all natives that were under the yoke of the *Encomiendas*. Due to this action most *Palenques* disappeared at least tremporarily, starting in 1549.

[139] A *Sanbenito* was a penitential garment or blessed sackcloth, worn upon orders of an *auto-de-fe* ceremony; it consisted of a pointed hat decorated with crosses, flames and devils; wearers had to tie a rope around the neck and carry a tallow candle in their hand in order to acknowledge the personal errors of their ways.

Francisco de Zayas (1567), was an aloof, remote and unimaginative governor; the *Cabildo* acknowledged it had been appointed by a communications mistake.

Pedro Menéndez de Avilés (1567-1574); Spanish Admiral, Captain General of the Fleet of the Indies in 1554, born to an old noble family in the kingdom of Asturias, *Adelantado* and governor of Florida, fleet organizer and founder of San Agustin. He was the man chosen by Felipe II –his good friend and sponsor- to punish the *Hugonotes* that had established settlements in the Americas. He reinforced the towns of San Agustín, Havana, Santo Domingo, Puerto Rico[140] and Santiago de Cuba. He died in Spain in 1574 of a heart attack;

Diego de Rivera (1572), was a colorless and brief governor of Cuba; he served on an interim basis whenever Menéndez was too busy. For this service he was granted by Felipe II all the lands around present day Güines, southeast of Havana, on both sides of the Mayabeque River. A city was not founded there, however, until 1737;

Sancho Pardo Donlebún (1572-1574). A protégée of Menéndez de Avilés and a second choice as interim governor; a talented cartographer who made the first marine chart of Cuba.

The years from 1574 to the end of the century brought a series of important events in Cuba.[141] One of the most encouraging of these was the appointment of Gabriel de Montalvo as governor of the island. He was a *Caballero del Hábito de Santiago* and had been a fair-minded conservative Catholic leader (*Alguacil Mayor*) of the Inquisition in Granada. As it becomes to

---

[140] The name of the current city of San Juan was Puerto Rico, while the name of the island was San Juan.

[141] During the first half of the XVI century, the Spanish Conquistadores perceived their residence in Cuba as strictly temporary. They did not bother to find good materials of construction to make their residences more comfortable; with the possible exception of Puerto Príncipe (where a tile factory was built as early as 1544), they lived in *bohios modificados*, i.e., Taino structures in which the kitchens and sanitary facilities were segregated. In Havana, in 1587, the Church that later became the Convento de Santo Domingo was built out of *pencas de guano y barro* (palm fronds and mud).

a respectable and well intentioned man, nothing upsetting or regrettable occurred during the three years he occupied the position; his term in office was a stabilizing interlude in the chaotic curse of events in Cuba. He was followed by men of the same caliber: Francisco Carreño, Gaspar de Torres and Gabriel de Luján.[142] The late 1500s were also the years when the future *Catedral de la Habana* was consecrated and when the *Zanja Real*, bringing water from the Almendares River to the capital, was first placed in service. The protection of Havana was increased with plans to build the *Torreón de San Lázaro* at the intersection of today's Malecón and Marina streets, inside today's Antonio Maceo Park. Catholic education in the island got started when Dominican, Franciscan and Jesuit friars began to open primary schools in the city, soon to be expanded to the rest of the island.[143]

Native Tainos, until then moving from place to place outside the cities, were offered land and housing under the protection of Hernán Manrique de Rojas, a *"Caballero hijodalgo de linaje ilustre descendiente de los señores de la casa de Poza."* (A Knight – hijodalgo- of illustrious lineage, descendant of the lords of the

---

[142] In 1581 Spain declared war against England, France and Holland. Havana was attacked and its residents defended the town with valor and resiliency, whether they were Spaniards, native Tainos from Guanabacoa or Black slaves. The concerted effort was made possible by a new sense of honesty inspired by Montalvo, Carreño, Torres and Luján.

[143] The first Cuban reference to popular education took place in Santiago de Cuba, where the priests of the Cathedral were «teaching grammar to clerics and Church leaders, as well as anyone who was willing to pay attention.» Juan de las Cabezas Altamirano (1565-1615, Bishop of Santiago, Guatemala and Arequipa, Perú) opened a school for boys in Havana, to teach «grammar, arts and other virtues.» As an amateur sociologist, Bishop Altamirano indicated in a letter to the Kings of Spain in 1608 that there were 1,000 natives left in all of Cuba: 300 in Guanabacoa, 100 in Baracoa, 250 in Bayamo, 150 in Puerto Príncipe, 100 in Sancti Spíritus, 77 in Santiago de Cuba and 50 in Trinidad, for a total of 6.5 % of the total island's population. Many of them had not been born in Cuba but were inserted in the island from *Nueva España* (North America south of Canada, all of present-day Mexico and Central America except Panama, most of the United States west of the Mississippi River, plus Florida). They were exempted from taxes, lived very poorly, cultivated small plots or worked as laborers in farms, or acted as lookouts in the coasts looking for corsairs. Many males had to serve in remote locations, far from their wives and children.

House of Poza.) His public service included serving the King with his weapons, which he did in the 1550s fighting *Cimarrones* in Cuba, in the 1560s defending Granada against the attempts of the Muslims to recover it, in the 1570s fighting Lutheran corsairs in Jamaica and in the 1580s preparing Havana for the defense against Francis Drake's attack in 1586.

In spite of Martínez de Rojas protection, the Tainos in Cuba never had the same rights and status as the Spaniards. Even in 1580, when their numbers had decreased by almost 30%, Bishop Juan del Castillo (who served the Diocese of Santiago de Cuba[144] from April of 1564 to October of 1578) asked King Felipe II ...

«...que les quiten los protectors y que las justicias tengan mucha cuenta con ellos, porque darles un protector es darles un encomendero, siendo ellos pobrísimos, que toda la tierra donde puede haber granjerías, las tienen tomadas los Españoles, y ellos están allí como extraños y parece convener que se descarguen de todas molestias...»

(...lets remove the protectors and may justice give many deserved rights to them, because to give them a protector is to assign an *Encomendero*; they are very poor. All land with good sowing has been taken by the Spanish, and they (the natives) are there as strangers; it appears convenient to dispense them from any and all hassles ...)

The island of Cuba continued through the rest of the century to be the target of French corsairs. In 1582 a corsair simply known as Richard attacked Bayamo. The residents fought decisively, apprehended Richard and hung him from a Ceiba. His son escaped, turned eastward and demolished and burned Santiago de Cuba to the ground, including the Cathedral, City Hall, the recently inaugurated San Francisco Convent and most of the houses. Within 2 years, it was not only the French but also the British attacking Spain's property. Francis Drake left

---

[144] Santiago de Cuba became a Diocese in 1518. At the time it included all of present day Cuba. In 1570, at the request of the *Cabildo de la Habana*, today's capital city became a separate Diocese. Other Dioceses were segregated from Santiago in 1912 (Camagüey), 1979 (Holguín), 1995 (Bayamo and Manzanillo), 1998 (Guantánamo and Baracoa).

Plymouth for the peninsula, burned Vigo (Spain) to the ground and, on the way to the Caribbean, destroyed the town of *Santiago de las Azores*. Once in the New World he made his presence felt in Santo Domingo and Cartagena de Indias. Having overextended his supply lines, his fleet took refuge in Bahia Honda and Mariel, in Cuba, where it was received with multiple cannon rounds. For the first and last time Drake took an eastern course out of western Cuba, took a look at heavily fortified Havana and continued to Matanzas, where the residents were well prepared to receive him. He decided to tack north to Florida, but before reaching the peninsula changed his mind, took an easterly course and returned to England.

Other news before the century was over were favorable to the development of the island:

In 1578, Felipe II was shown some samples of Cuban-grown woods and issued an order that his new palace of *El Escorial* [145] would use precious Cuban woods rather than from any other source.

In 1589 work started in the construction in Havana bay of the forts of *San Salvador de la Punta* and *Tres Reyes del Morro*, both under the design and direction of Juan Bautista Antonelli (1527-1588),[146] the best known military engineer of the times.

In 1594 Juan Maldonado Barnuevo was appointed by the King as Governor of Cuba; he was one of the governors of Cuba that successfully defended the island from pirates; he was also instrumental in developing the copper mines in the mountains surrounding Santiago de Cuba. Both for agricultural development and work in the mines, Maldonado Barnuevo promoted the importation of Black slaves to Cuba. It was at those

---

[145] *El Escorial*, constructed between 1561 and 1569, is a multifunctional architectural complex where Felipe II lived his last years. It is notable for its woods, pastures, meadows, artificial waterways, ponds and gardens, as well as chapels, towers and palatial interiors.

[146] Antonelli designed and supervised the fortresses in Cartagena de Indias, Colombia, as well as ports, dams and forts in Valencia, Benidorm and Alicante.

times when the construction of independent small and crude sugar mills, later called *trapiches*,[147] became a good business in Cuba.

In 1595 Felipe II granted a series of tax exemptions to the operators of *trapiches azucareros*.

In 1598 Felipe II died, the copper mines of *El Cobre*, near Santiago de Cuba, began to produce enriched ores and a Royal decree authorized Cuba to start commerce with other Spanish possessions in the Americas.

Image above:
a typical **Taino settlement** in western Cuba;

---

[147] A *trapiche* was a primitive mill to extract juice from the sugar cane, to be later concentrated and crystallized to make sugar. On his third trip to Cuba, Columbus imported a few cane stalks that were the seeds for a nacient sugar industry in the island. By the end of the 1500s there were more than 60 *trapiches* functioning in Cuba. The *trapiches* were modernized to *ingenios* (XVII century, larger and more mechanized sugar processing facilities); by 1800 there were more than 1000 *ingenios* in Cuba. By the end of the 1800s, the *ingenios* gave way to the *centrales*, modern and highly automatised factories for sugar production. In 1898, there were, in addition to 500 modern *ingenios*, some 50 *centrales azucareras* en Cuba. In other places in the Americas a *trapiche* was also a milling machine used in the wine and mining industries.

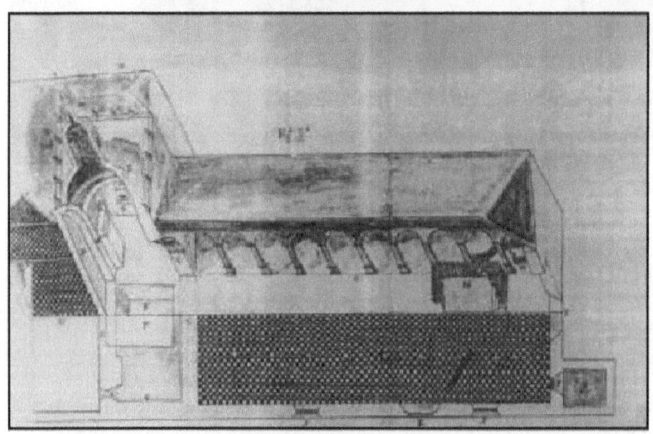

Images, top to bottom:

A XVI century Map of Havana, showing on the left side (South) two of the seven **lomas de la Habana** (hills of Havana), *el Chaple, los Zapotes, Jesús del Monte, 10 de Octubre, Luyanó, el Mazo* and *el Burro*;

a settlement of bohios *modificados* preferred by the Spaniards;

the 1523 plans for the **first Cathedral of Santiago de Cuba**.

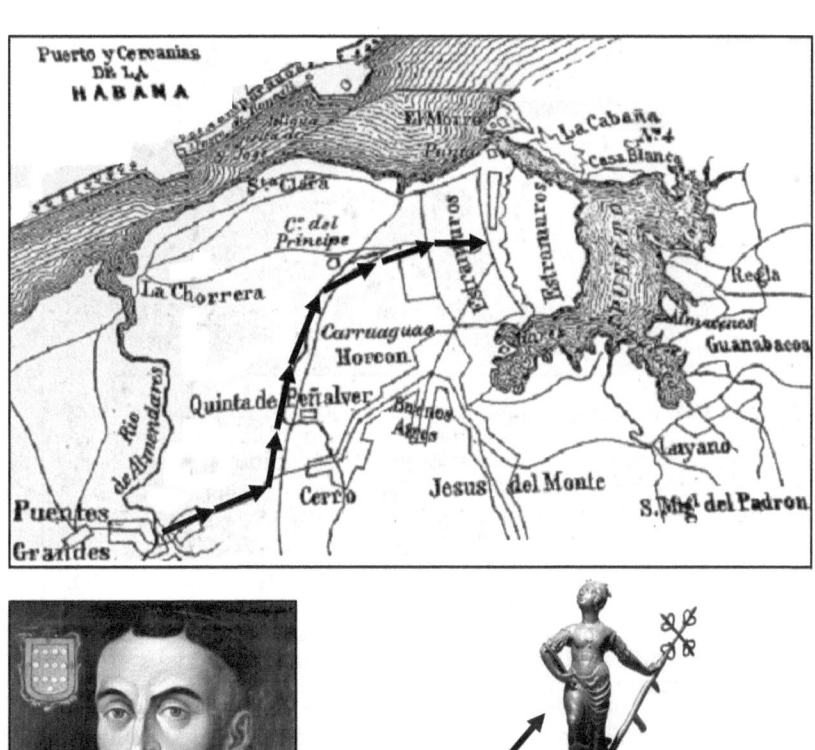

Images, top to bottom, left to right:

An **old map of Havana** showing the path of the new aqueduct inaugurated in 1574. The last stretch was under today's Zanja Street;

Silvestre de Balboa, author of *Espejo de Paciencia*, the first book dealing with Cuban history;

the statue of the **Giraldilla**, Inés de Bobadilla herself (?), wife of Hernando de Soto and interim governess of Cuba in his absence. She was the Cuban version of Homer's *Penelope*;

the *Castillo de la Fuerza* where, on top of its tower, Inés had the *Giraldilla* installed.

In Cuba, catastrophes such as hurricanes, earthquakes, fires and tidal waves became in the seventeenth century important issues with theological and philosophical implications. "Moral causes" seemed to justify natural phenomena that were sent by God to punish Cubans for their sins. It was a phenomenon widely spread in all Spanish colonies.

In Santiago de Chile in 1647, Cuzco and Guatemala in 1650, Lima in 1682 and 1746 and Argentina in 1692, recent quakes were considered either a punishment or at least a test for the faithful. All catastrophes were clear gestures of divine wrath in response to moral failings. On June 11, 1766 in Santiago de Cuba, Bishop Morell de Santa Cruz wrote in a pastoral letter that the 1776 quake that trashed the city had been a punishment for the moral evil and loose morals by most of its inhabitants. Years later José Antonio Saco made the following comment:

«The state of manners, the prevailing sins indulged by our grandparents and the spirit of the times can be deducted from this fervent declamation of the venerable Prelate. One would incur in serious mistakes, however, if we were to take the hype of the Pastoral to the letter; it was definitely conditioned by the terror that this catastrophe had instilled in all souls. He was the same dignitary that warned Havana of divine plagues with which Cubans would soon be flogged.»

The longest poem found in Cuban literature since 1608, when the *Espejo de Paciencia* was written by Silvestre de Balboa, was *Poètica Relazion Christiana and Morality*, written in *décimas* (ten-line stanza poetry) in 1796 by a Cuban-born priest, Francesco Maria Colimbini. Despite being handwritten, it had a huge circulation, from the Captain General, to whom it was addressed, to Crown employees and military superiors. It attributed to moral causes a recent hurricane with which "God had punished Havana." In the 1700s Havana was a city in which the floating population prevailed half of the year. It made the city a cosmopolitan and wicked place. Many in Cuba saw the British assault on Havana, for instance, as one of the divine plagues intended to punish the mischievous Cubans.

Catastrophes and the tendency to be alarmed in Colonial Cuba

Images, top to bottom, left to right:

Hernando de Soto (1496-1542), first Spanish explorer of today's USA;

Ponce de León (1476-1521), leader of the first expedition to Florida;

Francis Drake (1540-1596), British Vice Admiral, privateer, slaver and politician in the Elizabethan era;

Felipe II of Spain (1527-1598), King of Spain, Portugal, Naples, Sicily, England, Ireland, the Netherlands and the Philippines (named after him), son of Charles V;

Pedro Martínez de Avilés and a painting showing the first Mass celebrated in St Agustin, Florida, September 8, 1565.

COLONIAL CUBA - 153

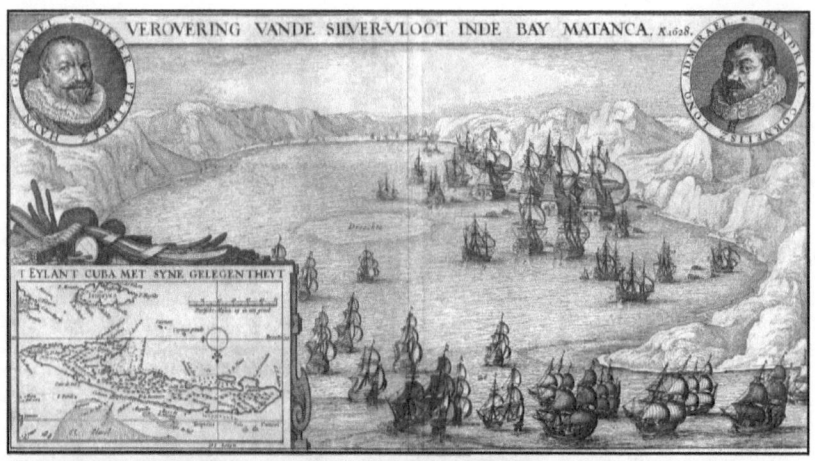

Images, top to bottom, left to right:

The **looting of the Spanish fleet** anchored in Matanzas bay by Dutch corsairs;

a XVI century drawing showing a victorious **Carlos V** surrounded by his subjects, with François I of France to his right;

the **Torreón de San Lázaro**, a Spanish fortification on the north of Havana;

a scene of **Black slaves** cutting sugar cane in Cuba.

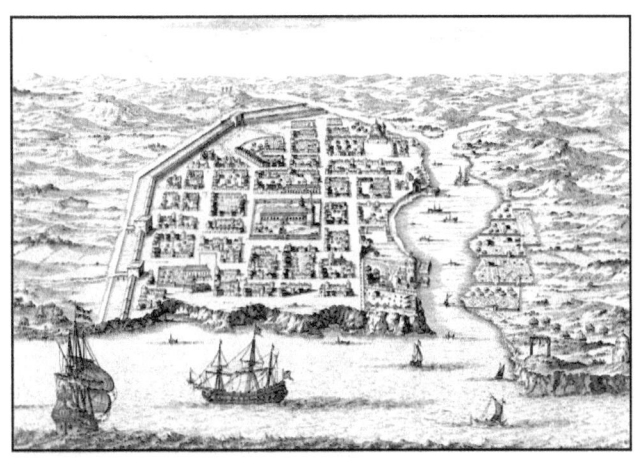

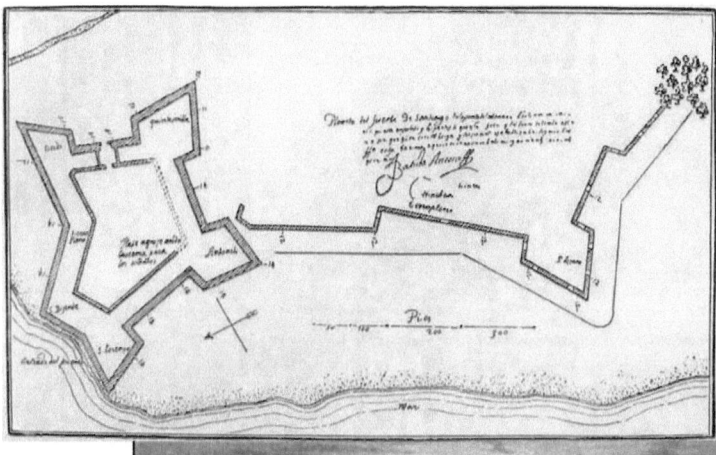

Images, top to bottom:
A 1560 view of **Santo Domingo**, capital city of the island of *Hispaniola*;
the 1593 Antonelli's plan for the **Castillo de la Punta**;
a 1558 engraving of the **Spanish fleet** assembled in Havana harbor.

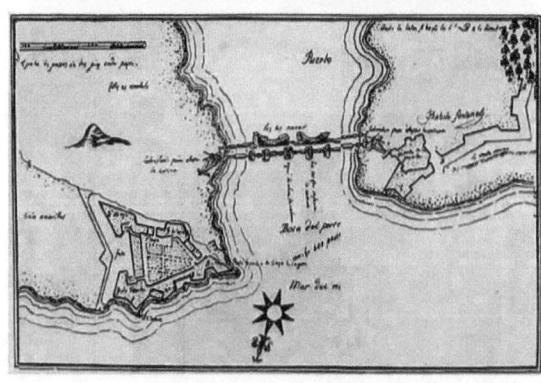

Images, top to bottom, left to right:

The library of **El Escorial**, with bookcases made with precious woods from Cuba, as preferred and ordered by Felipe II;

a late XVI sugar **trapiche**, a primitive sugar cane mill;

José de Acosta's 1590 **Historia Natural y Moral de las Indias**;

the plan of **Juan Bautista Antonelli** to prevent corsairs to access the port of Havana with a chain that would be extended from both sides of the entrance;

a 1590 drawing of a Black **Cimarrón**.

From 1600 to 1700

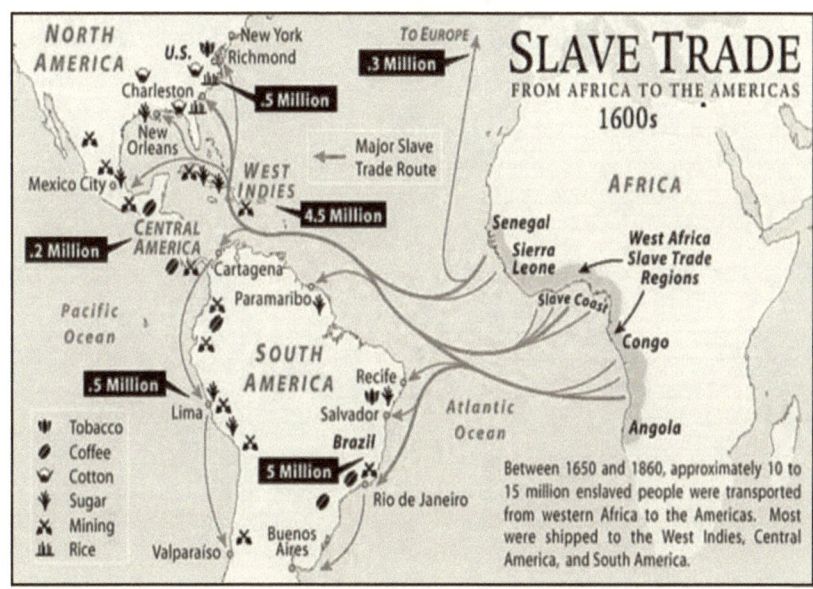

The Slave Trade in the 1600s

14
A Stable Population with Diminishing Chaos

AS THE SEVENTEENTH century rolled by, things seemed to stabilize in Cuba. Pedro Valdés was appointed governor and Captain General of the island; Bishop Juan de las Cabezas Altamirano became the Bishop of the island.

In 1606 Valdés wrote to King Felipe III:[148]

«I am alone against the entire island. From the Lieutenant Governor and the wealthiest hacendados, down to the humblest of residents, everyone is guilty of smuggling. Under those conditions, punishment is impossible since the interior parts of Cuba would be reduced to desolation if the smugglers were penalized according to the severity of their crimes.»[149]

Felipe III responded issuing a general pardon to smugglers in Cuba, Venezuela and Hispaniola.

The corruption situation had no end in sight. In 1604 a notorious case exploded in Cuba. The captains of four merchant vessels who carried African slaves from Senegal to Cuba with-

---

[148] Felipe III, son of Felipe II and his fouth wife Anna, daughter of Emperor Maximilian II, was known in Spain as *Felipe el Piadoso*. He was an "undistinguished and insignificant man, a miserable monarch, whose only virtue was the total absence of vice." He has been charged with the sorry decline of the Spanish Empire. He was not considered particularly intelligent or academically gifted.

[149] The same situation was occurring in the British colonies. The governor of Bermuda in 1602 had complained to his King that his settlers «will not give evidence against each other in any public venue, for they are akin both by consanguinity and villainy.» The governotr of New York reported to London that «everyone is conniving with the smugglers and people are so accustomed thereto that, as I tried to stop it, the whole city was in an uproar and looked at actions against smuggling as a violent violation of their property.» Officialy, the Portuguese authorities in Brazil looked the other way as long as the smuggled lots were silver from Potosí and a portion was left behind; the Dutch exempted merchandise brought in from Spanish colonies from custom duties, provided they got a fair cut.

out a license, bought back their cargo after the authorities in Havana had it confiscated. A pro-forma trial increased the smugglers' expenses but they still reaped a substantial profit. This type of action took the name of *blanqueo* (whitewashing) and occurred frequently all across Cuba. It became important for the local economy and it filled the colonial treasuries. In Cuba it probably accounted for 7 to 15 percent of the net income of the town of Havana.[150] Those moneys probably never arrived in Spain.

When it was found that most local tobacco and sugar from Cuba, Venezuela, Trinidad and Hispaniola was carried to Europe by illegal Dutch and English ships, the Spanish crown tried to stem this flow of contraband by ordering the depopulation of northern Hispaniola and forbidding tobacco and sugar cultivation in Venezuela and Cumaná. By virtue of the smarts of Dutch Calvinists and *conversos*, there was no shortage of tobacco in Europe. Before long, Amsterdam spawned a sugar refining industry three times as large as Spain's, although the Dutch had no lands in the Americas with sugar cultivation. It was the Portuguese, however, who dominated smuggling from Cuba in the early 1600s. They forged bills of lading and import papers, disguised shipped freights, adulterated terms of delivery and consignment, hid cargo and thinned out waybills. It came to the point when the crown ordered Cuba's governor to banish all Portuguese from the island, except those married or who had lived there for at least ten years. [151]

Although all towns in Cuba participated in the smuggling frenzy, *San Salvador de Bayamo* and not Havana was the capital

---

[150] The *Casa de Contratación de Sevilla*, the Spanish House of Trade, had been established in 1505, to monitor foreign commerce, which was absolutely prohibited, and to curb any efforts to trade with other non-Spanish colonies in the Americas. It presumably registered all ships, crews, equipment and merchandise arriving in Cuban ports. It was completely impotent to stop the trade in slaves, linen, wines, hides, precious metals, wood and exotic foods.

[151] A very similar situation occurred in Buenos Aires, where 370 out of 1,500 residents were Portuguese; they were all involved in illegal trade.

of gunrunning and contraband. It was reported to the crown in 1606 that there were twenty four Dutch, one English and four French ships in the fluvial port of Bayamo.[152] In fact, in 1606 Bayamo had the same population than Havana and was favored as a residence by the Spanish governors. By the end of the century, smuggling in Bayamo was so widespread that all landowners, council members and clerics were imprisoned for contraband.

The main event in the first years of the XVII century, however, was the abduction of Bishop Fray Juan de las Cabezas Altamirano. He was a graduate of Salamanca and had arrived in Cuba in 1592 at the age of 27. His initial appointment was as general vicar of the Dominican order for Hispaniola. King Felipe II of Spain appointed him as the third Bishop of Havana in 1603. The first order of business for Bishop Altamirano was to visit his congregations in the different towns of Cuba. On April 29, 1604, he was abducted with his secretary, a *canónigo* named Puebla, as they made the rounds close to the town of Yara, near Bayamo. The kidnapper was a French corsair, Gilberto Girón, *Señor de la Ponfiera*; his intention was to secure an enormous ransom from the town residents. The Bishop was taken to a prison that had been seized by the corsairs in the town of Manzanillo. 24 people from Bayamo, however, joined forces and under the direction of a resident captain, Gregorio Ramos rescued the Bishop; in the process Gilberto Girón paid with his life when he had a *mano-a-mano* with a huge Black slave, Salvador Galomón. The incident was the subject of *Espejo de Paciencia*, a long poem by Silvestre de Balboa Troya y Quesada (1563-1649), the court clerk of the *cabildo* of Puerto Príncipe.

As a phenomenally long poem, *Espejo de Paciencia* followed the Renaissance epic mold but introduced purely Cuban elements. Classical mythological animals, fauns, centaurs and

---

[152] *San Salvador de Bayamo* was the second village ever founded in Cuba by Diego Velázquez, on November 5, 1513. It is inland, on the margins of the Bayamo River. The name *Bayamo* probably comes from the existence of a local tree called *Bayam*; the Tainos considered it a tree of wisdom; it is leafy and provides a good shade.

mermaids that abound in the poem, did not offer the newly released Bishop grapes or apples, but guanábanas and mameyes.[153] They did not give him lilies or roses but heliconias and yellow morning glories, typical Cuban flowering bushes. The beautiful mermaids did not organize banquets with lamb or quail but with iguanas, ducks and jutías (a kind of rat). Balboa recounted a real event in a mythological and supernatural context; the bishop kidnapping was real, as was the reward that the pirates demanded for his release: one thousand tanned animal skins, one hundred pounds of meat and two hundred gold ducats. It was the last action of privateer Girón. When it came to changing the hostage for ransom, fierce fighting ensued that cost Girón his life; his head was then set on a stick and paraded triumphantly through the town of Bayamo.

When *Espejo de Paciencia* was published by Silvestre de Balboa, it was preceded by six sonnets by local authors, three of which were native Cubans: Pedro de las Torres Sifonte, Cristóbal de la Cova and Lorenzo Lasso de la Vega. All six

---

[153] In this long poem, Silvestre de Balboa characterized the French corsair Gilberto Girón as «*el conquistador de Cayo Romano y terror de las costas de Cuba.*» (Conqueror of Romano Key —the largest island in the Cuban archipelago after Cuba itself and the Isle of Pines— and the scourge of Cuban coasts). After his rescue, Bishop Altamirano fell out of favor with colonial authorities and was transferred to Guatemala in 1610, where he died at age 50. Silvestre de Balboa, by the way, was one of the public officials accused of participating in contrabands in Puerto Príncipe. He was fined 648 reales by the crown in 1607.

The poem *Espejo de Paciencia*, written in 1606, was lost for many years. It was found by accident (after fears that it was a hoax) and was first published in 1765 as part of the book *Historia de la Isla y Catedral de Cuba* by Bishop Pedro Agustín Morell de Santa Cruz y Lora. Bishop Morell's book was also lost and found by chance, in an ancient library, in 1838. The man who found it was Esteban Echeverría, a well known literary critic who was a regular member of Domingo del Monte's famous tertulias in Havana. Del Monte a man well versed in mythological literature, called *Espejo de Paciencia* the equivalent of *El Cantar del Mio Cid* in Spanish literature.

Morell de Santa Cruz, by the way, left a document before expiring where he revealed his life long secret: he was born in Hispaniola of a Jewish mother and a Spanish father. His body was interred in the *Iglesia Parroquial Mayor*, the church that preceded the Havana Cathedral (It was situated where the *Plaza the Armas* was later built). When that church was demolished and everything was transferred to the new Cathedral in 1777, his cadaver was lost, never to be found again.

sonneteers had been participants in the skirmish that cost the life of Girón and all six had been found actively engaged in contraband and fined by judge Manso de Contreras, the envoy of Felipe III. A Royal Letter of Pardon was issued by the crown in 1607. [154] It read in part

«Our joy is justified [after the victory over Gilberto Girón] and we are happy to make these men beneficiaries of our Royal Mercy.»

As the 1600s advanced, construction works in the island, particularly in Havana, the newly designated capital, progressed very slowly. The *Castillo de la Punta*, ordered to be constructed by Felipe II at the same time as *El Morro* (1588), was particularly defective.[155] A tidal wave during the hurricane of August 28, 1595, destroyed whatever had been built. As for *El Morro*, the crown was informed in 1638 that

«...quedan por construir los alojamientos para la tropa, almacenes de municiones, rampas, aljibes, plataformas para emplazar baterías y muchas otros detalles complementarios...»

---

[154] It was Gilberto Girón, by the way, who lent his name to the now famous *Playa Girón*, a beach in the Bay of Pigs, in southern Cuba, frequented by the French corsair for rest and recreation purposes.

[155] Part of the problem was attributed to constant infighting between Governor Juan Maldonado Barnuevo and Juan Bautista Antonelli, the master builder.

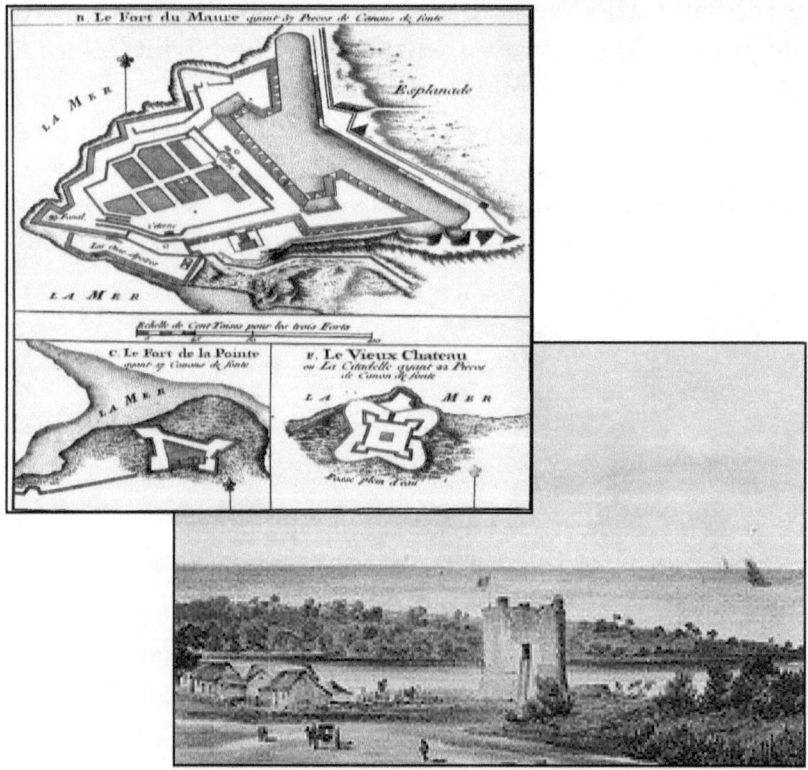

Images, top to bottom, left to right:

Casa de Contratación de Sevilla, Spain's trading monopoly with all American possessions;

Juan Bautista Antonelli's original plans for **El Morro** and **La Punta** fortresses in Havana;

the **Torreón de San Lázaro** at the mouth of the Almendares River in Havana.

Images, top to bottom, left to right:

French corsair **Gilberto Girón**, the abductor of Bishop Morell de Santa Cruz;

Bishop **Pedro Agustín Morell** de Santa Cruz y Lora;

Felipe III of Spain, son of Felipe II and *Anna de Austria*, known as *Philip the Pious*, an "undistinguished and insignificant man;"

Jean- François de la Roque de Roberval, a French adventurer, *protégé* of Francis I, King of France;

Spanish coat of arms of the **Habsburgs**, to which Philip belonged.

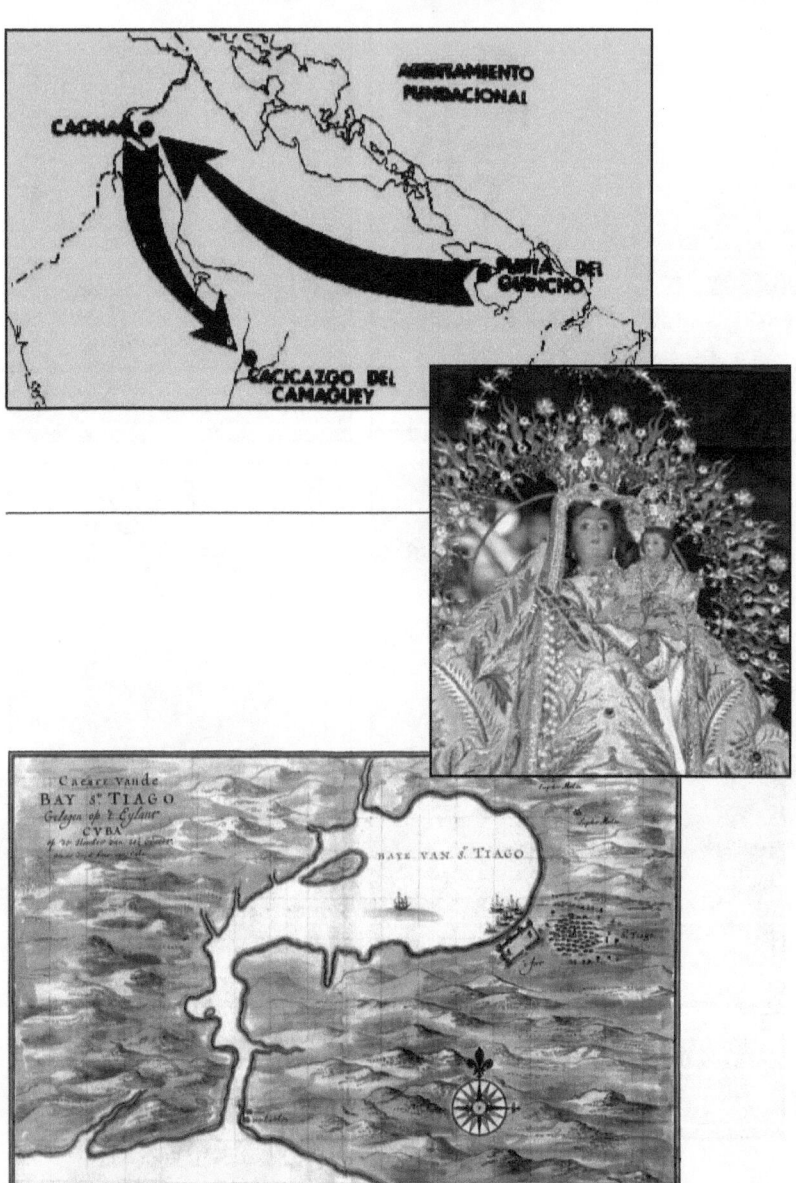

Images, top to bottom, left to right:

The three successive relocations of Puerto Príncipe (today's City of Camagüey). In 1514 it was founded at **Punta de Guincho**, Nuevitas. It was then moved to the native settlement of **Caonao**, and after a rebellion it was moved to the Taino settlement of *Camagüey*;

the original image of **Our Lady of Charity** (Virgen de la Caridad del Cobre) found in the Bay of Nipe, Oriente in 1606;

one of the oldest maps of **Santiago de Cuba**, showing the initial settlement of residents.

Images, top to bottom, left to right:

One of the oldest engravings of **Havana**, showing the hills around town;
Diego Grillo (1558-1640), a Black liberto, Cuba's most notorious native pirate;

Some books that created the romance of pirates and buccaneers in literature:
Sir Francis Drake Revived, London, 1653;
Piratas de la America by Alexander Olivier, Cologne, 1681;
Bucaniers of America by Alexander Olivier, London, 1684;
A New Survey of the West Indies by Thomas Gage, London, 1684.

15

Spain Considers the Worth of Cuba

SEVERAL IMPORTANT EVENTS and historical trends during the first half of the XVII century showed an increased interest on the part of Spain to defend, protect and organize a secure life and a minimal economic development in the island of Cuba.

More and more, Spain's economic power was based on exploiting the precious metals obtained in America; the British, French and Dutch, in the meantime, began to create products and techniques to be marketed in Europe, including Spain; the Spanish were forced to buy the goods and technical skills that were not produced or created on the peninsula or the colonies. Inevitably, Spain fell behind in industrial arts compared to other European countries. It participated in the global market as buyers and not manufacturers or developers of products and new technologies. The situation, of course, would make a turn for the worst in 100 years, when the industrial revolution would sweep Europe.

In 1606, at the Bay of Nipe on the northern coast of Oriente, three fishermen (Taino descendants Rodrigo and Juan de Hoyos, and Black slave child Juan Moreno) found an image miraculously floating in the middle of a storm in the bay. It was fastened to a board with the inscription *"Yo soy la Vírgen de la Caridad,"* (I am Our Lady of Charity). They were looking for salt needed for the preservation of meat at a small town called *El Cobre*.

In 1607, the Spanish crown divided the government of Cuba into two areas, one of which, lying west of an imaginary line drawn across the island fifty leagues east of Havana, was left under a governor and captain general resident in that city; everything eastward from that line was placed under a second governor who was expected to make his headquarters at Santiago de Cuba. Roads across Cuba, however, were impassable in the rainy season and the two areas were incommunicado part of the year. The mails were carried out by native runners. Cuba was an immense region very sparsely populated, with a dangerous and untrustworthy diversity of races, beset from enemies from outside pretending to be peaceful traders.

In 1616, the town of Puerto Príncipe, until then the most developed and well built of the original seven towns founded by Velázquez, was completely destroyed by a sudden, fast and fierce fire.[156]

In 1618 Dutch fleets made numerous incursions into Cuban territory, mostly due to Spain-Netherlands rivalry during the Thirty Year War. Upon the death of Governor Sancho de Alquízar (1616-1619), the Havana cabildo appointed its own auditor Diego Vallejo as governor. A few weeks later the cabildo changed its mind and Vallejo was replaced for incompetence by Jerónimo de Quero, former warden of *El Morro* and *La Fuerza*. King Felipe III disagreed and fined every cabildo member with a $100 penalty.

In 1620 the crown imposed a duty of goods entering Santiago de Cuba and Havana of two and one half percent, presuma-

---

[156] *Santa María del Puerto del Príncipe* was originally founded in 1514 in the north coast of the island, in the *Cacicazgo de Caonao* (today's Nuevitas). It originally consisted of 17 houses made of straw and wood. Water along the coast was found brackish and the location very humid. The town was moved in 1528 to the *Cacicazgo of Camagüeybax* after natives from the island keys of the north were continuously attacking the original Spanish settlement. The chosen location was in a sabana, halfway between the Tínima and Jatibonico rivers. Its first illustrious resident was Vasco Porcallo de Figueroa, founder of Sancti Spíritus and Sabaneque (today's Sagua la Grande), a powerful and rich *Encomendero*, married to Tínima, the child of a Cacique. It is said he was the most hated and feared of all *Conquistadores* in Cuba. Sabaneque became the city where old buccaneers would retire and enjoy their loots. Over the years, retired or frequent visitors to Sabaneque were Francis Drake (1540-1596) and Henry Morgan (1635-1688), from Britain; Cornelio Jol (aka *Pata de Palo*) and Laurent Graff (aka *Lorencillo*) from the Neatherlands; Juan Davies Nau (aka *El Olonés*) and Jean Lafitte, from France; and last, but not least, Diego Grillo (1558-1640), a Black liberto and Cuba's most famous autochthonus pirate.

bly for public works, munitions and payments for look-outs. It increased contraband and even dealings with corsairs and privateers. In the meantime the governors of both areas of Cuba continued their larceny unabated. It was said that the captain general of Santiago had ordered all property of Portuguese families —notorious black marketeers— to be sold at cheap prices and bought it for himself.

Starting in the 1620s, the presence of buccaneers and corsairs in Cuba increased fivefold as the uninhabited island of Tortuga, north of Hispaniola, became the headquarters of all scoundrels, rogues and villains trying to rob Spain of peninsula-bound treasures. Governor Francisco de Venegas, governor of Havana from 1520 to 1524, accused Governor Velasco of Santiago de Cuba of living in Bayamo —town of *contrabandistas*— instead of Santiago, and issued an order giving Velasco 15 days to move to Santiago and reside there. He was supported by the King and Velasco was replaced after he refused to comply with the royal mandate. In the meantime, buccaneers and privateers were raping towns all around Cuba given the internal fights among those commissioned by the crown to supervise the integrity of the Spanish highly prized Cuba.

In 1628, the *Compañía Holandesa de las Indias Occidentales* were organized in the Netherlands; within few months it launched three new fleets against Spanish possessions in the Americas. One of these, led by Piet Hein (*Pata de Palo*) attacked towns from Pinar del Rio to Matanzas in the northern part of Cuba. Spain responded by sending 32 ships under the leadership of Admiral Juan de Benavides from Veracruz against the Dutch. Unfortunately Benavides found the Dutch in front of Havana, followed their ships to the bay of Matanzas, attacked them and lost, leaving behind all his ships. After the battle, *Pata de Palo* found out that the bay of Matanzas was full of Spanish merchant ships with a substantial amount of gold. He proceeded to commandeer the treasures. Benavides was arrested, taken to Spain, indicted, condemned and executed for his cowardice.

In 1629, good news arrived in Madrid. A fleet under the direction of Don Fadrique Alvarez de Toledo, 4th Duke of Alba,

Grandee of Spain and Commander of the Spanish Army during the Eighty Years War (1568-1648) against Spain, surrounded the island of Tortuga and destroyed ships from England, France and the Netherlands that frequently sought refuge there. It continued to Pinar del Rio, from where it expelled the fleet of Cornelius Jols,[157] the Dutch privateer and admiral of the Dutch West India Company, who was waiting for the Spanish galleons carrying silver to Cádiz.

The year 1640 was witness to several unprotected Caribbean Leeward and Windward Islands taken from Spain by England, Holland and France. The Dutch took control of Aruba, Bonaire, Curacao, Saint Eustatius, Saint Martin and Saba; the British claimed Antigua, Barbados and Nevis and the French took over Martinique and Guadeloupe.

In 1645 Juan Bautista Antonelli continued his plans to protect Havana from pirate attacks and built the forts *Santa Dorotea de la Luna* (*La Chorrera de San Lázaro*) at the mouth of the Almendares River and the *Torreón de Cojímar* on the eastern coast of Havana.

In 1648, yellow fever, a virus brought to the western hemisphere from Africa by slaves, decimated the populations of Cuba (fiebre amarilla) and Mexico (black vomit or *xekik* in Maya). Eventually it affected the eastern US, the Caribbean, New Orleans and the lower Mississippi valley and, of course, Panamá, where it competed with malaria to cause the ruin of the French company building the canal. In Cuba it caused the death of one third the population of Havana.

In 1651, to counteract pirate attacks and following a royal decree that made it obligatory, all ships headed for Spain (carrying gold, silver and, alpaca wool from the Andes, emeralds

---

[157] Cornelius Jols was also called *Houtebeen, Pé de Pau* or *Pata de Palo*. He defeated the Spanish in Cabañas, Cuba, in 1638, when he captured five Spanish ships full of silver. A Spanish song lyrics at the time were: «*Patapalo es un pirata malo que come pulpo crudo y bebe agua del mar cuando tiene sed.*» (pegleg is a bad pirate who eats raw octopus and drinks seawater when he is thirsty). Cornelius was eventually defeated, captured and executed when he attacked Santiago de Cuba in 1645.

from Colombia, mahogany from Cuba and Guatemala, leather from the Guajira, spices from Caribbean islands, sticks of dye from Campeche, corn, manioc, and cocoa from Mexico) were required to assemble as one large fleet in Havana Bay, and traverse the Atlantic Ocean as a group. Ships arriving from May through August had to wait for good weather conditions, and together, depart as a fleet for Spain by September. It decisively boosted commerce and development in the then humble villa of Havana.

After the signing of the Peace of Westphalia ending the Thirty Years' War in 1648 (Spain vs. the Dutch Republic, The Holy Roman Empire vs. France and Sweden), the British started its policy of harassment of Spain. The town of Remedios was sacked. A large fleet organized by Oliver Cromwell made its presence felt in the Americas beginning with the taking of Jamaica. They repelled a 500 man expedition sent from Santiago de Cuba.

In 1656 Juan Montaño Blázquez, following the dictates of Madrid, started the construction of a wall protecting Havana.

In 1659 Cuba was attacked by British filibusters and buccaneers from Port Royal in Jamaica, while the French took Tortuga, the old privateer's refuge. The stalking of Cuba continued until 1667, when François L'Olonnais, aka Jean David Nau, *el Olonés*, attacked several towns and settlements in the northern coast of Cuba.[158]

In 1664, the crown of Spain began to issue *Patentes de Corso* (the French *Lettre de Marque*) to any Spanish resident willing to equip a ship, hire a crew, and harass and torment the French

---

[158] His friends attributed to him the motto "*Yo soy El Olonés y valgo lo mismo vivo que muerto.*" (I am *El Olonés*, worth the same dead or alive). He survived a shipwreck in the coasts of Panamá and with his men went inland. Soon he found *Kuna* or *Guna* natives (indigenous people of Panamá and Colombia, nowadays famous for their molas, which are colorful textiles with appliqué) who fought and eventually captured them. The Frenchmen were all tortured, killed, dissected and (according to legend) eaten by the *Kunas*. In modern times, the *Kunas* are also famous for their almost total resistance to cancer and cardiovascular deseases and their consumption of 30 to 40 oz. of flavanol-rich cocoa per day.

and British settlements in the Caribbean, particularly those in Tortuga Island. [159]

Images, left to right:
The chaos and fire in **Puerto Príncipe** in 1616;
The construction of a fort in **Nuevitas** in the 1580s.

---

[159] Tortuga Island is located on the north shore of what is now modern-day Haiti. It was baptized with that name by Spanish explorers since its outline resembled the shell of a turtle from a distance. When the French bucaneers were forced from their home on Hispaniola, they migrated to Tortuga, which had a solid port, a harbor with a clear, sandy bottom, lots of timber and an abundance of herbs and plants, tobacco, fruits, and vegetables.

In time, the French were joined on the island by criminals evading capture, runaway slaves and Europeans under punishment for crimes. All of them were bound together by a hatred of the Spanish. Tortuga continued to be ruled by the French throughout most of the 1600s, although four times was invaded and rescued by Spain; it always offered safe harbor to any non-Spanish ships, as long as they shared with Tortugan residents the booty they stole from the Spanish. Henry Morgan, Jean L'Ollonais, Jean le Vasseur, Pierre Le Grand, John Davis, and Roche Braziliano were just a few of the buccaneers and pirates who spent time in Tortuga. These and other lesser-known rogues made their way around the island, hiding from the Spanish when necessary, and attacking them whenever the opportunity arose.

By the 1680s, when Spanish treasure ships sailed past the island less frequently, the buccaneers angered the British by attacking Jamaican plantations and English merchant ships; they became full-fledged pirates, attacking passing vessels except those belonging to the French. When the French and the Spanish ended decades of hostility in 1684 (Treaty of Ratisbone), Tortuga's residents were quickly caught and hanged. Nowadays, Tortuga is known as the *Commune of Île de la Tortue* in the *Port-de-Paix arrondissement* of the Northwest Department of Haiti.

Leprosy (St. Lazarus desease) was a major health issue in colonial Cuba since the XVII century. Leprosy had been brought by European immigrants and especially by about 50,000 African slaves imported from 1500 to 1570. Spain established its first leprosy hospital at Hispaniola in 1520. Leprosy spread from Hispaniola to Colombia,  Equador, Cuba, Mexico and southern United States within a few years. In 1526 Hernán Cortés founded the first leprosy hospital in Mexico City. In 1616, the hospitals in Havana accepted their first leprosy patients. From 1613 to 1680 the records of the Havana's Cabildo showed many references:

«Let people with the evil St. Lazarus disease be forced outside the city... Velázquez de Cuellar is hereby authorized to ensure that after all available medical checks are made, people with St. Lazarus are to be sent without delay from our city to hospitals in the City of Mexico... All those touched by the St. Lazarus syndrome should come together in one place to stay, with no visiting by anyone and without any of them authorized to enter or return to the city under severe punishment.»

Years later, in the minutes of a council meeting held in February 1691 dealing with lepers circulating on the streets of Havana, the following was recorded:

«Lepers are to be picked up in an appropriate place and be examined by Dr D. Moner, who will provide results under oath, before they are taken to the St. Lazarus hospital. In this city and beyond, there are different people who are currently suffering from the evil disease of San Lazaro; one is a Jacinto Hernández. He is ordered to stay on the other side of the Luyanó river; another is Horacio Mora, son of Maria Manuela Soledad, aged eleven years or so. He is here authorized to roam the streets securing alms for the hospital, but always separated from his family and any other person. He is not to touch anyone»

In 1681 these patients began to be accommodated in a poor house, with a chapel and several huts, founded by a Spaniard, D. Pedro Torres Alegre, at the Calzada de Infanta between Tejas and Carlos III, near the old Villarín bridge. The first leprosy lazaretto in Cuba dates back to 1554 when it opened in the town of Guanabacoa. Two mulatto lepers who worked in the city were the first to be admitted and isolated.

Leprosy, a XVII Century Serious Health Issue

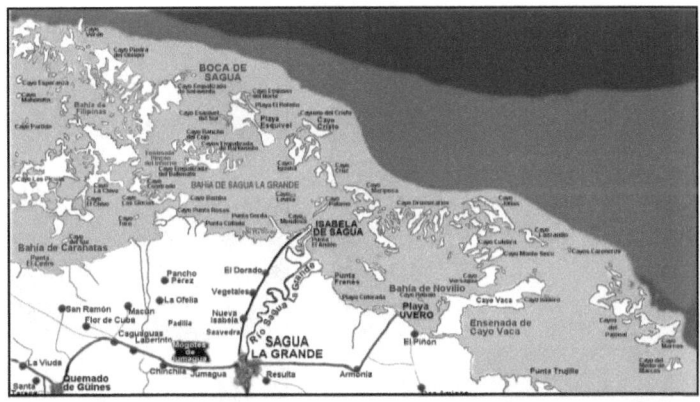

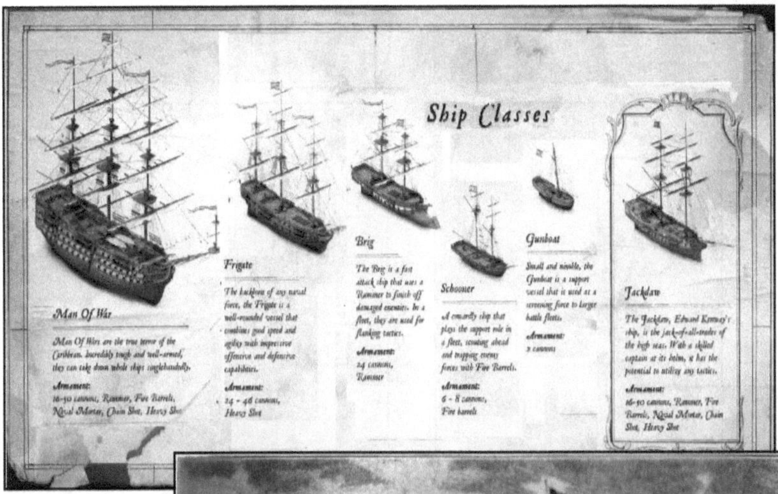

Images, top to bottom:

A map of the region of **Sagua la Grande** and the keys, the area of Cuba favored by pirates and corsairs because the multitude of hideaways in the coasts;

different types of **ships used by pirates** and corsaries;

Spain's Silver fleet on its way across the Atlantic.

Images, top to bottom, left to right:

Piet Hein, aka *Pata de Palo*, a Dutch privateer who became the terror of the island of Cuba around 1620;

Don Fadrique of Toledo, 4th Duke of Alba, conqueror of Granada, Grandee of Spain, mortal enemy and hunter of French, English and Dutch pirates;

a **Dutch postage stamp** showing Piet Hein;

Piet Pieterszoon, *el Olonés*, the pirate who sacked Matanzas on Sept 5, 1628;

Oliver Cromwell (1599-1658), the British Prime Minister who succeeded in the occupation of Jamaica after failing to take Cuba and Hispaniola.

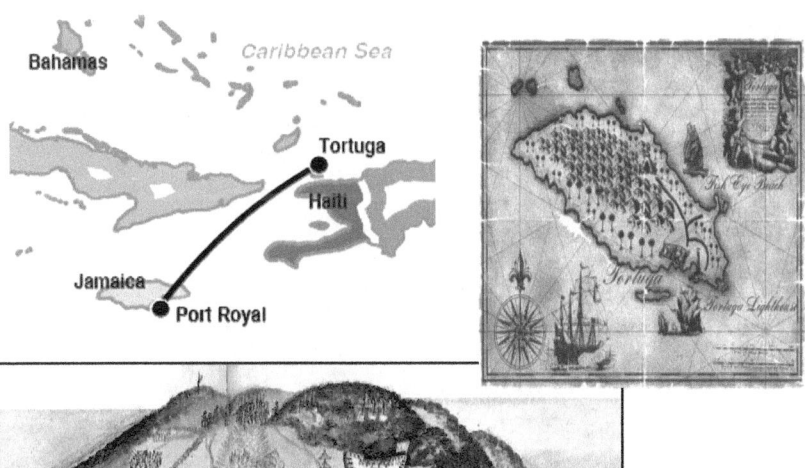

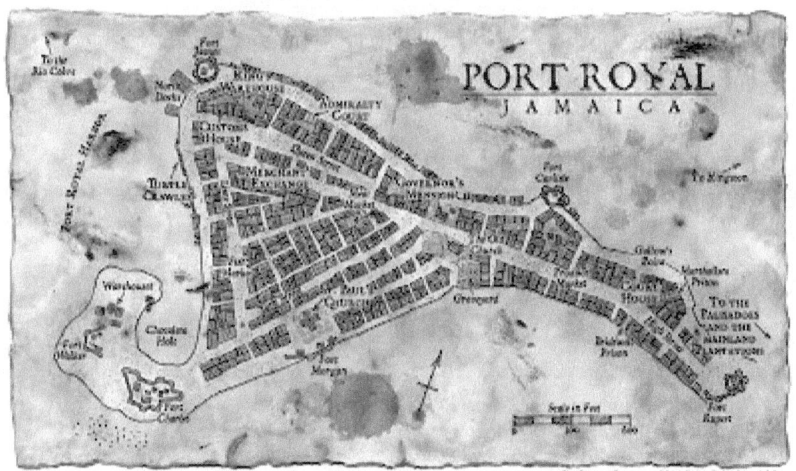

Images, top to bottom:

The two strongest sanctuaries for pirates and corsairs around Cuba: **Port Royal** and **Tortuga**;

a contemporary map of **Tortuga**;

Tortuga as seen from the **Caribbean sea** (with the shape of a turtle);

a map of **Port Royal**.

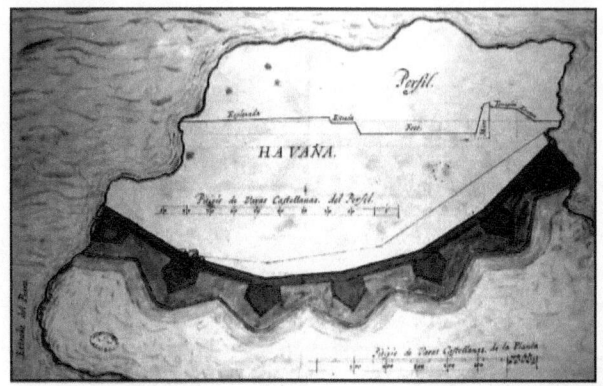

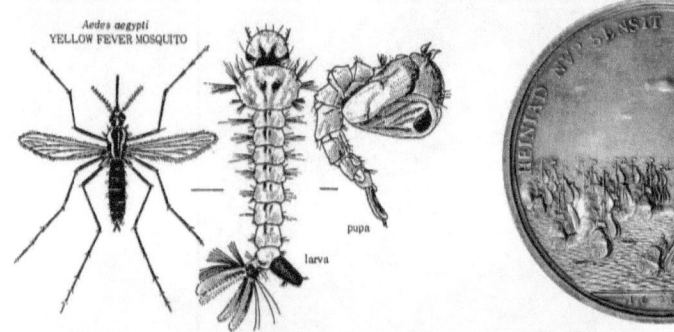

Images, top to bottom, left to right:

Juan de Síscara's 1656 plans for the projected building of a wall on the land side of Havana;

Aedes ægypti, the mosquito that transmitted Yellow Fever in Cuba and the Americas;

a medal commemorating the **sacking of Matanzas** by Piet Pieterszoon, *el Olonés* in 1628;

an **Ancient Map of Santiago de Cuba Bay** viewed from the North. On the circle, the town of *El Cobre*.

16

Cuba's Growth Began to Show Up

THE XVII CENTURY IN CUBA was characterized by the constant threat, intimidation and real danger by corsairs, pirates and buccaneers and by the extraordinary growth of the island, particularly the towns of Havana and Santiago de Cuba. On a letter to his mother in Seville by Hernando de la Parra, an employee of Juan Maldonado (el Mozo),[160] he related

«San Cristóbal [la Habana] is progressing in spite of too many pirates and little business. The town is been built with little order or structure. All houses are made of straw and cedar boards. Everybody has fenced an area for fowl and has planted fruit trees. This has produced an infernal plague of mosquitoes, larger and more annoying than those of Seville.»

Whatever business came to Havana during the XVII century, it was always related to commerce. The island population was growing from 25 thousand in the early 1600s to 50 thousand by the end of the century. Commerce consisted of the exportation of sugar, tobacco, feedstocks and precious woods. On a typical day there were 25 to 40 ships anchored on the port of Havana. It necessitated an abundance of services: housing, temporary lodging, food and entertainment. It also had undesirable consequences: a floating irresponsible and loafing population, petty thieves, dirty pavements and prostitution. Escaping from these realities, which also happened in Santiago de Cuba, several small towns began to develop around the two capitals: Alquízar in 1618, Guanajay in 1650, Santiago de las Vegas in 1685, Holguín in 1689, Matanzas in 1693. In other

---

[160] Juan Maldonado Jr. (el Mozo) was the son of Governor Juan Maldonado Barnuevo (1594-1602), one of the great promoters of the importation of Black slaves from Africa. Junior was an entrepreneur, owner of *ingenios* and the first to set up a sawmill in the Almendares River, at the point of the present location of Puentes Grandes.

places, people running away from the large towns or needing closer access to agricultural land were setting clusters of "improved" bohíos, which later would become towns in their own right: Cojímar, Bejucal, Pinar del Rio, Santa Clara, Guane, Manzanillo, to name a few.

On a larger scale, the construction of *El Morro, La Punta* and the *Muralla*,[161] brought to the island the skills of professional stonecutters, masons and quarrymen. They began to make possible the construction of mansions, churches, convents and roads. Houses in big towns began to be constructed with bricks, wood columns and beams,[162] and tiles, cemented with quicklime or lime (calcium oxide) and sand. Many residences in Havana and Santiago began to be stuccoed with mud with colored pigments like mustard, sienna, vermilion and red. The *bohíos* continued to be the best options for poor residents, both in towns and in the countryside.[163]

Across the island many towns and cities showed a significant progress:

On July 14, 1601, the *Ermita de la Merced*, a wooden structure dedicated to the *Virgen de Altagracia*, was built on a farm in *Manga Larga,* near the town of Puerto Príncipe. A larger building made of mortar and bricks replaced this 1601 church in Puerto Príncipe itself in 1604. Black slaves from a nearby *Palenque* set the town on fire in 1616; only the church, the bell from the *ayuntamiento* (City Hall) and a large cross that had been

---

[161] The *Muralla* of Havana turned out to be the largest, most expensive and worthless project ever undertaken by the Spanish crown in Cuba. It consumed 180,000 tons of stone. Its usefulness lasted less than 100 years. It destroyed the lives of men like Juan de Síscara, who labored at the *Muralla* for over 30 years without ever visiting Spain again.

[162] Before the end of the XVII century, a public facility for milling wood was established in the southern part of the port of Habana: *el Arsenal*. It was powered by hydraulic means; a circular saw rotated by its connection to a large wheel that was moved by water brought there from the *Zanja Real*.

[163] Construction financing was made possible by a combination of *Situados* (funds sent to Cuba by the Virreinato de Mexico under orders from the Spanish crown), the crown's benefactions to the Church and the private profits from tobacco, hides, woods, sugar and livestock exports.

placed in the central plaza survived. It was not until 1748 that a new and larger *Iglesia de la Merced* was built.

In 1626 the Havana *cabildo* authorized the construction of a house "on the road leading to La Punta," on the corner of today's Baratillo and Obrapía Streets, by Don Pablo de Pedroso, "*capitán de caballos, alguacil mayor del Santo Oficio de la Inquisición y Alcalde ordinario de la Habana.*" For many years it was the best house in Havana.

In Havana, in 1632, on the corner of Cuba and Acosta streets, the second Havana Parish was founded, the *Ermita del Espíritu Santo*. It measured 9.2 by 43 meters. It had to wait until 1729 and Bishop Jerónimo Valdés before it would be expanded.[164]

On December 20, 1632 and on February 27, 1668, the *Convento de Santa Clara de Asís* [165] and the *Hospital, Convento e Iglesia de San Francisco de Paula* [166] were built; the last one on the grounds of the former *Ermita del Humilladero*.

In 1640 the *Plaza del Santo Cristo del Buen Viaje*[167] was built, a residential place for well to do residents. On one of its sides the *Ermita del Humilladero* (Chapel of the Cavalry) took a prominent place.

---

[164] In 1936, the remains of Bishop Valdés were found on a cript under the Church.

[165] In 1922 the Republic of Cuba bough the four-city-block property for US $ 1 million and turned it into the *Ministerio de Obras Públicas*.

[166] The original church was of heavy wood construction and was lost during a 1730 hurricane. In 1937 the church was bought by *Ferrocarriles Unidos*; they were prevented from demolishing the church when the Cuban legislature declared it *Monumento Nacional*.

[167] **Defined by today's Villegas, Teniente Rey, Bernaza and Lamparilla Streets.** The square was filled by worthy neighbors whose houses were built according to their hierarchy, proud lineage and illustrious ancestry. The square changed its name many times: *Plaza Vieja,* **Plaza Real, Plaza Mayor,** *Mercado de las Lavanderas, Plaza del Mercado, Plaza Fernando VII, Plaza of the Constitution, Parque Juan Bruno Zayas.* In 1930 President Machado built an underground garage under it. As *Plaza Vieja*, it was the site of executions, processions, bullfights, and *fiestas* - all witnessed by Havana's wealthiest citizens, who looked down from their balconies.

In 1655, next to an old *ingenio azucarero* called *San Francisco de Paula*, on a small hill bordered by what was to be the *Calzada de Jesús del Monte*, a small church was built that would later be called the *Iglesia Parroquial de Jesús del Monte*.

In 1673, on swamp land that was so prone to flooding that received the name of *Plaza de la Ciénaga*, several of the richest families in Cuba drained the area and began to acquire land to construct sumptuous mansions: the Conde de Lombillo, the Marqués de Arcos, the Marqués de Aguas Claras, the widow of Fernández de Velasco, Captain General Luis Chacón, among others. Their dreams were realized early in the 1700s. The Jesuits, who had built a humble church with the assistance of Bishop Compostela, bought land on the square to construct a temple in 1727.[168]

In 1687 Bishop Diego Evelino de Compostela arrived in Havana. He was the 20th Bishop appointed to the Dioceses of Habana and Florida and remained 18 years with that status. His work in Cuba was extraordinary: he directed the renovation of the Hospital San Juan de Dios; opened the Casa-Cuna (foundling asylum) for abandoned children, founded the Colegio San Francisco de Sales; as well as several public schools, hospitals, charitable institutions and churches across the island

In 1690 *Consolación del Sur* had a church even though it only had three masonry houses and 65 made of wooden planks and tree stalks.

---

[168] Their initial request to the Havana *cabildo* was denied in 1704. They persisted and were granted a permit in 1727. Unfortunatelly they were expelled from all Spanish lands by Carlos III in 1767 and never took possession of their church; it first became the *Parroquia Mayor* of Havana and later, in 1793, today's Havana Cathedral. Carlos III adduced that

«I am moved by weighty reasons, conscious of my duty to uphold obedience, tranquility and justice among my people, and also acting for other urgent, just and compelling causes, which I am locking away in my breast...»

The actual reasons for the Jesuit expulsion have been shrouded in mistery. The most plausible theory is that Freemasons, Voltarians and Manteistas (poor university students) accussed the Jesuits of conspiracies against the throne of Spain; they were all resentful of the snobbism of Jesuit education.

In 1690, on a small hill called *Peña Pobre* at the time of the founding of Havana, later called *Loma del Angel*, Bishop Evelino de Compostela (1687-1704) erected the *Iglesia del Santo Angel Custodio*.[169]

On September 25, 1690, the King of Spain authorized the founding of a *villa* on the margins of the San Juan and Yumurí Rivers, close to the Guanima bay (today's bay of Matanzas), where a small settlement of contrabandistas had built their dwellings. Thirty intrepid residents received *solares*; the *Leyes de India* clearly specified that there had to be a minimum of 30 neighbors and the future city of Matanzas was founded. The following year Bishop Diego Evelino de Compostela sponsored the construction in the town of a wooden church with palm tree stalks on its roof. [170]

In 1694, in the southern side of Matanzas bay, the crown ordered a fort to be constructed to protect shipments of sugar from the docks in the bay. It was called the *Castillo de San Severino* in honor of Governor Severino de Manzaneda.

Many other churches and settlements were built, notably in Sancti Spíritus in 1680, Melena del Sur in 1655, Holguín in 1692, Santiago de las Vegas in 1694 and Remedios in 1692, to mention a few. Practically no town or moderate size settlement in Cuba was left without a house of worship. The tradition was to start with wooden structures while solid buildings made of stone or bricks were constructed.

Aside from construction of housing, public works, defense infrastructure and the erection of more permanent churches and decent roads, an important transformation was taking place in Cuba during the XVII century. If reading and writing

---

[169] At the Santo Angel Church Father Félix Varela and José Martí were baptized. The church also gave its name to *Cecilia Valdés*, the famous Cuban operetta, also known as *La Loma del Angel*.

[170] The original Matanzas church was on the other side of where is now the Cathedral, facing the city's *Plaza Mayor*, which had been delineated in 1693. The initial church was destroyed by a hurricane in 1730, when the new Cathedral was about ready to be placed in service.

were an attribute of the rich and the nobility in the XVI century, the XVII century made it very difficult for residents of Cuba to progress without knowing how to write and read. By the 1680s and further, those who could not contribute to the advancement of trade and commerce in such towns as Havana, Santiago de Cuba, Puerto Príncipe and Holguín, had as their only *modus vivendi* the hard work in agriculture, side by side or supervising the work of slaves and native Indians.

At the turn of the XVII century, the colonial authorities began to show a healthy interest in building educational establishments and in the diffusion of instruction, particularly language, arithmetic, geometry and literature. The *cabildos* dedicated a portion of *propios* (local tax collections) to pay for teachers, inspectors, school construction and school materials.[171]

Presiding over the Spanish Empire at the end of the XVII century, at a time where the Spanish domains included little of Europe but almost the entire American continent, was Carlos II of Spain (1661-1700). His reign marked the end of his family line; he was born in 1661, and was so genetically unstable [172] and challenged that his looks were similar to the offspring of incestuous unions between brothers and sisters or fathers and daughters. His mother, *Mariana de Austria*, was a niece of his father, Philip IV and the daughter of *María Ana de España* and Emperor Ferdinand III. Thus, *Emperatriz María Ana* was simultaneously his aunt and grandmother, while *Margarita María Teresa de Austria* was both his grandmother and great-

---

[171] The first reference to *maestrescuelas* in the island was that of the personnel of the Cathedral of Santiago de Cuba, who in 1604 were charged with the responsibility to «teach grammar, arts and other virtues to church clerics, as well as anyone who volunteered to listen to them.»

In 1648, Diego de Villalba y Toledo, *Marqués de Campo*, wrote to his Majesty in Madrid «This year, during the carnival in Havana, every man on horse, all youngsters and all students, showed up with signs and messages written in perfect Castillian.»

[172] Royal families have always increased their inheritances by marrying cousins and nieces among themselves or with aunts and uncles, a custom that has lasted until present times.

grandmother.[173] Notable forebears of Carlos II were *Juana de Castilla* (also fondly known as *Juana la Loca*); she was an ascendant of two of Carlos II 16 great-great-great grandmothers, six of his 32 great-great-great-great grandmothers, and six of his 64 great-great-great-great-great grandmothers.

Charles II of Spain's jaw was so deformed from inbreeding, it reportedly was unable to function in any sense. Nicknamed *El Hechizado* (the Hexed) because of his deformities, Charles was saddled with an extreme version of the jutting, tapering Habsburg chin.[174] It was at the lower end of an oversized head, whose mouth struggled to contain an oversized tongue that left him with a propensity to mumble and drool and an inability to chew. He suffered from intestinal upsets, convulsions, premature ejaculation (according to María Ana de Neuburg, his first wife) and impotence (according to Marie Louise de Orléans, his second). «He was unable to speak until the age of four, and couldn't walk until the age of eight. He was *menudo, débil y muy delgadito*,» said Gonzalo Alvarez, who led the *Universidad de Santiago de Compostela* in a desperate study of the King's infirmity. «He looked like an old person when he was 30 years old, bald and senile and suffering swellings on his feet, legs, abdomen and face. During the last years of his life he could barely stand up and suffered from hallucinations and seizures». He died at the age of 38, hairless and heir-less, taking the Habsburg line down with him. French Bourbons moved in to fill the resulting power vacuum, and there were never Habsburgs in Spain again. When Charles II died, the military was practically non- existent, consisting of one division, burdened by corruption, sloth and inefficiency; the treasury was bankrupt, and there was no promotion of commerce or industry. Spain had

---

[173] Margarita María Teresa de Austria was *Infanta de España* and Empress of the *Sacro Imperio Romano Germánico* because of her marriage to her uncle Emperor Leopold I.

[174] His two rows of teeth could not meet. The Habsburgs were immortalized mercilessly in portraits by Titian and Velazquez.

effectively slipped from the ranks of the great powers. Cuba was in the hands of governors that served for their own political and financial good, not for the benefit of Cuba or Spain.

Even before the death of Charles II, the European powers were already positioning themselves to see which noble house would inherit the Spanish throne with its vast empire. Louis XIV of France asked for, and gained, the Pope's consent for his grandson, Philip of Anjou, a grand nephew of Charles II, to ascend the throne. On his deathbed Charles II willed the crown to this French-born successor. The transfer of the Spanish Crown to the Bourbons, in 1700, did not go uncontested; it precipitated the War of the Spanish Succession (1701–1713). All things French came into fashion for over a century, and gave rise to a new type of Cuban and Spaniard: the *afrancesados*. For Cuba the worst consequence of the rise of the Bourbons was that all ports in the island were blockaded by British and Dutch fleets, even though Cuba was comparatively free from the hostilities.

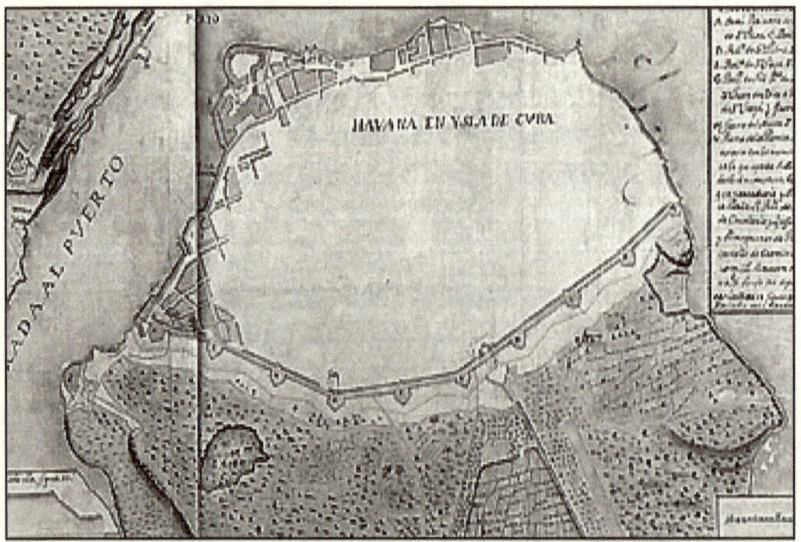

Image above:
The initial **settlements** in Havana shown on a 1620 map.

The Ancestry of King Charles II of Spain (1661-1700)

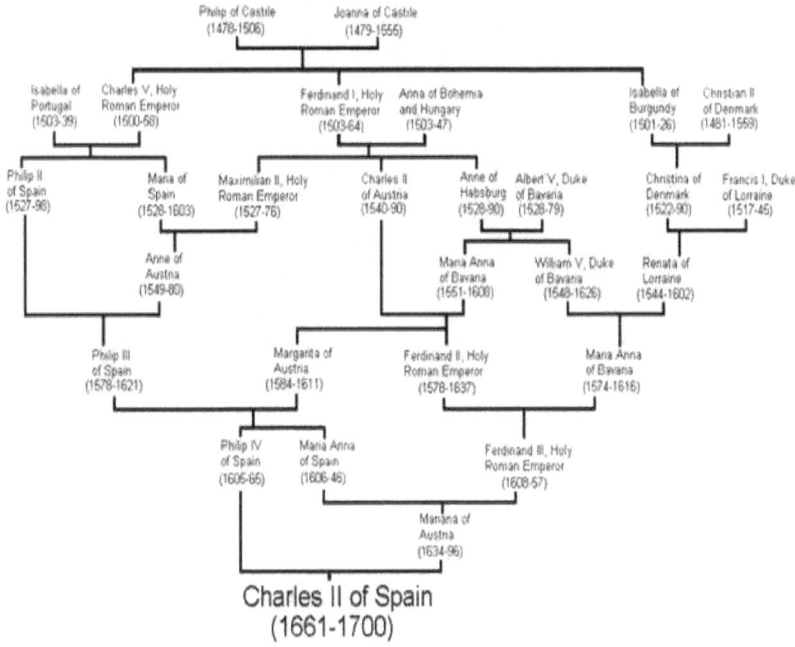

WAR OF THE SPANISH SUCCESSION

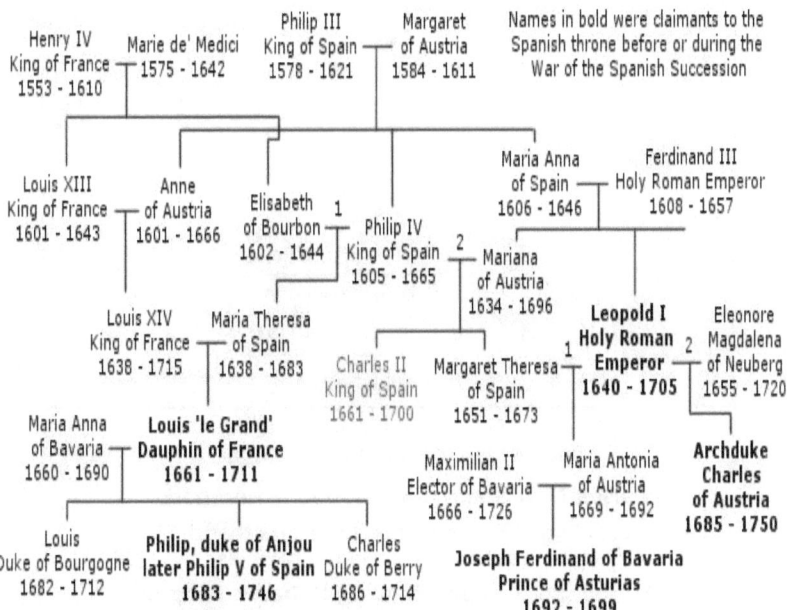

Names in bold were claimants to the Spanish throne before or during the War of the Spanish Succession

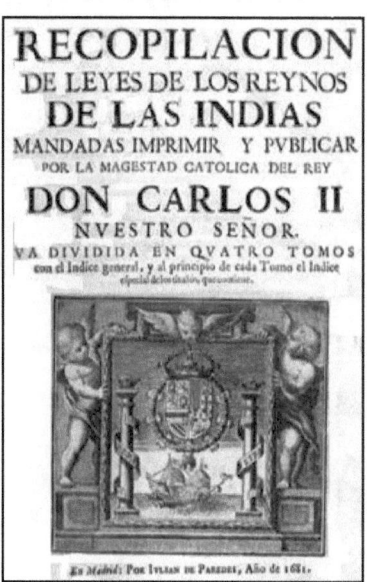
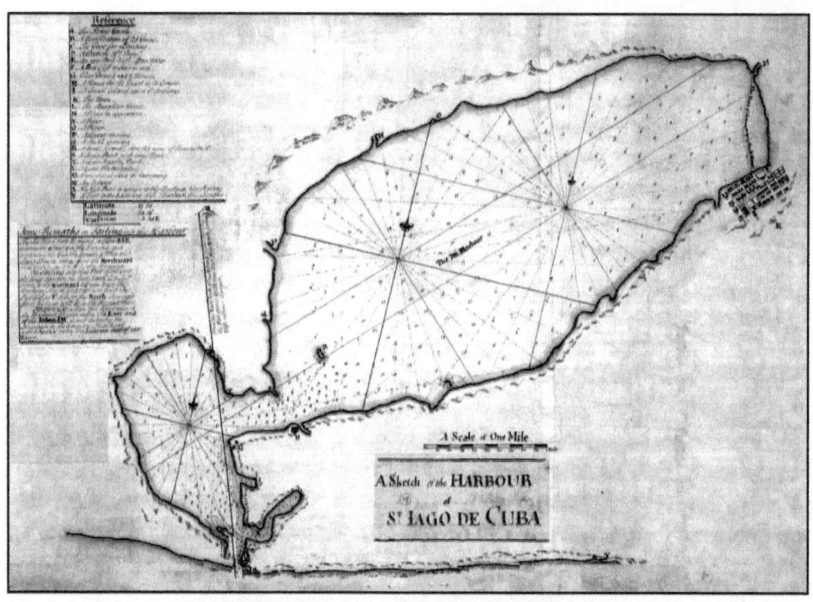

Images, top to bottom, left to right:

Carlos II of Spain (1661-1700), *el Hechizado*;
the compendium of **rules and regulations** that the Spanish crown set up for use in the colonies;
A 1660 sketch of **Santiago de Cuba**, with lots of rules for harbor users.

Images, top to bottom, left to right:

two of the **garitas** (sentry boxes) on the wall protecting Havana,
Santo Angel and *Maestranza*;

Hospital de San Felipe y Santiago, later called *San Juan de Dios*;

the church of **Santo Cristo del Buen Viaje**;

the **Plaza del Cristo**, a sketch in the Miahle style.

Images, top to bottom:
The **fortifications** of Havana over time;
An **architectural rendering** of the wall of Havana in 1625.

Images, top to bottom:

The church of **San Francisco de Paula**. It was built in 1665, with a Baroque façade. It was said that the multitude of Baroque churches in Havana was due to the coarseness of local stones not allowing boldness of form;

A scene of some of the **first settlements** in Havana according to an engraving dated 1583;

The **Iglesia del Santo Angel Custodio**, built in 1695. Its pure vertical lines contrasted with the clumsy Baroque structures of most other old churches in Havana.

Images, top to bottom, left to right:

Three great bishops of Colonial Cuba: **Juan José Díaz de Espada y Fernández de Landa** (1756-1832), **Diego Evelino de Compostela** (1685-1704) and **Jerónimo Nosti de Valdés** (1646-1729);

A view of the **Almendares River** from *La Chorrera*. On the far background, the first wood mill that supplied wood boards to builders in Havana;

A **physical geography map** of what was later the province of Havana.

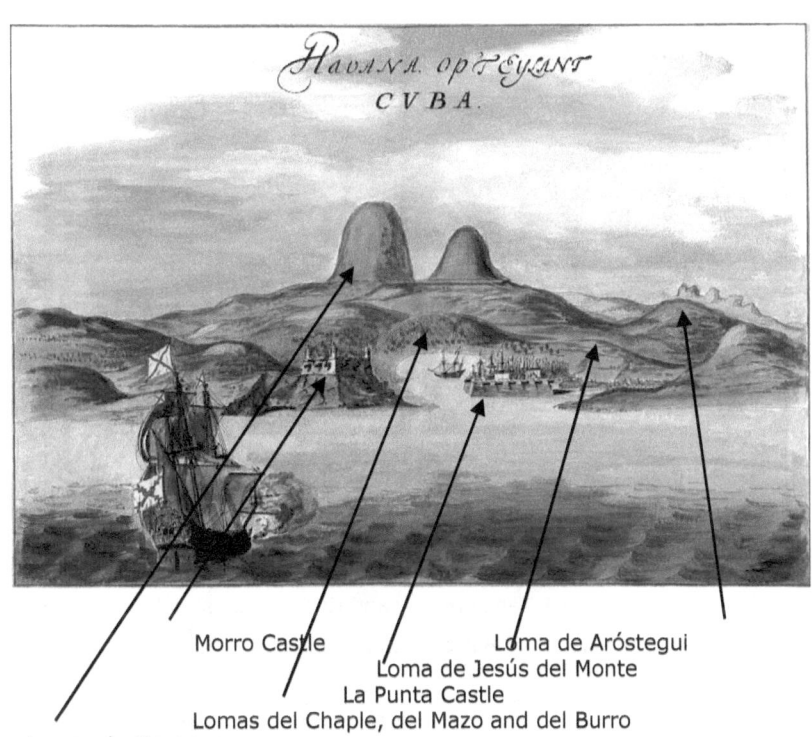

Morro Castle
Loma de Aróstegui
Loma de Jesús del Monte
La Punta Castle
Lomas del Chaple, del Mazo and del Burro
Lomas de Managua

Images, top to bottom, left to right:

One of the **oldest depictions of Havana** with the relative locations of its distinct hills;

a **1685 engraving** showing Spain lovestruck with Havana;

the new **Coat of arms of Havana** in 1665, when Queen *Mariana de Austria*, widow of King *Felipe IV* of Spain, ratified a popular heraldic shield showing the three protective castles: *La Punta, El Morro* and *La Fuerza*, as well as the motto *Siempre Fidelísima* (Always faithful).

Casa de Beneficencia, San Lázaro & Belascoaín, 1901 photo.

In the last years of the XVII century in Havana, Bishop Avelino Diego Velez, better known as the Obispo Compostela, moved by the tragedy of a newborn baby devoured by stray doga in the streets of Havana, opened the first *Casa-Cuna* or *Casa de Beneficencia* (House for Abandoned Children). It was at the corner of today's Teniente Rey and Compostela streets.

Upon the death of Bishop Compostela in 1704, his successor, Bishop Fray Jerónimo Valdés, built in 1711 a new *Casa de Beneficencia* in the block limited by Oficios, Muralla, Mercaderes and Teniente Rey streets. On his testament, he bequeathed his last name —Valdés— to all current and future abandoned children raised in the *Casa-Cuna*.

In 1823 the *Casa de Beneficencia* was moved to Reina and Campanario streets. A *torno* (turnstile) was installed for the first time to facilitate access and anonimity to those wishing to place a child there. The *Casa* joined forces with the *Casa de Maternidad* in 1852 and moved to Prado and Trocadero streets, the original place of the San Isidro Hospice, where Bishop Juan Espada had installed the *Casa de Maternidad* (home for unwed mothers and their children) in 1831. The consolidated houses moved years later to a much larger building at San Lazaro and Belascoain streets. The Countess of Jaruco donated the land. Luis the las Casas was governor and contributed funds for its construction. There were initially 62 girls, 66 indigent boys, 13 nuns and 51 Black slaves. Among some of the best known children that were received over the years in the *Casa de Berneficencia* were Fermín Valdés Domínguez (1852-1910), José Martí's best friend and Fray Olallo Valdés (1820-1889), a Cuban priest consacrated as *Beato* by Pope Benedict XVI in 2008.

The new *Casa de Beneficencia* lost all government support in 1950, when the children were moved to the *Escuela Cívico-Militar* and the nuns were displaced first and eventually let go.

Havana's Foundling Home

From 1700 to 1800

The British under Lord Albemarle attacking Havana in 1762

17
The XVIII Century Opens a New Era in Cuba

THE BELIGERENTS IN the War of the Spanish Succession met in the Dutch city of Utrecht during March and April of 1713 to sign a series of individual peace treaties which gave birth to the *Peace of Utrecht*. Present in the negotiations were representatives of Louis XIV of France and his grandson Felipe V of Spain (the country's first Bourbon), as well as agents acting on behalf of Anne, Queen of Great Britain, the Duke of Savoy, the King of Portugal and the United Provinces of the Netherlands. The presumed purpose of the meeting was to establish in Europe a balance of power.[175] Its real intention was to slow down and end the territorial ambitions and hegemony of Louis XIV of France, *Le Roi Soleil* (the Sun King) or *Louis le Grand*.

With the closing of the XVI century, Cuba ended its first 100 years of colonial status. In many ways the century had not been a successful experience. The native population was almost exterminated. The island remained unpopulated and insecure. Cuba was an appropriate launching station for discovery and colonization of other lands but other than commerce, little was done to develop its potential. Corsairs, privateers, buccaneers

---

[175] The strongest claim to the throne of Spain upon the death of King Charles II, *el Hechizado,* was his second cousin Louis, the Grand Dauphin of France, the eldest son of Louis XIV and evident successor of his father to the throne of France. The Austrians were also possible claimants to the Spanish throne. In order to improve the chance of the Bourbons, Louis gave up his rights to the throne of Spain in favor of his second son Philip, Duke of Anjou, who later became Philip V of Spain. It worked out well since Louis would die of smallpox in 1711, at the age of 49. Had Louis been chosen as Spain's King it would have concentrated both thrones –France and Spain- in the same person. The monarchs of Europe would have opposed such unbalance of power. Philip V went on to rule as King of Spain for 45 years, from 1700 to 1746.

and pirates kept the population *in vilo* (on tenterhooks). Few of the governors the metropolis had sent to Cuba were interested in nothing but profit, lucre and financial deals, even if it meant participation in smuggling, trafficking and contraband. In the best of cases, Cuba became a training station for Spanish officials aspiring for positions in the government of the peninsula, a practice that would be followed by most governors and captain generals of Cuba all the way to the end of the XIX century.

Some events at the close of the XVII century merit mentioning:

In 1652, San Juan de los Remedios, a town located less than 5 kilometers from the northern coast in the center of the island, founded around 1515 by Vasco Porcallo de Figueroa,[176] was savagely sacked by pirates.

In 1656 Juan Montial, Bishop of Santiago, started a campaign to put an end to the scandalous life of clerics and friars in his diocese; within a year he was assassinated by unknown person or persons.[177]

In 1662 British Admiral Christopher Myngs attacked and took possession of Santiago de Cuba and Guantánamo. He was known for his unnecessary cruelty, plundering and slaughtering entire towns as he commanded large fleets of buccaneers with as many as 700 pirates aboard. He was considered a mass murderer by Spanish authorities; in 1665, however, he was knighted in England. He died victim of musket balls fired by a Dutch sharpshooter in 1666.

---

[176] Most likely, Remedios –founded as *Santa Cruz de la Sabana*- was the second town founded in Cuba, after Baracoa and earlier than Trinidad. For many years Porcallo kept Remedios hidden from the crown to avoid the corresponding taxes. His ego was such that in 1518 he renamed the village *Santa Cruz de Vasco Porcallo*, an action objected by his wife, the daughter of the *Cacique de Sabaneque*.

[177] A similar fate occurred to Bishop Gabriel Díaz Vara Calderón, who perished under strange circumstances in 1676. It prompted a letter from Bishop Juan García de Palacios to the crown where he stated «*nos estan matando los Obispos.*» (they are killing our bishops).

In 1665 the buccaneers Edward Mansfield (British) and Pierre Le Grand (French) [178] took turns ransacking the town of Sancti Spíritus. The following year Henry Morgan, pirate and governor of Jamaica, took and destroyed Puerto Príncipe. Also that year, coming from Tortuga Island, Jean-David Nau, aka François Nau, *el Olonés*, harassed the entire northern coast of Cuba.[179]

In 1670 and 1673 Spain signed peace treaties with England and Holland; they presumably ended all British and Dutch pirate attacks sponsored and backed by Spain's enemies in the Caribbean. Five years later, however, British privateers living in Jamaica were laying waste to the town of Trinidad and also assaulted Puerto Príncipe.

In 1680 The British and the Dutch governments retired all support to the privateers in the Caribbean but France did not.[180] British Admiral Robert Holmes began to cooperate with Spain to protect and defend the coasts of Cuba. The French continued to besiege the coasts of Cuba.

In 1682, Havana surged as the most important city in Cuba, superseding the importance and control of Santiago de Cuba.

---

[178] It was said that Le Grand –imitating what Cortés had done in Mexico– always ordered his men to sink the boat they used to board an enemy vessel, making it imperative to fight hard since it would be impossible to make a retreat.

[179] Henry Morgan acted "legally" as a pirate because he was protected by a *Patente de Corso* (*Lettre de Marque* or Letter of Commission) issued by the French. He promoted the island of Tortuga as a base of operations where gold could be "laundered" in the largest multinational venue for the disposal of booty in the known world.

[180] France and Spain finally made peace with the *Tregua de Ratisbona* (1684); Spain recognized its lower political and military status in Europe and agreed to the demands of Louis XIV. Prior to Ratisbona, Spain had made numerous concesions to other European kingdoms: the Treaty of Lisbon (1668), the War of Devolution and the Treaty of Aquisgran (1668), the Peace of Nimega (1678). Following Ratisbona, Spain went trough the Nine Years War (1688-1697) and the Peace of Ryswick (1697). The results were a much diminished Spanish empire and an almost total loss of influence. The final *coup de grace* (blow) was yet to come one hundred years later with the Napoleonic invasion of the peninsula. In 1697, the French newspaper *La Gazette* showed a headline "*l'aigle a pris le coq*" (the eagle has taken the rooster).

Bishop Compostela had come to Havana in 1687 to take over the Bishopric, as the twentieth Bishop of Havana. He discharged his duties as such for eighteen years, during which he established, among other things, a *Casa-Cuna* (foundling home) and San Francisco de Sales, a school for poor and indigent children.

Concerned about the situation prevailing in *Hospital San Juan de Dios* (many paupers were leaving without full recovery), he founded the Convent of Our Lady of Bethlehem, a home for the convalescent poor. He asked the *Belemitas*, an Order of Franciscan tertiaries approved by the Holy See, to manage the instritution.

Construction of the building began in 1712, with costs borne by Juan Francisco de Carballo, who purchased the land to be occupied by the Convent. Just like Bishop Compostela, Carballo did not see the completion of the works to which he contributed so much, as he was assassinated in 1718.

In 1720, the church, the cloister and the convalescent home, became the nucleus of the *Convento Nuestra Señora de Belén*. The *Belemitas* applied for a permit in 1772 to build an arch over Acosta street in order to facilitate the transfer of patients from the convent to the hospital; health authorities had banned the movement of sick people across the street. The *Belemitas* remained in this building until 1842 when the community disappeared and the convent and hospital were expropriated by the city. For almost ten years, starting in 1843, the buildings were used for government business, housing the offices of the Segundo Cabo and Military Cavalry inspectors.

When in 1852 Queen Isabel II restored the Society of Jesus in Cuba, she asked that a school be created in the convent buildings that the city of Havana had expropriated. In 1853, the *Convento de Nuestra Señora de Belén* was turned over to the Jesuits; the order established there the Royal College of Havana. It was in 1854 that the first forty children were admitted. The building and the school kept *Belén* as their original name.

The Arch over Acosta street in Havana

In 1693 and 1696 there were internal scuffles and disorderly fighting in Cuba. In Oriente the miners de *El Cobre* revolted in Santiago de Cuba and took hostage governor Juan de Villalobos, who was considered too feeble and returned to Spain. In Remedios, a group of residents responded violently to what they perceived as hostile incursions of residents of Santa Clara on their rights.

In 1697 Spain and France signed the Peace of Ryswick, with England and the United Provinces. France returned Cataluña and Luxembourg. Spain ceded the western side of Hispaniola to the French.

Cuba and the entire Caribbean were a lawless and anarchical territory during most of the XVII century. Recurrent and complicated wars in Europe retarded its growth for almost a century. Very few new immigrants arrived; they were predominantly adventurers and not settlers. The notable exception was several thousand Spanish colonists who had been expelled from Jamaica when that island was invaded by the British in 1655.[181] Not finding sufficient gold or silver in Cuba, its residents turned to agriculture and the raising of cattle. Sugarcane had been planted and began to be cultivated on a small scale. It was not until the Treaty of Ryswick in 1697, that the European powers temporarily settled their differences, and the threat of pirate attacks was lifted from Cuba.

Havana became a prominent city and port; a period of substantial wellbeing and good fortune set in, based primarily on the cultivation of sugar cane, coffee and tobacco. Shipbuilding

---

[181] In 1655 Spanish Jamaica only had 1,500 settlers, men, women and children. It was entirely unprotected. The islanders were caught completely off guard when a British fleet showed up on May 19th. The British faced an inexperienced defender that exchanged a few shots with the 60 gun ship Swiftsure. Once the British disembarked and occupied Santiago de la Vega (present day Kingston) they issued orders to all residents to abandone the island within a fortnight since it had just became part of the Commonwealth of England. The invading English were supposed to proceed to Hispaniola and the Cayman Islands and undertake a similar action. They did not and Prime Minister Cromwell threw them in the Tower of London. For the British, Jamaica became a gold mine, producing sugar cane for the home and international markets.

increased more than 50% within fifty years after the Peace of Ryswick; legal trade with Spain and contraband with other Spanish colonies increased abruptly beyond expectations. Cuba's tobacco business was so successful that the Spanish crown turned it into a monopoly. In time, the severe controls of Madrid irritated merchants in Havana and *guajiros* (small agricultural land owners), mostly immigrants from Islas Canarias. Several open revolts resulted; the monopoly was ended more than one hundred years later, when Cuba was about to become a free land. Cuba became so important in the eyes of Europeans that Britain and Spain again found themselves at war (the Seven Years' War); a huge British force was dispatched to conquer the island in June 1762; after a prolonged siege -marked by heroism on both sides- the British captured Havana and stayed there for a year, ending with the Peace of Paris in 1763.

Under Spanish authority, Havana's defenses were heavily strengthened and Cuba's capital became the most strongly fortified city in the Americas. Its strategic value was clear during the 1776 American Revolution. As a tacit ally of the rebellious American colonies,[182] Spain went again to war with England in 1779. Havana became an important base of operations and several expeditions went forth from its waters to capture Mobile, Pensacola and the Bahamas from England. On one crucial instance French Admiral Comte François de Grasse's fleet departed from Havana to cut off General Cornwallis' troops at Yorktown; it brought a final victory that assured American independence.

Aside from its strategic importance, Havana had become by far the largest and most beautiful city in the Americas. By the middle of the XVII century it had 76,000 residents, more than twice the number of New York. It was dressed up with beautiful parks and imposing churches and palaces at the time when many American cities –North, Central and South- were all but

---

[182] Spain's alliance was with France, against the British. The French were formal allies of the American Revolutionaries.

glorified crossroads. Most of Havana's prosperity began to penetrate into the Cuban countryside; new methods for faster and more efficient processes to cultivate and manufacture sugar were tried and succeeded. Not always with the best intentions, Spanish edicts allowed and legitimized free trade in slaves. It boosted the prospects of making Cuba the Queen of sugar production; it sadly saddled Cuba as a one-crop economy.

Images, top to bottom:

Henry Morgan (1635-1688), privateer, pirate and admiral of the English Royal Navy. He was trained by Commodore Chistopher Myngs to plunder Spanish possessions in America. In 1668 he landed and sacked Puerto Príncipe but found little to take because the residents had been warned;

two views of the **Spanish Armada** destroyed by Henry Morgan in 1678, from a book published by William Crooke, London, 1684.

Images, top to bottom:

Map of Jamaica in 1698. Since 1494 it was a Spanish possession known as *Santiago* but in 1655 it came under British rule after an attack by Sir William Penn that forced the Spaniards to flee to Cuba;

British ships arriving in Jamaica. Under the British, Jamaica became one of the world leading sugar exporters and slave-dependent territories. Many of its merchants and traders were Jews whose ancestors had been expelled from Spain. They decided the best defense against a return by the Spaniards was to welcome pirates and buccaneers to the island in order to forestall any aggressions by Spain or the Dutch.

Images, top to bottom, left to right:

A gold coin celebrating Louis XIV as **Pacificador del Mundo** (World Peacekeeper). With the weakening of Spain, France began to grow as the strongest power on continental Europe, while its rival England held superiority in naval power. During the War of the Spanish Succession, England, allied with Austria and Prussia, were able to prevent the French house of Bourbon from assimilating the Spanish Empire as part of France;

A copy of the document signed during the **Peace of Ryswick** in 1697. It settled the war that pitted France against England and Spain;

Michel de Grammont (1645-1686) counting his loot. He was a nobleman that decided to become a pirate when he came into disfavor after killing his sister's suitor in a duel. He fled to *Hispaniola*;

Monsieur Michel de Grammont, **leader of the French buccaneers** in Tortuga and *Hispaniola* in the late 1670s. He harassed the coasts of Cuba with impunity for over 20 years.

COLONIAL CUBA - 205

Images, top to bottom, left to right:

Christopher Myngs (1625-1666), English Admiral and pirate. He attacked Santiago in 1662, commanding the largest fleet of buccaneers ever assembled;

Pierre le Grand catching a Spanish captain by surprise while they were playing cards, painting by Howard Pyle;

Iglesia de la **Villa de la Santísima Trinidad**. Together with *Valle de los Ingenios* the town has been selected by UNESCO as a World Heritage site;

Main altar of **San Juan de los Remedios** church. Remedios was the only town in Cuba with two churches on the same central plaza.

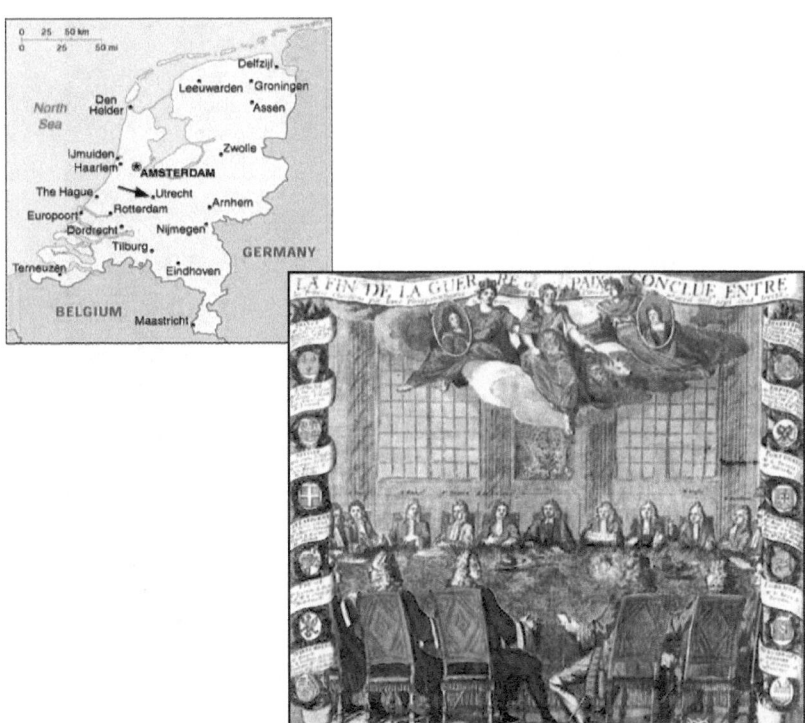

Images, top to bottom:

City of Utrecht in Holland, where the beligerants in the War of Spanish Succession (Spain, England, France, Portugal, Savoy and the Dutch Republic) signed several peace treaties ending hostilities;

A view of the signing ceremony at **Utrecht**. The treaty gave England a 30 year right to supply Black slaves to Cuba and other Spanish colonies in America;

The city of Ratisbona, capital of the **High Palatinate**, where in August of 1684 France and Spain (Louis XIV of France, Leopold I, for the Holy Roman Empire and Charles II of Spain) signed a truce lasting 20 years.

Images, top to bottom, left to right:

Philip V of Spain (1683-1746), on a painting by Louis Michel Vanloo. He was a Bourbon, the grandson of Louis XIV of France and son of Louis the Grand Dauphin. Charles II of Spain named him his successor and he was proclaimed King of Spain, at age 16, at a ceremony in Versailles;

Louis XIV (1638-1715), aka *Louis le Grand, Louis-Dieudonné* and *le Roi-Soleil*. He reigned in France for 72 years and 110 days. Marble bust by *Gianlorenzo Bernini*;

British Admiral **Sir Robert Holmes** (1622-1692). In 1687 he was given a powerful squadron of fast-sailing ships and the command to clear the coasts of Cuba, Hispaniola and the rest of the Caribbean from pirates and buccaneers. The scoundrels soon left for the South Seas and Madagascar, ending the days of piracy in the Caribbean.

A **Lettre de Marque**, a government license to attack and capture enemy vessels. In the XVII century it was considered an honorable calling.

The War of Jenkins' Ear (known as *Guerra del Asiento* in Spain), was a conflict between Great Britain and Spain lasting from 1739 to 1748. Its unusual name, coined by Victorian Scottish writer Thomas Carlyle (1795-1881) in 1858, refers to an ear severed from Robert Jenkins (1730-1799), captain of *Rebecca*, a British merchant ship.

In 1738 Jenkins testified before Parliament that on September 12, 1731, while returning home from the island of Cuba, Captain Juan de Leon Fandino, master of the Spanish ship *La Isabela*, had boarded his ship, harassed him and his crew under suspicion of smuggling and took up all his money leaving him «without those necessities which were essential to safely carry the ship home.» Jenkins said Fandino had tied him up to a mast and sliced off one of his ears with a sword, telling him to say to his King «this will happen to his highness if he is caught on illicit trade in these waters.»

The severed ear was subsequently exhibited (on a pickled jar) before Parliament. The tale of the ear's separation from Jenkins, following boarding of his vessel by Spanish coast guards in 1731, provided the impetus to declare war against the Spanish Empire, which started on October 19, 1739, after a 257 to 209 vote in Parliament.

The war, rather than seeking redress from Spain, had the intention of encouraging the Spanish not to renege on its lucrative *Contrato de Asiento* with Britain (permission to sell slaves in Spanish America). When a Parliament member asked how Jenkins reacted, Jenkins said «I commended my soul to God knowing my country would protect me.» Jenkins' story created a sensation and public outcry forcing Prime Minister Robert Walpole (1676-1745) into declaring war on Spain. Called the War of Jenkins's Ear, it amounted to little more than a few skirmishes at sea, but eventually developed into the cross-continental War of the Austrian Succession.

Jenkins' Ear shown to Parlament in 1738

18
The Effervescense of the XVIII Century in Cuba

AS THE XVIII CENTURY approached, a substantial economic transformation was taking place in Cuba. The island was no longer important just as a defensive base of operations for the Spanish fleets in the Caribbean; it became a thriving colony exporting sugar, coffee and tobacco to Europe. The revelation of the potential of Cuba as a commercial emporium surprised Madrid and surpassed the resident's best expectations. The 1700s was the century when maritime affairs proved to be the key to wealth and development. The thirteen British colonies in North America were partly responsible for Cuba's emergent success; after the brief occupation of Havana by the British in 1762, commercial exchange with the north became almost unstoppable; more so after 1776, when the newly independent United States could no longer get its sugar, tobacco and coffee from British colonies in the Caribbean.

In addition, the Haitian revolution of 1802 [183] strengthened the technology and commercial prospects of Cuba's sugar industry. By 1795, almost 500 North American commercial vessels entered the port of Havana yearly, compared with about two dozen Spanish ships. The level of business reported by Havana's customs jumped from less than 5 million pesos in the mid 1750s to close to 30 million by the end of the century. The population of Cuba increased from 50 thousand at the beginning of the XVIII century to 150 thousands in the mid 1700s

---

[183] At the start of the XVIII century, the French colonies in the Caribbean included Haiti, Guadalupe, Martinica, San Martín, Saint Bartholomew, Dominica, Saint Lucía, Saint Vicente and Granada. All these islands were sugar producers. After the Seven Year War (1756-1763), the British had conquered all these islands except Haiti (Guadalupe in 1759, Dominica in 1761, Martinica, Saint Lucia, Saint Vicent and Granada in 1762).

and over half a million by the end of the 1700s; 40% of them lived in Havana. Half the population was Black throughout the XVIII century, as there was an unceasing demand for slave labor in the sugar industry.

During most of the XVIII century, the government of Madrid appointed authoritarian former military leaders to the position of Captain General in Cuba. Many of them received their positions as rewards to military performance in Europe; some of them eventually were promoted to higher positions in Spanish America, such as Revillagigedo and Bucarelli as Viceroys of Mexico.[184]

A major change of strategies occurred in 1762, the year the British took Havana and kept it for a few months.[185] After recovering its Cuban possession, the Bourbons reorganized the military structure in Cuba and initiated a series of reforms.[186] Ambrosio de Funes Villalpando, *Conde de Ricla*, Grandee of Spain, became the first Captain General after the recovery of the Island. He arrived in Cuba with Marshal Alejandro, *Conde de O'Reilly* (1722-1794), Inspector General of the Spanish infantry for the entire Spanish Empire; such was the importance that Spain now conferred to Cuba.

---

[184] Cuban born Juan Vicente Padilla, *Conde de Revillagigedo* (1740-1799), was Viceroy of Mexico from 1789 to 1799; Fra Antonio María de Bucareli, *Marqués de Vallehermoso*, was Viceroy of Mexico from 1771 to 1779.

[185] Ever since Oliver Cromwell became Lord Protector of the British Commonwealth in 1653, the British formulated the so-called "Western Design," a plan to attack and acquire Spanish territories in and around the Caribbean and to plant them with English settlers. In 1654 British General Robert Venables and Admiral William Penn were given the task of turning this policy into reality. In 1760, Sir George Keppel, Count of Albemarle, was added to that list; one of his first actions was to attack Havana in 1762.

[186] The reforms included giving slaves the ability to buy their freedom and giving slave owners an easier way to grant freedom to slaves, which at the time was a complicated legal operation. The voluntary freeing of slaves (manumition) was seen as an incentive for slaves to behave well and earn this priviledge. It was a difficult legal process but its complexity increased the value of manumition in the eyes of slaves.

O'Reilly analyzed what had gone wrong with the defense of Havana during the successful British siege in 1762, and recommended sweeping reforms to improve the fortifications, training practices and troop organizations, which were quickly approved by the Spanish Crown. Ricla's actions included increasing the number of veteran troops, undertaking large fortification improvements at *El Morro*, *La Cabaña*, *El Principe* and *Atarés*, and allowing exports from the ports of Santiago, Trinidad and Batabanó. Cuba continued to receive the *Situado* [187] from Mexico in spite of its now larger local income due to the reforms of Ricla; two years after he arrived, the *Real Hacienda* (the royal treasury) declared that Cuba's income had doubled to 316 thousand pesos. By the end of the XVIII century it would amount to over 3 million.[188]

Sugar was responsible for Cuba's economic boom; it had been cultivated in the island since the XVI century but in the 1700s it became the primary source of income. Livestock, tobacco and coffee were distant sources of wealth. The great growth of the sugar business was the result of new technologies and technicians coming from Haiti and Dominica, and the timely acquisition of lands[189] by enterprising and ambitious men that decided not to invest as much time and money in the cities, as less adventuresome residents were doing. Due to competition from Mexico, Venezuela and islands in the Caribbean, it was essential for Cuban based growers to lower the cost of sugar cultivation; to achieve that it was necessary to import cheap slave labor.[190] Once this was accomplished, the issue

---

[187] The *Situado* was a semi-regular shipment of gold from the Viceroyalty of New Spain (Mexico) that was sent to Cuba as a way to provide economic support.

[188] The Borbonic reforms in Cuba, when found successful, were extended to all Spanish colonies in the Americas. In that sense Cuba became a testing ground for colonial management strategies.

[189] Starting in the late 1600s and lasting well until the 1730s, lots of cattle raising lands were torn down and turned into sugarland.

[190] The British, for instance, had imported 10 thousand Black slaves in the brief months they occupied Havana. After 1765, slaves were introduced in Cuba at the rate of 2 thousand a year.

of selling sugar abroad was easy to resolve. Cuba was a long island with dozens of harbors close to the cane fields, hence land transportation was inexpensive. The geographical situation of the island at the crossroads of international commerce (both to North America and Europe) did the rest. To even improve the lot of the sugar growers, in 1789 the free trade of slaves was authorized by Madrid and the importation of slaves was declared free of taxes for both Cuban residents and Spanish merchants.

To maximize profits sugar planters began to bring automation to the island. By the end of the XVIII century most sugar producers had introduced steam engines on the *ingenios azucareros*. From a production of half a million pounds of sugar in the 1750s, production grew to 2.5 million by the end of the century. A new wealthy class became powerful in Cuba: it was appropriately call the *sacarocracia*.

Tobacco was also making important inroads in the Cuban economy. Originally the seedlings were planted in the flat, wet and fertile lands of riverbanks. Profits were enough to justify going inland. The necessary capital was much smaller than those required for sugar fields, therefore the initial tobacco planters were small producers relying on the family for the intensive nature of tobacco cultivation. After moving inland with expanded plots, the necessary capital was usually lent by merchants. Europeans went wild in their addiction for tobacco and snuffs[191] but tobacco never truly competed with sugar. By the

---

[191] Tobacco leaves were rolled to produce cigars, which ther Europeans knew as *Habanos*. Snuff (also called *rapé*) was made by pulverizing dried, cured and matured tobacco leaves and packaging them for inhalation through the nose, delivering a swift hit of nicotine. It is said that *rapé* inhalation was a favorite treatment of Catherine de Medicis (1519-1589) for her persistent headaches. She called it *Herba Regina,* and with her seal of approval it was popularized among the French nobility. The practice became so popular in Europe that Pope Urban VIII (1568-1644) baned it inside churches under the penalty of excommunication, and Louis XV (17110-1774) banned its use in the Royal Court of France under the penalty of banishment and exile.

end of the 1700s, there were 100 "modern" sugar mills in Cuba and only 20 factories manufacturing tobacco finished products.

The Spanish crown established a monopoly of tobacco and snuff in 1717.[192] It was opposed in 1717, 1720 and 1723 by successive *Sublevaciones de Vegueros* (planter's revolts) and led to the forced resignation of Vicente Raja, Captain General of Cuba in 1718 as well as encounters with Spanish troops in Guanabacoa, San Miguel, Bejucal and Santiago de las Vegas that claimed the life of 20 planters.[193] Spain's militia captain Ignacio Barrútia, under orders from Captain General Gregorio Guazo, took 12 prisoners during the revolts; all of them were hanged and their cadavers exposed near the church of Jesús del Monte.

Later, in 1739, the Spanish crown reluctantly agreed to transfer the tobacco monopoly to a local entity, the *Compañía de la Habana*; after realizing substantial profits for a few years (1740-1752), the *Compañía's* profits declined and returned the control of tobacco to the crown. It was an ill-timed action since the real tobacco boom (cigars and cigarettes rather than snuff) took place in Europe after 1790.

Other businesses brought capital and wealth to Cuban enterprising residents in the XVIII century; Coffee began to be a profit-making crop in the mountains of central and eastern Cuba and was almost exclusively sold into the North American market. The *Astillero* (dockyard) of Havana built 18 large ships during the first half of the century and earned substantial profits repairing ships transporting Cuban products to Spain and North America.

---

[192] On April 11, 1717, Spain proclaimed the *Estanco del Tabaco* (Watertight control of tobacco cultivation and products). On August 21 more than 500 tobacco farmers revolted in Jesús del Monte, a hilly area south of Havana.

[193] Vicente Raja was replaced by his Lieutenant Governor Gómez Maraver, who had orders to discontinue the *Estanco*. In 1718 Gregorio Guazo y Calderón arrived to Havana as newly appointed Captain General, with orders to resume the *Estanco*, hence the new revolts. That back and forth was typical of the crown's poor administration of Cuba.

As early as the first years of the XVII century, the British had the intention to seize Havana. The island of Cuba was an important strategic point for navigation in the Americas, particularly because important and functional ports in both the North and the South coasts, as well as its position as the key to shipments in the Caribbean. They had studied its topology and the location of all its defenses.

When England and France became formal enemies, the alliance of the French with the Bourbons in Spain became unacceptable; war was declared against Spain. In May of 1762 the British placed a fleet of 53 warships in the Bahamas; they were manned by 25 thousand men, 15 thousand of which were regular soldiers.

On June 6 British Count of Albemarle moved the fleet in front of Havana, with most of the ships blocking the bay's entrance. Juan Prado Mayena, the island governor, was alarmed by the strength of the siege and began to reinforce the defenses of *El Morro* and *La Cabaña* forts. Inside the bay he only counted with 14 Spanish warships —a good part of the total Spanish naval forces. The entrance to the bay was closed with chains and three ships were sunk between *El Morro* and *La Punta* to frustrate any intent to enter the bay. Albemarle ordered six of the ships to remain at the bay's entrance. They threatened the *Morro* and attempted to land men at *La Chorrera*, on the west of the city. A group of men landed near the *Torreón de Cojimar* and began to shell the small fort. Carlos Caro, the Spanish man in charge, had no choice but withdraw his 400 defending men and seek refuge at *La Cabaña*.

Luis Vicente de Velasco, a navy captain in charge of *El Morro*, resisted several thrusts by the British but on the third day of the attack he was wounded and died within 24 hours. From the land side, on the eastern side of the bay, the British continued to besiege *El Morro*. They finally dug a tunnel from *La Cabaña* and exploded numerous charges of dynamite under *El Morro*; that made it possible to seize the now defenseless fortress. On August 12, 1762, Havana capitulated; one thousand Spaniards and *Criollos* were lost; close to eighteen hundred British soldiers were killed or wounded.

Havana's Morro Castle and Lighthouse

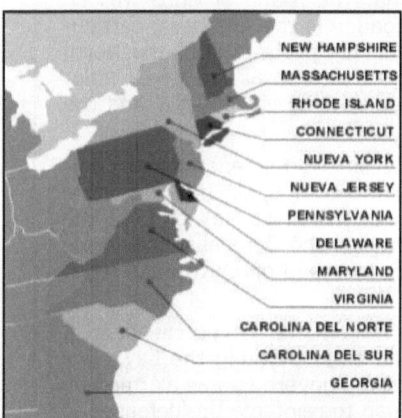

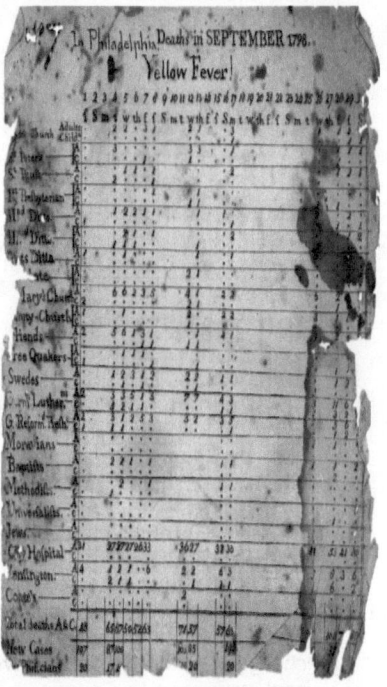

Images, top to bottom, left to right:

The **Haiti revolt** of 1802;

The **13 North American Colonies** in 1776;

A listing of victims of **Yellow Fever** in 1798;

The **city of Havana in 1686**, an engraving by Allain Mallet, Frankfurt.

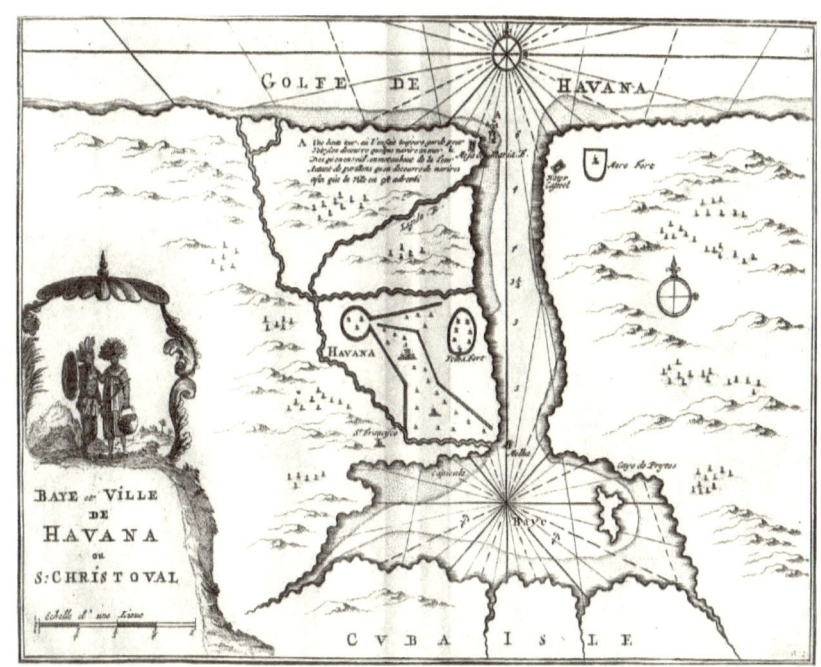

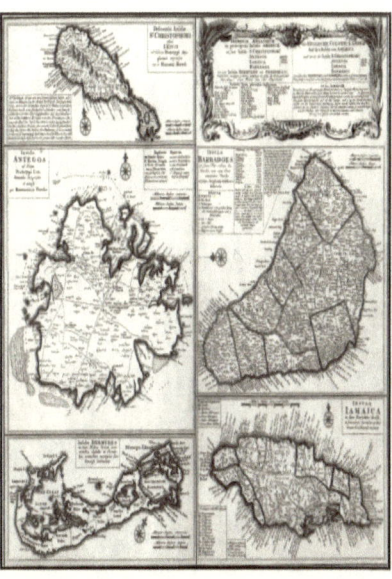

Images, top to bottom, left to right:
A **plan of Havana** in 1702;
A stock certificate of the **Real Compañía de La Habana**, dated 1791;
English island colonies in 1731. Engravings by Homann Nuemberg.

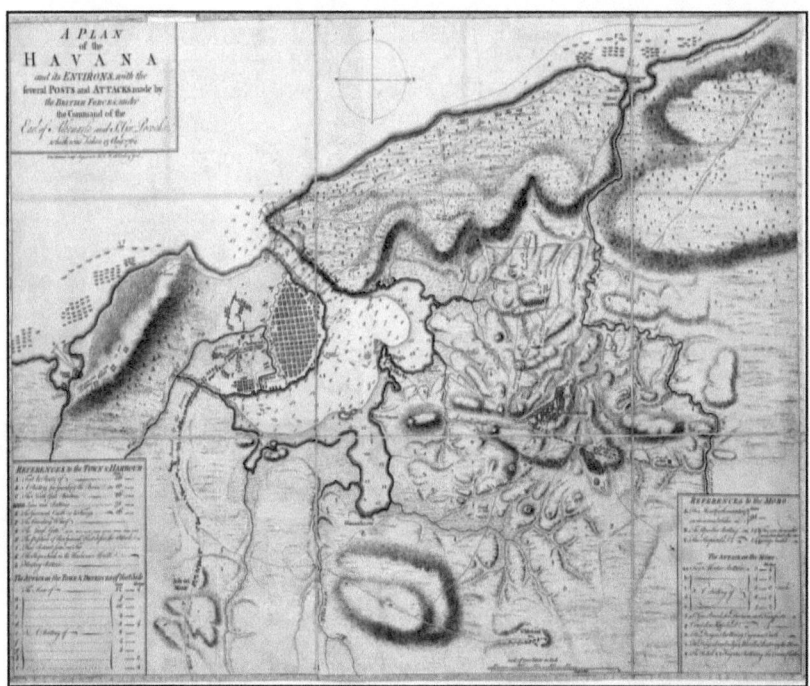

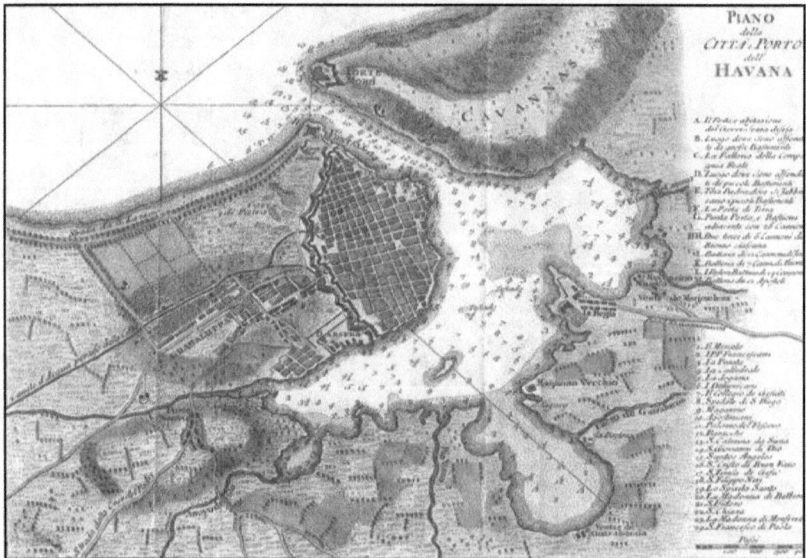

Images, top to bottom:

A plan of Havana showing the disposition of the **defenses** and the British ships during the attack of 1762;

The **port of Havana** and its surroundings in a 1763 drawing by Coltellini.

Images, top to bottom, left to right:

A **1780 map of Cuba** by M. Bonne, published in Paris;

French forces under General Charles Leclerk, husband of Pauline Bonaparte, Napoleon's sister, invading Cap Français in Haiti with 40 thousand troops in 1802. He captured Touissant Louverture and took him to France, where he died in 1803.

Images, top to bottom, left to right:

Marshal Alejandro, Conde de O'Reilly (1722-1794), born in Dublin, Ireland, governor of Louisiana; he married into the Cuban family of Luis de las Casas, governor of Cuba. He started the construction of *Castillo de la Cabaña* to further fortify Havana after the British siege of 1762.

Ambrosio de Funes Villalpando, Count of Ricla, first Captain General of Cuba after the British left in 1763. He organized the department of finances, the police, the hospitals, and in 1764 he founded *La Gaceta de la Habana*.

The **city of Havana** at the close of the XVII century. On the extreme left the *Arsenal*. Few buildings or roads beyond the *Muralla* under construction. On the right, a very lively commercial activity in the port entrance.

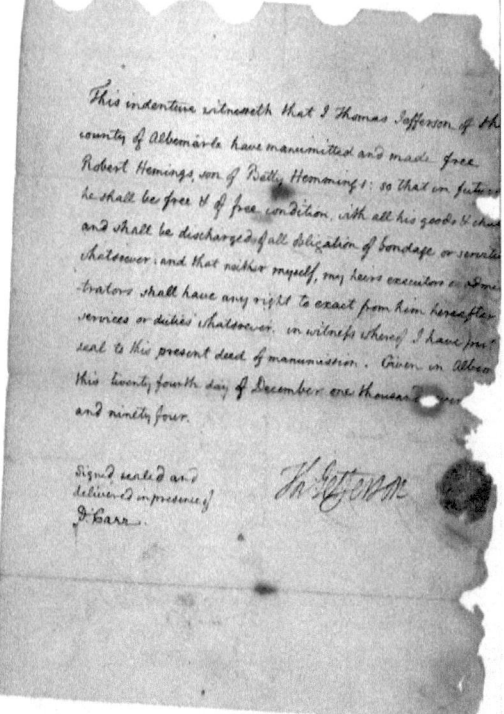

Images, top to bottom, left to right:

Two 1680 views of a **sugar mill in Cuba** before modernization;

Two views of **Black slaves** during the tobacco and sugar harvests in the 1700s;

A **manumition** (voluntary liberation of a slave) document for the Hennings signed by Thomas Jefferson in 1794.

COLONIAL CUBA - 221

19

The British and Sugar Created a New Cuba

THERE IS NO DOUBT that once Havana was recovered by Spain, the crown transformed the city into the most heavily fortified place in the Americas and turned Cuba into one of the most economically progressive areas under the Spanish domain. *La Cabaña* became the largest fortification in the New World. At a dreadful cost, the work took 11 years to be finished. Once completed it was considered an impregnable and invulnerable fortress that could withstand the power of any European army. *La Cabaña* was equipped with a large number of state-of-the-art cannons cast in the best armament workshops in Spain. Other defense fortifications surrounded an unassailable Havana: the *Atarés* castle defended the shipyards (*El Arsenal*), [194] deep inside the bay; the *Príncipe* castle guarded the western part of the city; the batteries of *San Nazario* and the *Doce Apóstoles* made sure that no enemy could remain free from fire if it tried to storm its way into the bay. The *Santa Clara* battery [195] guarded the western approach to the harbor entrance.

---

[194] *El Arsenal,* built in 1725 and located at today's Egido and Factoría streets, was a strong economic force in Havana thanks to the lumber resources available close to the bay, in what are now the neighborhoods of *El Vedado, El Cerro, Marianao, Luyanó* and *Lawton*. In 1769 the *Santísima Trinidad*, a warship measuring 62 meters long, with four decks and 150 cannons, was built at the *Arsenal* at a cost 40,000 *Pesos Fuertes* (US $ 125 thousand in today's money). It was one of over a hundred ships built at the *Arsenal* between 1750 and 1850. Unfortunately, it was sunk during the Battle of Trafalgar.

[195] *Santa Clara*, named after Count of Ricla (also known as Count of Santa Clara), was one of the most formidable artillery defense units in the New World. It stood 300 ft along the waterfront, west of what is now the *Calzada de Infanta*, at the northern end of a range of hills extending from the water to the *Príncipe* fortress. Its parapet was 10 ft thick, the wall of the fort was six feet in depth, all built with stones and cement in what became to be known as *mampostería*.

Aside from the surge in crown expenses for defense fortifications and infrastructure, Havana began to see administrative reforms that stimulated growth in both urban and rural economic sectors; they led to rapid demographic expansion as well as the spatial scattering of the city in all directions. It was mostly due, but not exclusively, to an expanding sugar economy and the sensational growth of plantation slavery.

As a reaction to the 1762 English occupation of Havana, the reforming Bourbon monarchs, mostly Charles III (1759-88), directed a fundamental administrative, military and commercial overhaul of the vast Spanish colonial empire with a number of objectives: assure military security, bring about economic growth, and ensure the administration's efficient fiscal regimes through extensive managerial reforms.

Barely three years after recovering Havana in 1765, the Spanish crown proclaimed Cuba as a *zona de comercio libre*. Additionally, in 1771, the *fuero militar* [196] was extended and protections and privileges were granted to both the regular army and the locally recruited *milicias*.[197] As a broad spectrum of the population benefited through the *fueros* bestowed by the crown, loyalty to Spain increased among residents of Cuba, and with it an unprecedented and wide spread material prosperity. A late XVIII century census indicated that white Europeans were 85% of Cuba's population; it was all due to considerable immigration of military personnel from the peninsula after the recovery of Havana, as well as intermarriage within the Spanish white population. In that sense, Cuba was becoming unique among all Spanish colonies; there, mixed marriages

---

[196] The concept of *fuero* dates back to the feudal era. A monarch would concede to groups of his choosing (towns, regions, social classes, individuals) certain rights and privileges (not contestable in civil courts) in exchange for their acknowledgment of his authority. The equivalent in the Anglo-Saxon world would be the Charters.

[197] This was important since a large share of Cuba's free population was recruited into the *milicias* irrespective of racial origins; at the time, 40% of Havana's adult white male population and over 65% of the adult free population of Blacks were initiated in the *milicias*. They all benefited and were protected by the privileges of the *fueros*.

were more prevalent and loyalty to Spain was conspicuously vanishing.[198] Cuban-born aristocrats, however, were sharing in the political and military destinies of the Spanish empire: Francisco Díaz de Pimienta, for instance, became Admiral in the Royal Spanish Navy and Viceroy of Sicily, Gonzalo O'Farril Herrera was twice the Spanish Minister of War, Calvo de la Puerta and the Count of Santa Cruz both reached the level of Marshals in the Spanish Army.

Charles IV, by all accounts an inept King, appointed Luis de las Casas y Aragorri (1745-1800) as governor of Cuba in 1790. He had been a field aid to *Conde de Ricla* and served under Alejandro O'Reilly, his brother in law. Las Casas worked to abrogate the *fueros militares* and to impose labor obligations among the free population. He also founded the first newspaper in Cuba, *El Papel Periódico*, began construccion of the *Paseo del Prado* and established the public lighting system in Havana. His political record is not as clean as many of his followers believed.[199] He, nevertheless, established the principle that «*los nacidos en la Isla tenían los mismos derechos a la gobernación que los peninsulares.*» (Those born in Cuba had the same rights to be part of government than those born in the peninsula). He was the man that first opened the public square to Francisco de Arango y Parreño. (1765-1837).

---

[198] During the XVIII century the upper classes in Cuba did not feel the weakening and disintegration of the Spanish Empire and residents of Cuba found no contradictory interests with those of the peninsula. The crown goals were to increase income, protect its commercial benefits and control the governance and the burocratic *status-quo*; the resident's goals were free commerce, freedom of crops and industry, reform of taxes and duties, priority for local appointments and full powers to the *cabildos*. Yet no sensible disparity was yet felt. The phase "*La Siempre Fiel Isla de Cuba*" (the always faithful island of Cuba) was coined in the last years of the XVIII century as it became evident other colonies from the Americas were indulging in independence hopes. All sorts of publications in Cuba repeated the phrase *ad nauseam*.

[199] The Alejandría sugar mill in Güines, ostensibly property of the Count of O'Reilly, was actually owned by his brother-in-law Don Luis de las Casas.

Other developments before the end of the XVIII century were:

For the first time in 300 years, commerce with Cuba was approved on October 16, 1765, from the ports of Santander, La Coruña, Sevilla, Cádiz, Málaga, Cartagena and Barcelona, and a mail service was established between Havana and La Coruña.

In 1766 Carlos III of Spain approved that natives and halfbreds (his words) could enter religious orders and be ordained. Almost simultaneously he decreed the expulsion of Jesuits from all possessions of Spain in the Americas.

In 1767 Architects Augusto Crane, Silvestre Abarca (the builder of *La Cabaña*) and Louis Huet designed and supervised the construction of the *El Principe* fortress[200] on a hill west of Havana, and Atarés fortress on the southern side. El Príncipe was the most modern fort in the Americas; within the shape of an irregular pentagon, it included two bastions, two semibastions, a *rediente* (redans, top of the defensive walls in zigzag), deep trenches, mine galleries, warehouses, offices, a cistern and a housing area large enough to accommodate a garrison of over a thousand soldiers. Its defensive artillery had 60 cannons of various calibers and a special system of underground red brick-lined tunnels that allowed communications with all the outposts and most remote positions of the castle. *El Principe* was under construction until 1779.

In 1768, Jerónimo Enrile y Guerci, *Marqués de Casa Enrile*, brought to Cuba the last of more than 14 thousand Black slaves he had purchased in today's Senegal. Only José Villanueva, Pere Labat and Luis de las Casas managed to import more Black slaves (up to 500 thousand) to Cuba.

In 1769 Alejandro O'Reilly left Havana with a strong fleet to take over the Louisiana, the territory given by France to Spain after the Seven Year War. The territory had been founded by

---

[200] Named after Charles of Bourbon, Prince of Asturias, son of Charles III.

Pánfilo de Narvaez in 1528 and explored by Hernando de Soto in 1542. In 1682 La Salle named the region after France's Louis XIV; it included today's states of Louisiana, Mississippi, Arkansas, Oklahoma, Missouri, Kansas, Nebraska, Iowa, Illinois, Indiana, Michigan, Wisconsin, Minnesota, North Dakota, South Dakota. France ceded most of the territory to the British after the Seven Year War (1756-1763); it came into Spain's hands by the Treaty of Fountainbleau in 1763. Napoleon reacquired it in 1800 by the Treaty of San Ildefonso and sold it to to Thomas Jefferson in 1803 for a pittance (828,000 square miles for US $15 million, less than 3 cents an acre, probably the worst Real Estate deal in history), using the funds to invest in Hispaniola and Haiti.

In 1772 the Paseo del Prado was built in Havana and in 1777 the new Cathedral of Havana was inaugurated at the former Swamp Plaza, a site where the runoff of the city was collected. In 1796 it received and kept the remains of Chistopher Columbus, later transferred to Seville after Spain's loss of Cuba.

In 1779 Carlos III of Spain declared war against England. He began to send funds and weapons to the North American rebels via New Orleans, in what was called the Bourbon family Pact. In 1783 the Treaty of Paris acknowleged the independence of the United States of America.

Next year, 1780, a serious Yellow Fever epidemy scourged Havana. Over 2 thousand residents reportedly died.

A royal edict in 1784 prohibited Cuban-born youngsters to study law in Cuba; they are approved to study in Mexico and Santo Domingo.

Several important leaders of future Cuba were born before the end of the XVIII century: in Tournai, France, in 1784, Jean Baptiste Vermay, the founder of Academia de Bellas Artes San Alejandro; in 1787, in Caracas, Venezuela, Narciso López, the filibuster that created the National Flag of Cuba; in 1788, in Havana, Father Félix Varela Morales, Vicar General of New York, theological consultant to American Bishops, Cuban deputy before the Court of Spain, champion of anti-slavery and independence leader in Cuba; in 1789 author María de las Mercedes Santa Cruz Montalvo, Countess of Merlín, daughter of the Count of Jaruco and Mompox; in 1797 José Antonio Saco (1797-1879), the founder of *Revista Bimestre Cubana* and numerous political, anthropological and historic essays was born in Bayamo; in 1799, Felipe Poey Aloy (1799-1891), zoology professor at the University of Havana and founder of the Cuban Academy of Sciences, was born in Havana.

In 1793 the *Sociedad de Amigos del País* opened its library in Havana. José Agustín Caballero (1762-1835), whose best student were Félix Varela, José Antonio Saco and José de la Luz Caballero, dictated the first round of lectures in the Society's libray. The same year governor Las Casas opened all Cuban ports to trade with the US.

The first pro-independence revolt took place in 1795 in Bayamo under the leadership of Nicolás Morales and Gabriel José Estrada. It failed and they were imprisoned.

The century ended in 1799 with the appointment of Salvador Muro y Salazar, Marqués de Someruelos (1754-1813) as governor of Cuba.

Images, left to right:
A Cuban postage stamp honoring the **Sociedad Económica**;
Don Luis de las Casas Aragorri (1745-1800), founder of the
Sociedad Económica de Amigos del País and
El Papel Periódico de La Habana.

It may be said that until the eighteenth century the island of Cuba remained indifferent to the intellectual and technological devel-
opments in Europe. From the earliest days of the conquest, Cuba was considered a comercial factory and a stopover point for the rich and promising regions of New Spain. What absorbed the attention of the metropolis was to take possession of America's extensive territories, ignoring the inglorious island whose population and wealth paled when compared to what was available in other parts of the continent.

The opening of the University of Havana and the jesuit school, both around 1728, were the first signs that there was room in Cuba for culture, industrial arts and applied sciences. In 1735 the first printing shop (known as *Boloña's*) was established and in 1747 the government established a second one, known as *Arazoza*. Pamphelts and announcements began to be printed in Cuba and in 1761 **Don José Martín Félix de Arrate**, published the first historical and demographic essay about the island; it was lost and not published until 1830.

A few years later a *Sociedad Económica* was opened in Santiago de Cuba and, during the government of Luis de las Casas Aragorri (1790 to 1796), culture and technical skills in the island finally took a large progressive step following his challenge: «Habaneros, protejed las letras, learn the sciences, illustrad la patria.» In 1792 the *Sociedad Económica de la Habana* began publishing its *Memorias* and the first newspaper, the *Papel Periódico*.

On the scientific and engineering front some headway began to take place in the early 1800s. The pioneers were men like **Francisco de Arango y Parreño**, publisher of a seminal treatise on the state of Cuban agriculture; **Gonzalo O'Farrill**, diplomat, uncle of the Countess of Merlin, heavy investor in sugar; **Sebastián Calvo**, *Marqués de Casa Calvo*, future governor of Louisiana, importer of one of the first steam engines for his sugar estates; **Ignacio Montalvo**, *Conde de Casa Montalvo*, known for his "journey of sugar espionage" to Barbados and Jamaica; and **Joaquín de Ayesterán**, Cuban expert in sugar milling and refining, who was a major force in the modernization of sugar making in Cuba, as well as the top industrial spy on British industrial developments.

There was Room in Cuba for Culture

Notable Cubans born in the XVIII century, top to bottom, left to right::

José Agustín Caballero (1762-1835), theologian, philosopher and educator;
Pbro. Félix Varela (1788-1853), precursor of the independent movement, notable Catholic figure in Cuba and the US;
Dr. Tomás Romay y Chacón (1764-1849), founder of medicine in Cuba;
José Antonio Saco (1797-1879), statesman, Deputy to Spanish Courts;
Francisco de Arango y Parreño (1765-1837), scholar, champion of public education in Cuba;
Dr. Felipe Poey (1799-1891), zoologist founder of the *Academy of Sciences*;
José de la Luz y Caballero (1800-1862), father of Cuban intellectual life;
The **Countess of Merlín** (1789-1852), novelist, travel writer.

Images, top to bottom, left to right:

Carlos III of Spain (1716-1788). He was the champion of Enlightened Absolutism in Spain, and tried to reescue the empire through far-reaching reforms in trade, education and agriculture;

the seal of the *Sociedad Económica de Amigos del País*;

a 1789 view of the *Plaza de la Catedral* in Havana.

Images, top to bottom:

San Carlos de la Cabaña fortress, built by Carlos III, completed in 1774;

the entrance to **El Príncipe** fortress in Havana, built from 1767 to 1779, named after Charles of Bourbon, Prince of Asturias, son of Carlos II of Spain;

the **Santísima Trinidad**, a 5 thousand ton warchip built in Havana in 1769. It was designed by Mateo Mullán, the top Irish naval architect, with four decks of eight pounder guns, the largest ship of its kind in the world. Its first commission was to support the US independence on the English Channel.

Images, top to bottom:

Two views of the **Santa Clara battery** in Havana. On the top, soldier placing an *Ordoñez cannon* in possition, on the bottom a close view of the emplacement. The Ordoñez cannons were developed by Spanish captain Salvador Díaz Ordoñez. In 1898 they fired the first shots (against the US Coastguard Vicksburg) in the Hispano-Cuban-American War. The Santa Clara battery was built in 1717, named after the Count of Santa Clara, governor of Cuba. It was at the site now occupied by *Hotel Nacional* in Havana;

a view of the **Paseo del Prado** in Havana, started in 1772, re-designed by Jean-Claude Nicholas Forestier (master landscape architect of Paris) in the early 1900s. It was the first paved street in Havana.

On February 15, 1769, days after the death (not without suspicion of poison) of Pope Clement XIII (1693-1769), a conclave was called under the influence of the Bourbons, with the paramount purpose of electing an anti-Jesuit cardenal as the new Pope. The Spanish cardinals were committed to the defenestration of the Jesuits and had openly stated: «We will not go there to elect a Pope; we expect the abolition of the Jesuits. Either a Pope to the like of the Bourbons or schism in the Church.»

After three months of conclave and 179 ballots, Cardinal Gian Vincenzo Ganganelli de Rimini (1705-1774) was elected. He was frightened by the schismatic threat. Indecisive, timid, insincere and inclined to bend and change colors as a chamaleon, he signed as Clement XIV, on July 21, 1773, an infamous decree titled *Dominus ac Redemptor* (Lord and Savior), expelling the Jesuits from all European countries and all American colonies. It affected 11,293 priests, more than 2,000 of which were in different parts of America, teaching, converting natives, establishing contacts with the ruling and wealthy classes and everywhere openly meddling in state affairs.

The moment Ganganelli stamped his signature in his ominous decree he cried anxiously: *Compulsus feci!* (I was forced). He died in 1774, convinced that he was destined for eternal damnation. As his corpse decomposed rapidly with great stench, his friends commented that the Jesuits had been avenged.

In France, under the siege of Jansenists led by Blaise Pascal and the writings of Voltaire, Louis XV complied with Ganganelli decree and secularized all Jesuits. In Austria, Queen Maria Teresa, a devout catholic, did not oppose the decree and Jesuit heads rolled, to the satisfaction of Louis XV and his son the Dauphin (future Louis XVI), who was later to marry her daughter Marie Antoinette. A similar reaction took place in the Portugal, Naples, the Two Sicilies, Malta, the Low Countries and Parma. The suppression of the order had longstanding economical effects in the Americas; in Cuba the main negative impact was in the area of public education and health.

The suppression of the Society of Jesus

Images, top to bottom:

View of the **Old Plaza of Havana** under British occupation, a painting by Dominic Serres;

a 1767 engraving showing the **expulsion of the Jesuits** from the Portuguese Empire, France, the Two Sicilies, Malta, Parma and all Spanish posessions, more for political reaasons rather than theological controversies. After the fall of Napoleon in 1815, with the political climate of Europe changed and more stable, and with the powerful monarchs who had called for the suppression of the Society no longer in power, Pope Pius VI I issued an order restoring the Society of Jesus in the Catholic countries of Europe.

From 1800 to 1895

The European reaction to the Monroe Doctrine in 1823

20
The Decade when Spain Lost its Empire

THE NAPOLEONIC INVASION of Spain was a traumatic event for the Spanish Empire. It demolished the economic, political and social weave of Spain. In the colonies, the Empire began to unravel as a weakened Spain's could not keep its hold over its possessions; this opening allowed many revolutionary idealists in Spanish America to declare independence from the peninsula.

After the execution of Louis XVI during the 1789 French Revolution, Austria, Sardinia, Naples, Prussia, Spain and Britain formed in 1793 a First Coalition that was defeated by the French, even in the midst of its own civil war. Two events contributed to the French victory: the revolution's *levée en masse* (total conscription) and the extraordinary campaigns in Italy and Austria by General Napoleon Bonaparte. A Second Coalition was formed in 1798 by Austria, England, Naples, the Ottoman Empire, Portugal, Russia, Sweden and Spain. It ended in defeat in spite of the internal divisions within the governing French Directory and France's lack of a suitable war chest. This time the event contributing to French victory was the return of Napoleon Bonaparte from Egypt and his *coup d'état* of *18 Brumaire* (November 9, 1799); he had reorganized the French military, defeated the Austrians at Marengo and forced the British to sign the *Paix d'Amiens* (Peace de Amiens) on March 25, 1802.

Five years later, Napoleon engaged France in an additional military conflict: the Peninsular War (1807-1814), also called by Spaniards *la Guerra de la Independencia Española* (Spanish War of Independence). It started when French and Spanish armies occupied Portugal in 1807,[201] escalating in 1808 when France, with its army already in Spanish territory, turned on its ally Spain. The war began on May 2, 1808 and ended on April 17, 1814. It took a Sixth Coalition (Austria, Prussia, Russia, Britain, Portugal, Sweden, Spain and several German States) to defeat Napoleon in 1814. A large contributor to this defeat was the burden that Spanish guerrillas imposed inside Spain on France's *Grande Armée*, harassing it, interrupting its communications and hounding it into isolation.[202] The war destroyed the Spanish government and administration. Before the end of the war, the Spanish Constitution of 1812 had been established on 19 March 1812 by the *Cádiz Cortes* (Spain's first national sovereign assembly, the *Cortes Generales* or General Courts), which were in a secured location in Cádiz during the Peninsular War.[203] The Spanish Constitution of 1812 established the principles of universal male suffrage, national sovereignty, constitutional monarchy and freedom of the press, and supported land reform and free enterprise. This constitution, one of the most liberal of its time, was the first ever being close to going into effect in Spain. It was never recognized in the American territories resulting in a power vacuum that lead to the independence of most colonial territories, with the exception of Cuba and Puerto

---

[201] On 27 October 1807, Spain's prime minister Manuel de Godoy, on behalf of King Carlos IV of Spain, had signed the Treaty of Fontainebleau with France, agreeing that after Spain and France had defeated Portugal, it would be split into three kingdoms; the new Kingdom of Northern Lusitania, the Algarve and a rump Kingdom of Portugal. France, in payment for Spain's cooperation, would have received some of Portugal's territories. Napoleon had decided to attack Portugal because it ignored his mandate to stop commerce with Britain.

[202] Napoleon used to call the pestering of the Spanish partisans — repeatedly beaten but never overwhelmed— the Spanish Ulcers. Napoleon had warned earlier in his career that the conquest of Spain would be «too hard a nut to crack.»

[203] The Cortes drafted and adopted the Constitution while in the middle of an outbreak of yellow fever surrounded by 70,000 French troops in southern Spain, first on *Isla de León* (now *San Fernando*), an island adjacent to the bay of Cádiz, on the Atlantic coast, and then on a small, strategically located building within the city of Cádiz itself.

Rico. On March 24, 1814, Ferdinand VII returned from exile in France and abolished the constitution a month later. He had originally promised to uphold it; in numerous towns across Spain he was welcomed by crowds asking him to reign as an absolute monarch. To please them he ordered to torn down all monuments celebrating *La Pepa*. [204] Crowds all across Spain began to smash the markers that had renamed many central plazas as *Plaza de la Constitución*.

The 1812 Constitution was an attempt to govern a far-flung composite Empire, from the Atlantic to the Pacific. According to many scholars it was decidedly a premature experiment in representative government for the American territories. Most of Spain's colonial possessions were represented in the Cadiz Cortes that promulgated the 1812 Constitution: the Viceroyalties of Mexico (7 deputies) and Perú (5), the territories of Central America (2), Cuba (2),[205] Puerto Rico (1), Chile (2), Argentina (3), Venezuela and Colombia (3) and the Philippines (2). [206] The total number of representatives was 303, of which a minority were born abroad. Most of the colonial representatives were *Criollos*, i.e., colonial-born. The representatives from peninsular Spain decided to limit their weight by opposing equal rights for them, particularly since there were so many mixed-race people and slaves. At the time, the population of continental Spain was between 10 and 11 million, while the colonial areas had a population of 15 to 16 million. The Cortes ultimately approved a distinction between nationality (all Spaniards, regardless of birthplace) and citizenship (those nationals with the

---

[204] Since it had been adopted on Saint Josephs day (March 19) Spaniards baptized the 1812 Constitution *La Pepa*. The rallying cry of Spain's constitutionalists became *¡Qué Viva La Pepa!*, an expression of joyful indifference that became popular in Cuba.

[205] The two deputies from Cuba to the Cadiz Courts were Andrés de Jáuregui as the delegate from Havana and Juan Bernardo O'Gaban for the Captaincy of Santiago de Cuba

[206] The Philippines and Cuba did not achieve independence from Spain until the end of the XIX century; in Argentina the 1812 Constitution was never implemented.

right to vote). Without doubt, the short-lived 1812 Constitution had redefined Spanishness. Spain, however, missed the opportunity to make citizens of all native American peoples and failed to offer citizen status to free Black men and women of "virtue and merit," according to José Antonio Saco.[207] No one in the Cortes of Cadiz suspected that one of the strong weapons of the independence movements across the Americas was to cultivate the support of natives and Blacks in the wars against Spain.[208]

On April 11, 1814, Napoleon Bonaparte relinquished its position in France and accepted to be imprisoned in the island of Elba on the western Mediterranean sea. On July 21, the Inquisition was restored in Spain. Havana began to receive thousands of troops from Spain, ready to fight Simón Bolívar in Venezuela and Colombia. At that point in time José de la Luz y Caballero was 14 years old; Gaspar Betancourt Cisneros and José María Heredia were 11; Domingo del Monte, born in Maracaibo, Venezuela, had just turned 10 years old; Gabriel de la Concepción Valdés (Plácido) and Francisco Frías y Jacott, Conde de Pozos Dulces, turned 5; José Luis Alfonso, Marqués de Montelo, celebrated his 4th birthday, while writers Ramón de la Palma and Antonio Bachiller y Morales became 2 in Havana and Cirilo Villaverde 2 years old in Pinar del Rio.

The first decade of the XIX century was also witness to important events:

In 1800, France received *La Louisiana* from Spain after the secret San Ildefonso Treaty of October 1st.

Cuba received before the end of 1800 the first visit of Prussian geographer, naturalist and explorer Alexander von Hum-

---

[207] José Antonio Saco, leader of Cuban exiles during his entire life, would be chosen to represent Cuba in the Spanish Cortes in 1835. He published in 1870 a multivolume history of slavery in the Caribbean.

[208] In 1810, according to a census ordered by Francisco de Arango y Parreño, member of the *Junta de Instrucción de Cuba*, the population of the island was 600,000 residents, 326 Blacks and mixed-race and 274,000 whites.

boldt (1769-1859), the man who first described Cuba from a modern scientific viewpoint. He was a close friend and colleague of the brightest scientific minds of the times, including the eminent chemists Joseph Louis Gay-Lussac and Justus von Liebig. Humboldt returned to Cuba in 1806.

Bishop Juan José Díaz de Espada y Fernández de Landa, was appointed Bishop of Havana in 1800. Four years later, he started the construction of a *Campo Santo* (cemetery) outside the city walls, near the coast, about a mile west of Havana, at the place later confined by San Lázaro, Vapor, Espada and Aramburo streets. [209]

In 1801 Toussaint L'Ouverture took control of Haiti and claimed the eastern part of Hispaniola from Spain. Three years later Jean Jacques Dessalines proclaimed the independence of Haiti, causing a large migration of Spaniards from Hispaniola to Cuba.

In 1804 Thomas Jefferson threatened to take Cuba by force if Spain did not grant title to eastern Florida to the US. Spain complied and a large number of Spaniards emigrated from Florida to Cuba.

The Spaniards in Cuba lamented the October 21, 1805 defeat of the Spanish armada in the Battle of Trafalgar, were some 33 of the best and largest warships of Spain and France were sunk. A dozen of Cuban-born Spanish marines were taken prisoner or died in Trafalgar, off the south west coast of Spain. England suffered the death of its brightest and best Admiral, Lord Nelson, aboard HMS Victory. The loss of so many large Spanish ships affected the commerce between Spain and Cuba

In 1807 the US congress passed a law limiting foreign commerce; the prices of sugar and coffee from Cuba plummeted.

In a surprising move, Carlos IV relinquished the throne of Spain on March 19, 1808. He had succeeded Carlos III after his

---

[209] The Espada Cemetery, as people called it, was adequate for Havana's needs until a cholera epidemic in 1868. It was then decided to build a new cemetery that was inaugurated in 1871, the Colón Cemetery.

death. He liked to hunt more than he liked to govern and was very distressed after the popular revolt at the winter palace in Aranjuez, a facility built by Felipe II in 1560 at the Tajo River, 42 km south of Madrid. The throne of Spain was occupied after June 6, 1808 by José Bonaparte, brother of Napoleón.

In Cuba, Salvador José de Muro y Salazar, *Segundo Marqués de Someruelos*, governor of the island from 1799 to 1812, reaffirmed his loyalty to the deposed Fernando VII and not to the Bonapartes. As 150,000 French soldiers invaded Spain, Someruelos sent into exile to New Orleans over 15,000 French residents in Cuba. The British took the side of Spain against José Bonaparte's troops and were defeated and thrown from Spain after a battle in *La Coruña*.

In 1809 an envoy from US president Jefferson met in Havana with Someruelos offering to incorporate Cuba to the American republic. Someruelos refused and sought support from the *Virreinato de Nueva España* (Viceroyalty of New Spain).[210] Both France and England let the US know that they would oppose the annexation of Cuba.

A rare and unprecedented uprising occurred in Cuba in 1809: Román de la Cruz, Luis Basave and Joaquín Infante, all residents of Bayamo, appealed to Cuban residents to rise against Spain. It was the first pro-independence conspiracy in Cuban history. Three years later, already in exile in Caracas, they published a pamphlet with the title "*Proyecto de Constitución para la Isla de Cuba.*"

Closing the first decade of the XIX century, in 1810 Pierre Toussaint Frédéric Miahle (1810-1868) was born in Bordeaux, France. He would travel and live in Cuba from 1838 to 1854. He is best remembered for his exquisite portraits of life in Cuba published in *Album Pintoresco de la Isla de Cuba* in 1855. He excelled as painter, engraver, printer, scientist, professor of draw-

---

[210] The Viceroyalty of New Spain included present day Mexico, Central America except Panamá, Florida and most of the US west of the Mississippi and south of Canada.

ing at the Literary and Artistic Lyceum, and director of San Alejandro Art Academy in Havana. During his long stay on the island, he earned consideration and appreciation from the highest figures of the Cuban intelligentsia. Felipe Poey, a former tour mate on many of his visits to places along the island, recalled: «Mialhe always had with him a blank drawing book and pencil. He mostly worked alone.»

Images, top to bottom, left to right:

Napoleon Bonaparte (1769-1821), the French consul, general, emperor and dictator that rose to prominence in France after the 1789 revolution;

José Bonaparte (1768-1844), brother of Napoleon, briefly king of Sicily, Naples and Spain;

Manuel de Godoy (1767-1851), *Prince of the Peace*, despite many disasters, he used corruption to maintain power. He was probably responsible for the disastrous war against England that cut off Spain's Empire and ruined its finances;

Charles IV of Spain, *el cazador* (the hunter, 1748-1819), second son of Carlos III. He abdicated on behalf of his son after *the Revuelta de Aranjuez*;

Fernando VII of Spain, *el Deseado*, (1784-1833), the eldest surviving son of Charles IV. Rumor was he was the son of Manuel de Godoy.

Since the arrival of the Spanish in Cuba, the usual funerary practice was to bury the important dead inside churches. The general population was content to be buried around church buildings, but the rich insisted to be buried inside. This religious practice, which was also the norm in Europe, was extremely harmful; the parishioners were not only exposed to the fetid stench of corpses inside the churches, but also the practice of church burials were a significant cause of expanding epidemics. It was not until 1798 that King Carlos IV signed a Royal Decree establishing the obligation to open cemeteries away from the towns.

Havana had its first cemetery in 1806. A few years earlier (1802) the new Bishop Juan José Díaz de Espada y Landa had come to Cuba. He was a restless spirit who was comfortable in the circles of the Spanish Enlightenment. Bishop Espada suffered an attack of yellow fever soon after he arrived on the island. Under care by doctor Don Tomás Romay he survived the fever. This event encouraged him to worry about the health of the island. He dried swamps and marshes, supported the dissemination of an innovative method of vaccinations and sponsored the construction of cemeteries outside churches. The cemetery of Havana, bearing his name, was founded in 1878 and served the capital until it was demolished in 1901. The architect in charge of the work was a French architect, Etienne Sulpice Hallet.

The chapel of the Espada Cemetery mimicked an Etruscan temple. It was painted pale yellow with black stripes to simulate marble, in a Baroque and Neoclassical style until then unknown in Havana. The entrance had almost classical pilasters and a square door. By design of Bishop Espada, the door was between two rectangular panels representing Religion and Medicine. Above the door was a bronze relief with allegories of Time and Eternity. The only remains today are a wall fragment in the corner formed by Vapor and Hospital streets.

The Espada Cemetry in Havana

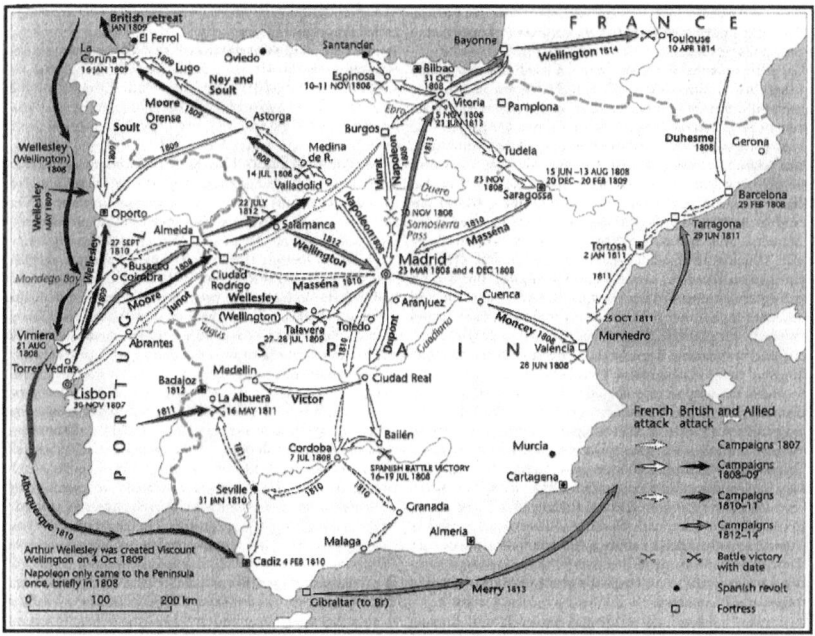

Images, top to bottom, left to right:

François Dominique Toussaint L'Overture (1743-1803), leader of the Haitian revolution, died in jail in France, leaving Jean Jacques Dessalines to complete the Haitian rebellion;

a view of the **Black rebellion in Haiti**;

a **map of Spain** showing the action durting the Peninsular War (1807-1814), also called by Spaniards *la Guerra de Independencia Española*.

Images, top to bottom, left to right:

The front page of the **1812 Constitution** published in Spain by the Cortes Generales on March 19, 1812;

graffiti on behalf of the constitution;

a group of **Black slaves**, proclaimed by the constitution to be nationals but not citizens of Spain (no right to vote);

Alexander Humboldt (1769-1859), younger brother of a Prussian minister, geographer, naturalist and explorer, the man who *"rediscovered Cuba;"*

the **Humboldt book** on Cuba, written during his work in the island between 1801 and 1826, a study on the thoughts of landholders and colonial functionaries from Havana.

Images, top to bottom:

A page from the ***Illustrated London News*** showing the location in the city and the inside of the *Spanish Cortes* in the 1800s.

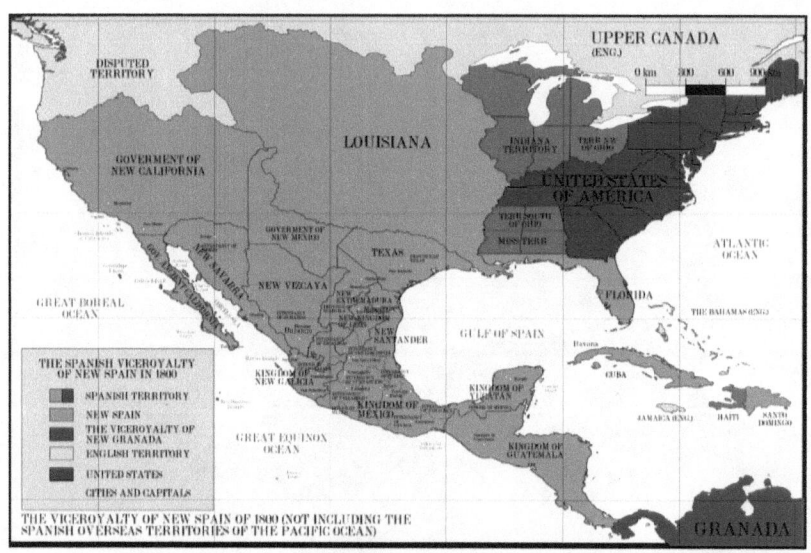

Images, top to bottom:

A map showing the extent of the **Viceroyalty of New Spain** (Mexico +) in the 1800s;

the extent of the territory (828,000 square miles) comprised in **the Louisiana purchase** of 1803;

the front cover of **Album Pintoresco de la Isla de Cuba** by Frédéric Miahle (1810-1868).

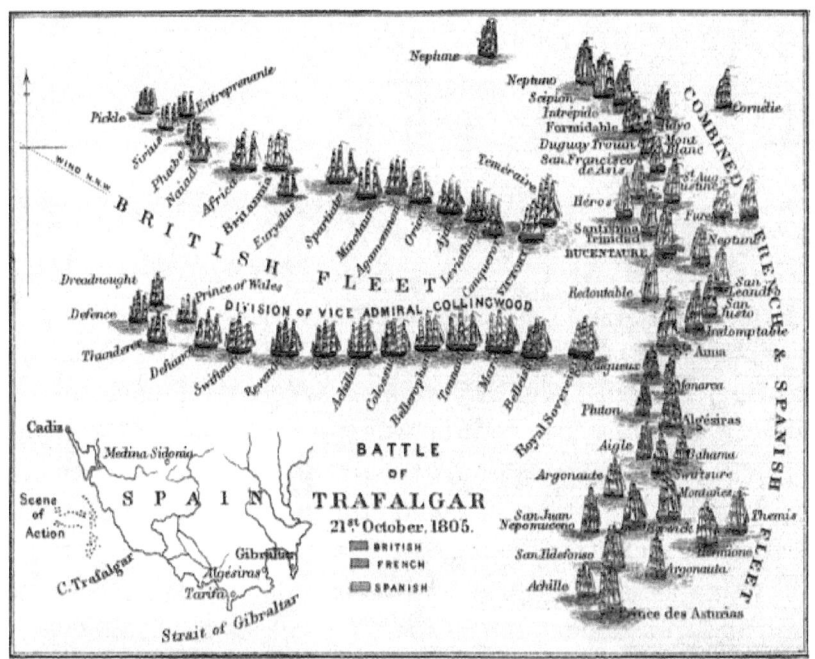

Images, top to bottom, left to right:

The positions of the British, French and Spanish naval forces at the start of the **Battle of Trafalgar** in 1805;

José María Heredia, a portrait;

a **1939 Cuban postage stamp** honoring José María Heredia;

Salvador de Muro y Salazar (1754-1813), Marqués de Someruelos, Captain General and Governor of Cuba from 1799 to 1812.

21

A Constitution Enlivened Things in Cuba

GIVEN THE SITUATION in Spain after the Napoleonic invasion, it is not difficult to understand why most of the American colonies became independent in the first years of the XIX century. The only large city in Spain where the French troops were not in absolute control was Sevilla. Most of the loyal Spanish army was quartered in the city.[211] A *Junta* had been organized there with hopes to coordinate the fight against the invading French troops. In Cuba, Someruelos was not only improvising policy but was also coordinating the defense of Jaruco, Bahía Honda, Canasí and other coastal towns that were under attack from the British.

In the midst of this chaos, Someruelos received in Havana an unexpected visit by Don Juan Aguilar Amat, the crown's appointed intendant for Cuba.[212] Aguilar brought Someruelos up-to-date about the situation in the peninsula and brought him letters, orders and newspapers. It helped the Cuban *Capitán General* to align his strategies in harmony with the emergency policies of the captive Spanish government. As people found out the happenings in Spain from the mouth of other passengers in Aguilar's ship, the gardens, hallways and meeting rooms of the *Palacio de los Capitanes Generales* filled up with concerned citizens. Someruelos, with the acquiescence of obispo Espada, general Villavicencio and brigadier Don Fran-

---

[211] Spain's loyal army had assembled 50,000 troops in Sevilla. Over 200,000 French soldiers had occupied Madrid and Barcelona while 250,000 were in smaller regional capitals and in Lisbon.

[212] The title of intendant (Spanish *intendente*) was used by Spain and other colonial countries through history. Traditionally, it refers to the holder of a public administrative office that cared for the crown's resources, an individual in a managerial position, generally having control over all financial aspects of the government.

cisco Montalvo, the highest military authorities in Cuba, proclaimed the loyalty of the island to Fernando VII and declared war against France. The news was sent to Veracruz, Cartagena, San Agustín and towns in Central America, with a plea to do likewise. What other regions in colonial America saw as an opportunity to free themselves from the Spanish burden, in Cuba became a show of patriotism and an opportunity to acclaim and extol the virtues of the new King. Printed materials from the Sevilla Junta began to be widely distributed. There was never any movement to replace or challenge the authority of Someruelos as the leader of loyalty to Spain; in fact, a certain extra limitation of his powers was tolerated.

Havana, nevertheless, was isolated and no Spanish or even North American ships arrived for months at a time; the British navy had a solid blockade of the Cuban coasts. Groups of people concentrated daily at the *Plaza de Armas*, the docks and the governor's residence, but Someruelos had nothing new to inform. [213] It got to the point that people stopped figuring out what was happening in the peninsula. Many had a feeling that Cuba would become a French colony. Finally, on September 27, 1808, the *San Justo*, a ship of the Spanish navy, arrived with the news that the French army had been defeated in Andalucía by Don Francisco Javier Castaños, half brother of former Cuban governor Don Luis de las Casas. The elation and joy in the streets of Havana had no parallel, even if some public administrators had shown a wavering and erratic support for Spanish sovereignty. In the harbor of Havana, several *Salvos de Artillería* (artillery outbursts) were fired every hour for an entire day.

---

[213] From the day he found out there was a Junta in Seville, Someruelos contributed a fair portion of his salary to support Spanish loyal troops in the war in the peninsula. He had resisted the exhortations of general Marie-Louis Ferrand, governor of Santo Domingo who, when he learned that Carlos IV had abdicated in Bayona, pleaded with him to support José Bonaparte. Ferrand, believing that the French would recover Santo Domingo, had sent troops to combat militias loyal to Spain in Dominican territory. In personal command of a 1,500 men he was defeated at *Palo Hincado* by these militia troops fighting under Don Juan Sánchez Ramírez, an hacendado from Santiago de los Caballeros. Humilliated, Ferrand committed suicide before entering the capital as a prisoner.

The French army eventually crossed the Ebro River after its defeat in Bailén; the Portuguese began to fight the French within its borders; by the end of August, Fernando VII entered Madrid and the Cortes began to meet regularly. At the Aranjuez Palace, the *Junta de las Indias* met for the first time in months on September 25th. The only thing the French left behind was *La Pepa*, the constitution that King José Bonaparte had proclaimed in Bayona, following orders from his brother Napoleon.

As the uncertainty of the ties with Spain grew larger, some *criollos* began to look at the US for a permanent alliance. It was the first symptoms of what would become a powerful annexionist movement. They flourished side by side with a separatist, pro-independence movement that was taking hold in the masonic lodges. On December 17, 1804, the Grand Lodge of Pennsylvania opened in Havana a branch, the *Templo de las Virtudes Teologales*. Six other lodges opened acoss the island.[214] In 1812 the first anti-slavery conspiracy, led by a free Black former slave, José Antonio Aponte, openly defied Someruelos' authority. Criollos and Spaniards in Cuba panicked, feeling that a repetition of the Haiti experience was about to happen. It was a main obstacle in the plans of the independentistas.

José Antonio Aponte, aka *Aponte el Negro,* was a Cuban activist, military officer and carpenter, leader of a local *Yoruba* association. In February of 1812 he lead an uprising by Afro Cubans; he was aprehended, tortured and hanged on April 9, 1812, his head placed inside an iron cage and displayed around Havana. He had been a member of the Francisco de Miranda troops that fought in the US war of independence. He took arms in Guanabo, at the Ingenio Peñas Altas, on March 15, 1812.[215]

---

[214] Any assembly of Freemasons was forbiden by Spanish law under the penalty of deportation. Its members had to practice their rites in secret, yet some of the Captains General of Cuba were masons and from time to time the craft was tolerated.

[215] Historian Elías Entralgo Vallina in his book *La Liberación Etica Cubana*, called Aponte «*el Espartaco Cubano*,» for his anti-slavery ideals. His organization reached Blacks, Mestizos and Whites in «*San Antonio de los Baños,*

On April 14, 1812, a Basque naval officer, Juan Ruiz de Apodaca (1754-1835), first Conde de Venadito, was appointed new governor of Cuba. He was a man of tact and good judgment. After leaving Cuba in 1815 he was appointed Viceroy of New Spain (Mexico) during a moment of great turbulence in the Mexican War of Independence. In Cuba, he implemented the 1812 Constitution and contested Bonaparte's order prohibiting the export of Cuban sugar to Europe. It coincided with the first trip to Paris of the Countess of Merlin (1789-1852, later married to General Cristobal Antonio, a Bonaparte supporter). [216] She left for Paris in 1812, where she lived until her death in 1852.

Other events in the second decade of the XIX century were:

In 1812 Félix Varela began to publish his *Instituciones de Filosofía Ecléctica para Uso de la Juventud*, an important metaphysical treatise. José Agustín Caballero had been the first Cuban writing against scholasticism but Varela was the first to teach true philosophy at the *Seminario San Carlos*.

In 1814, governor Apodaca imposed press censure in Cuba as soon as he learned that the 1812 Constitution had been abrogated by Fernando VII.

In 1815 the Jesuits returned to all Spanish territories. By then the old political order of Europe had been restored at the Congress of Vienna after years of revolution; the Church had been

---

Alquízar, Güira de Melena, el barrio de la Salud y el de Jesús María, la Plaza de Santo Cristo, la Punta, la Plaza de Armas, la Alameda de Paula y el muelle de Luz, atravesando la bahía y continuando su trayectoria con más vigor por Casablanca, Guanabacoa y sus barrios rurales, Bacuranao, Guanabo, Jaruco, Río Blanco del Norte y Aguacate, alcanzando fuera de la Habana las poblaciones de Holguín, Bayamo, Santiago de Cuba y Baracoa.»

[216] María de las Mercedes Beltrán de Santa Cruz y Montalvo, Countess of Merlin, held a well-attended literary salon in Paris, offering recitals, benefit galas and grand balls. Her apartments on the *Rue de Bondy* became a customary meeting place for Balzac, George Sand, Alfred de Musset, Strauss, Rossini and other literati. Her husband died in 1839. The following year she returned to Cuba to claim her inheritance. She was a close friend of Gertrudis Gómez de Avellaneda. At the time of her visit, residents of Cuba were in perpetual fear of a Black slave rebellion.

persecuted as an agent of the old order and abused under the rule of Napoleon. With the authoritative monarchs who had called for the suppression of the Society no longer in power, Pope Pius VII issued an order restoring the Society of Jesus in the Catholic countries of Europe.

Also in 1815, a new *Intendente de Hacienda* arrived in Cuba: Alejandro Ramirez (1777-1821). As a *Supervisor de las Finanzas de la Corona*, a position he had held in Puerto Rico, he eliminated the *Estanco del Tabaco* (monopoly) and established in 1818 the right of Cuban merchants to trade with everyone. He was the founder of the *Escuela Gratuita de Dibujo y Pintura de la Habana*, later, in 1832, called San Alejandro in his honor.

For a brief period (100 days) Napoleon Bonaparte returned to power in France. He was defeated on June 18, 1815 at Waterloo and sent for the rest of his life into exile at Saint Helena. 1815 was also the year when Juan Bautista Vermay arrived in Havana. He became director of San Alejandro Art School in 1818.

In 1816 José Cienfuegos Jovellanos (1763-1825) was appointed governor of Cuba. Fernandina de Jagua, in the southern coast of Cuba, would be later named Cienfuegos in his memory. Cienfuegos' main mission was to review and updsate the defenses of the island, particularly Havana's and to protect Florida from the expansionary wishes of the US. He formed a disciplined and no-nonsense team with Intendente Alejandro Ramírez.

After Napoleon's downfall, in 1816, the Congress of Vienna [217] (September 1814-June 1815) rejected a motion to abolish the slave trade and decided the critical issue of prisoners of war during the French invasion of Spain. Talleyrand, the unsinkable French bureaucrat, proved to be an able negotiator for

---

[217] The Congress of Vienna was the first time in history that representatives from several nations came together to formulate treaties. Prior to Vienna all countries relied mostly on messengers and messages between capitals instead of face-to-face meetings.

12,000 *afrancesados* that had sworn fealty to Joseph Bonaparte. Cuban supporters of defeated France were never touched.

Also in 1816, José Silverio Jorrín (1816-1897) was born in Havana. Originally a reformista and a member of the *Partido Liberal Autonomista*, he authored in 1896 *Cuba y los Cubanos*, a solid endorsement for Cuban independence. He was called the champion of public instruction in Cuba. He died in exile in New York in 1897.

Cuba, with a population of 650,000 residents, counted in 1816 with 190 schools where less than 7,000 students attended clases. Of these, about 300 were descendant of Black slaves.

A 1817 census revealed that only 45% of the population were white and Cuba was running the risk of repeating the Haiti experience. To prevent this, the Spanish crown offered white peninsulars a *caballería* [218] of land, two cows, one horse and a mule, as well as 15 years of tax exception, to anyone willing to move to Cuba. A large immigration of families from the Canary Islands turned the demographic balance in favor of Whites.

Two tecnical improvements that would affect the economy of Cuba took place in 1817: Francisco de Arango y Parreño, a representative of the island in the Spanish Cortes, founder of the *Sociedad Económica de Amigos del País* and member of Spain's *Supremo Consejo de Indias*, introduced steam engines in the sugar *trapiches* in Cuba. Alejandro Ramírez, intendente of Cuba, hired Ramón de la Sagra (1798-1871) as professor of Natural History at the University of Havana. He was a disciple of the world's leading anarchist thinker Pierre Joseph Proudhon and a close friend of Kar Marx and Friedrich Engels. The following year the chairs of Economy and Philosophy were inaugurated at the University, with Father Félix Varela occupying the later.

On February 22, 1818, Spain sold Florida to the US for a net price of US$ 5 million. Over 3,000 Cuban-born floridians re-

---

[218] A Cuban *caballería* of land is equivalent to 33.16 acres.

turned to the island, many of them with new skills they had learned in agriculture, cane cultivation, tobacco and cattle raising.

As a direct result of the flourishing sugar industry a merchant vessel began to make regular rounds between Matanzas and Havana in 1819. The year was witness to the birth in Bayamo of Carlos Manuel de Céspedes, future leader of the 1868 war of independence. The following year, Miguel Teurbe-Tolón was born in Matanzas.

In 1820 Cuba ignored the proclamation of the 1812 Constitution, even after Fernando VII had been forced to accept it on March 7. A batallion from the *La Fuerza* castle asserted and swore its loyalty to the constitution and surrounded the see of government to force governor Juan Manuel de Cajigal y Niño (1754-1823) to accept it. Enthused about the freedoms granted by the constitution, the *Seminario de San Carlos y San Ambrosio* created a chair for constitutional studies and appointed Father Félix Varela as its first incumbent.

An old engraving of the **Seminario de San Carlos y San Ambrosio** in Havana. It was made possible with rents from properties confiscated to the Jesuits.

On November 16, 1771, the *Cabildos Eclesiástico y Secular* approved the creation of a ***Colegio Grande*** (modelled after the *Colegio de Monserrat* in Cordoba) to educate noblemen as well as indians.

The **Real Colegio de San Carlos** (named in homage to Carlos III of Spain) was inaugurated on February 10, 1772. On the 28th, it began to teach courses in Latin, Philosophy and Arts.

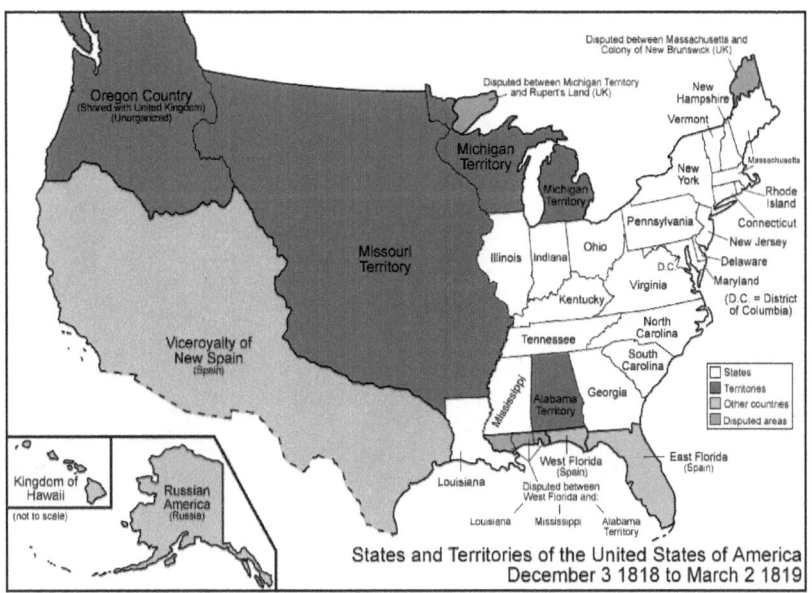

Images, top to bottom:

The territories and States of **North America** in 1818, important because of its evergrowing trade and commerce with Cuba;

the **Surrender at Bailén**, a village by the Guadalquivir river in Jaén, Spain. The Spanish army (on the left), led by Francisco Castaños, had a decisive victory over the French *Grande Armée*, led by Pierre Dupont, who was taken prisoner along with the bulk of his troops. It infuriated Napoleon and proved his army was not invincible. Painting by José Casado at *El Prado*.

Images, top to bottom:

The ceremony of installing the **Cortes de Cádiz** on September 24, 1810. It was the first national assembly ever to claim sovereignty in Spain;

the **Palacio Real de Aranjuez**, near Madrid, bult by Felipe II. In 1808 Spaniards were hungry and frustrated by the French invasion and they revolted in Aranjuez. The royal family, with Manuel Godoy, Spain's strong man, took refuge in the *Palacio de Aranjuez*.

Images, top to bottom, left to right:

Intendent (Supervisor of Crown Finances) **Alejandro Ramírez**, who broke Spain's tobacco monopoly in Cuba, opened the island to world commerce, was a leader of the *Sociedad Patriótica* and founded *San Alejandro Art School*;

Minutes of the Congress of Vienna (1814), where the Holy Roman Empire was dissolved and a new map of Europe was established;

Charles Maurice de Talleyrand Périgord, Napoleon's advisor who deceived and betrayed him with flattery, courtesy and an appalling straight face;

Juan José Ruiz de Apodaca, Captain General of Cuba during 1812 to 1815, the years when Spain lost its Colonial Empire.

Images, top to bottom, left to right:

José Cienfuegos y Jovellanos, General during the Spanish War of Independence (1808-1814), governor of Cuba during 1816 to 1819, close colaborator of Intendent Alejandro Ramírez. He was honored by giving his name to today's city of *Cienfuegos*;

Ramón Dionisio José de la Sagra, eminent botanist, writer, sociologist, economist and political anarchist. Born in Galicia, Spain, went to Cuba in 1821 where he was advisor to governors and professor of Natural History;

José Antonio Aponte, a Cuban-born political activist who organized the first large scale conspiracy. He was leader of the *Yorubas* in the island in the 1810s;

José Silverio Jorrín, in the 1810s was the leader of public education in the island and an advocate of scientific agriculture.

Images, top to bottom, left to right:

Pope Pius VII reinstating the *Society of Jesus* in 1814. The Jesuits had been suppressed in 1767 by the papal brief *Dominus ac Redemptor*. After the fall of Napoleon in 1814 (who persecuted the Church as an agent of the old order), they were restored when their powerful monarchical enemies were no longer in power;

an early engraving of the **Palace of the Captain Generals** in Havana, built in 1773 by the *Marqués de la Torre*. The Parroquial Mayor church had to be demolished and the *Plaza de Armas* redesigned in order to open space for the Palacio.

Images, top to bottom, left to right:

Barnaba Niccolò Maria Luigi Chiaramonti, **Pope Pius VII** (1741-1823), head of the Catholic Church from 1800 until his death. He was in permanent conflict wit Napoleon (who exiled him) after snubbing Napoleon's marriage to Princes Marie Louise;

General **Francisco Gabriel Castaños**, Duke of Bailén, the first Spanish General that defeated the *French Grande Armée*;

an early picture of the masonic **Templo de las Virturdes Teologales**, founded in 1804, supporter of the rebellion by José Antonio Aponte;

a US postage stamp conmemorating the **Louisiana Purchase**.

French painter Jean Baptiste Vermay (1784-1833) was born in Tournan-en-Brie, near Paris. Very young, 11 years old, he was enrolled by his parents in the painting school of Jacques-Louis David in Paris. As a teacher of Hortense de Beauharnais, stepdaughter of Emperor Napoleon, he was exempted from military service to devote himself entirely to art. He won a gold medal for his painting *The Death of Mary Stuart* at the Exhibition of Painting in Paris, competing with his teacher David. The final defeat of his protector Napoleon at Waterloo, however, radically changed his life. He traveled to Germany and Italy, visited North America and from there went to the island of Cuba, where he arrived with his expertise in architecture and decoration, half a dozen of his paintings, a Masonic endorsement, a commission to paint a portrait of an aristocratic lady and a letter of recommendation from the great painter Goya.

In Cuba he met Bishop Juan José Díaz de Espada y Landa, who bought some of the oils he had painted in Havana and placed them in several churches. Among these were the chapel of *Cementerio Espada*, the *Espíritu Santo* Church and the Cathedral of Havana, where Vermay painted three frescos: *La Ultima Cena*, *La Ascension* and *Las Llaves de la Ciudad*. Bishop Espada also commissioned him to finish the paintings started by the Italian artist Giuseppe Perovani (1765-1835), in the Cathedral of Havana. Perovanii had died of cholera on a brief trip to Mexico. Vermay taught several classes in the education section of the *Sociedad Económica de Amigos del País*. He founded the *Academy de Dibujo y Pintura de la Habana*, later called the *Escuela de Artes San Alejandro* in honor of Alejandro Ramírez, Quartermaster General of the Army and Intendant of the Royal Treasury, to whom the Academy owed its foundation and progress.

More importantly, Vermay was the author of three paintings inside the *Templete*; the neoclassical building built in 1828 to mark the spot where, under the shade of a leafy *Ceiba* tree, the first mass and the first meeting of the council of Havana were held in 1519.

Two Vermay paintings inside the *Templete* in Havana

22
Peaceful Normality Briefly Returned to Cuba

ON AUGUST 29, 1819, general Don Juan Manuel de Cagigal (1754-1823) replaced Don José Cienfuegos as Captain General of the island of Cuba. Don Francisco Dionisio Vives had arrived in Havana on July 2, 1816, the day the Spanish warship *Atocha* burned to ashes in Havana harbor. Don Alejandro Ramírez, new Intendant for the island, also landed in Cuba that day, having received a promotion as intendant of the island of Puerto Rico. Cienfuegos was responsible for four of the most propitious measures to assure prosperity in Cuba. They became high stakes for Cagigal to follow.

1) A treaty was signed with England to do away with slavery and slave markets; it moved sugar owners in Cuba to adopt modern technologies to compensate for the coming scarcity of slave labor.
2) On June 23, 1817, Cienfuegos decreed the end of Spain's tobacco monopoly, opening the doors to wide world sales of Cuban tobacco products.
3) On February 10, 1818, Cienfuegos legalized Cuban commerce with any country in America and Europe. Within a year it produced a 400% increase in exports from the island.
4) The Cienfuegos administration ended three centuries of contraband and complicity with pirates and corsaries along the coasts of Cuba. A fleet of armed coastguard vessels and watchtowers in Jaruco, Mariel, Cabañas and Bahía Honda, manned by retired navy officers, aggressively stopped wrongdoers from doing business in the island.

Cagigal assumed the governorship of Cuba at very critical times. He was 65 years old and frail, and could not impede the implantation of the 1812 Constitution in Cuba. At the insistence of many liberals in Havana, [219] he decided to swear loyalty to the document in order to avoid a serious conflict. Two months later, on June 12, he renounced his position and temporarily left the governorship to Don Juan Hecheverry, his *Segundo Cabo*. On March 3, 1821 general Don Nicolás de Mahy arrived in Havana as the new governor of Cuba and Cagigal retired to Guanabacoa, where he died in his colonial mansion.

The first order of business for Mahy was to define the conditions about transfer of ownership of Florida to the US and end the speculations about annexation of Cuba to the US territory. Mahy resolved both issues by speeding the delivery of Florida to the US and closing any conjectures that Spain would ever sell the island to the North Americans.[220]

Unexpectedly Mahy contracted yellow fever and died on July 19, 1822, leaving the Segundo Cabo as interim governor of the island. His first decision was to send troops to Bahía Honda, where corsairs from Mexico and Venezuela had taken over and sacked the town.

Don Sebastian de Kindelán, Cuba's Segundo Cabo, immediately faced difficulties of his own; as several political parties presented candidates for the election of deputies to the Spanish Courts, he had to disqualify a slate of candidates campaigning for the independence of Cuba. Loyalists and separatists, for the first time, battled each other on the streets of Havana, and only Kindelán's skillful diplomacy averted a tragic end; luckily for him, in May of 1823, field marshal Don Francisco Dionisio Vives arrived in Havana as the new governor of the island.

Vives began his term with an in depth look into the political groups in Havana; he unearthed a clandestine society promot-

---

[219] As well as the April 16, 1820 invasion of the Palacio de los Capitanes Generales by a batallion from *La Fuerza* castle in Havana.

[220] Mahy's staff had unearthed a report with evidence that agents from the US had bought from a functionary in Cuba several maps showing the fortresses that protected Havana. The payment to the traitor had been 150 ounces of gold.

ed by Venezuelan sympathizers, the *Rayos y Soles de Bolívar*.[221] His leader, José Francisco Lemus, was immediately detained and deported to Spain with a group of his followers. Once the news of the restoration of Fernando VII arrived in Havana, Vives swore allegiance to the Spanish crown, the political uncertainty vanished and the island returned to tranquility. [222]

The political, security and loyalty uncertainty persisted in Cuba almost until the 1880s. Mexican and Colombian corsairs continued to threaten and ambush Cuban coastal towns. A Colombian promoted pro-independence conspiracy in Puerto Príncipe in 1826 resulted in the capture and hanging on March 16 of its leaders Francisco Agüero (Frasquito, 1793-1826) and Manuel Andrés Sánchez (1805-1828), who had disembarked in Santa Cruz del Sur from the British ship *Maryland*.[223] On October of 1826 US Commodore David Porter gathered troops in Mexico and explored the southern coast of Cuba, presumably under orders of the US government «to aid local authorities in the suppression of piracy and for no other object.» On February of 1828 the Spanish warship *Lealtad* boarded the 22-cannon Mexican brigantine *Guerrero* in front of Havana, apparently intent on storming the city. In May of 1829, 3,500 Spanish soldiers sailed into Havana harbor on their way to attempt the second conquest of Mexico.[224] Months later, Mexico financed and promoted a new conspiracy to liberate Cuba under the name of *Aguila Negra*; several members were condemned to death; their

---

[221] One of the arguments of the leaders of *Rayos y Soles de Bolívar* was that Spain was preparing the sale of Cuba to the British. This absurd fantasy persisted in Cuba for years, well into the later part of the century.

[222] On August 23, 1824, however, Gaspar Antonio Rodríguez, an officer in the Spanish army, with 8 of his subordinates, took to the central plaza in the town of Matanzas, firing their weapons while extolling the Constitution. They found no followers and returned to their posts.

[223] Agüero and Sánchez were hung in the Plaza de Armas of Puerto Príncipe. Agüero was 33, Sánchez 21 years old.

[224] The expedition to Mexico, comanded by brigadier Isidro Barradas, failed miserably. Only 1,400 soldiers returned from Tampico, less than half those that departed.

sentences were commuted by governor Vives, acting magnanimously, once more seeking royal pardons for conspirators, invoking the name of Fernando VII's infant daughter, the future Queen Isabel II of Spain.[225]

Other important events in the third decade of the 1800s were:

Once the independence of Mexico became a reality on February 24, 1821, Cuba lost the *situados* (gold shipments) from Mexico to help the island's economy.

On March 26, 1821, in a decision under pressure by Cuban constitutionalists, Intendant Alejandro Ramírez and Francisco de Arango y Parreño, *Consejero de Estado* since 1820, ceased in their functions at the request of governor Don Nicolás de Mahy, who had assumed his functions 23 days earlier.[226]

On April 28 of that year, Pbro. Félix Varela, Tomás Gener Buigas (1787-1835), and Leonardo Santos Suárez y Pérez (1795-1860) were elected as Cuba's representatives to the Spanish Cortes; for the first time the *criollos* prevailed over the Spanish-born.[227]

In the decade of the 1820s, Rafael María de Mendive was born on October 24, 1821, the same day Francisco Vicente

---

[225] Vives was an extraordinary governor of Cuba. He tried to solve all problems politically, without violence. He reorganized Cuba's defenses and its troops; managed economic and geographical studies of the island; published the best census and demographic studies ever done in Cuba; opened Isla de Pinos to development; increased the budgets and brought about an era of prosperity and hope. His top aide and right hand since 1825 was Don Claudio Martínez de Pinillos y Ceballos (1782-1853), Count of Villanueva. He was the first leader of *reformismo* in Cuba (an increase of benefits and rights for Cubans without a break with Spain).

[226] Alejandro Ramírez would die on May 20 due to undefined high fevers. Arango y Parreño, considered in Spain as "*un español de ultramar*," (an overseas Spaniard) would return to Cuba as Superintendent of the Treasury in 1824.

[227] On June 11, 1823, Varela, Gener and Santos Suárez, the delegates to the Cortes from Cuba, voted in favor of dismissing King Fernando VII of Spain for incompetence. They were purged once the King was restored to his position; they had to escape to Gibraltar and seek refuge in the US as exiles.

Aguilera was born; Louis Pasteur was born on December 27, 1822 in Dole, eastern France; Esteban Chartrand was born in *Ingenio Limonar*, Matanzas; Nicolás Azcárate was born on July 21, 1828, Salvador Cisneros Betancourt in Puerto Príncipe and Juan Cristóbal Nápoles Fajardo (el Cucalambé) in Las Tunas;

John Quincy Adams, as Secretary of State of US president James Monroe, fearful of England's reaction, turned down a plan to purchase Cuba in September of 1822. Adams would be elected president of the US in 1825.

During the 1820s, with the Spanish New World in revolt, Simón Bolivar led independence movements in Venezuela and Colombia, and José de San Martín fought for independence in Argentina and Chile, both working together for the liberation of Ecuador. Britain, knowing that these new countries would be more likely than Spanish-dominated colonies to trade with them, acted out in economic self-interest and offered them its political support.

Tomás Gutiérrez de Piñeres, párroco de Jaruco, also known as the "Marat of the Constitutional era," became a best-seller author and polemicist in Cuba under the pseudonym *Liberato*.

The French crown, since 1814 under Louis XVIII, was convinced by Talleyrand to grant the people a Constitutional Chart. It upset the royalists (also known as *ultras*), who had offered Spain full support to recover their lost American colonies. In 1823 France pledged not to support Spain on any efforts to recover the colonies in America.

In Havana, several conspirators in "*Soles y Rayos de Bolívar*," led by José Francisco Lemus, were captured and sent to exile. José María Heredia escaped to the US where he obtained exile status.

President Monroe began to formulate the Monroe Doctrine, i.e., European powers must stay out of the Americas. It was proclaimed on December 2, 1823.

The *Templete* was inaugurated in Havana on March 19, 1825. The remains of Jean Baptiste Vermay were deposited there after his death. One of his last actions was to design the *Diorama* theater in Havana, later part of the Manzana de Gómez.

In May of 1825, a group of *criollos* led by José Agustín Arango and José Aniceto Iznaga (1791-1860) [228] asked Simón Bolívar to intervene in favor of the independence of Cuba. Bolívar brought the subject at the *Congreso de Panamá* in 1826 but whatever help was appropriate was postponed for a future date.

Claudio Martínez de Pinillos, Count of Villanueva and supporter of Fernando VII, was appointed Intendant in Cuba in 1825.

José Antonio Saco and Félix Varela began to publish the magazine *El Mensajero Semanal* in New York in 1828. It ceased publication in 1831. Also in 1828, Ramón de la Sagra began to publish *Anales de Ciencias, Agricultura y Artes* in Havana. The University of Havana opened its own printing shop and book publishing operation that year.

A royal decree abolished all expressions of *Masonería* in Cuba, meetings, organizations, publications, membership, in 1828.

From 1829 until early 1830 Cuban philosopher José Antonio Saco, eminent and combative social researcher and writer, and Don Ramón de la Sagra, director of the Botanical Garden of Havana and editor of the Annals of Science, Agriculture and Arts, engaged in one of the fiercest intellectual controversies that ever took place on Cuban territory. The Subject was Sagra's disparagement of José María Heredia's poetry, recently lauded on an article published in *El Mensajero Semanal*, Varela's weekly magazine in New York.

---

[228] José Aniceto Iznaga was born in Trinidad, Cuba. With Narciso López, Miguel Teurbe Tolón, Cirilo Villaverde and Juan Manuel Macías, he participated in the design of the Cuban flag: two white and, three blue stripes, a red triangle with a white star. In 1848, with Gaspar Betancourt Cisneros, he travelled to Washington for two meetings: the first with president James K. Polk on June 23, the second with Jefferson Davis the following day. Davis favored helping the cause of Cuban independence but president Polk — hoping to perhaps buy Cuba from Spain— remained uncommitted. Nothing ever came out of those meetings.

Madrid, in the early years of the XIX century was a city in the fringes of chaos. Fernando VII, after the reluctant abdication of his father Carlos IV, ingratiated himself with the Spanish nobility by adding "heroic" to all the titles that Madrid had granted since the Middle Ages; the Heroic Duchess of Alba, etc.

El Parque del Retiro began to be conditioned; new groves were planted; trenches were covered, ruins of the old hermitages and the *Buen Retiro* palace were demolished. An animal house was built for the exhibition of exotic and wild beasts. Large parts of the park were opened to the public; they could now enjoy a space exclusively reserved for the Royal family until then. The *Conservatorio Musical* was created, the Stock Exchange founded, a Turtle fountain was planned and the *Puerta del Sol* and its surrounding streets were illuminated. The *Plaza de Oriente* was to be refurbished, with the existing Royal Palace on one side and a new Royal Theater taking the place of the old *Caños del Peral* theater on the other side.

It was not to last long. At Aranjuez, south of Madrid, on the night of March 17, 1808, a huge crowd stormed and ransacked prime minister Godoy's home. Within a month the courts had left Madrid upon the arrival of the French army and the Royal family had moved to Sevilla. Spain belonged now to the French.

It was King José Bonaparte and not Fernando VII who continued the modernization of Madrid; he set the first stone on the *Puerta de Toledo*. Inside he placed a copy of the Bayonne Constitution he was granting Spain. That day Spain became a constitutional monarchy with a senate, state council, cortes, and a single tolerated religion...Catholicism.

When his time came to come back, Fernando discontinued all initiatives that José Bonaparte had started and returned confiscated convents and churches to dioceses and orders that were supporting his absolutism and intransigence. In 1820 he swore the 1812 Constitution in front of the court and the people cheered. He had the first stone of the *Puerta de Toledo* unearthed and a copy of the 1812 Constitution and some new coins replaced the Bayonne memento. By 1823 there were protest rallies in the streets of Madrid demanding an interim regency to replace Fernando VII. Chaos had finally arrived.

La Pepa, **the 1812 Spanish Constitution**

Images, top to bottom, left to right:

Juan Manuel Cagigal y Niño, the Captain General of Cuba who oversaw the restoration of the *1812 Constitution*;

Francisco Dionisio Vives, Captain General of Cuba when all the Spanish possessions had been lost. He preserved Cuba for Spain and was rewarded with the title *Count of Cuba*;

The *Iglesia Mayor* at the Plaza de Armas in Puerto Príncipe in 1813.

In 1819, Governor Don José Cienfuegos and Intendant Don Alejandro Ramirez approved the founding of a town at an abandoned Siboney enclave next to río Saladito in Las Villas. In 1829 the town was baptized *Fernandina de Jagua* in honor of the King, but later was renamed **Cienfuegos** in honor of Cuba's Captain General and Governor.

Images, top to bottom, left to right:

A **tobacco warehouse** during the *Estanco* (Spain's monopoly);

Tomás Gener y Buigas, one of the first promoters of culture in Matanzas, elected to the Cortes in 1820, went on exile in 1823;

Francisco Agüero Velazco (Frasquito), one of the first conspirators in the 1823 *Liga de la Cadena*. Captured and hung in the Plaza de Armas of Puerto Príncipe;

Andrés Manuel Sánchez, conspirator of *Liga de la Cadena* with Frasquito, was hung with him on March 16, 1826.

Images, top to bottom, left to right:

Claudio Martínez de Pinillos, Count of Villanueva, leader of the *reformistas* in Cuba. Promoter of Cuba's first railroad, the mechanization of the sugar mills, the improvement of the aqueduct and many public works;

the seal of the **Masons**, established in Cuba in 1804 with the founding of the *Templo de las Virtudes Teologales*;

a cartoon depicting the effects of the 1823 **Monroe Doctrine** (US prohibition of European countries to meddle in New World countries).

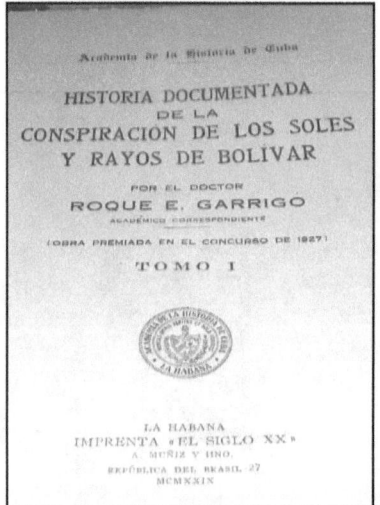

Images, top to bottom, left to right:

Rafael María de Mendive, founder of *Revista de la Habana* in 1853, active member of the *Sociedad Económica de Amigos del País*, teacher and mentor of José Martí;

Nicolás Azcárate Escobedo, lawyer, eloquent speaker, one of Cuba's reformist leaders, founder and writer for many newspapers, expelled from Cuba by governor Blas Villate, Count of Valmaseda, for his pro-independence viewpoints and active support;

A history of the **Rayos y Soles de Bolívar** conspiracy, published by the Cuban Academy of History in 1929;

The coat of arms designed and used by **Joaquín Infante**, the author of *Proyecto de Constitución para la Isla de Cuba*, the first Constitution project in Cuba, published in 1812.

Images, top to bottom, left to right:

José Aniceto Iznaga Borrell, one of the men who visited Simón Bolívar in 1827 to talk him into helping the independence movement in Cuba;

Juan José Nápoles Fajardo (*el Cucalambé*), journalist, author of *Rumores del Hormigo*, the poet who popularized the term *guajiro* to designate *campesinos* (countrymen or peasants), a term only used in Cuba;

The monument to **Francisco Vicene Aguilera** in Bayamo. He was a lawyer and the richest hacendado in Cuba in the 1800s, and donated his entire fortune to the cause of independence;

A rare image of **Aguilera** as a young man in the 1840s.

Images, top to bottom:

Paisaje, a painting by Esteban Chartrand, the best XIX century painter in Cuba, born in Limonar, Matanzas, traveled several times to Paris to study classical painting. He had his first solo exhibition in Charleston, South Carolina in 1870;

a 1828 drawing of **Havana's jail building** and the execution grounds in front of the jail.

the **Havana Jail and Prison** years later, in 1903, before it was demolished.

Images, top to bottom, left to right:

Salvador Cisneros Betancourt, *Marqués de Santa Lucía,* president of the *República de Cuba en Armas*, freed his slaves in 1868 and placed his fortune in the hands of the Independence army;

Joaquín de Agüero, joined the insurrection against Spain after freeing his slaves in 1843, was captured and shot in 1851;

José María Heredia y Heredia, arrested in 1823 on a charge of conspiracy, sentenced to banishment from Cuba for life, sought refuge in Mexico where he became a magistrate, wrote the celebrated *Oda al Niágara*;

Esteban Chartrandt Dubois, the best painter of rural scenes in the history of art in Cuba, graduate of San Alejandro Art Academy, considered one of the best painters of the French Barbizon school.

23
Peace and Prosperity Finally Arrive in Cuba

ASIDE FROM HIS HUMANE treatment of residents of the island, Francisco Dionisio Vives was a rare example of what Spain could do to seek and gain the loyalty of Cubans. He improved the defense systems and lifted a sense of uncertainty and perpetual fear by residents; it took the development of «a military machine consisting of eight corps of rural militias, each with 3 companies and 70 horses.» In addition he organized the compilation of economic, geographic and demographic data in 1828 to serve as guide for needed infrastructure improvements in the island. On May 15, 1832, he returned to Spain crowned with success, after several spontaneous homage in his honor by groups of businessmen, artists and common citizens. Although he had been reluctant to give up his previous mission as Spain's ambassador to the US (from 1820 to 1821), he felt his most rewarding assignment in the service of Spain had been the years he spent in Cuba.

After Vives, General Don Mariano Ricafort Palacín y Abarca (1776-1846) took his turn as governor of Cuba. He had been since 1816 in Alto Perú, Caracas and Cartagena de Indias, fighting against Simón Bolívar. Wounded by a rifle shot on his right leg, he retired from active duty and became governor of the Philippines in 1825. By all accounts he had been a good public servant there and, after brief stints in Guam and the Marianas, he was promoted to the top post in Cuba. Ricafort's years were uneventful, except for a terrible scourge of Asian Cholera that in 1833 spread from Havana to the entire island, at a cost of more than 25,000 lives. He acted prudently after the death of Fernando VII; due to his skillful political maneuvers, Isabel II was quickly accepted in the island as the new Spanish sovereign.

On June 1, 1834, Ricafort yielded the governorship of Cuba to Lieutenant General Don Miguel Tacón y Rosique (1775-1855), Vizconde de Bayamo, a favorite of Spanish liberals. Historians would say of Tacón «*governó a Cuba a taconazos,*» (a play of words, "governed Cuba kicking with his boots" -*Tacón* meaning in Spanish the back part of the sole of a boot).

To expedite and make things easier for Tacón, the Spanish crown, in accordance to *the Estatuto Real de 1834,* [229] proceeded to give the governor of Cuba the power to award nobiliary titles to any *criollos* he deemed worthy. The list in Cuba was flooded with prestigious *criollos*: **Claudio Martínez de Pinillos**, Count of Villanueva, **Luis Juan de Clouet**, Count of Fernandina de Sagua, **Marshal Alejandro**, Count of O'Reilly, **Antonio Vaillant**, Marquis of Candelaria del Yayabo, **Andrés Arango y Nuñez del Castillo, Juan Montalvo y Castillo, Serapio Mojarrieta, Prudencio Hechevarría y O'Gabán** and **Juan de Kindelán**, to mention a few. [230]

In spite of these offerings to Cuba, Tacón had to deal with several revolts and insurrections: on June 17 and 29 of 1835, Blacks from outside the walls in Havana revolted and de-

---

[229] The *Estatuto Real* was a law promulgated in Spain by María Cristina de Borbón, widow of Fernando VII, regent of Spain during the childhood of the future Isabel II. The *Estatuto* made no mention of the abolished 1812 Constitution but established that the Crown could agree voluntarily to transfer certain functions that were exclusive rights of the Monarchs. One such powers was the dispensation of nobility titles, which the Crown could transfer out of the King's will to local entities, such as regional governors.

[230] The nobility titles in Cuba followed the Spanish designation and resembled those of the rest of Europe. They were, in descending order of power, importance and social standing: Duke (*Duque*), Marquis (*Marqués*), Count (*Conde*), Viscount (*Vizconde*), Baron (*Barón*), Lord (*Señor*). The title of *Grande de España* (Grandee of Spain) was usually in conjunction with another title but at times was also granted to a person without any other nobility title, in which case the person would have *Grande de Eapaña* added at the end of his name; all Grandees were to be addressed as *Su Excelencia*, the title being at the same level as that of a Duke; infact, and all Dukes were considered *Grandes de España*. Noble titles in Cuba had a designation of a physical place. i.e., *Marqués de Bayamo, Conde de Canimar*, or the surname of the family as in *Marqués de Casa Sandoval, Conde de Casa Lombillo*, or were designated to recognize some good deed to the Royal family, as in *Marqués del Real Agrado* or *Marqués del Socorro*.

stroyed property. Tacón captured, judge and sentenced them to death within 4 days of the uprising. In Oriente, in 1836, Mariscal de Campo Don Manuel Lorenzo, governor of Santiago de Cuba, ignoring orders from Tacón, proclaimed his loyalty to the 1812 Constitution. Tacón sent an army of 3,000 to overpower him and succeeded. Within days he sent Lorenzo back to Spain aboard an English ship.

On the positive side, Tacón fought against gambling, contraband, corruption, indolence and laziness, annihilating several rings of bandits and outlaws that accosted the citizens in Havana and Santiago. He created an effective police force and ignored lineages, hierarchies and wealth. He was graciously remembered as a governor who built theaters, markets, jails and beautiful avenues, as well as the man who built in Cuba the first railroad in the Spanish domains.

Tacón was granted Spain's *Toison de Oro* [231] and the titles *Duque de La Unión de Cuba* and *Duque de Bayamo* at the end of his term in 1838. He was rewarded by Cubans of all classes with multiple homages and celebrations by the time he left the island on April 22, 1838. His successor was General Don Joaquín Ezpeleta Enrile (1788-1863), his Segundo Cabo. Ezpeleta was the son of a previous Cuban governor and nephew of the governor of the Philippines. He had been made prisoner by the invading troops of Napoleon in 1808 and remained prisoner in France until 1812. He presided over an era of economic prosperity in Cuba, none of which was related to his administrative or executive skills. On January 10, 1840 he was replaced by General Don Pedro de Alcántara Tellez Girón (1786-1851), Príncipe of Anglona [232] and Duke of Osuna.

---

[231] The *Orden del Toisón de Oro* (England: *Order of the Golden Fleece;* Dutch: *Orde van het Gulden Vlies*; Portuguese: *Ordem do Tosão de Ouro*; French: *Ordre de la Toison d'Or*; German: *Orden vom Goldenen Vlies*; Italian: *Ordine del Toson d'Oro*; Spanish:*Orden del Toisón de Oro)*, is an order of chivalry founded in Bruges by Philip III, Duke of Burgundy in 1430, to celebrate his marriage to the Portuguese princess Infanta Isabella of Portugal, daughter of King John I of Portugal. It evolved as one of the most prestigious orders in Europe. Today's holder is Juan Carlos I of Spain.

[232] Anglona is a historical area of northern Sardinia in Italy

Other events of importance in Cuba during the 1830s and 1840s were:

On May 12 and August 1, 1831, two important regular publications began in Havana: *El Lucero de la Habana* and *Revista Bimestre Cubana*. They were short-lived, as few residents had use for essays and politico-economic analyses. José Antonio Saco directed the *Revista Bimestre* with the financial help of the *Sociedad Económica*.

On August 13, 1832, Bishop Juan José Díaz de Espada died in Havana. He had been a priest for 51 years and Bishop for close to 31 years. He had encouraged universal vaccination, endowed many public schools with his own funds, founded in 1727 an asylum for the insane and was indefatigable in his efforts to promote public education. In his honor, in 1833, a Memorial dedicated to him was published in Havana; it was authored by the best writers in Cuba.

In 1832, knowing that Fernando VII of Spain was in his last days, the Basque ultra-conservatives, supporters of the King's brother Carlos María Isidro de Borbón as heir to the throne, revolted as they learnt of the ambitions of Isabel II, daughter of the King, to be Queen of Spain. They became known as the *Carlistas*; they relentlessly fought the establishment in Spain well until after the 1936-1939 Spanish Civil War.

On March 30, 1833, Jean Baptist Vermay died in Havana, the result of a cholera contagion, and on September 29, King Fernando VII of Spain, *el deseado*, [233] died in Spain. He had married four times: in 1802 to his cousin María Antonieta of the Two Sicilies; in 1816 to his niece María Isabel de Portugal, daughter

---

[233] Fernando VII became *el deseado* (the "coveted" or "wished for") as the people of Spain were hoping to get rid of the Napoleonic troops and recover their King from his exile in Paris. Fernando did not deserve that hope. As he abdicated the throne of Spain on behalf of Jose Napoleón, he declared: «*Doy sinceramente en mi nombre y en el de mi hermano y tio a vuestra Majestad Imperial y Real la enhorabuena de la satisfacción de ver instalado a su hermano el Rey José en el trono de España.*» (On behalf of myself, my brother and my uncle, I sincerely give to your Imperial and Royal Majesty my congratulations, with the satisfaction to see your brother King Joseph on the throne of Spain).

of his older sister Carlota; in 1819 to María Josefa of Saxony, daughter of Maximilian, prince of Saxony, the only wife not previously related to him; in 1829 to another niece, María Cristina de Bourbon, daughter of his younger sister María Isabel.

On March 6, 1834, the *Academia Cubana de Literatura* had its first session. It had been authorized by Queen Regent María Cristina de Borbón; Domingo del Monte was elected Secretary and Nicolás de Cárdenas president. 27 members were accepted, among them Luz y Caballero, José Antonio Saco and Felipe Poey. From the beginning there was a rivalry with the *Sociedad Patriótica*,[234] supported by the Intendant and Claudio Martínez de Pinillos, Count of Villanueva. The board of the *Sociedad Económica de Amigos del País*, had promised to fund the *Academia Cubana de Literatura* but became irritated when the *Academia* contacted the Queen Regent without consultation. Their support vanished and the *Academia* ceased to exist, in spite of Saco's defense in a 1834 article, which cost him a long exile in London, Paris and finally Madrid. When José de la Luz tried to contact Tacón on behalf of Saco, he was also sent into exile. [235]

---

[234] The concept of *Sociedades Patrióticas*, *Sociedades Económicas* and *Sociedades de Amigos del País* was born in 1775 in Madrid. By the end of the century there were more than 80 such societies in the Spanish colonies. They all had the purpose of supporting the liberal ideas of the *Ilustración* (the Enlightenment) and to fund important social and humane activities in their cities and capitals. In Cuba the *Sociedades* evolved in their names and functions: *Sociedad Patriótica de la Habana* (1793-1795; May 1838-April 1843); *Real Sociedad Económica de la Habana* (1817-1823; January 1846-June 1849); *Sociedad Económica de la Habana* (1824-1825; May 1843-Nocvember 1845); *Real Sociedad Patriótica de la Habana* (November 1835-April 1838); *Real Sociedad Económica de la Habana* (January 1846-June 1849); *Reales Junta de Fomento y Sociedad Económica de la Habana* (July 1849-1850); *Real Junta de Fomento y Sociedad Económica de la Habana* (1851-1853); *Real Junta de Fomento y Real Sociedad Económica de la Habana* (Noember 1853-1857); *Real Junta de Fomento y Real Sociedad Económica* (1858-1863); *Real Sociedad Económica* (1864-1866); *Real Sociedad Económica de Amigos del País de la Habana* (November 1877-December 1896).

[235] Saco was a man of limited means. His exile was mostly financed by José Luis Alfonso (1810-1881), *Marqués de Montalvo*, a wealthy *hacendado* who would marry Miguel de Aldama's sister María de los Dolores in 1835.

1835 saw the passing of Father José Agustín Caballero (1762-1835), uncle of José de la Luz y Caballero, and pioneer of Cuba's cultural and political transformation. He had been the publisher of the *Papel Periódico*, an alumnus of the San Carlos and San Ambrosio Seminary, a teacher and mentor of Félix Varela, José Antonio Saco [236] and José de la Luz.

On August 13, 1836, the 1812 Constitution was reestablished in Spain by a liberal government. It was proclaimed immediately in Santiago by Governor Manuel Lorenzo on September 20. Tacón, in Havana, received orders from Spain on October 21 to «take whatever measures you dispose of in order to detain the governor of Santiago and derogate and revoke his unlawful proclamation.» A state of civil war prevailed in Cuba for a few days as the British consul tried to mediate. Manuel Lorenzo assembled a small battalion of Black slaves and free men but lost.

On December 14, the *fuerzas vivas* (literally the living forces, i.e., sugar magnates, church leaders and members of the *Sociedad Económica de Amigos del País* in Havana) appealed to Tacón for reconciliation. [237] The troops in Santiago let the governor know they were not willing to fight their brothers from Havana. Bayamo took a stand favoring Tacón and Manuel Lorenzo resigned and left for London, ending the stand-off.

As the Madrid Cortes opened their 1837 session, José Antonio Saco showed up and presented his credentials as deputy. He was not admitted to his chair; neither were Ignacio Montalvo or Francisco Escovedo, the other two deputies. It, of course, created great discontent among the people in the island.

---

[236] In 1835 Saco was reelected three times to the *Cortes* in Madrid, even though he had been in exile for years at a time. He had won a competition sponsored by the *Sociedad Económica de Amigos del País* in 1831 with *La Vagancia en Cuba*, a brilliant essay about the factors that contributed to youth vagrancy in the island; it was one the reasons Saco lived almost life-long in exile.

[237] It is worth noticing that sugar cane harvest in Cuba usually started at the end of the year, between Christmas and New Year's at the latest.

In June of 1837, the conspiracy *Soles de la Libertad* was denounced by an unknown traitor. As many others of the time, the conpiracy failed.[238] Among its leaders were José Antonio Saco, Narciso López, Manuel Molina, Manuel Rojo, Rufino Izquierdo, and Laureano Angulo, all residents of Cádiz at the time. Its strategy was to produce chaos in Cuba with the assassination of Miguel Tacón. Molina, Rojo, Izquierdo and Angulo were captured in Havana as soon as they disembarked. They suffered prison until Tacón was replaced as governor and Captain General in 1838.

Before 1840, Cuba saw the birth of several people that were destined to play an important role on its road to become a modern republic: on February 24, 1832, poet **Juan Clemente Zenea** was born in Bayamo. He would find a tragic death in 1871; also in 1832 compositor and pianist **Nicolás Ruiz Espartero** was born in Havana. Besides classical compositions he wrote many barcarolles, nocturnes and popular songs; in Puerto Príncipe, **Carlos J. Finlay** was born. He was the main discoverer that yellow fever was transmitted by the mosquito *Aedes aegypty*; on July 9, 1835, future first president of independent Cuba, **Tomás Estrada Palma**, was born in Bayamo; on the same year composer **José White Lafitte**, author of *La Bella Cubana*, was born in Matanzas; on November 18, 1836, future top military leader of 1898 Cuba's war of independence **Máximo Gómez Báez** was born in Bani, Santo Domingo; on August 25, 1837, **Luisa Pérez de Zambrana** was born in Santiago de Cuba. She was an outstanding elegiac poet, chosen in 1860 to render a tribute to Gertrudis Gómez de Avellaneda; on August 4, 1839, **Calixto García** was born in Holguín. He was one of the few men that fought in all three Cuban Wars of Independence.

---

[238] Other notable failed conspiracies in the first half of the XIX century were: the *Expedición de los Trece* (Expedition of the 13) in 1826, the *Gran Legión del Aguila Negra* (Great Legion of the Black Eagle) in 1829, the *Cadena Triangular* (Triangular Chain) in 1837 and the *Conspiración de la Escalera* (Conspiracy of the Ladder) in 1843.

There were also important individuals that strived to develop Cuban society and relentlessly labored to set Cuba free without getting their wishes come true: on August 13, 1832, **Bishop Espada** died in Havana; *Jean Baptist Vermay*, founder of the San Alejandro Art School in Havana, died on March 30, 1833 after contracting cholera; on March 21, 1837, the top XIX century *reformista*, **Francisco de Arango y Parreño** died in Havana. The Spanish crown granted him in 1834 the title of *Prócer del Reino* (National Hero); On May 7, 1839, *José María Heredia* died; he had been the most celebrated Cuban-born poet and patriot of the XIX century.

Two views of the **Convento de Santo Domingo**, seat of the *University of Havana*, founded by the order of Dominican Priests in 1728 and run by them until 1842. After its secularization, the Rector and all professors were appointed by the Captain General of Cuba.

In 1851, at the peak of anexation feelings in Cuba, the students supported and demonstrated for Narciso López. At the start of the Ten Year War, many students joined Carlos Manuel de Céspedes and Ignacio Agramonte (both alumni) supporting the insurrectos. During the War of 1895 the Spanish authorities chracterized the University as a *foco de insurrección* and restricted the number of annual admissions.

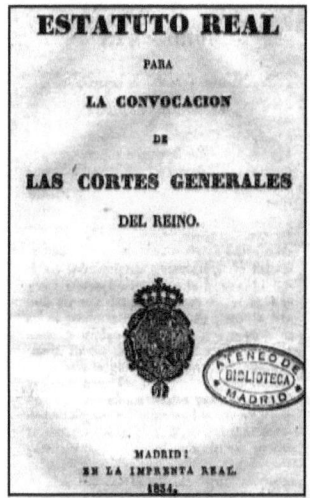

Images, top to bottom, left to right:

The tower and entrance to the **Real y Pontificia Universidad de San Gerónimo de La Habana**, the old *University of Havana*, established in 1728 at the Convent of *San Juan de Letrán* on *Mercaderes* street. The University was secularized in 1842;

the brochure published by the **Academia Cubana de Literatura**, written by José Antonio Saco in defense of José María Heredia;

the **1834 Estatuto Real** convening the Cortes to meet after the death of Fernando VII;

the classified section of a 1803 issue of the **Papel Periódico de la Habana**.

Images, top to bottom, left to right:

The front two pages of the ***1812 Spanish Constitution*** established and published by the Cádiz Cortes, Spain's first sovereign assembly;

a ***2012 Spanish postage stamp*** honoring the 1812 Constitution;

a rare photo of ***Francisco de Arango y Parreño***, c.1795;

Don Miguel Tacón y Rosique, governor of Cuba from 1834 to 1838.

Images, top to bottom, left to right:

Don Carlos María Isidro de Borbón, brother of Fernando VII, objected to Isabel II, (daughter of Fernando VII) ascending the throne of Spain, in 1833, launching the first *Guerra Carlista*;

Intendente **Alejandro Ramírez Blanco**, main promoter of economic diversification and free commerce in Cuba, supporter of the *Escuela de Dibujo y Pintura*, later named in his honor;

Bishop **Juan José Espada**, bishop of Havaba in 1800, indefatigable in the promotion of public education;

a cartoon showing governor **Mariano Ricafort**. Rumors had it that *Refugio* street in Havana got its name for the hospitality and refuge that a Cuban lady offered to Don Mariano during his years as governor;

Venerable **Félix Varela**, Cuban independence leader, teacher, writer and politician. An exile, he held the second most important position of the Catholic Diocesis in New York.

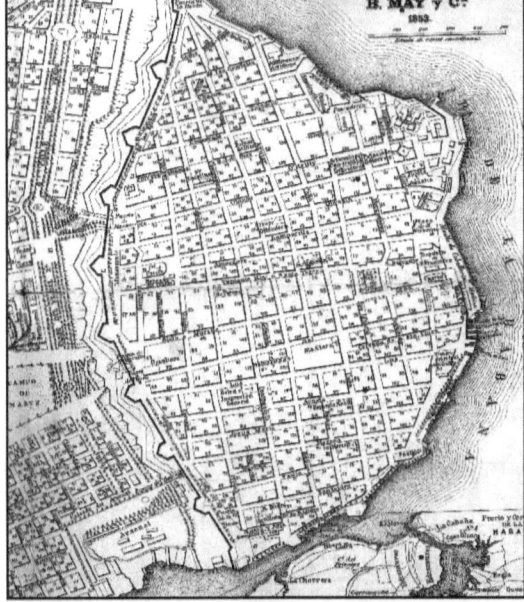

Images, top to bottom, left to right:

María Cristina de Borbón, widow of Fernando VII, regent of Spain until her daughter Isabel II (on her lap) was proclaimed an adult at age 13;

Havana in 1838, during the times of Domingo del Monte. A look from the town of Casablanca, on the other side of the bay. On the distance, the Atarés hill, on the left, the Alameda de Paula;

a **1853 map of Havana**, showing the growth of the city outside its walls;

Felipe III, Duke of Burgundy, the monarch who established the order of the *Toisón de Oro* (Order of the Golden Fleece), wearing the collar of the order.

A selection of Newspapers published in Cuba in the early 1800s.

Images, top to bottom, left to right:

The **Villanueva railroad station**, seen from the North in 1867;

Francisco de Goya, Spanish painter to the royalty in the 1800s;

Isabel II and husband Francisco de Asis y Borbón (Paquito);

The **Duke of Osuna,** painting by Goya;

A cartoon dealing with Isabel II, Her succession to the throne of Spain was always disputed by the *Carlistas*. Finally she was deposed by the Glorious Revolution in 1868 and went into exile in France.

Teatro Coliseo, Havana, 1877

The first theater built specifically for opera in America was the **Coliseo** or **Teatro Principal**, built in Havana in 1772. On October 12 of 1776, the **Coliseo** opened with an inaugural work by Pietro Metastasio entitled **Didone Abandonata**, in celebration of the island discovery by Columbus. Prior to that date, in 1750, **La Opera del Mendigo** (The Beggars Opera), a satirical musical in three acts written by John Gay with music by Johann Christophe Pepusch, opened in New York on December 3 at the **Theater on Nassau Street**, a two story wooden structure that held about 280 people. The work was more a musical anti-opera than an opera; instead of the grand music and themes of opera, the work used familiar tunes and ordinary, uninteresting people as its characters. The venue, on the other hand, was not a building specifically constructed for the acoustics, illumination and visibility demanded by a professional operatic experience, as was the **Coliseo** in Havana. The US had to wait until 1793 when the New Theater at Market street, in Baltimore, was built with all the rigors of an opera locale.

Starting in the late eighteenth century there was continued operatic activity in Havana, but it was not until the early 1800s that Havana became a true musical center, not only for the Americas, but for the entire world. That musical and cultural effervescence spread to other towns such as Cienfuegos, Matanzas, Camaguey and Santiago de Cuba, attracting famous operatic singers and musicians to the island and even entire companies from Spain and Italy.

(continued)

Opera in Colonial Cuba

Giovanni Bottesini and Luigi Arditi

(continuation)

The first Cuban opera, with libretto by Manuel de Zequeira and an unknown musical author, was **America y Apollo**, which opened in 1807. In 1811 a stable company was created with Spanish singers. Several Cuban composers authored operas and operettas, as well as European composers visiting Cuba, such as the Italian Stefano Cristiani, who presented several operas in the late 1810s, and the Spanish José Serrano, who did the same in the early 1820s. The effort of these men was complemented by two extraordinary composers and conductors visiting Havana for long seasons: **Giovanni Bottesini** and **Luigi Arditi**. They both became musicians at the *Teatro Tacón*; Nottesini as first violin and Ardini at the contrabass. At the time, the *Teatro Tacón* was the largest in America and third largest in the world. Both Bottesini and Arditi took turns as directors of the Tacón orchestra.

The arrival of Bottesini and Arditi brought about an instant credibility for Havana as an opera city. Tecnicians, sound experts, supporting actors and musicians, stage designers and technical specialists began to arrive in Havana for the opera seasons. Curtain mechanics, sound amplifiers, set mechanics and scene painters began to seek Havana as a profitable and secure place to work. The Tacón Theater became a world class venue with electronics and internal communications (stage to warehouses, front desks and ticket booths) invented by Antonio Meucci. For several decades in the 1800s Havana had tne most complete and ambitious opera seasons in America. Rafael María de Mendive, Martí's teacher, wrote librettos and Cuban and international composers such as Manuel Saumell wrote masterful songs. Many of these musicians made sure that Verdi's operas, for instance, were opening in Havana a few weeks after they opened in Italy. Such was the case for *Lucia di Lammermoor* by Gaetano Donizetti, *Norma* and *I Puritani* by Vincenzo Bellini; all three had their American premiere in Havana.

Opera in Colonial Cuba

24

Cuba Got a Fresh Look but no Independence

Between 1853 and 1870, Baron Georges-Eugène Haussmann (1809-1891), commissioned by Napoleon III, renovated Paris and turned it from a city of narrow, dark and smelly streets into the City of Lights that it is today. Something similar was done in Havana, nine years earlier, by governor Miguel Tacón y Rosique, *Duque de la Unión de Cuba* and *Vizconde de Bayamo*. [239] Until his appointment in 1834, Havana had had several good governors like Someruelos, Cienfuegos, Cajigal, Vives and Ricadort, but their main concern was always to ensure that Cuba remained forever a *siempre fidelísima isla*, firmly under Spanish control. Don Miguel Tacón, in less than four years [240] literally transformed Havana and the entire island, enabling Cuba to show substantial progress in urban development, architecture, education and the arts, with the evident exception of political freedom.

During his first year of rule, [241] Tacón ordered a strikingly modern public lighting system installed in Havana; it caused a sensation among visitors from the peninsula and from the US and other European and South American countries. The old

---

[239] Leyend had it that he had been a combatant in Trafalgar and that, as governor of Popayán, had received a severe beating from the patriots in Nueva Granada (present day Colombia), arriving in Lima with only 25 men. His enemies called him *el derrotado de Popayán* (the loser of Popayán).

[240] Appointed by Queen Regent María Cristina, widow of Fernando VII on June 7, 1834; his mandate ceased on April 21, 1838, under the reign of Isabel II.

[241] In his first year, Tacón's followers repeated in papers, announcements and *tertulias* the phase: *Llegó Tacón, se acabó el relajo* (Tacón is here, no more laxity). Of his two previous predecesors people used to say: *Vives vive solo para las peleas de gallos* (Vives only has eyes for cockfights) and *Ricafort solo gasta tiempo en su refugio* (Ricafort spends all his time with the lady on Refugio street).

fashioned lamps, reeking smoke, bad odors and grease, were replaced by clean and practical gas lamps of rare beauty, in numbers that astonished the population. There were reports that more than 500 such lamps were placed *intramuros*, within the territory protected by the walls of the city. Orders were to light all lamps one hour before sunset and stay lit until dawn. It practically deterred crime in the city during the night.

Supplementing the new lamps, Tacón created a *Cuerpo* de *Serenos* (Night Watchmen Corps), with specific responsibilities drafted by Tacón himself. The city was divided in four districts, each with its own brigade of *serenos* and sixty watch stop-points. Each *sereno* carried a gun, a whistle, a hand held oil lantern, a trained dog and a pike. They would announce the time at each stop-point: i.e., *las tres en punto y sereno* (three in the morning and everything is quiet). They had powers to arrest anyone during their patrol duties and had the means to re-start lamps that had gone out. To further eliminate hide-outs for bandits, all doors in Havana were to be closed at the sound of the 9:00 pm *cañonazo* (artillery blank gun-shot) and stay locked until dawn. Civilians were prohibited to carry concealed weapons after the *cañonazo* and were detained by the *serenos* if they did so.

In addition, Tacón also set up a *Cuerpo de Bomberos* (fire brigade), consisting of eight three-men units, two for each district, as well as three units for areas outside the city walls. The men in these brigades were laborers from maintenance guilds moonshining for a salary. They knew the entire water supply network [242] and had field practices every last week-end of the month. The *Cuerpo de Bomberos* placed safety advisory notes on public announcement boards that Tacón had ordered placed

---

[242] The network consisted of emergency water outlets placed on the sides of corner buildings linked to the new Fernando VII aqueduct, inaugurated in 1827 to replace the so-called Royal Ditch of 1575. The Fernando VII aqueduct was in turn replaced by the Albear aqueduct in 1858, a more modern gravity-fed water supply taking water from the Vento springs of the Almendares river. Since Tacón's times, the water outlets were also used to wash and sweep all paved streets and to wet the non-paved streets to eliminate dust raised by passing carts and *volantas*.

every six blocks on every street in Havana and other large Cuban cities.

To control crime, eliminate contraband and import duty violators and to stop and prevent disaffected and rebellious people to enter Cuba to propagandize or recruit separatists, Tacón organized a unit of custom inspectors in Havana and other cities with facilities to receive passenger ships. They would collect passports or landing papers, took them to an office and inspected them against lists of potential offenders. No one was allowed to disembark until their passports were returned. The only way to be excluded was if an island resident would personally vouch for the visitor's conduct during his/her stay in Cuba. In Havana these arrangements took place at the *Muelle de Comercio*, later known as the *Muelle de Caballería*, situated opposite the harbor office.

To provide visitors a good first impression, Tacón paved the entire *Muelle de Comercio* with Catalonian granite and placed a beautiful and practical marble Italian fountain at the center of it. This *Fuente de Neptuno* provided drinking water to residents, tourists and mooring ships. [243]

These beautification and practical projects by Tacón stimulated the wealthy classes in Cuba to build palaces that would blend well with the surroundings: *Palacio de los Marqueses de Aguas Claras* and *Palacio de Luis Chacón*, both situated on San Ignacio street, abutting the *Plaza de la Catedral*, between Empedrado and O'Reilly streets; the *Casa de Baños* (bathhouse); the *Palacio del Marqués de Arcos*, also situated on Mercaderes street between Empedrado and O'Reilly streets; the *Palacio de los O'Farrill* (later sold to Havana's Archbishop), on Habana street, between Chacón and Tejadillo; the *Palacio Pedroso* on today's Cuba street, between Peña Pobre and Cuarteles streets; the *Casa del Marqués de Monte Hermoso*, south of the *Plaza de Armas* on Obrapía street, between San Ignacio and Mercaderes streets;

---

[243] Years later it was placed at a park in Havana limited by Calzada, Quinta, C and D streets in *El Vedado*.

the *Casa del Conde Barreto* on Oficios street, between Luz and Santa Clara streets; the *Casa de los Condes de Jaruco* with huge, exquisite mosaic windows overlooking the park limited by Muralla, Teniente Rey, San Ignacio and Inquisidor streets. Finally, the beautiful and inspiring *Alameda de Paula*, where the *Teatro Principal* was situated.

All those streets in Havana were unpaved, very muddy when it rained and very dusty when it did not. People moved around the city in *volantas* (two wheel vehicles pulled by a good looking horse) or *a caballo* (riding horses). Ladies never descended from their *volantas*; clerks, waiters, porters and servants approached the vehicle to serve ladies with refreshments, purchases, messages or to pick up their bags.

On the other side of the social scale, notices with rooms to let were posted on the announcement boards placed by Tacón, particularly those closest to the docks. $24 *pesos fuertes* for the monthly rent of a room; 6 RS (*reales*) for dinner, 4 RS for breakfast or lunch. [244] The rent for a four or five room house was about 80 to 100 *pesos* a month.

One of the favorite eating spots for tourists and merchants was the *Plaza del Vapor*. It was a hundred or so yards outside the city walls, limited by Aguila, Dragones, Reina and Galiano streets. At the end of Dragones, the street merged with *Calzada de Zanja*, [245] the open aqueduct or ditch bringing water to Havana from *La Chorrera*, on the mouth of the Almendares River. In 1835 Tacón, for hygienic reasons, covered the *zanja* and had the water run inside cast-iron pipes of large diameter.

Near *Plaza del Vapor*, the *Calzada de Galiano* went over the zanja by means of *Puente Galiano*. Before Tacón, all around the

---

[244] A *peso fuerte*, equivalent to a US dollar, was broken down into 8 RS (*reales*). A *duro*, was a silver coin worht 5 *pesos fuertes*. The *centavo*, one hundredth of a *peso*, was a copper coin used in all Spanish posessions. Tourists from the US could pay their purchases or consumption in Cuba either with US dollar or *pesos fuertes*. All merchants accepted both without preference.

[245] *Calzada* was the name given to a large paved street or avenue.

Plaza merchants and traders from far away brought their products to their own dilapidated *casillas* (wood huts) where they exhibited their goods. By 4:00 AM they were heaping with fruits, grains and vegetables; by 12:00 noon the place reeked to heaven; by 6:00 PM the place was empty. Tacón built a modern market framed by a double colonnade made out of masonry and marble, calling it the *Mercado de Tacón*, although people referred to it as the *Mercado del Vapor*. At the center were a *carnicería* and a *pescadería* (a butcher and a fishmonger), both run by Tacón's favorite friend, 49 years old Don Francisco Marty y Torrens, future owner of *Teatro Tacón* and, at the time, the man who controlled most of the food trade in Havana. On Galiano and Reina streets Tacón provided buildings with large windows where merchants displayed ornaments and trinkets, as well as linen and exotic fabrics. In was a happy anticipation of today's shopping centers and malls.

Aside from the *Mercado del Vapor*, the only two other places where people could buy fresh produce in Havana were the *Mercado del Santo Cristo* in *Plaza del Cristo* (or *Plaza Nueva*) next to the *Iglesia del Santo Cristo*, and the *Mercado de Maria Cristina or de Fernando VII* in *Plaza Vieja*. They were also controlled by a friend of Tacón, Don Manuel Pastor, who had invested 100,000 duros (500,000 *pesos fuertes*, equivalent to US $500,000). From those investments Mr. Pastor earned US $60,000 a year for about 23 years. [246]

There were also woeful decisions during Tacón's time as governor of the island. In his quest to develop a strong economy in Cuba, Tacón authorized in 1839 the going ashore in Havana of the Portuguese slave ship *Tecora*, with 500 Blacks that had been kidnapped in Sierra Leone; 53 of them were re-

---

[246] These investments were inside dealings of palace favorites (all born in Spain), but there was no way the colony could make those investments with public funds, which were managed tidily and with diligence by Count Villanueva, a clean man completly independent from governor Tacón.

embarked in the schooner *Amistad* to be taken to Puerto Príncipe.[247]

Other important events in the decade of 1840 to 1950 were:

The town of Ciego de Avila was founded and the *Teatro Brunet,* one of the best in Cuba, was inaugurated in Trinidad,.

Lieutenant General Pedro Téllez Girón and Anglona, Prin-ce and Marquis of Santo Mauro Javalquinto, Vera and Villadarias, took over as captain general of Cuba on January 10, 1840. He supported the arts and literature and introduced important urban and social improvements in the island. His son brought to Cuba from Paris the first daguerreotype camera [248] and made the first pictures of the island on record.

On March 7, 1841, Jerónimo Valdés y Sierra was appointed Captain General of Cuba. He appointed a Venezuelan general, Narciso López de Urriola, as president of the military commission and chief military man in Matanzas and Trinidad. He ordered all slave dealers to close their businesses.

Also in 1841, former US president John Quincy Adams gained the absolution and liberation of the slaves that had mutinied in the ship *Amistad*; they were repatriated to Sierra Leone in November. Inspired after knowing these news, the slaves building the *Palacio de Aldama* revolted and were accommodated in their petitions by the Aldamas.

Cuba's population reached 1,000,000, with 59% Blacks.

---

[247] Two of these slaves assaulted and killed the cook and the captain; they tried to force the ship's navigator to take them back to Africa. They were tricked and taken to the eastern tip of Long Island where they were captured by the cutter USS Washington and were subject to a long process that threatened to disrupt the Martin van Buren presidency in the US. They were finally taken back to their country in 1842. On September 2, 1839 a play entitled *The Long, Low Back Schooner*, based on the *Amistad* story, played in New York to full houses; in 1997 *Amistad*, a film by Steven Spielberg also dramatized the incident for world audiences.

[248] First practical photographic technology, invented by Frenchman Louis Daguerre in 1839; direct positive pictures were made on Sheffield plates, which were silvered copper plates produced by cold-rolled cladding of silver foil on a copper support.

As president of the military commission, Narciso López, brother-in-law of the Count of Pozos Dulces, a slave-owner, found guilty several abolitionists accused of misdeeds.

Juan Manuel de Manzanedo and González de la Teja, returned from Cuba to Spain with a fortune obtained in the slave trade; he became the first *Indiano* [249] celebrity, as he became in Spain a successful investor, builder and patron of the arts.

In 1843 a town in Oriente called *Santa Catalina del Saltadero del Guaso* changed its name to Guantánamo. Also in 1843, Joaquín de Agüero freed his 8 slaves and gave them tracks of land where they could make a decent living for themselves.

Leopoldo O'Donnell y Jorris became Captain General of Cuba on October 20, 1843; one of his first decisions was to dismiss Narciso López from all his military positions in the island: the deposed Narciso López made common cause with farmers that tried to annex Cuba to the US to maintain slavery.

The *Conspiración del Triunvirato* (after the Triunvirato Sugar mill, property of the Alfonsos) exploded in Cuba; it was also known as *La Carlota* (the name of its best known lady leader) and *La Escalera* (a ladder was used to place a torture victim); it lasted from 1843 well into 1844. Del Monte and Luz y Caballero were accused as *provocateurs*.

In 1843 Ignacio Agramonte was born in Puerto Príncipe; in 1844, Emilio Bacardí Moreau was born in Santiago de Cuba, the Countess of Merlín published *La Havane* in Paris and the *Diario de la Marina* was founded in Havana..

In Havana, the old fashioned lighthouse of *El Morro* was demolished and a new one built (the *Columna de O'Donnell*, still working today).

---

[249] The term *Indiano* became popular in Spain in the 1830s; it designated young Spanish fortune-seekers that succeeded with hard work in Cuba, went back to their hometown in Spain and built large, colonial-style houses, where they lived out the rest of their days, basking in the glory of their huge fortunes as reflected in the grandeur of their mansions. They usually contributed substantially to the wealth of the towns where they had been born.

In 1844 Captain General O'Donnell subdued the *Conspiración de La Escalera* in Matanzas; Carlota, one of the leaders, was quartered with horses pulling on all her extremities; poet Gabriel de la Concepción Valdés (Plácido), who was probably not involved, and 10 other Blacks, were tortured and executed by *garrote vil* on June 28. The year would be remembered on the island as *el año del cuero* (the year of the whip). The repression sparked a mass exodus to the United States.

A new railroad between the mining town of El Cobre and the tip of the bay, in Santiago de Cuba, was inaugurated on November 1, 1844, when Spain still had to wait 4 years to have its first railroad.

Isabel II issued on September 13, 1845, a Royal Order authorizing the transfer to Spanish Guinea of any free Black who wished to return to his/her native town. The order had no effect for lack of interest of the former slaves. Antonio Maceo was born in San Luis, Oriente, on June 14, 1845.

The frigate *Oquendo*, with the first 206 Chinese hired to address the lack of black slaves in Cuba, arrived in Havana on July 29, 1847, from the port of Amoy (today's Xiamen, Fujian, China). Days later 330 additional Chinese arrived in the Duke of Argyle ship.

Rafael María de Mendive inaugurated his newspaper *El Artista*; Governor Federico Roncaly y Cerruti was appointed Captain General of Cuba on February 20, 1848.

US President James K. Polk, at the behest of Miguel Aldama and other members of *Club de La Habana*, [250]authorized Romulus Mitchell Saunders, his ambassador to Spain, to offer US $100 million for the island of Cuba; the offer was rejected.

---

[250] The *Club de la Habana* was openly pro-annexation of Cuba to the US. Its illustrious members included José Luis Alfonso, Cristobal Madan, Cirilo Villaverde, Domingo Goicuría, José Antonio Echeverría, Ramón de la Palma, Rafael María de Mendive, Gaspar Betancourt Cisneros and Miguel de Aldama, among many others. The pro-annexation sympathies and active memberships were mostly in Havana, Trinidad and Camagüey.

Narciso López organized a pro-annexation uprising in Cuba called *La Mina de la Rosa Cubana*. It failed to find followers in the island and all conspirators had to reembark and take refuge in the US.

An August 11, 1849, by order of Zachary Taylor, US president, the participation of its citizens in the filibustering expedition being organized by Narciso López to invade Cuba was prohibited. Narciso's ships had sailed from New York and New Orleans but were detained and confiscated.

Despite President Taylor's orders, Narciso Lopez, with the support but without the presence of John Quitman, governor of Mississippi, landed in Cardenas with 600 Americans and took over the city on May 19, 1850. The Cuban flag, designed by López like the flag of Texas, was flown for the first time. López' defense of slavery (he was an agent of the slaveholders landowners, seeking to expand slave territories under the US flag), halted support to his cause. Navy lieutenant Francisco Armero y Peñaranda, future Prime Minister of Spain, captured two of López' supply ships, forcing him to retreat and re-embark after only a few hours.

José Gutiérrez de la Concha e Irigoyen son of an Argentinean governor who was shot by pro-independence troops in 1810, was appointed Captain General of Cuba on November 11, 1850. He intended to suppress all attempts to change the status quo in Cuba. Narciso López intended a new invasion of Cuba from Mantua, Pinar del Rio. Once more, he failed to attract support from the people of Cuba and had to leave the island.

In the middle of the XIX century, Cuba looked like an idyllic place to live, far away from an Europe full on conflicts. The only cause of concern of its residents were hurricanes, one of which, in 1844, devastated several areas of the island. Eye witnesses from the *Torreón de San Lázaro* reported that a huge black twisting plume of clouds advanced unexpectedly towards the city of Havana, bringing with it a gigantic swell of the waters, reaching over 100 feet in size. Havana, at the time, had no natural barriers; the Cabaña hill diverted water into the harbor channel, where it rushed with destructive fury towards the wharfs of the port, wreaking destruction on the moored ships. People called it «worst than the breath of Satan.» 114 people were killed, 79 wounded, 120 disappeared. More than 200 ships were destroyed, close to 1000 houses were seriously damaged or left roofless. Of the 200,000 residents, close to 25% were affected. Trees fell, the *Jardín Botánico* lost more than half its plants, the Tacón Theater had its roof damaged, the Teatro Principal and the Gran Diorama in Alameda de Paula were razed to the ground.

But worst things were happening in Europe. In Italy, the *quarantotto* (forty-eight) became a symbol of relentless turmoil; in France Louis Philippe d'Orleans was forced to abdicate giving way to the Second Republic; In Hungary, the liberals earned their independence from Austria, as emperor Ferdinand I was forced to ratify a new Constitution; in the Americas, Mexico was engaged in a war against the US, where the North American giant was completing its geographical expansion; in Florence the republicans were proclaiming the Republic of Tuscany. In the midst of all these, Havana residents were enthusiastically planning for the best of all previous celebrations of the Spanish Queen Mother's birthday.

Images, top to bottom:

A 1799 **Carlos III Silver Real**. Ocho *Reales* were worth a *Peso Fuerte*. A *Peso Fuerte* was equal to one US dollar;

a 1823 **Fernando VII gold Medio Escudo**. One *Escudo* was worth 80 *Reales*. Each Medio Escudo was worth US $5 dollars;

a 1808 **Fernando VII Silver Duro**. One *Duro* was worth 5 *Pesos*. At the time an ounce of gold was worth 16 *Pesos*. All these coins were circulating in Cuba, given its status as one of the world's busiest international ports.

In 1817, freemasons of the "Suns and Rays of Bolívar" lodge in Cuba organized a conspiracy to create the Republic of Cubanacán with the help of Venezuela and Colombia. Among its main leaders were Colombian ex-president José Fernández Madrid, Ecuador's future president Vicente Rocafuerte and Peruvian writer Manuel Lorenzo Vidaurre. José Francisco Lemus, a Cuban-born Colombian army colonel was the leader in Havana. Plans were to organize an invasion by a 3000 men Bolivarian army under a high rank general loyal to Bolivar.

Lemus with the collaboration of Colombian officials, used subterfuges common to the meetings of Masonic lodges, such as secret taps, signs, rituals and Freemasonry salutes. Each conspirator, a *Sol*, before becoming a *Ray* had to recruit at least seven new followers; these practices secured the conspiracy and prevented its detection.

During the second half of 1822 and early 1823, the movement spread from Havana to Matanzas, Las Villas and Camagüey, linking with other lodges and secret organizations. The political platform attracted many illustrious natives: Miguel Teurbe Toulon, José María Heredia, Mariano Segui and others, among whom were judges, priests, military officers, small business owners and, as Vives described, «tenants, field hands and people of color, including town mayors, council members and high class neighbors .»

Throughout almost four years of conspiratorial activities, stocking weapons and ammunition, they designed a flag and issued several proclamations signed by Lemus as generalissimo in chief of the Cubanacán Republican troops.

The organization, however, had been penetrated since 1821 by the intelligence services of Captain General Nicolás Mahy. In 1824, when the restoration of absolutism in Spain could cause a revolutionary outbreak, the governor decided to liquidate the threat of the conspiracy.

Arrests throughout Cuba began on August 14, 1824; Lemus was arrested in Guanabacoa. The case involved 602 defendants; Captain-General Mahy, acting with great tact, decided to avoid shedding blood to prevent greater evils. Lemus was sent to Spain; other conspirators were sentenced to heavy fines. Heredia, Francisco Agüero, Andrés Manuel Sánchez, José A. Iznagas, Gaspar Betancourt Cisneros, José A. Arango and others were allowed to escape abroad.

The Republic of *Cubanacán*

Images, top to bottom, left to right:

The **Teatro Villanueva** in 1850, at the block comprissed by Zulueta, Colón, Morro and Refugio streets, scene of the disturbances for which José Martí was detained in 1869;

the **Teatro Principal** at the *Alameda de Paula*;

the **Teatro Tacón**, on the *Paseo del Prado*, today enclosed inside the *Centro Gallego*;

the inside of the **Teatro Tacón**. It could accomodate 1500 spectators.

Death of Capt. Ferrer, the Captain of the Amistad, July, 1839.

Don Jose Ruiz and Don Pedro Montez, of the Island of Cuba, having purchased fifty-three slaves at Havana, recently imported from Africa, put them on board the Amistad, Capt. Ferrer, in order to transport them to Principe, another port on the Island of Cuba. After being out from Havana about four days, the African captives on board, in order to obtain their freedom, and return to Africa, armed themselves with cane knives, and rose upon the Captain and crew of the vessel. Capt. Ferrer and the cook of the vessel were killed; two of the crew escaped; Ruiz and Montez were made prisoners.

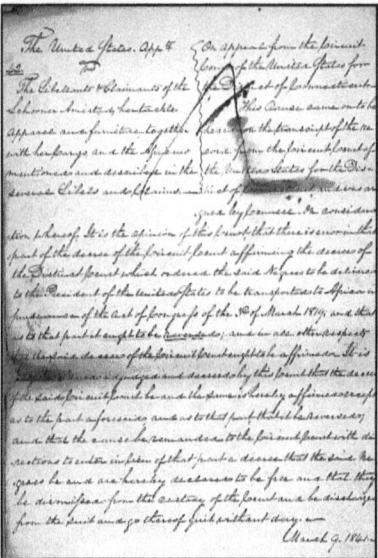

Images, top to bottom, left to right:

An engraving published in 1840 in several US newspapers showing the mutineers on the ship **Amistad**;

the Supreme Court opinion on the **repatriation of the slaves** illegally imprissoned in the *Amistad* ship;

a Cuban postal stamp commemorating the death of **Plácido** in 1844 during the conspitacy of the *Soles y Rayos de Bolívar*;

A Cuban postal stamp honoring **Joaquín de Agüero**. In 1851 he headed one of the first insurrections against the Spanish government in Cuba.

Images, top to bottom, left to right:

An engraving showing the torture method known as **La Escalera**;

the **Palacio de los Condes de Santovenia**, at 9 Baratillo street, on Havana's *Plaza de Armas*, built in 1784;

three noteworthy men in early XIX century Cuba: **Francisco Frías**, Count of Pozos Dulces, director of the newspaper *El Siglo*; **Leopoldo O'Donnell**, *Gran Duque de Tetuán*, Captain General of Cuba in 1843, the man who repressed La Escalera conspiracy; **José Gurtiérrez de la Concha**, Viscount of Cuba, three times Captain General of Cuba;

a rare cartoon of **Domingo del Monte**, writer, lawyer, critic, patron of the arts, advocate for public education in Cuba. He was at the center of the conspiración de *La Escalera*.

Jean Baptiste Vermay (1784-1833), the first world class painter that visited and stayed in Havana.

Images, top to bottom, left to right:

A drawing by Miahle showing Havana's **Customs House**;

Tacón's 1836 **Fuente de Neptuno** in Havana, formely at the *Alameda de Paula*, later at *Paseo del Prado*, on the block between Zulueta and Neptuno, nowadays back at its original location;

the **Alameda de Paula**, oldest promenade in Havana, in 1850;

the **Casa de Beneficencia** in Havana, founded by Bishop Jerónimo Valdés. Until 1959 it was at the corner of Belascoain and San Lázaro streets.

Photo of the Havana-Güines railroad in 1835.

Claudio Martínez de Pinillos, Count of Villanueva, was Chairman of Havana's Board of Public Works. Among his official duties was to ensure the promotion of agriculture and the adequacy of roads and access everywhere in the island. He was a *criollo* born in Havana in 1782. He had fought in Spain against the Napoleonic invasion and had returned to Cuba in 1813 as Treasurer of the Spanish Army. In the 1830s, knowing of the problems of moving sugar, coffee, corn and rice from the fertile Güines valley to the port of Havana, he became the main proponent of railroads to improve the economy of Cuba. He found the funds necessary by a loan from an English banker named Alexander Roberts, with the support of many of the landowners.

Martinez de Pinillos, however, found Miguel Tacón, Captain General of Cuba, as an impenetrable obstacle to the establishment of the Havana-Güines railroad. At 59, Tacón was a tired but important personality, an egomaniac, authoritarian and sour man, always bragging about his past involvement in the Battle of Trafalgar. He soon clashed with the Count, an illustrated and popular man. Twenty years earlier Martínez de Pinillos had sent a letter to Tacón accusing him of abuses during his assignment to quell the insurgents in the Viceroyalty of Rio de la Plata. He had ended the letter saying: «You are a coward and, if ever our lives intersect, I will challenge you to a duel.»

The hatred between the two men seethed for more than two decades. When Havana's Board of Public Works sent Tacón the proposed path of the Havana-Güines railroad, Tacón vetoed the project. « Villanueva will not have his train,» were his words. Work on the Iron Road project, which had already started and was close to Bejucal, was cancelled, citing a number of strategic reasons without any foundation. He requested the dismissal of Villanueva to the government of Madrid.

(continued)

The Remarkable Story of Cuban Railroads

(continuation)

La Habana was 320 feet higher than Güines at a distance of 16 miles; half the path was in uneven terrain, full of small hills on which workers had to build embankments. It was an epic effort. The railway bridge over the Almendares River became known as the Santería Span. Every night, Babalawo slaves prayed to their orishas for protection; one or two men fell every week from its 200 ft tall pillars into the river. Hundreds of men were needed to carve the rock for the 330 feet long tunnel at Vento.

When the crown ignored the objections of Tacón, the Captain General forced the terminal in Havana to be at a place called *Quinta de Garcini*, a block limited by today's Oquendo, Estrella, Marquéz González and Maloja streets, more than 3 miles from the Ensenada de Atarés, the nearest potential wharf location. At a meeting with Tacón Martínez de Pinillos objected; he was dismissed by the Captain General with a strange grin on his face.

Martínez de Pinillos kept his cool and told Tacón: «the time has come for you to have a chance to finally get rid of me. I challenge you to a duel. If the result is favorable to you, take credit for the construction of the railroad. If it is favorable to me, the crown will never absolve me for having killed the most important functionary in Cuba. Either way you destroy me.»

The duel took place at the city bloc Tacón had designated as the terminal for the railroad, at half an hour before dawn. José Antonio Saco and Julián de Zulueta were Tacón's godparents. Wenceslao Villaurrutia and Antonio Escovedo were Martínez de Pinillos'. Escovedo did the counting. Tacón was to fire first, at 10 paces, as specified by Tacón who was short sighted. Tacón failed his shot, barely scratching the Count's face by an inch. Martínez de Pinillos raised his arm and said: «General, I will be content if you stop interfering in the affairs of the railroad.» Tacón answered «Villanueva, you win. I am satisfied.»

Martínez de Pinillos pointed his weapon straight up and fired. The duel was over.

On the following November 19, 1837, members of the Real Development Board, chaired by the Count of Villanueva, solemnly inaugurated the first Spanish railway throughout Latin America, the first under the Spanish flag and the seventh worldwide.

The Remarkable Story of Cuban Railroads

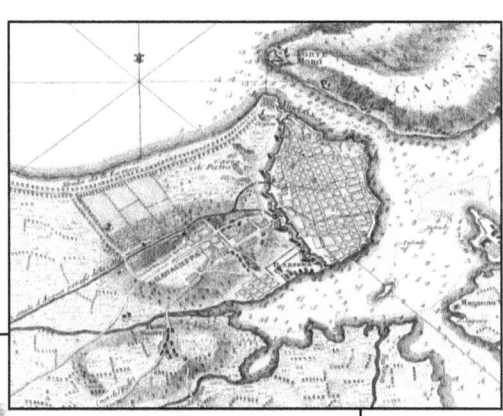

Images, top to bottom, left to right:

A **1838 Plan of Havana** bay;

a **1855 view of Havana** from the *El Chaple* hill;

Don Francisco de Albear, engineer of the first large scale aqueduct serving the city of Havana, commissioned by governor La Concha in 1852;

Louis Moreau Gottschalk, an American composer and pianist, celebrated figure in Europe, friend of Chopin, Victor Hugo, Spain's Queen Isabel II, France's Empress Eugenia de Montijo, US president Andrew Jackson, composer Berlioz. Jazz precursor and musical director of *Tacón Theater*.

Images, top to bottom, left to right:

Mercado de Tacón, or *Plaza del Vapor*. Francisco Marty, owner of *Tacón Theater*, had a 20 year fish monopoly granted by Tacón; the only other markets in Havana were *Colón's* (Monserrate, Zulueta, Animas and Trocadero streets, where the *Palacio de Bellas Artes* is today) and *Cristina's* (San Ignacio, Teniente Rey, Mercaderes and Muralla streets, where a park and an underground garage are today);

first street car in Havana, drawn by horses, in June 1862,

the railroad **Station of Villanueva**, built in 1839 on land bought from Havana's Botanical Garden, originally owned by *Caminos de Hierro*, which later merged with *Ferrocarriles Unidos*, a Canadian company.

Images, top to bottom, left to right:

A denunciation of an **illegal sale of slaves** in Havana on 1847;

an advertisement for *La Dominica*, a **Havana store**, in 1840;

a **Cuban Royal Lottery ticket** in 1845, with proceeds destined for street paving in Havana;

a **firefighter's car** during the times of governor Tacón in 1835.

In the 1840s, rebellious slaves incited by the British consul, David Turnbully and his secretary, Ross Cocking, erupted in a series of riots across the island but mainly in Havana and Matanzas. Even though these disturbances were never characterized as a conspiracy, they fueled the apprehension of slave owners who believed the violence were the initial manifestations of a revolt due to start on Christmas Day, 1843; the fear was it could be a repeat in Cuba of the Haitian Revolution of 1802. On November 20, 1842, Domingo del Monte shared his feelings with his friend Alejandro Everett, a powerful lawyer from Boston. Everett passed the information to Daniel Webster, US Secretary of State, as well as to the Spanish ambassador in Washington, several US representatives and the US consuls in Madrid and London. Webster offerred to send two ships to support the threatened colonial government in Havana, and to quell the projected rebellion by force, should it be necessary. Captain General Jerónimo Valdés never believed that a conspiracy was brewing; he attributed the news to slave merchants trying to stop the suppression of the slave market and to end the numerous manumissions taking place around the island.

Subsequent events made it clear the rumors were unfounded, but that did not allay the fears of the residents; as soon as the new governor General Leopoldo O'Donnell took posession, he was greeted with the rumors. This was credible enough for him; witin two weeks he began to unleash a ferocious campaign of arrests and tortures to obtain implausible confessions of membership in the conspiracy. José de la Luz y Caballero, at the time under medical treatment in París was incriminated, along with Felix Tanco, the Guiteras brothers, Manuel Castro Palomino, Benigno Gener, Domingo del Monte and dozens of white *Creoles*, almost all of them economically solvent. Their fate was to be sent into exiled. Free mestizos, Blacks and hundreds of slaves were not expelled from Cuba but assassinated.

The False Revolt of Christmas Day, 1843

25

The First Pro-Independence Movements in Cuba

WHILE INDEPENDENCE MOVEMENTS were exploding in South America starting in 1809, local Cuban elites in the island remained silent and peaceful in spite of the power vacuum created in Spain by the Napoleonic invasion. Cuban planters, artists, poets and intellectuals felt the anxiety of their former neighbors from Santo Domingo when they arrived in Cuba escaping from the horrors of the Haitian Revolution of 1790. The Spanish authorities tried to prevent any contact of Cuba's population with the exile's ideals and experiences, even though several Haitians generals like Jean François Papillon and Georges Biassou, and Dominican generals like Gil Narciso, had fought on the Spanish side against the French armies.[251] Among those who welcomed Haitian officials who sought refuge in Cuba in 1796 was José Antonio Aponte y Ulabarra; he led a Black fraternal society called *Shango Tedum*.

By 1810, sugar *hacendados*, coffee planters, and slave owners in Cuba decided to tighten their ties with the Spanish authorities convinced that Madrid was the only power capable of defending their economic interests (slave ownership) and ensure plantation security in the face of potential revolts. It was left to non-slave-owning planters and other representatives of the middle class, such as writers, peasants, artisans to figure out how to start an independence movement. The first conspiracy supporting independence in Cuba was led by Román de la

---

[251] The Spaniards backed the Haitian revolution from the beginning, giving arms and food to the insurgents, as well as logistics and intelligence reports. Spain's aim was to recover Haiti; it had been taken by the French after the Peace Treaty of Ryswick in 1697. Spain was officially neutral during the Haitian uprising and kept its contacts with the rebels in secret; it only declared war on France and sided with the rebels after Louis XVI was executed by the French National Convention in 1793.

Luz, Joaquín Infante and Juan Francisco Bassave. All three were white *Criollos* from wealthy families; Bassave, in particular, was *capitán de milicias* and had a following in poor neighborhoods and among the battalions of Blacks and mulattos, on one of which Aponte was a first corporal. An indiscretion by Román de la Luz' wife, however, caused the conspiracy to be discovered; Luz and Bassave were not able to escape and were exiled and sentenced to prison. Infante, who made his living carving beautiful religious images, evaded his captors, escaping to Venezuela; in 1811 he drafted the first constitution for an independent Cuba.

In early 1812, new conspiracies started in Cuba; they were led by José Antonio Aponte, along with his lieutenants Hilario Herrera, Francisco Javier Pacheco, Clemente Chacón, Salvador Calf, John Barbier, José del Carmen Peñalver and Juan Bautista Lisundia. They became the backbone of a vast movement of free blacks and slaves throughout the island, whose actions reached Remedios, Puerto Príncipe, Bayamo, Jiguaní, Holguín and Baracoa. In Havana, some conspirators would distract police attention by setting fires outside the walls, while their associates would take weapons from the main barracks to supply the insurgents among the workers of the sugar mills. Supporting these activities were King Henry Christophe of Haiti [252] and Dominican General Gil Narciso.

On March 15, 1812, Barbier, Pacheco and Lisundia successfully got the Black workers in the *Peñas Altas* sugar mill, near Matanzas, to revolt but failed to do the same in other mills. A few days later Aponte and his followers were captured and in early April 1812, after a quick process, they were hanged. Aponte's head was cut off and displayed in a cage on a busy

---

[252] Henry Christopher (1767-1820) was a former slave and key leader in the Haitian Revolution of 1804. In 1805 he took part under Jean-Jacques Dessalines in the unsuccessful invasion of Santo Domingo (today's Dominican Republic) against French forces under the command of French officer Marie-Louis Ferrand.

corner of Havana as a warning. [253] Unexpectedly, the conspiracy of Aponte in 1812 was a severe blow to independence plans; it fueled among criollos a fear that any strong pro-independence effort on the island would provoke a general revolt by the slaves.

Those fears continued in Cuba until August 12, 1851. On that day the city of Puerto Príncipe awoke to the sound of 12 rifle shots that ended the lives of four insurgents that had been captured in *Sabana de Méndez*, on the northern side of the city. The calm of the city was shaken. Rumors began to spread. The names of the men were Agüero, Zayas, Betancourt and Benavides. They were all members of the best and oldest families in the city. Agüero, in particular, had been closely watched by Spanish authorities since 1843 when he had set free his eight Black slaves and given them tracts of land from his own properties. With his wife Ana Josefa Perdomo he had founded a free public school in Guáimaro, the town that was in 1869 to become the venue of the first Cuban Constitution.

Harassed by Puerto Príncipe's authorities, Agüero and his wife had moved temporarily to the US; they returned to Cuba in 1849 and founded the *Sociedad Libertadora de Puerto Príncipe*.

Within a few months, on July 4, 1851, he was back to his farm *El Redentor*, and had recruited 40 "able men" who took to the mountains near the town of San Francisco de Jucaral, near Guáimaro. It was the first well armed and organized effort to

---

[253] It has been speculated by Cuban historian Fernando Portuondo, that Aponte was betrayed by one of his lieutenants, a man called Esteban Sánchez in whose house the conspirators had met. Commenting on these events, another Cuban historian, Ramiro Guerra, atributed the disorganized haste of the Aponte conspiracy to «the need to stop the dissapointment of Blacks after a 1811 decision of the Spanish Courts not to abolish slavery and slave trade; deceived in their hope, Blacks resolved to organize a rebel movement to win freedom by force or by any other means.» Elías Entralgo, a historian not easily given to superlatives, looking at the Aponte conspiracy, praised his organizational capabilities and listed Aponte's talents: «calm, patience, courage, intuition, skills, caring, subtlety and careful observation of people and things, but, above all, his binding power. He knew how to bring together individuals from diverse trades and means: cobblers, bagaseros, saddlers, carpenters, ringers, rickshaw pullers. He triumphed as a conspirator but failed as an insurgent.»

seek the independence of Cuba. A proclamation was issued that read in part...

«*Declaramos estar abiertamente en contra de todo acto o ley que surja de nuestra antigua metrópolis: no reconocemos ninguna clase de autoridad, sea cual sea su rango, cuyo nombramiento y facultades no hayan nacido de la mayoría del pueblo de Cuba, que es el único con facultades para dictar leyes a través de sus representantes.*» (We openly declare to be against all acts or laws that emerge from our former metropolis: we do not acknowledge any kind of authority, regardless of its rank, whose appointment and faculties are not born from the majority of the people of Cuba, the only body with faculties to dictate laws through their representatives).

The Agüero insurrection failed within a few days, mostly for lack of adequate support. They were counting with the help of *criollos*, free Blacks and slaves; it never materialized in the quantities needed. By the time they were encircled and ready for their first battle, they had only 300 men, 100 lancers and 200 infantry. After an initial sharp engagement, the Spaniards fled, their captain and 20 others being killed, 18 wounded. Agüero and his men had 3 wounded and none killed. Twelve Spanish soldiers had come over to Agüero's side. Legend had it that after this initial victory many men from the region joined their ranks, reaching close to 1000. They followed the Spaniards until they reached *Cascorro*, 17 kilometers from Puerto Príncipe.[254] Eventually the stronger and reinforced Spanish forces from Puerto Príncipe prevailed. They encircled the three units organized by Joaquín de Agüero, Francisco Agüero y Estrada and Ubaldo Arteaga Piña. All men were taken prisoners after suffering 16 casualties. All their arms were captured by Spanish troops.

---

[254] These events were reported by the *New York Herald* on the edition of July 28, 1851. It indicated that «similar movements have taken place in Las Tunas, Sabanicú, Bayamo, Trinidad and Pinar del Río. The government has placed a black-out on news as great number of its troops have gone over to the insurgents. All war vessels have gone out to sea and the steamer Blasco de Garay sailed from Havana at 10:00 PM last night, with 2000 additional men; they will join 4000 soldiers available to General Lemory in the barracks of Puerto Príncipe.»

Days later, on August 21, 1851, the *New York Herald* reported from Key West:

«General Narciso López,[255] aboard the steamer *Pampero* with 450 followers, came through the North West Pass on Sunday last at 5:00 PM, anchored off our light house, communicated with shore and left at 10:00 PM. It is understood that it landed about 12 miles eastward of Bahia Honda, in Cuba, where they were joined immediately by people from the surrounding country. López left at 7:00 AM and marched against the nearest military post. A Spanish smack,[256] sent by Francisco Marty, manager of the Havana Opera House and close friend of the governor, was there picking up intelligence. This expedition appear to have been planned with a good deal of skill; those engaged in it seem to have a determination to survive or perish.»

The *Pampero* was commanded by a Captain Lewis, the same man who had directed the steamship *Creole* in the Cardenas successful expedition of May 19, 1848, and who had been fined US $5000 as the commander of the failed expedition of the *Cleopatra* in 1850. Months later, the *Pampero* landed on August 12, 1851, in Bahia Honda, Pinar del Rio, the same day Joaquín de Agüero was shoot in Puerto Príncipe.

Forty four out of the 400 men aboard the *Pampero* were Cubans. The Americans were grouped in two battalions of 232 and 122 men each, commanded by Colonel Downman, a veteran of the Mexican war, and Lieutenant Colonel William Scott Haynes from Tennessee. Most of their staffs were foreign officers of distinction, mostly Hungarians and Germans. One of

---

[255] In an article in *La Gaceta de la Havana*, December 27, 1848, Narciso López had been characterized by Captain General Federico Roncalli, Count of Alcoy, as follows: «*El Mariscal de Campo Don Narciso López, es tan conocido por los arrebatos temerarios e imprudentes de su caracter como por la veleidad e inconstancia de sus sentimientos y opiniones.*» (Field Marshal Don Narciso Lopez, is as well known for its reckless and imprudent outbursts of character as for the fickleness and skittishness of his feelings and opinions). Earlier, the wife of Southern US General Jefferson Davis, who in 1848 had been offered by Narciso López the command of the 1851 expedition to Cuba, had said of López... «this dark man is remarkable for his glowing eyes and snowy hair.»

[256] A smack was a small sailing ship rigged like a sloop or cutter used for fishing and sailing along the coast.

them was a nephew of the US Attorney General, another had graduated from West Point with honors. Landing on Bahia Honda was at 8:00 PM on August 12, 1851 and lasted until 9:00 AM. Men aboard the Spanish frigate *Esperanza* were waiting for them. Within hours they were reinforced by the frigate *Pizarro* and the schooner *Victoria*; the first one carrying 750 men, the second was transporting 30 horses and a large load of weapons. They were following orders from Captain General Concha, who had known for weeks about the expedition. By 11:00 AM Lopez' men were surrounded, 45 Americans were killed or wounded, 4 officers were killed and 7 were wounded. The rest wondered about the countryside or were taken prisoner. The only thing worrying Concha was that not all invaders had been shot as soon as they were captured and he now had to contend with the turmoil that an execution in Havana would produce. He was particularly interested in the capture and execution of Narciso López; he was garroted in front of 20,000 spectators that were gathered for the occasion. The *Gaceta de la Habana* reported on September 2, 1851...

«*Veinte mil hombres permanecieron en silencio hasta que la cabeza llena de canas del hombre en la silla cayó hacia adelante bajo el garrote.*» (Twenty thousand men stood quiet until the grey head of the man in the chair fell forward under the garrote).[257]

It was, until then, the bloodiest day of the Cuban's struggle seeking independence.

The news of the executions were received with rage in the US. In Spain, however, the news was received with glee. In Cuba, mobs attacked the newspaper *Union*, as well as several coffee houses sponsored by Spaniards. The office of the Spanish consul in New York was attacked in the evening of September 3rd. The Spanish Consul Laborde, in fear for his life (or for

---

[257] The punishment of the *Garrote Vil* is imparted by placing the victim in an easy chair, clamping his limbs, placing a band around his neck, and gradually pressing a screw until the neck is broken. His last words were «Adieu, dear Cuba.» In all, of the men landed by the *Pampero*, 556 were killed and 436 jailed.

effect) took refuge in the home of a friend and later fled to Havana. At the Palace of the Captain General in Havana a mob broke open the doors, defaced the portraits of the Queen of Spain and the Captain General of Cuba. On a smaller scale a similar destruction of Spanish property took place in Key West. In Mobile, Alabama, only the quick action of several influential citizens could quiet a rabble trying to execute a Spanish lieutenant. Public meetings took place in Louisville, Cincinnati, Baltimore, Philadelphia and Pittsburgh, where long lists of resolutions were adopted.

On the other side of the coin, Captain General Concha saw the events of 1851 as an opportunity to urge strong measures to suppress future insurrections. He began to build great roads, a strong army and navy and a completely centralized military administration. In Madrid, the affairs dealing with Cuba were placed in the hands of the prime minister and an special advisory council was created. Among other things, the newspaper *El Faro Industrial* [258] was suppressed, its American director brought before a military court and, without delay, found guilty of aiding the *filibusteros* and condemned to 8 years imprisonment in Ceuta. He was later pardoned under pressure from Washington.

A few months later, the *Conspiración de Vuelta Abajo* was organized by friends of Narciso López. It was instantly suppressed by Concha. Cuba, for a few years, became an outwardly quiet island.

---

[258] Originally called *Diario de Avisos políticos, Mercantiles, Económicos y Literarios*, *El Faro Industrial* was one of the most important publications in Cuba. Its proprietors were Cirilo Villaverde and Antonio Bachiller y Morales; the director was José María de Cárdenas, a disciple of José Antonio Saco and Félix Varela. Its correspondents in Spain were Gertrudis Gómez de Avellaneda and José Jacinto Milanés. Some of the frequent writers were Gaspar Betancourt Cisneros and Rafael María de Mendive. The paper was published between 1841 and 1851, when it was closed because *quebrantaba la tranquilidad ciudadana* (it was affecting public peace).

After the execution of Gabriel de la Concepción Valdés (Plácido) in 1844, a young man, 25 years old Eduardo Facciolo, began to openly express his condemnation of the tight tyranny of the Spanish colonial regime in Cuba. His godfather, a captain of police in the town of Regla and a man fully devoted to the Spanish crown, reprimanded him severely and remainded him of his obligations as the best typographer of the government printing shop situated across the street from the *Palacio de los Capitanes Generales*.

Facciolo's answer to this dilemma was to secure employment at the printing shop of Domingo Patiño on Obispo street, where he met Cirilo Villaverde, Juan Bellido de Luna, Anacleto Bermudez and other writers and colaborators of the newspaper *Faro Industrial de la Habana*.

After *Faro Industrial* was outlawed and closed by the government of Captain General Concha in 1852, Bellido talked Facciolo into being the typographer of a clandestine new paper called *La Voz del Pueblo Cubano*. The first issue was printed on June 13, 1852. Two thousand copies were distributed in Havana hand-by-hand. The authorities were bewildered and set up to find and punish the transgressors of the rigid censorship impossed by the Concha government. *La Voz* followed with a second issue, this time three thousand copies distributed across the entire island, New York and even Madrid and Barcelona. Such an audacity had to be punished severely. By then a new Captain General was in power in Cuba, Valentín Cañedo. He gave strict orders to the military to find the press, destroy it and take all those implicated under custody. Cañedo was irate; the second issue of *La Voz* refered to him as *General Salchicha*.

The printing press was moved to a sugar warehouse on Teniente Rey street, property of Bellido's brother, and hidden on a huge trunk that the conspirators refered to as *el sarcófago*, the coffin. A third issue was printed in an empty store on Galiano street. A fourth issue was planed to be printed on the home of a poet that lived on 44 Obispo street. Luck ran out and the *sarcófago* was discovered by the watchman in charge of the street lamps as it was transported across Dragones street. All those implicated were detained. Cañedo sentenced Pacciolo to death as the printer and worst culprit. He was garroted at 7:00 AM on Tuesday, September 28, 1852. His last wish was to be allowed to write a good by letter to his mother, which he did.

Eduardo Facciolo's Printing Press in 1852

Images, top to bottom, left to right:

Map showing the area of the **1851 rebellion** by Joaquín Agüero;

a plaque, now lost, commemorating the **1812 rebellion** of Aponte. It was situated at the corner of Monte and Aponte streets in Havana;

the 1812 Project for a **Cuban Constitution** written by Joaquín Infante;

one of the few contemporary images of **José Antonio Aponte**;

Salvador del Muro y Salazar, **Marqués de Someruelos**, Captain General of Cuba during the Aponte rebellion;

a 100 Gourdes bill showing **King Henry Chistophe** of Haiti.

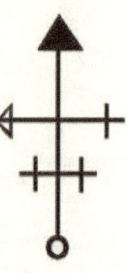
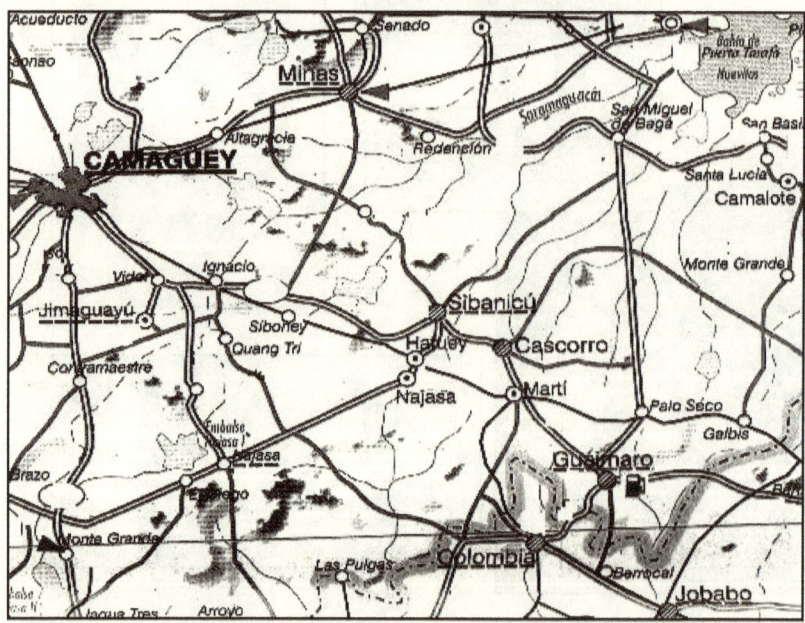

Images, top to bottom, left to right:

A Cuban postal stamp commemorating the 100 anniversary of the 1851 Joaquín de Agüero rebellion in **Jucaral**, Camagüey. It ocurred 17 years before the 1868 War of Independence;

a contemporary image of **Joaquín de Agüero**;

the *abakuá* symbol used by the men of **José Antonio Aponte** to verify the authenticity of internal communications;

a map of the **areas of rebellions** in Puerto Príncipe showing Guáimaro, Cascorro, Jimaguayú, Sibanicú and Najasa.

Images, top to bottom, left to right:

Eduardo Facciolo Alba (1828-1852), typographer and printer of the newspaper *El Faro Industrial*, first martir of journalism in Cuba. He was executed for violating the censorship of the press in 1852;

an engraving showing the **execution of Facciolo**;

Domingo Goicuría and **Cirilo Villaverde**, conspirators for Cuban independence in the 1850s;

The New York Journal, a newspaper reporting independence efforts in Cuba;

the first edition of Cirilo Villaverde's **Cecilia Valdés** o **La Loma del Angel**.

Images, top to bottom, left to right:

An engraving showing **Cárdenas** on fire on May 19, 1850;

a map of the area near **Bahia Honda** where Narciso López and his fellow filibusters made their last and disastrous attempt to invade Cuba aboard the *Pampero* on August 12, 1851;

an engraving of young **Narciso López** in 1840, when he served Spain as governor of Matanzas;

a 1812 copy of the ***Diario de la Habana***, describing the events surrounding the rebellion of José Antonio Aponte in Camagüey;

an image of **Colonel William Logan Crittenden** (1823-1851), West Point graduate, former US Army Lieutenant, second in command to Narciso López in 1851. He was executed August 17, 1851, on *Atarés Castle* in Havana.

Images, top to bottom, left to right:

The area near **Bahia Honda** where Narciso López landed in 1851 aboard the *Pampero*;

a **cartoon** showing Spain trying to keep the US out of their property;

a **cartoon** presenting Narciso López as a mercenary, published by Spanish loyalists in New Orleans;

Don José Gutiérrez de la Concha, Captain General of Cuba at the time of Narciso López' invasions;

the **Cuban coat of arms** as designed by Narciso López. It was a close precursor of the coat of arms adopted after independence in 1898.

Images, top to bottom, left to right:

Narciso López at the time of his unsuccessful Cuban invasions;

enlargement of the engraving showing the execution of Narciso López;

the New Orleans engraving showing the **execution of Narciso López**;

the **chair** of Narciso Lopez' execution, showing the tourniquet that would break the neck of the condemned;

postal stamps celebrating the **centenary of the Cuban flag** in 1951.

In the early years of the XIX century, rich merchants and planters in Havana were frequent visitors of the *Teatro Principal*, opened since 1773 at the *Alameda de Paula*, and the *Teatro Diorama* designed by Juan Bautista Vermay in 1827 at the place near today's *Capitolio*. Popular classes enjoyed variety and light comic shows at the *Teatro Villanueva*, outside city walls, on the block limited by today's Zulueta, Colón, Morro and Refugio streets, as well as some small circus-like theaters in what is now *El Cerro*. A growing city, however, demanded an institution worthy of great capitals like Madrid, Paris, London and Barcelona.

Two men took the initiative in the 1800s: Governor and Captain General Miguel Tacón, first Duke of Cuba, and Catalan grocery merchant Francisco Marty y Torrens, supplier of the Spanish Navy. Tacón provided quarry stone for a majestic theater and sponsored "six masked balls;" Marty provided the funds and his management skills. The chosen location was the corner of today's Prado and San Rafael streets. Carpentry was trusted to Miguel Nin Pons, patriarch of a *criollo* family that would include writer Anaïs Nin (1903-1977) in time. The theater opened on schedule and under budget on February 28, 1838.

The inaugural performance was on April 15 with *Don Juan de Austria* by Mariano José de Larra. It had been chosen by José Antonio Saco: the story of Don Juan, brother to Felipe II, hero of the Battle of Lepanto, graduate of Alcalá de Henares. Culture, romance and valor, a combination that pleased Saco. From the start, Tacon became the best venue for Opera in Havana; the *Teatro Principal* was not large enough for audience room and a grand stage. Paris-scale Grand Opera became the norm, with plenty of extras, stage resources and the best lyric stars of the times like Marietta Gazzaniga on the main role in Verdi's *La Traviata*, and Erminia Frezzolini in Bellini's *La Sonnambula*. During the 1859 season, Louis Moreau Gottschalk, Tacón's musical director, staged *Fête Champëtre Cubain*. The orchestra had "650 performers, 87 choristers. 15 solo singers, 50 drums, 70 violins, 11 contrabasses, 11 violoncellos and 80 trumpets, a total of 900 persons bellowing, singing and blowing to see could do it best," according to a review in the *Gazeta de la Habana*. It was equal to laying a plan for a military campaign, requiring money, time, diplomacy, muscles of steel and an iron will.

Havana's *Teatro Principal*

26

A Precarious Tranquility in the Late 1800s

DURING THE REIGN OF ISABEL II, the *Partido Liberal Moderado* was in power in Madrid except for brief exceptions. It was a period of time called *La Década Moderada* (1843-1854) in the history of Spain. The crown had a strong intervention in the political life of the country, second only to the Army; all groups, aristocracy, church and conservative bourgeoisie, had to resort to the Army's blessings to reach political power in Spain.

The next biennium (*el Bienio Progresista*, 1854-1868) led to the crisis of the Elizabethan system. A military *pronunciamiento*, supported by progressives and moderates and led by General Don Leopoldo O'Donnell, Duke of Tetuan,[259] Grandee of Spain, did away with the Espartero [260] government in 1856. Queen Isabel II asked him to form a government as the 44th Prime Minister of Spain. O'Donnell dutifully accepted after founding the *Partido Union Liberal*, which was a happy cross of Progressives, Moderates and even *Carlistas*.[261]

---

[259] In 1860 he commanded the Spanish army at the battle of Tetuan during Spain's invasion of Morocco. He was rewarded for this campaign with the title Duke of Tetuan. In 1843 he was sent to Cuba as Captain General, where he was responsible for the 1844 repression of the *La Escalera* revolt.

[260] General Joaquín Baldomero Espartero was the man who had lost the Battle of Ayacucho in Perú to Antonio José de Sucre (*el Gran Mariscal de Ayacucho*), securing the independence of most of South America. Sucre was one of Bolivar's generals, 2nd President of Bolivia, ambushed and assassinated in 1830 near Quito.

[261] The *Carlistas* had been very strong in the 1830s, after the birth of Isabel II and the opposition of heir-presuntive Carlos, her uncle, who felt robbed oif his right to succession and took asylum in Portugal. The *Carlistas* recovered their popularity with the dissatisfaction with Alfonso XII after the loss of Cuba during the Hispano-Cuban-American war of 1898. They would remain popular during the Spanish Civil war (1936-1939) and until the end of the Franco regime in 1975.

The next important event in the peninsula was *el Sexenio Revolucionario* (1868-1874), when Spaniards attempted to establish a democratic regime, overcoming moderate liberalism and introducing democratic practices. It began on the same year that the 1868 War of Independence in Cuba, with a revolution that Spaniards called *La Gloriosa*. Queen Isabel II was deposed [262] and the revolutionary leaders recruited as King an Italian Prince, Amadeo de Savoy.[263]

The rebels of *La Gloriosa* belonged to marginalized groups: unionists, progressives and democrats. They came together and signed the *Pacto de Ostend*, in an effort to democratize political life and bring about economy recovery. The movement was led by two military men, General Juan Prim y Prats, Grandee of Spain (progressive), [264] who had found Amadeo after searching all the European courts for a Prince that would not be opposed to being democratically elected,[265] and General Francisco Serrano, Grandee of Spain (Unionist, like O'Donnell), who had helped Espadero overthrow the regency of Maria Cristina and convoked the Cortes to declare Isabel as an adult at age 15.

After the abdication of Amadeo I of Savoy, the Spanish parliament voted by a large majority the proclamation of the Republic in February of 1873. The majority of the House were

---

[262] It was said that she had fell more and more under the influence of the Jesuits and had become increasingly tyrannical.

[263] Amadeo I would be the only Spanish King from the House of Savoy, a royal family that emerged in the 11th century in what is now Switzerland and lasted until the end of World War II. Amadeo was the second son of King Vittorio Emanuele II of Italy. He reigned in Spain from 1870 to 1873, under a regime fraught with republicanism, Carlist rebellions in the peninsula and independence movements in Cuba. He could not take the stress and abdicated and returned to Italy after declaring before the Cortes that «the Spanish people are ungovernable.»

[264] On December 28, 1870, General Prim, president of the Spanish Cortes, recently promoted to Marshal, was shot and killed by unknown assassins as he left the Cortes' chambers; he died two days later.

[265] In the words of General Prim «looking for a democratic monarch in Europe is like trying to find an atheist in heaven.»

monarchists, however and, from the beginning, the republic never had much with real support. On January 4, 1874, a military coup by General Manuel Pavia[266] took place; the parliament, under occupation by the *Guardia Civil*, was dissolved and General Serrano suspended the Constitution. By the end of the year General Arsenio Martínez Campos [267] proclaimed Alfonso de Borbón, son of the exiled Isabel II, as Alfonso XII; the Bourbon monarchy had been restored.

Once the monarchy was restored, two major parties dominate political life: the Conservative Party of Canovas, supporter of political stability, defender of the Church and the social order; and the Liberal Party of Sagasta, more democratic, secular and socially active. Both parties were run by remarkably astute men; both were essentially in agreement ideologically, i.e., they were politically centralist (supporting the concentration of power in a central authority) and strong defenders of the monarchy. A period of relative calm permeated Spain, hoping for the end of both wars, the *Carlista* and the Cuban first War of Independence.

Conservatives and Liberals agreed to govern taking peaceful turns. The parties realized that winning the election was not as important as being the party chosen by the king to rule. Unfortunately this was possible by a corrupt electoral system that manipulated elections, falsified records, bought and sold votes, used coercive practices on the electorate, and disregarded polit-

---

[266] General Pavia had been mentored by General Prim. He repeatedly offered his services to put an end to the anarchy that was raging in Madrid as well as in all provinces. He was particularly alarmed by the disorganization prevalent in the Cortes. His argument was that «Spain has to choose between a restoration of the monarchy under Alfonso XII or a dictatorial, military and political republic for the foreseable future.»

[267] Martínez Campos had fought under General Prim and after the revolution of 1868, requested to be sent to Cuba, where he fought in the Cuban War of Independence. Considered too soft to win, he was replaced by Blas Villate, Count of Valmaseda. He returned to Spain and backed the *coup d'état* of General Manuel Pavia in favor of Alfonso XII. In 1876 he was sent back to Cuba, this time with the reputation of a diplomatic and savvy military man.

ical and economic abuses over certain sectors on the population, especially in rural areas.

All thorough *la Década Moderada* (1843-1854) and *el Bienio Progresista* (1854-1868), life was becoming temperate and less severe in Cuba and among Cubans, when compared to the uncertainties created by Narciso López' and Joaquín de Agüero's insurrections and rebellions. In 1852 the Countess of Merlín died in Paris and in 1853 Domingo del Monte died in Madrid; Federico Miahle left the island; José Julian Martí was born in Havana, Juan Gualberto Gómez was born in Matanzas and Félix Varela died in San Agustín, Florida.

A brief period of excitement broke out in Havana in March of 1854 when the steamer Black Warrior stopped in the capital on a regular trading route from New York to Mobile, Alabama. The ship's captain did not produce a cargo manifest in time and Cuban officials seized their vessel, its contents and its crew. Washington saw the incident as a violation of its sovereign rights and Pierre Soulé (1801-1870), the French-born US Minister to Spain, issued an ultimatum to Madrid to return the ship or else. Although he was chastised by the US government, the action strained US and Spain relations; at the time President Buchanan had authorized Soulé to negotiate a US purchase of Cuba with the provision that

«...if a purchase could not be negotiated you will then direct your effort to the next desirable object, which is to detach that island from the Spanish dominion and from all dependence on any European power, in accordance with our doctrine of Manifest Destiny.»[268]

---

[268] Manifest Destiny was the widely held belief that American settlers were destined to expand throughout the continent. Historians have for the most part agreed that there were three basic themes to Manifest Destiny:
First, the special virtues of the American people and their institutions; second, America's mission to redeem and remake the new continent in the image of the founders; and third, the belief in America's irresistible destiny to accomplish this essential duty. Manifest Destiny was not a universally accepted concept among Americans; many prominent American politicians, such as Lincoln and Grant did not agree with it. Most Whigs rejected it, while most Democrats supported it. Soulé's reaction to the Black Warrior affair was consistent with Manifest Destiny, as were the wars against Mexico to seize part of its territories.

The rationale for the United States to purchase Cuba from Spain while implying that the U.S. should declare war if Spain refused, was written into a document known as The Ostend Manifesto, named after the town of Ostend, in Belgium, where it was signed by James Buchanan, American minister to Great Britain, John Y. Mason, minister to France, and Pierre Soulé, President Pierce's appointed minister to Spain.[269]

Behind the appearance of peace and tranquility, however, several *criollos*, knowing of the renewed US interest to acquire Cuba, began to accelerate their plans for independence. On the morning of October 19, 1854, the pailebot [270] *Charles T. Smith* arrived in Baracoa from New York. It carried a cargo of wood and feed stocks owned by a Don Juan Enrique Félix, a covert member of the *Junta Cubana de Nueva York*. Inside some of the boxes were numerous weapons and war materials. Two days later, another pailebot, the *John E. Whit*, arrived again in Baracoa with merchandise property of Francisco Estrampes. They were both managing expeditions organized in New York by Domingo de Goicuría; their mission was to join Don Ramón Pintó, president of the *Junta Revolucionaria de La Habana*, and his fellow conspirators Juan Cadalso, Anacleto Bermúdez, José Antonio Echeverría, Esteban Santa Cruz, Benigno Gener and José Ignacio Iznaga; all were in charge of extending Pintó's secret plans across the entire island. Unfortunately the port pilot denounced them with the help of a man called Claudio Maestro who, pretending to be a recruiter for the rebels, travelled

---

[269] Southerners, who had long feared that Cuba might become an independent Black republic, applauded the document, but it was vigorously denounced by the Northern press as a plot to extend slavery. William L. Marcy, US President Pierce's Secretary of State, immediately repudiated it for the American government.

[270] A *pailebot* was a schooner, a type of sailing vessel that had many important uses as a merchant, fishing or pleasure boat. Its rig was a variant of the schooners', as it had two or more masts rigged with uncrossed sails. Its design allowed it to achieve maximum speed. Its name came from the English *pilot's boat*, because its speed and maneuverability. It was widely used by pilots of British ports during the second half of the nineteenth century.

around the island looking like a peddler with a horse loaded with trinkets.

So many patriots were captured and imprisoned that all the jails in the island were full to capacity and the Spanish authorities had to imprison conspirators aboard an old ship called *El Pontón*, anchored in Havana harbor. In 1855, Spain-born Don Ramón Pintó, was taken prisoner in Havana. In spite of his high position and well known talents, he was executed by *garrote* on March 22 under orders from his close friend, Don José de la Concha, Captain General of Cuba. [271] When Pintó's family asked for the Christian burial of his corpse, Concha refused to cooperate and Pintó had to be laid to rest in an unmarked tomb.

On the 31st of March, Francisco Estrampes was also executed and the *Junta Cubana de Nueva York*, informed about a meeting of General John Anthony Quitman [272] with the US president, broke the agreement it had made with him to direct an invasion of Cuba. A year later, 1856, Gaspar Betancourt Cisneros and Francisco Frías, *Conde de Pozos Dulces*, closed the *Junta Cubana de Nueva York* and travelled to Europe. Domingo Goicuría, not knowing what to do with the loads of weapons in his charge, donated them to William Walker (1824-1860) the

---

[271] On a letter dated three years earlier, on August 10, 1852, Concha had written at the end of a very appreciative letter to Pintó : «*puede usted estar seguro que nada me sería más agradable que se me presentáse [sic]una ocasión de ocuparme en su obsequio ó en el de su familia.*» (you can be sure that nothing would be more pleasing to me than having a chance to bestow an honor to you or to your family).

[272] John A. Quitman (1798-1858) was an American politician and soldier who had participated in the Mexican War of 1846, reaching the rank of Major General. He had been approached by Narciso López to lead the failed filibuster expedition of 1850, but decided to instead serve as Governor of Mississippi. He helped López to recruit men and obtain weapons, however, and promised to organize an expedition in 1853. Once more, with López dead, and the *Junta de Nueva York* having everything ready for such expedition, Quitman did not deliver, alleging that in view of the Kansas-Nebraska Act, any action in Cuba would be interpreted as helping a would-be slaveholding territory. The *Junta de Nueva York* broke with him after Quitman simply left Washington and went home without telling anyone he was quitting.

American lawyer, journalist, adventurer and Nicaragua's president-to-be, who was organizing his last filibuster expedition to Central America.

In spite of these early unsuccessful attempts to launch a pro-independence military campaign across Cuba, the seeds for self-rule had been planted and were there for future time. In the meantime, important things were happening in the island that would eventually impact the destiny of Cuba:

In 1856 the railroad lines began to expand eastward into the provinces most likely to organize independence rebellions.

In 1857 a world financial crisis affecting the US began to impact trade with Cuba. Cuban producers saw their export levels diminished to almost half of the volume in previous years. Coffee exports went down to zero. Banks and commerce houses began to declare insolvency. The business world was in panic and an unexpected overpowering fear led to total immobility. For Cuba, it was the worst business climate of colonial times.

In the midst of this chaos, a school for teachers was founded by the Piarist fathers in Guanabacoa; it would be the first of several catholic schools known as *Escuelas Pías*. The Jesuits, on the other hand, opened an observatory at their Belén school in Havana. In Santiago de las Vegas Martín Morúa Delgado was born and Juan Cristóbal Nápoles Fajardo (el Cucalambé) published *Rumores del Hormigo*. Miguel Teurbe-Tolón, a renowned Cuban playwright and poet, creator of Cuba's flag and coat of arms, died in Matanzas, aged 37. His book *El Laúd del Desterrado*, written with Heredia, Turla, Castellón, Santacilia, Quintero and Zenea, would be published the following year.

The year 1858 saw the first Cuban Chinese immigrants opening stores on Zanja street in Havana. Last names like Lin Pao and Chan were replaced —for clients' benefits— by Pérez, Rodríguez and Suárez. With the laundries, grocery markets and ice cream outlets, a famous Chinese doctor, Cham Bombiá, opened a consulting office and became famous.[273] By 1860, many Chinese were revolting against abuses by non-Chinese employers, leading to a culture of seeking employment only with Chinese patrons.

The following year Cuba had a new governor, Don Francisco Serrano, Duke of La Torre and *Grande de España*. He authorized Juan Martínez Villegas (1816-1894), one of Spain's best known political journalists, to publish the conservative and satirical newspaper *El Moro Muza*.[274] On a more serious note, in 1860 Gertrudis Gómez de Avellaneda began to publish *Album Cubano de lo Bueno y lo Bello*. It lasted only 12 issues.

In 1861 and 1862, Cuba had a new drop in exports due to the uncertainty created in the US by the secession of southern states and the war between the states. Mexico, also an important additional market for Cuban exports, was also under the intervention of Britain, Spain and France and lowered its business with Cuba.

1861 was the first year of extraordinary musical events at *Teatro Tacón*, under the direction of musical director Luis Moreau Gottschalk. His symphony *Una Noche en el Trópico* opened with 40 grand pianos played by world renown grand masters like Espadero, Saumell, Cervantes, Desvernine, Edelmann and Laureano Fuentes.

In 1862, Miguel Aldama, Francisco Frías, José Silverio Jorrín and José Morales Lemus began to write on a new reformist newspaper, *El Siglo*. Aldama and Morales Lemus financed the paper, Frías (*Conde de Pozos Dulces*) assumed its direction. As many other efforts to publish in Cuba, the paper only lasted for

---

[273] His fame was inmortalized by the popular phrase "*no lo salva ni el medico chino*," (not even the Chinese doctor can save him, a proverb Cubans began to use to characterize lost causes).

[274] Martínez Villegas founded in Cuba *El Moro Muza* as a nationalist, anti-separatist paper. He set up other critical and satirical weeklies elsewhere: *El Tio Camorra* and *La Charanga* in Madrid and *Antón Perulero* in Buenos Aires. His papers were regularly closed by censors; he died poor and ignored by the public, although his works were praised by literary men like Domingo Faustino Sarmiento and Ricardo Palma.

six years. 1862 was the year when José de la Luz y Caballero died in Havana at age 62. He had numerous articles published in *El Faro Industrial* and *La Revista de la Habana*, which likewise were publications lasting one year or less. Cuba, at the time, had 1.4 million residents, 800 thousand Whites, 600 thousand Blacks. Of 35 thousand Chinese residents, only 60 were women and less than 400 men had married or had stable relations with Cuban ladies.

In 1863 Armando García Menocal (1863-1942), was born in Havana. He would grow up to be "the painter of the making of the Republic." [275] Poet Julián del Casal was born on November 7 of that year; poet and dramatist José Jacinto Milanés died a week later, on November 14.

In 1865, three years before the outburst of the 1868 war of independence at Yara, members of the Reformist Party in Cuba, with the authorization of governor Domingo Dulce, sent a letter with 24,000 signatures to General Francisco Serrano, as former governor of Cuba between 1858 and 1862, asking him to intercede before the Madrid Courts and the government to grant political and economic reforms in Cuba. Life in Spain was in turmoil, with O'Donnell reassuming power in Madrid. He appointed Antonio Cánovas del Castillo as Minister of Ultramar, promising quick reforms. In March of 1866 José Antonio Saco was elected to the *Junta de Información* [276] from Santiago de Cuba; with him 12 reformists were elected for 16 positions; José

---

[275] In 1893, when he was a young man of 30, Menocal painted *Reembarque de Colón por Bobadilla*, showing the Admiral in chains on a ship deck as he was taken prisoner to Spain on October 1500, after his third trip to America. The Spanish colonial governor asked him to remove the chains but Menocal refused; as a challenge to authority, he moved to an earlier date the initial exhibition day in Havana. Two years after the closing of the exhibition, he joined the independence forces as an aide to Máximo Gómez.

[276] The *Junta de Información* was a consulting organism set by the Spanish government between October of 1866 and April of 1867 to attend petitions for political (freedom of the press), social (end of slavery) and economic (open markets) reforms in Cuba. No action was taken by Madrid on any of the recommendations other than a new 10% tax. This rebuff consolidated the will for independence.

Morales Lemus was elected as the president of the Cuban delegation. On November 6, the *Junta* celebrated its first session in Madrid.

Spanish Prime Minister O'Donnell, however, pressured by anti-reformists, replaced liberal governor Domingo Dulce with conservative Francisco Lersundi,[277] the man who would be in power in Cuba when the 1868 War of Independence exploded.

Things began to look bad for the *Junta de Información* as 1876 began; on February 12, barely three months after the start of its meetings, the crown proclaimed a *Ley de Reforma Tributaria* without even the courtesy of consulting with the *Junta*. The law was printed in *La Gaceta de la Habana* in its March 1867 issue. On May 5, the *Junta* met for the last time in Madrid. All its members were advised to go home. By July 1st —under severe protests— the law began to take effect in Cuba. As the prospects of concessions from Spain faded out after the failure of the *Junta*, Cuban planters, cattlemen, intellectuals and merchants began to seriously consider independence as a necessary and viable solution. No one in Madrid was willing to look seriously at the reforms demanded by the Cubans; the impact of increased taxation by Madrid was heavier than ever; and the island was under the weight of an international economic crisis. Cuban patriots in Oriente began to mobilize.

---

[277] Francisco Lersundi had replaced Federico Roncali as Prime Minister of Spain in 1853. He was appointed by Isabel II, upon the recommendation of María Cristina de Borbón, her mother and former crown regent. María Cristina was so involved in salt and railroad swindles in Spain and America that she was expelled from Spain in 1854 and had her pension revoked. At the time it was said in Spain that «*no hay proyecto industrial en el que la Reina madre no tenga intereses,*» (there are no industrial projects in Spain where the mother Queen does not have a cut).

Starting in 1863 and lasting until the founding of the republic, young people with separatist ideals became regulars at the sidewalk of *Café El Louvre*, where they had patriotic gatherings that captivated three generations of Cubans. La *Acera del Louvre* was a site located on Prado street between Neptuno and San Rafael streets, on the side-walk of *Hotel Inglaterra* in the heart of Havana, just opposite the statue of Queen Isabel II of Spain in what would later be Havana's Central Park. These gatherings produced many conflicts with Spanish authorities because the youngster's political positions were at odds with the official colonial policies. The young *criollos* meeting regularly at the Louvre sidewalk became known *as los Jóvenes de la Acera del Louvre*.

In 1871, the *Acera* was witness to Spanish Captain Don Nicolás Estévanez who, from his seat at the café heard the shots during the shooting of the eight innocent students of medicine on November 27. He broke his sword, gave up his military career and declared «Humanity and justice must stand before even the homeland.»

In the later part of the XIX century, José Martí, during a brief stay in Havana before moving to New York, became one of the *Jóvenes de la Acera del Louvre*. In 1890, by extraordinary coincidence, Antonio Maceo visited the *Acera* during his stay at the *Hotel Inglaterra* and also went into the sidewalk to dialogue with and inspire the youthful supporters of Cuban independence. Major General Ignacio Agramonte and Generals Sanguily and Aguirre were also an assiduous participant in the *Acera* meetings. No other place in Havana was ever close to these extraordinary and regular events.

Eight years after the Nicolás Estévanez affair, on April 26, 1879, in the sidewalk of the *Café El Louvre*, Martí gave his speech *Honor Honra*, during a tribute to Dr. Adolfo Márquez Sterling, organized by the Liberal Party. Martí was such an sensational and formidable speaker that Captain General Ramón Blanco, after knowing of his address, decided to go to the *Liceo de Guanabacoa* to personally listen to him the following day. His only comment was «This man is not only crazy, but dangerously insane.»

With time, more than 40 youngsters who met regularly at the *Acera del Louvre* gave their lives in the 1895 Cuban War of Independence. The Café continued to attract important personalities during and after the war: Sara Bernhart (1887), Julián del Casal (1890), Rubén Darío (1910), Raúl Capablanca (1920), Enrico Caruso (1920), Gabriela Mistral (1922), José Mojica (1931), among many others.

Havana's *Café El Louvre*

Images, top to bottom, left to right:

Scene from Madrid in times of **La Gloriosa**;

the **abdication of Isabel II** after the promulgation of *La Gloriosa* (also called *La Septembrina*) in 1868 by Prim and Serrano. Standing in front of her, the future King of Spain Alfonso XII, her son;

Baldomero Espartero, prince of Vergara, defender of Isabel II and victor over the *Carlistas* in 1839;

Queen Regent **Maria Cristina de Borbón**, mother of Isabel II.

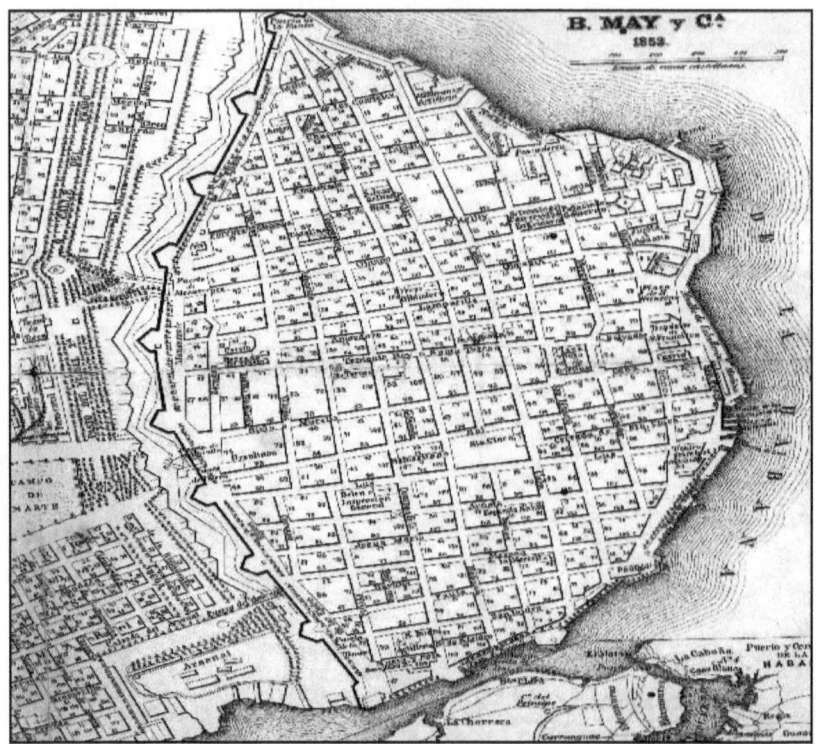

Images, top to bottom:
A map of **Havana** in the years prior to the 1868 War of Independence;
a **view of the city** taken from La Cabaña.

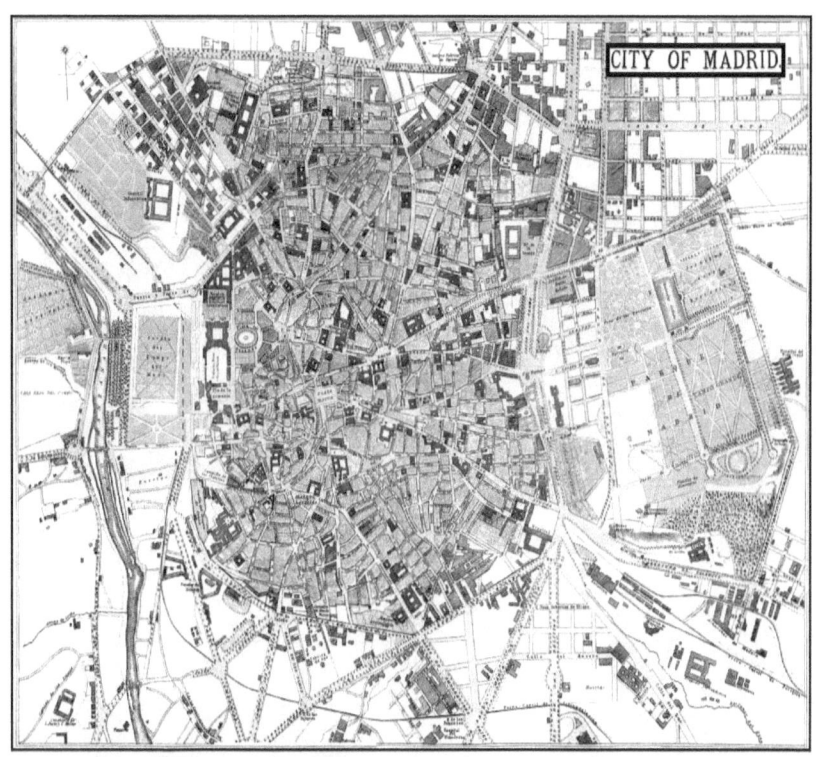

Images, top to bottom:
A Map of **Madrid** in the years prior to the 1868 Cuban War;
a **view of the city** from the south.

Images, top to bottom, left to right:

The provisional **Spanish cabinet in 1869**, after the triumph of *La Gloriosa*. The circles show (lef to right) Práxedes Mateo Sagasta, Juan Prim y Prats and Francisco Serrano;

a studio photo of **Isabel II** in 1869.

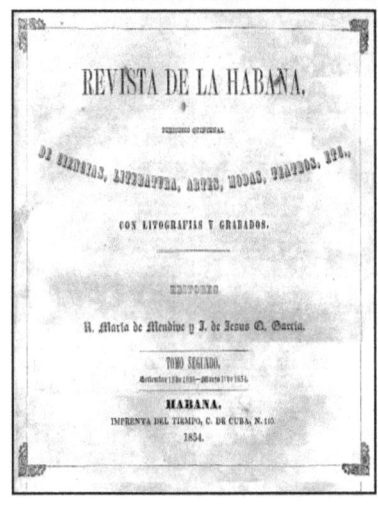

Images, top to bottom, left to right:

Cuban painter **Armando García Menocal** *(1868-1942)*;

a detail of Menocal's controversial painting of **Reembarque de Colón por Bobadilla** *(1893)*;

the ironclad **Tetuan** in 1860. It was built for the Carlist wars but saw action for the first time in the Cuban wars of independence;

the **Revista de la Habana** (1853), founded by Rafael María de Mendive, José Martí's mentor.

a typical *pailebot* designed for custody of the coasts of Cuba;

Images, top to bottom, left to right:

Antonio Cánovas del Castillo (1828-1897), a strong supporter of the Bourbons in Spain, main architect of the 1876 Spanish monarchical constitution, shot dead in 1897 by an anarchist;

an engraving showing the **shooting of Cánovas**;

An issue of **Album Cubano de los Bueno y lo Bello**, a publication by *La Avellaneda*;

a Spanish stamp honoring **La Avellaneda**;

the **Escuelas Pias de Guabanacoa**, first teacher's school in Cuba, founded by the PP. Escolapios in 1857.

Images, top to bottom:
Several images from a satirical magazine published by
Juan M. Villergas in Cuba.

El **Moro Muza** was a very successful magazine. In Cuba, in the 1860s, a popular saying was «*vete a contárselo al Moro Muza.*» (go, tell the *Moro Muza*, which meant «go to hell.») Another popular saying was «*¡Qué lo haga el moro Muza!,*» meaning «anybody but me.» It was also popular to induce children to do something by saying «*I am going to tell this to el Moro Muza.*» The term comes from a descendant of the visigoth Conde Casio called Muza Ibn Muza (788-863), who was known as *el Moro Muza*.

Images, top to bottom, left to right:

Juan Bautista Topete, Spanish naval commander, follower of Serrano and O'Donnell, led the naval conspiracy against the Bourbons in 1868; **Amadeo de Savoya**, elected Spain's King in 1870 following the overthrow of Isabel II; **King Alfonso XII**, reached the Spanish throne after an 1870 *coup d'etat*;

Juan Prim y Prats, leader of the Progressive Party that opposed Isabel II and deposed her in 1866; **Pierre Soulé**, US ambassador to Spain in the 1850s, sponsor of the *Ostend Manifesto* asking for the US purchase of Cuba; General **Manuel Pavia**, ultra-conservative follower of Prim and Amadeo.

Napoleon III of France, nephew of Bonaparte, challenger of the Monroe Doctrine; he invaded of Mexico to install Maximilian I as Emperor; **William Walter**, believer in the theory of Manifest Destiny, *filibustero*, invader of Nicaragua, where he was executred; **John A. Quitman**, Governor of Mississippi, friend of Narciso López.

Images of some of Cuba's Captain Generals from 1843 to 1879, top to bottom, left to right:

Leopoldo O'Donnell, backer of Maria Cristina, leader of the Progressive Party, governor of Cuba; **José Gutierrez de la Concha**, Captain General of Cuba on three ocassions;

Francisco Serrano, supporter of O'Donnell, leader of the Union Liberal Party, allied with Prim, Sagasta and Topete, rumored to be the real father of Alfonso XII, son of Isabel II; **Domingo Dulce Garay**, governor of Cuba in 1862, married to a Cuban lady, enemy of Isabel II; **Francisco Lersundi**, trusted friend of Maria Cristina, as Captain General of Cuba he was surprisingly unprepared for the 1868 War of Independence;

Blas Villate, Count of Valmaseda, three times Captain General of Cuba, supporter of the Spanish Bourbons; **Arsenio Martínez Campos**, *"pacificador"* of Cuba in 1878, a failure in 1898.

Images, top to bottom, left to right:

Antonio María Claret, Isabel II's confesor, appointed Archbishop of Santiago de Cuba by Pope Pius IX, founder of schools; **Don Facundo Bacardí**, founder of the Bacardí emporium;

Isidoro de Armenteros, partner of Narciso López in the *Conspiración de la Mina de la Rosa* in 1848; he was executed in 1851; **Gertrudis Gómez de Avellaneda**, talented writer and intense political activist; **Miguel Teurbe Tolón**, writer, poet, teacher, exiled in the US in 1848;

Ramón Pintó, friend of governor Concha, businessman, conspirator for Cuban freedom, sentenced to death by Concha; **Francisco Estrampes**, sent to Cuba by Domingo Goicuría to prepare an invasion, he was captured and garroted in 1855.

The XVIII and XIX centures in Cuba were a dramatic counterpoint of light and shadow; on one hand were the seductive lights of the Enlightenment —printers, newspapers, patriotic societies— on the other, the infamous silhouette of the slave ships and slave quarters behind every economic activity.

Cuban culture, for better or worse, relied mainly on imported works of Spain, in spite of the efforts of the eminent minds of the San Carlos and San Ambrosio Seminary (1723), the University of Havana (1728) and the Patriotic Society (1793).

Cuba became the richest colony in the world after the destruction of Haiti and the growth of Cuban trade with Europe and the United States. Newspapers in Havana, particularly *El Papel Periódico,* featured things that people wanted to sell or buy; ads for entertainment performances; details of all vessels entering or leaving Havana; in a word, everything that people needed in a progressive colony.

The *Papel Periódico*, however, could not reach everyone; illiteracy reached 90 percent in the 1700s and was still 70 percent by late XIX century, when information was already considered a must-have commodity intimately linked to the "comforts" of life.

When Varela decided to renew the curriculum of the San Carlos Seminary, sharing the truths of the Catholic faith with the truths of reason, his tactic was to replace Latin in favor of Castilian and to supersede old scholastic traditions with the broad ideological landscape that Bacon, Locke, Newton and Descartes were contributing to changing times.

As for Spanish literature, Valera replaced the old Castilian poems with modern works: Cervante's *Don Quijote* and *Novelas Ejemplares*, Jorge Manrique's *Coplas*, Garcilaso's poetry and the works of Lope de Vega. Included in Varela's new canon were Fenelon's Adventures of Telemachus (1776), numerous dictionaries and grammars and, giving credit to America, *La Araucana* (1776) de Alonso de Ercilla. In Varela's words...

«Telemachus, with seventy-three editions, is undoubtedly a great book of adventures, the most read during this century; no other educational novel criticizes the excesses and weaknesses of the monarchy like Fenelon does. The Araucana, on the other hand, is one of the great successes of epic literature, arousing a special enthusiasm among Spanish settlers in America; a real literary monument dedicated to the Conquest.»

The seductive lights of the Enlightenment in Cuba

Domingo del Monte
1804-1853

Spain's *Siglo de Oro* (the golden years) in literature started with the publication of *Gramática de la Lengua Castellana* (Grammar of the Castilian Language), authored by Antonio de Nebrija, in 1492. It ended with the death of the last great writer of the period, Pedro Calderón de la Barca, in 1681. One wonders how much of the *Siglo de Oro* was enjoyed or known by Spaniards living in Cuba. To the best of our knowledge, thirty-two percent of the 179 titles requested by librarians in Cuba, even during the 1800s, were missals, church histories, lives of saints, and titles like Kempis' *Imitación de Cristo*, Loyola's *Ejercicios Espirituales* and St. Augustine's *Confesiones*.

It is not easy to list the best-sellers in Cuba before Domingo del Monte, who in 1830 was making lists of books he had found in his friend's homes. He knew that a member of the staff of governor Luis de Unzaga y Amezaga (1782-1785), had brought to Cuba 84 titles, 10 of them in French, comprising 280 volumes, distributed in four categories: devotional books, masterpieces of antiquity, scientific treatises and works of poetry and novels. Among the devotionals were some works of Bossuet, the thirteen volumes of Fray Luis de Granada's *Prayers for Seven Days a Week* and *Catechism* by Fleury. The Latin classics were represented by the *Epistles of Cicero*. The scientific treatises included Abad Noel Pluche's *Spectacle of Nature* and *Conversations about Natural History*. The bulk of the shipment, however, were history books like *Historia de la Conquista de Mexico* (25%), Spanish and French contemporary literature like *Poemas de Garcilaso* and *Fábulas de Iriarte* (20%), and legal treatises like *Leyes de Indias* (15%).

By the time Del Monte organized his *Tertulias Literarias* in the 1830s, hundreds of books were entering Cuba from Spain, France, the US and England. The regulars to the *Tertulias* travelled often to Europe and were up-to-date in the developments of science, literature, economics and politics in the old world. Del Monte, for instance, was able to read Victor Hugo's *Contes Sous la Tente* (Tales under a Tent) and *Bug-Jargal* in 1826, at almost the same time others were reading them in Paris; in 1830 he was reading in French *Scènes de la Vie Privée (Scenes from Private Life)* by Balzac, almost before the French public had access to the work.

Domingo del Monte's *Tertulias Literarias*

27

The War Against Spain Exploded in 1868

IN 1866, WHILE ACROSS the island of Cuba numerous residents were voting for delegates to the *Junta de Información*, Gaspar Betancourt Cisneros (1803-1866), one of the most enlightened citizens of Puerto Príncipe and a relentless conspirator against the Spanish government in Cuba, was dying from cancer in Havana on December 7. He had favored the establishment of a liberal constitutional regime in Cuba. Influenced by French Physiocrats, [278] he believed that the most important basis to create a rich and prosperous society was to support and defend the natural desire of every individual to better his/her own situation. It led him to condemn any Spanish political interference in the economic decisions of Cuban landowners; he was an ardent believer in the illegitimacy of any state regulation of economic activity. He had established a horse-drawn railway service in Camagüey in 1836, which by 1924 became *Ferrocarriles Consolidados de Cuba*. By the time he died he had become a renowned writer (using for his articles and essays the nicknames *el Lugareño* and *Homobono*), a popular newspaperman, teacher and businessman. In his time, he was identified as an annexationist, [279] even though he felt that

---

[278] *Physiocracy*, Greek for Government of Nature, is an economic theory developed by 18th century French economists; it sustains that the basic pillar of society for the production of wealth is individual productive work and views land (not commerce or accumulation of gold), as the basis of all wealth.

[279] *Gaspar Betancourt (el Lugareño)*, in a notable controversy about annexationism, became the most fervent adversary of José Antonio Saco, a passionate defender of independence. Gaspar Betancourt Cisneros opposed Saco, joining José Luis Alfonso, José Aniceto Iznaga and Cirilo Villaverde, at the time all proponents of annexationism as a practical solution to the lack of freedom in Cuba. Before his death, el Lugareño joined the pro-independence cause.

«*anexionismo es un cálculo, no un sentimiento.*» (annexationism is a rational calculation, not a feeling.)

Betancourt Cisneros had viewed the convocation of Cuban delegates to the *Junta de Información* on November 25, 1865, as the final triumph of *reformismo* in Cuba. He died before the Royal Decree of February 12, 1867, increasing taxes in Cuba, was issued by the crown. He would have approved the protest letter sent by Francisco Frías, Count of Pozos Dulces, to Queen Isabel II on February 17, 1867: [280]

«The Cuban commissioners protest, in a respectful but energetic way, the statutes of this Royal Decree, more so since in the preamble of this document there are two or three references to the Commissioners, in terms that could be interpreted as giving their approval to the statutes... the Commissioners of Cuba decline any responsibility and solidarity with the resolutions imposed by the government of Spain... the present rulers of Cuba constitute a *gobierno de hecho, no de derecho* (a *de facto* and not a *de jure* government), and therefore, all its acts are illegal and subject to challenge, invalidation and nullification.»

On the receiving end of that protest letter was no other that Cánovas del Castillo, "the most acerbic enemy of the freedom of Cuba," according to José Antonio Saco.[281] He had appointed all the delegates of the Spanish government to the *Junta de Información*, and had chosen individuals that were known in the metropolis for their opposition to any innovation —

---

[280] The letter from **Francisco Frías** was published in *El Siglo* in Havana; it was signed by Calixto Bernal, José Antonio Saco, Nicolás Azcárate, José Antonio Echeverría, Manuel Ortega, Agustín Camejo, Manuel de Armas, Antonio Fernández Bramosio, José Morales Lemus, Tomás Terry, Antonio Rodríguez and the rest of the members of the Cuban delegation to the *Junta de Información*. On April 14, 1868, Frías resigned as director of *El Siglo* in a letter to José Morales Lemus. The paper closed a year later.

[281] At that time **Cánovas del Castillo** was the Minister of Overseas Territories in the Spanish government. He had served in a number of posts during Isabel II and left the government after the 1868 Glorious Revolution. As a strong conservative supporter of the restoration of the Bourbon monarchy, Alfonso XII would choose him six times, between 1874 and 1897, as Prime Minister of Spain.

political, economic or social—in the relations between Cuba and Spain.

In December of 1867 Spain sent to Cuba a new Captain General, Francisco de Lersundi y Hormaechea, appointed for the second time to that position. On a letter from José Morales Lemus to Nicolás Azcárate dated May 15, 1869, the former owner of *El Siglo* [282] wrote from Philadelphia:

«Lest there is any doubt of the meaning and purpose of this appointment, let it be known that several of the seemingly and forever all-powerful Spanish institutions have been revived with all their former vigor and with greater force than ever; the old military commissions have been re-established and their powers have been expanded to almost cancel the ordinary courts. A military party organization, the *Cuerpo de Voluntarios* (Volunteers Corps) has been reorganized and energized, this time making sure by every conceivable means that no Cuban-born be retained in its ranks. The new recruits have begun to prepare for the dishonorable and detestable work that Spain expects to be carried out. The omnipotent sabre will now resolve all issues in Cuba.»

The bad news circulated across Cuba, particularly in Oriente province, when Azcárate sent a copy of Morales Lemus letter to Francisco Vicente Aguilera (1821-1877).

Aguilera had been born in Bayamo, the most combative pro-independence town in Cuba in the 1800s. He became a lawyer at age 23 at the University of Havana and returned east to Oriente province to manage his properties. He inherited a fortune from his father, increased it substantially and by 1867 was the richest *criollo* in all of Cuba. His properties included land, hotels, real estate in several cities, sugar refineries, livestock, and slaves; [283] it was calculated to be worth US $2.4 billion in

---

[282] During the period when **Domingo Dulce** was Captain General of Cuba (1862 to 1866) José Morales Lemus invited a group of friends to his home and asked them to contribute some capital to open a newspaper. He contributed a sizable sum and *El Siglo* was born, with Francisco Frías, Count of Pozos Dulces, as its first director.

[283] It has been documented that **Aguilera** never bought any slave regularly brought to Cuba from Africa. He eventually released the slaves inherited from his father and was the first sugar potentate who hired free workers to work in his sugar business.

2000 dollars. Only one other Cuban could compete with him in net worth: Miguel Aldama y Alfonso (1821-1888), son of a Spanish immigrant who made a considerable fortune in the sugar business and was the first industrialist that built a vertically integrated business based on saccharose: planting, harvesting, processing, refining, packaging, marketing and distributing worldwide the final product.

Francisco Vicente Aguilera became an ardent promoter of Cuban independence during his many trips to the US [284] and Europe, where he visited France, England and Italy. In 1851, at age 30, he began to actively conspire against colonial rule in Cuba and befriended Francisco Maceo Osorio, Carlos Manuel de Céspedes and Pedro (Perucho) Figueredo. At the time, the province of Oriente had not participated in the prosperity brought about in the western side of the island by sugar and tobacco crops. In New York, José Morales Lemus, upon his return from the failed *Junta de Información* meetings in Madrid, had re-established the *Junta Cubana*, a Committee pro Cuban independence which included Calixto Bernal and Nicolás Azcárate. The issue of Cuba's future had seemingly been relegated to the background due to the uncertainties of Spain's stability and the unknown resilience of the post-Civil War US markets.[285] Aguilera took the initiative to call for a meeting of leaders in Camagüey and Oriente to explore the best means to bring about a rebellion for independence in Cuba.

In August of 1868 the meeting took place in San Miguel del Rompe, near Las Tunas, with representatives of Puerto Prínci-

---

[284] As a young man visiting the US, Aguilera took courses at the University of Virginia and became a good friend of **Edgar Alan Poe** (1809-1849), who taught him the techniques of cryptography (secret encription of texts). Aguilera's interest in cryptography and Poe began when, as a child in Cuba, he first read **El Escarabajo de Oro** (The Gold Bug), a short story by Poe dealing with a man bitten by a gold-colored scarab-like bug; the key to the outcome of the story centered on one cryptogram.

[285] In Spain there were prospects of a revolution to depose Isabel II, particularly in Santander, Madrid and Cádiz; in the US most businessmen were hoping for a victory of **Ulysses Grant** in the coming elections before committing their capital.

pe, Manzanillo, Las Tunas, Bayamo and Holguín.[286] It became known as the *Convención de Tirsan*. Céspedes, as leader of the group from Manzanillo, proposed a September 3 date to start the insurrection. Some participants objected to the date, arguing that there would be more funds available to support the armed revolt after the 1868 harvest in the first months of 1869. The Manzanillo group prevailed and the date was chosen as October 14.[287]

In Havana, Captain General Lersundi found out about the projected uprising and issued a detention order against Céspedes. In Manzanillo the rebels learned the details of this order and met at Céspedes' *Hacienda La Demajagua*, anticipating the start of hostilities for October 10th. At the time, all 37 initial conspirators knew that most people in Cuba either wished to retain their union with Spain or were hoping for an annexation to the US. Starting a revolt under those circumstances was a clear act of courage and conviction. Fortunately for them, Captain General Lersundi had not comprehended the depth of commitment of the rebels; on the October 12 issue of the *Boletín de la Gazeta*, the official publication of the government in Cuba, no reference was made to any disturbances in the eastern part of Cuba. The central theme was the disturbances in the peninsula and the mutiny in Cádiz by admiral Juan Bautista Topete, one of the first steps of a September revolution which was supported by liberals, moderates and republicans.

By the end of October of 1868 the revolution in Cuba had gathered substantial momentum. Carlos Manuel de Céspedes

---

[286] The day after the meeting at **San Miguel del Rompe**, Aguilera published an ad in a newspaper in Bayamo stating: «all my properties, land, houses, buildings, and livestock, including 35,000 head of cattle and 4,000 horses, are for sale.» He indeed sold everything at firesale prices and turned 92 % of the proceeds to the revolutionaries, keeping the rest for himself, his wife and eight children. Years later, in 1877, he died in his small apartment at 223 West 30th street in New York City, destitute, after a brief bout with throat cancer. His wife and children had been working as seamstresses and laborers in the City since 1871.

[287] This initial agreement included Céspedes, Aguilera, Marcano, Izaguirre, Peralta and the Figueredos, meeting at the **Rosario** sugar mill.

took over Yara on October 11 and Bayamo on October 18, proclaiming the independence of Cuba; by December 27 he announced the freedom of all slaves, including his own, and accepted the title of captain general of *Cuba Libre*, thereby initiating the Ten Years War (1868-1878). The proclamation of freedom to the slaves was published on a new paper launched in Bayamo by José Joaquín Palma: *El Cubano Libre*.

A last minute attempt to prevent a bloody and contentious war between Cuba and Spain was made on October 24, when José Manuel Mestre, José Antonio Echeverría, Enrique Piñeiro and José Morales Lemus, the top rank of *reformismo* in Cuba, met governor Lersundi at his palace in Havana. According to witnesses, the governor was irritated, aggressive and uncompromising; it turned the *reformistas* into «*laborantes del independentismo*,» according to Morales Lemus. The war proceeded at an accelerated pace; by 1878 it would cause 200,000 deaths between *criollos* and *peninsulares*. By December of 1868 Céspedes had an army of 15,000 *mambises* armed with machetes, spears and some firearms sent by Cubans living in the US. On December 4, 1868, Ignacio Agramonte joined the revolt, took the town of Guáimaro and became the independence leader in the province of Camagüey.

Madrid reacted late but forcefully. Colonel Valeriano Weyler (1838-1930), a graduate of the Military School of Toledo and the winner of the *Cruz de San Fernando* for his participation in the Santo Domingo campaigns, was appointed chief of staff of general Valmaseda on November 5 and immediately departed for Manzanillo. Early in December Valmaseda presented a report setting the rules of engagement for confronting the Cuban's guerrilla fighting techniques. On January 27, 1869, Cuban General Manuel de Quesada y Loynaz, a veteran of the fighting against the French in Mexico, landed in the port of Guanaja, in Camagüey, with the first armed expedition sponsored from outside Cuba. Within the space of three months the war was totally defined.[288]

General Juan Prim, Minister of War from October 8, 1868 to December 27, 1870, proposed to General Francisco Serrano, Prime Minister, and Laureano Figuerola Ballester (1816-1903), Minister of the Treasury in Madrid,[289] a referendum where Cubans could vote for the independence of the island; he suggested an amnesty for Cuban patriots, both concessions to be depended on a hefty compensation to Spain guaranteed by the United States government. The project received strong opposition among the Spanish armed forces. The US responded with an offer to buy the island outright but Prim, visibly offended, refused to continue conversations. By then Domingo Dulce arrived in Cuba to assume the post of Captain General replacing an exhausted and demoralized Francisco de Lersundi. Dulce's first action was to try to gain the loyalty of the insurgents by offering freedom of the press and assembly. When the rebels refused to enter in negotiations, Dulce reposted by confiscating all their properties.

---

[288] During the Ten Years' Cuban War of Independence that was fought between 1868-1878, **Valeriano Weyler** served as colonel under General Arsenio Martínez-Campos; he returned to Spain before the end of the war to fight against *Carlistas* in the Third Carlist War in 1873. In 1878, he was made general and in 1895, Prime Minister Antonio Cánovas del Castillo would appoint him to replace Arsenio Martínez Campos when he could not pacify the new 1895 Cuban War on Independence.

[289] Laureano Figuerola is the man seated on the extreme left in the picture of the 1869 Spanish cabinet shown on page 344.

Images above: top to bottom, left to right:

Gaspar Betancourt Cisneros (1803-1866), writer, journalist, teacher, businessman, one of the most enlightened citizens of Puerto Príncipe;

a stock certificate of **Ferrocarriles Consolidados de Cuba**, the railroad company founded by Gaspar Betancourt Cisneros;

Francisco Frías, Count of Pozos Dulces, founder and first director of *El Siglo* newspaper, precursor of Cuban independence;

José Antonio Saco, statesman, deputy to the Spanish Cortes, writer, social critic, publicist, essayist, anthropologist, historian, and one of the most notable Cuban figures of the XIX century.

Images above: top to bottom, left to right:

A view of **Havana** in 1868;

Young **Antonio Cánovas del Castillo** (1828-1897), Spanish historian, statesman, and Prime Minister, whose political activity brought about the restoration of Spain's Bourbon dynasty in 1867;

Francisco Lersundi y Hormaechea (1817-1874), Spanish noble and politician who served as Prime Minister of Spain in 1853 and held other important offices such as Captain General of Cuba from 1866 to 1869. The first Independence War in Cuba exploded during his term in office.

Images above: top to bottom, left to right:

Nicolás Azcárate (1828-1894), lawyer, journalist, eloquent speaker, man of liberal ideas, freedom-loving politician and one of the reform movement leaders in Cuba;

Francisco Maceo Osorio (1828-1873), founder of the newspaper *La Regeneración*, consumate fighter for independence;

Pedro (Perucho) Figueredo (1818-1870), composer of *La Bayamesa*, Cuba's National Anthem on August 14, 1867, fighter for Cuban independence, was executed during the 1868-1878 War;

a 1869 issue of **La Voz del Pueblo Cubano**;

José Morales Lemus (1808-1870), head of the *Junta Patriótica de la Habana* in 1869.

Images above: top to bottom, left to right:

A 1867 engraving in *Centinela del Pueblo*, a Madrid newspaper, showing the main characters in the **1868 Cuban independence War**;

Ramón Céspedes, the lawyer that presided over the first motion to proclaim the abolition of slavery in Cuba, in Bayamo in 1868, a good friend and colaborator of Tomás Estrada Palma;

Tomás Terry of Cienfuegos, the *Cuban Croesus*, multimillonaire sugar baron, pioneer of electricity for sugar mills in Cuba;

Edgar Alan Poe, friend and mentor of Francisco Vicente Aguilera;

Francisco Vicente Aguilera, sugar potentate who donated all his fortune to the cause of Cuban independence.

Images above: top to bottom:

A contemporary drawing of the **occupation of Bayamo** in 1868;

the remains of **Bayamo** after it was burned down by the *mambises* in October of 1868;

photo of **Manuel Quesada, Miguel Aldama** and (seated) **Carlos Manuel de Céspedes**.

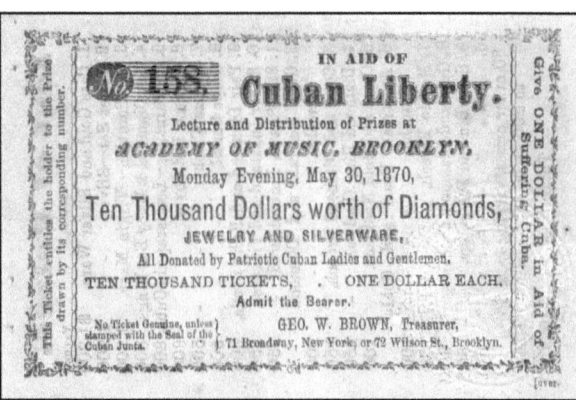

Images above: top to bottom, left to right:

A caricature of **Práxedes Mateo Sagasta** (1825-1903), eight times Prime Minister of Spain, always in the Liberal Party, political enemy of Isabel II, proponent of autonomy for Cuba;

an 1870 **ticket for a raffle** in New York to benefit the cause of Cuban Independence;

Domingo Dulce Garay, Marquis of Castell Florit (1808-1869), twice Captain General of Cuba. In 1868, during his second term in office, he decreed freedom of the press in the island for the first time;

Blas Villate, Count of Valmaseda (1824-1882), three times Captain General of Cuba. He was known for his violent policy against civilians in Cuba. He was fired and replaced by Lersundi.

España política interior

Images above: top to bottom, left to right:

Práxides Mateo Sagasta, famous for his rhetorical skills, close friend of Prim, met Carlos Manuel de Céspedes as a young man in Paris, took turns with Cánovas to govern Spain starting in the 1870s;

Antonio Cánovas del Castillo (1828-1897), six times Prime Minister of Spain, main supporter of the Bourbon restauration in the peninsula, leader of the conservatives, man of letters, was assassinated by an anarchist;

Laureano Figuerola Ballester (1816-1903), economist, Spain's minister of the Treasury, tried to aliviate Cuba's tax burden before the War of 1868;

a cartoon sarcastically showing Cánovas **teaching his "pupil"** Mateo Sagasta.

Cartoons published in Madrid criticizing the rebels in Cuba:

Manuel Quesada, José Morales Lemus

Benigno Goicuría

Carlos Manuel de Céspedes

Miguel Aldama

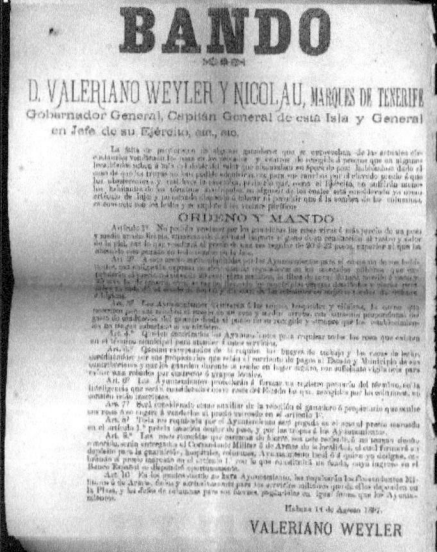

Images above: top to bottom, left to right:

Valeriano Weyler (1838-1930), Duke of Rubí, during his first visit to Cuba, serving under General Arsenio Martínez Campos in 1868;
the **book written by Weyler** after Spain's victory in the 1868 war;
a **proclamation** (*Bando*) by Weyler in his intent to "pacify" Cuba;
a **cartoon** of Valeriano Weyler from a Madrid paper in 1869.

28

The War of 1868 Began to Warm up

THE NEAR SIMULTANEITY of uprisings in Cuba and pronouncements in Spain in 1868, as well as the apparent similarity between the political platform of the Yara rebels and the interim government in Madrid, encouraged speculations of a secret agreement, signed somewhere in Spain, between Spain's Council President Juan Prim and Carlos Manuel de Céspedes, head of the Cuban insurrection. [290] The presumed conspiracy consisted of a projected dismantling of the rebellion in Cuba in exchange for broad autonomy for the island, with a political and economic status similar to Canada *vis à vis* Britain. These conjectures were never proven, but their very existence showed that Yara conspirators thought they had a liberal connection in the Peninsula which could be useful to negotiate political and economic reforms in the Island.

Serrano, Prim and Topete, the three ringleaders of the September 1868 revolt in Cadiz that deposed Isabel II, had close personal ties and prior service in Cuba: Captain General Serrano had been in Cuba on two occasions, 1859 and 1863, which earned him the title of *Marqués de la Torre*; he was also married to his first cousin, a lady of Cuban origin [291] who had a patrician Cuban ancestry. Prim had been in Havana, which was the

---

[290] Carlos Manuel de Céspedes had met Prim in Paris during his days as a student, when Prim was there in exile. Céspedes sympathized and supported the successful conspiracy that opposed the dictatorship of Espartero in Spain. After their brief friendship, Prim was promoted to Major General by Queen Regent María Cristina and entered victoriously in Madrid with General Serrano. Céspedes returned to Cuba.

[291] Antonia Domínguez Borrell Guevara y Lemus, 2nd Countess of San Antonio, born in Havana, daughter of María Isabel Borrell y Lemus, Padron y de la Cruz-Jiménez, a member of an illustrious Cuban family from Trinidad .

operational headquarters of his expedition against Mexico from late 1861 to mid-1862. Topete had been chief of the Naval Station in Havana from 1832 to 1838, and later chief of the Spanish Fleet Operations in Cuba.

While the war began to make progress in eastern Cuba, in Havana there were daily conflicts inspired by the war and brought about by Cuban-born students. To respond to these frequent disturbances, armed loyalists, the soon-to-be infamous and hated *Voluntarios*,[292] rushed to form quick response battalions prepared to quench any pro-independence revolts; the students were not intimidated, even after they were hunted treacherously from the rooftops.

Voluntarios were mainly recent immigrants called *peninsulares* and some of their island-born children, who decided to defend the Spanish homeland at any cost. They felt superior to the *criollos*; many of them were indeed better-off socially and economically. They defended the Spanish flag for fear of a race war that would turn Cuba into another black style dictatorship like Haiti. This fear, by the way, was also common in the rebel ranks. *Voluntarios* shared a strong loyalty to Spain with a deep hostility to the native population, and were typically intolerant and full of reactionary prejudices. Another important sector integrating this force of volunteers were public employees, members of the oversized colonial bureaucratic machine that wanted to preserve its enormous share on the jobs and benefits in the island. They feared that any reform that could change the *status quo* would not let them continue with their privileges.

Cuban insurgents fighting in Oriente and Camagüey had not forgotten the resolve and courage with which *habaneros* had met the *Voluntarios* on the aisles of Villanueva theater, fighting

---

[292] Spanish colonial powers in Cuba found out they could recruit numerous *Voluntarios*. At the outbreak of the 1868 insurrection, a body of 35,000 men enlisted for the defense of the capital, calling themselves *Voluntarios de la Isla de Cuba* (Volunteers of the island of Cuba). They were mostly drafted from Havana's Spanish Casino. Their initial manifesto read: «*Cuba será española o la entregaremos convertida en cenizas.*» (Cuba will always be Spanish or it will be delivered after being turned into ashes).

them one-on-one while displaying the Cuban flag. These rebellious youngsters were accused of provocations, rudeness, and insulting and outrageous behavior. It explained why, in the midst of so great excitation and passions, the Spanish colonial power approved the execution of some students that were accused of desecrating the tomb of Gonzalo Castañón, a Spanish journalist who had been killed in Key West on January 31, 1870. The relentless student harassment of colonial authorities in support of the war became the best argument to justify the draconian solution of cutting short the lives of eight students of Havana's School of Medicine for almost trivial reasons. [293]

Cuban rebels fighting in the eastern provinces also had not forgotten that a group of wealthy planters in the sugar zone of Matanzas (reformers, such as Julián Zulueta and Miguel Aldama, who would later become autonomists and finally separatists), had requested a meeting with Captain General Lersundi to avoid a disastrous war that could decimate their farms and Cuban economy. Lersundi dispatched them with disdain, claiming he was not interested on any reform agenda. Zulueta remained in Cuba to defend his interests, but Aldama fled with his family to New York, and became one of the leading spokesmen for the rebels. The planters' numerous mills and slaves, including Zulueta's, Aldama's and many others, whether they remained in Cuba or went abroad, were confiscated.

On another front, Spain continued to try to recover the good will of those that had not explicitly declared their support for the rebels. Madrid began to be very flexible with the sources of income due to corruption practices of those residents that fa-

---

[293] Several incidents were notable in the early history of resistance in Havana. On January 22, 1869, Juan Francisco Valero opened in the capital his drama *Perro Huevero aunque le quemen el hocico*. It resulted in a strong reaction by the Corps of Volunteers. On January 23, a theatrical performance at *Teatro Villanueva* resulted in another incident where 16 years old José Martí was sent to prison. On January 25, clients of *Café del Louvre* were assaulted by *Voluntarios*. On the same day, the house of Domingo del Monte at the *Palacio de Aldama* was stormed by a mob. Governor Domingo Dulce could not or would not control these unruly throngs. José Morales Lemus, fearing for his life, abandoned the island and moved to New York.

vored *a Cuba Española*, particularly Havana's civil employees. In January of 1869 Governor Dulce granted an amnesty to all insurgents deposing their arms in the next 40 days. There were few takers. The permissiveness for fraud, larceny and breach of trust extended into the issue of slave trade. Spain had signed a treaty with England in 1817 to abolish the trade, but the growing demand for manpower in the sugar industry led to extreme permissiveness and lack of compliance. Hundreds of smuggled slaves were landed on the numerous beaches and coves of the Cuban archipelago, bypassing customs without any controls. The flow of briberies proved to be unstoppable. Africans detected on the high seas by the British navy were nominally declared *emancipados* and presented to the Spanish authorities for their return to Africa. They were never returned to Africa; Spanish officials leased them for several years to private interests, presumably until they adapted to their new and strange environment.[294]

Exasperated, Governor Dulce decided to set aside his plans for conciliation [295] and decreed press censorship in the island and the establishment of military tribunals to punish the crime of *infidencia* (disloyalty).

In the meantime, on the war front, Carlos Roloff (1842-1907) joined the insurrection in February of 1869 opening a new front in Las Villas province.

Carlos Manuel de Céspedes addressed a letter to President Ulysses Grant seeking his support for Cuban independence and the recognition that there was a state of war between Cuba

---

[294] British consuls roamed the island of Cuba checking the status and treatment given to those *emancipados*. Receipts of fees paid by the individuals renting their services were falsified; the *emancipados* allowances were denied. Some of these blacks joined the forces of the *mambises* as a last resort to achive freedom.

[295] Governor Dulce had called his policy "*el olvido del pasado*," granting amnesty to all political prisoners that had in any way confronted the Spanish government. One of the first men condemned to prison after Dulce retracted his amnesty policy was 17 year old José Martí, who would start his 6 year sentence on October 21, 1869.

and Spain. Grant sympathized with the effort by the Cubans but took no action.

José Manuel Mestre fled to New York in March, 1869, and joined the *Junta Central Republicana de Cuba*, founded a month earlier by José Morales Lemus.

Two weeks later, Governor Dulce deported 257 Cubans to the Spanish island of Fernando Poo in Africa. A big commotion took place in Havana as members of the resistance fought a cadre of *Voluntarios* in the harbor. Close to 100,000 Cuban families began to seek refuge in the US.

In a new effort to smother the resistance in Havana and defeat the war in the eastern part of Cuba, Dulce decreed that no ships of any flag could get near Cuban territory. Madrid disapproved this unpolitical decision and voided the decree within 30 days. He fired back confiscating all properties of the insurgents and their sympathizers.

On April 9, an important member of the resistance in Havana, Francisco León y Nuez, was garroted at Cabaña Castle, in front of a large number of protesters. His last words supporting the war infuriated several *Voluntarios* watching the premises. They fired against the crowd killing seven demonstrators. The disturbances lasted three days. The *Voluntarios* began to disobey and neglect orders from Governor Dulce and even published leaflets criticizing his incompetence. On June 1st, they organized an act of protest at the *Plaza de Armas*. Dulce began to feel he had lost control of events in Cuba. He resigned his post the following day and returned to Spain.

On April 10, Céspedes convoked a Constitutional Assembly at Guáimaro, Camagüey; it established the three powers of the state (a legislative single Chamber, the Executive to be appointed by the Chamber and the Judicial courts); it divided the island in four provinces *(Oriente, Camagüey, Las Villas* and *Occidente)* and adopted as the national flag the one designed by Teurbe Tolón and first used by Narciso López in 1849. Céspedes was designated President and Manuel de Quesada General in Chief of the Army.

José Morales Lemus sent his first expedition to Cuba under the direction of General Thomas Jordan, a well known US Confederate officer; he landed in Cuba with 300 men and 4,000 weapons provided by Cuban exiles in the US. Jordan became a *de facto* Cuban Chief-of-Staff.

On June 28, Antonio Caballero de Rodas arrived in Havana, appointed by General Serrano as the new governor of Cuba. 60 days later Serrano rejected the offer of Hamilton Fish, US Secretary of State, to mediate between the Cuban rebels and the Madrid government. By the end of the year, US President Grant reiterated his reasons for not getting involved in the Cuban question. [296]

The US non-intervention policy was dramatically implemented with the interception of an expedition organized by the New York Junta, made up of 1,350 men equipped with Spencer carbines, revolvers, sabres, two 12-pounder batteries and several 60-pounder guns. All men were arrested.

Cubans in the *manigua* began to show signs of discord among themselves. General Manuel de Quesada was fired by the Legislative Chamber after he lost the battle of Las Tunas. [297] He was considered by many as arrogant and dictatorial in his relations with the legislators and the troops. Céspedes sent him to New York to help the support efforts of the *Junta Cubana*. Francisco Vicente Aguilera resigned as secretary of the Cuban legislature and Pedro Figueredo resigned as Sub Secretary of

---

[296] Grant conveyed to José Morales Lemus that «The US must observe perfect good faith to Spain, and whatever might be our sympathies with a people, wherever, in any part of the world, struggling for more liberal government, we should not depart from our duty to other friendly governments nor be in haste to prematurely recognize a revolutionary movement until it had manifested capacity of self-sustenance and of some degree of stability.» The only voice in Grant's cabinet that favored US intervention at any cost was Secretary of War John A. Rawlins, who died on September 5, 1869. By 1878, in spite of 10 years of self-sustenance of the *mambises* in Cuba, the US government never changed its position.

[297] Felipe Ginovés del Espinar, provisional colonial governor of Cuba, changed the name of this town from *Las Tunas* to *Victoria de Las Tunas* after the Spanish victory against Quesada on August 16, 1869.

War. At that point only Mexico, Perú and Chile were recognizing the legitimacy of the Cuban Government in Arms.

By the end of 1869, the Cuban army began a more organized and strategic war. What they lacked in numbers, experience, warfare training and arms and equipment, was amply compensated by their detailed knowledge of the countryside, their effective use of guerrilla tactics and a greater immunity to many diseases that thrived on the island. On the seas, however, the situation was different. Spain amassed a powerful fleet and sent it to Cuba: 50 vessels carrying 400 short and long range guns. It became a decisive advantage; Spain was now able to keep expeditions sent by the New York Junta from getting through.

In the peninsula, political support to the Cuban policy began to be questioned,[298] even after the insurgents had been forced to retreat from Las Villas, back to Camagüey.

On March 26, 1870, Cuban General Donato Mármol, one of the founders of Cuban independence, was stationed in Bayamo under the command of Máximo Gómez; from their position, Gómez and Mármol were controlling the entire valley of the Cauto River. Word came from advance observers that an entire division of Spaniards had left Las Tunas and were approaching Bayamo, then under the command of Blas Villate, Count of Valmaseda. Mármol ordered a tactical retreat from the city, not without setting it on fire with the enthusiastic consent of its residents.

---

[298] A March 1870 editorial in Madrid's newspwepar *La Discusión* read:

«For 18 months we have sustained a very difficult and bloody struggle in Cuba. Forty thousand Spaniards, at a cost of US $ 40 million, have put their feet upon that burning soil, and many of them are now dead. We have accomplished absolutely nothing. The insurrection is not defeated. It will hold out long enough to consume all the resources from our miserable coffers. It will cause the death of many Spaniards. It will be painful; we will probably meet in Cuba the same fate that we did in Santo Domingo. After lots of heroism and self-abnegation, we probably will leave in the hands of the enemy the sepulchers of our soldiers . Our reported victories may be real ones, but who can conquer a people fighting for liberty? »

Valmaseda responded to the more organized strategies of the Cuban rebels by increasing his repression of any signs of support for independence. A black slave, Cornelio Robert, shouted «*Viva Cuba Libre*» during a Holy Friday procession in Santiago de Cuba; he was identified, detained and executed. [299]

Valmaseda's best instrument of rebel control was a colonel that first showed his vehemence against rebels at an encounter on September 13 in the margins of the Salado River, near Santiago de Cuba. He took no clemency on a group of 21 hungry and poorly armed insurgents that surrendered after a desperate resistance. The victorious colonel was 31 year old Valeriano Weyler, who began to call his men the *Cazadores de Valmaseda*.

The Cuban army reorganized its ranks after a meeting of top chiefs at a farm called *El Potrero*, property of Mármol's father-in-law. Present were: Aguilera, Francisco Maceo, Carlos Manuel de Céspedes, Manuel de Jesús Calvar, Jaime Santiestean, Salvador Cisneros, Carlos Loret de Mola, Julio Grave de Peralta and Donato Mármol. General Máximo Gómez was given control of the army with Antonio Maceo under his direction. Calixto Garcia became second in command. Under García's direction, Cuban rebels attacked the town of Jiguaní and took prisoner the nephew of Captain General Lersundi, Francisco Muguruza Lersundi.

A few months later, on July 22, 1870, Donato Mármol, without medications or physicians to assist him, succumbed to smallpox on a field near Guantánamo. He was 27 years old.

---

[299] In one of the most interesting anecdotes of the 1868 War in Cuba, the Cuban army, knowing they were vastly outnumbered by the Spaniards, decided to abandon Bayamo. Marmol set his family home on fire and wrote to his mother, who had taken refuge in Camagüey: «Mother, I just had the pleasure to set your house on fire.» To which his mother, Doña María Mármol, an enthusiastic supporter of independence, simply replied, «Thanks.»

Images, top to bottom:

Stamps and Bonds of the Republic and the Republic in Arms;

An **allegory** published on the September 1869 issue of *Harper's Magazine* under the heading *Waiting for a Sail*.

Images above: top to bottom:

The area where the **Villanueva Theater** was located. The pole marks the intersection of Zulueta and Trocadero streets. On the right, the Church of *El Angel*;

a drawing of the **shootings** at the Villanueva Theater on January 21, 1869;

José Martí, at age 16, with his prison uniform and his shackles. They resulted in a lifetime of pain for his legs.

Images above: top to bottom, left to right:

The three men responsible for the 1989 **overthrow of Isabel II** in Spain: Juan Prim, Francisco Serrano y Domínguez and Juan Bautista Topete;

a group of **Voluntarios** marching in Havana in 1869;

an issue of pro-Cuban Independence newspaper **La Verdad** in New York.

Images above: top to bottom, left to right:

The **Acera del Louvre** (front façade of *Hotel Inglaterra*), a preferred place to meet for pro-independence youngsters in the 1860s;

a plaque locating the site of the **1868 Convention of Tirzan**, near Bayamo in Oriente;

a rare picture of young **Francisco Vicente Aguilera**.

Images above: top to bottom, left to right:

José Manuel Mestre Domínguez (1832-1886), disciple of José de la Luz y Caballero, member of the *Junta Cubana de Nueva York*, gave his entire fortune to the Cuban independence cause;

young **Juan Prim**, in the years he met Carlos Manuel de Céspedes in Paris;

one of the scholarly publications of **José Manuel Mestre** in 1862;

General **Thomas Jordan** (1819-1895), fighter in the *US Civil War Battle of Shiloh* (1862), Chief of Staff of the Cuban Independence Army in 1869, winner of the *Battle of Guáimaro* in 1870.

Images above: top to bottom, left to right:

The remains of the **La Demajagua** sugar mill, property of Carlos Manuel de Céspedes. He started the 1868 war from this estate;

a Cuban stamp conmmemorating the **presidency of Céspedes**;

General Donato Mármol (1843-1870), an exceptional independence leader in the 1868 War. He died very young at age 27.

Images above: top to bottom, left to right:

General **Carlos Roloff** (1842-1907), Polish-born former officer of the 9th Ohio infantry regiment in the US Civil War, fought in the three Cuban independence wars and survived to serve in the Republic;

General **Manuel de Quesada Loynaz** (1830-1866), member of Agüero's conspiracy in 1851, general of the Mexican army in 1861, General in Chief of the Cuban Independence army in 1869;

A Cuban stamp honoring **General Roloff**;

an aged **Blas Villate, Count of Valmaseda** (1824-1882). Three times Captain General of Cuba during the 1868 War, presided over the execution of Juan Clemente Zenea and the 8 students of medicine in 1871.

Images above: top to bottom, left to right:

A postage stamp honoring **Ignacio Agramonte y Loynaz** (1841-1873), head of the 1868 war in Camagüey starting in 1871, author of the *Guáimaro Constitution* in 1869, hero of the *rescate de Sanguily*;

Antonio Caballero de Rodas (1816-1876), Capitan General of Cuba in 1869, could not get along with the *Voluntarios* and resigned after a year;

a plaque commemorating the execution of **Pedro (Perucho) Figueredo** (1818-1870), the author of the *Cuban National Anthem*.

Images above: top to bottom, left to right:

The roster of leaders of the **Corps of Volunteers** in Havana in 1869;

the presentation card of **Pedro (Perucho) Figueredo**;

a 1869 **medal for Voluntarios** in Cuba;

a copy of Camagüey's clandestine pro-independence paper **El Cubano Libre** from 1869.

All along the northern coast of Havana, sideways with the road that led from the city wall to the Espada cemetery, the waters of the Florida straits broke into coastal dark, rough stone formations with jagged surfaces called *dientes de perro* (dog's teeth or beehive rocks), two to three feet in height, of irregular shape and full of holes. These rock formations, built by the erosion of sea waves over limestone strata, were on many places cut and transformed into small pools measuring 3 to 6 feet deep, in an area 6 ft into the sea by 15 to 20 feet along the coast. On the water side, the pools were open to the sea by 2 to 3 inches wide breaches in the wall that allowed the water to flow in and out. Fees were generally 25 to 50 cents for one hour of bathing, depending on whether the *baño* was covered or not within a wooden hut. A towel would normally cost one *real* to rent.

Gentlemen and their ladies (for no woman would use the facilities without the protection of a husband, a brother, a cousin or her father; never a male friend) would arrive to the shore on board their *volanta*. A weekly visit was a regular practice and the only practical way to seek some relief from the hot Havana summer. Like city cafés, the *baños de mar* were occasions to share a good time with friends and family. For those lucky enough to have a roof, they could venture in the deep end of their pool by holding to ropes hanging from the hut roofs.

The *Baños de Mar de La Habana* were so popular that in 1853 the newspaper *La Ilustración*, published in Barcelona and widely read in Havana, included an article by "reputable French physician M. Béranger" stating «a prudent temperature of these baths, particularly for children, must be from 25 to 29 ½ degrees; the salubriousness of the experience depends on the first bath of the season. A child, after a series of baths, should feel stronger and be more active, and should overcome the transparency of his skin and the bluish tint of his veins.»

The popular *Baños de Mar* in Havana

29
Madrid Realizes Cuba was Out of Control

AS MORE AND MORE sympathizers were joining the efforts of the Cuban insurgents, the press in Spain looked for ways to explain and justify what was happening in Cuba. They began to characterize the rebels as «*una muchedumbre abigarrada de blancos y negros*» (a black and white variegated swarm). They began to blame Lersundi as incompetent and inattentive, maligning him for claiming untruthful defensive actions in the *Gaceta* and gullibly anticipating he would crush the rebellions in eight days. In Camagüey the Spanish press disparaged the officers of the crown for seeking refuge in the municipal building instead of confronting and destroying the rebels. They reminded the powers in Cuba that the current revolt in 1868 was no different than those of 1851 and 1855 and had to be defeated with the same determination. Only Valmaseda and the *Voluntarios* were spared the scoldings in the Madrid press.

In many towns in Cuba, the mayors opened subscriptions to mobilize people to help in the war; ladies prepared first aid emergency kits with bandages, surgical instruments, disinfectants and stretchers. Recruiting posters were placed in many buildings asking residents to join the Corps of Volunteers. Nothing seemed to work. By the time Lersundi was replaced by Dulce [300] the districts of Oriente and Las Villas were under continuous siege and in Havana hundreds of demonstrators were questioning the permanence of Spanish rule.

No sooner had Dulce assumed the governorship of Cuba on January 12, 1869, he was reporting to Madrid that a new spirit

---

[300] Lersundi's December 21, 1868 report to authorities in Madrid, indicated that, with the possible exception of Oriente, where rebels had limited control of very few points, he was leaving the entire island pacified and safe.

of security and trust had spread across the island. Two days later he sent a request for reinforcements. To residents in the island he announced that the only thing needed in Cuba was to implement the rights guaranteed by the September revolution in Spain: full freedom of the press,[301] revocation of the military commissions,[302] expansion of the rights to assemble. He followed with a general political amnesty, considered by many Spaniards in Cuba «*una gran imprudencia.*»

Dulce later regretted he had opened a Pandora box. The insurgent armies grew in size; in many towns, including Havana, students became relentless upsetters of public order. A Madrid paper reported «Governor Dulce's friends have characterized the mood of the General as a mixture of embarrassment, sadness, guilt, shame, remorse, depression and annoyance.» Dulce's remedy to his mistakes was not to rely on Valmaseda and the *Voluntarios* but to approach the rebels to seek an arrangement «*de potencia a potencia.*»[303] It irritated his enemies and soon he was replaced. The *Diario de la Marina* was on his side; its rival paper, *La Voz de Cuba*,[304] an organ of the most radical *españolismo*, was against him. From that point on, it was evident that there were two wars going on simultaneously in Cuba. One war set the Spanish colonial government against the Yara

---

[301] During the war of 1868-1878, there were seven newspapers published in Camagüey, four in Havana and one in Sancti Spíritus providing news about the war. The most read were *Diario Cubano, Las Dos Antillas, La Estrella de Cuba, La Independencia, La Libertad, El Pueblo, La República, El Tribuno Cubano, La Verdad* and *La Voz de la Patria.*The freedom of the press decreed by Dulce comprised all subjects except news dealing with the Catholic Church and slavery, which were out of limits.

[302] Tribunals composed of officers of the army in different towns and cities, with attributions similar to those of justices of the peace.

[303] On January 13, 1869, a meeting took place at the home of the Marqués de Campo Florido with José Morales Lemus representing the *insurrectos*. The purpose was to design an electoral process agreeable to Spain. This project failed after the violence against Aldama and Del Monte in Havana.

[304] *La Voz de Cuba* had been founded in Havana by Gonzalo Castañón, the journalist whose grave was pressumably desecrated by the students of medicine executed in 1871. It represented the interests of the Spanish middle class in Cuba. *El Diario de la Marina* was said to represent the interests of the colonial government of Spain.

insurgents. The other was radical *españolistas* in Cuba against all liberal institutions. [305]

With Dulce out of the way and the *Voluntarios* empowered by their successful campaign to influence the Madrid government, the war continued with renewed impetus and cruelty.

On February of 1871 the *Cazadores de Valmaseda* decisively won a battle in Palmito, a town halfway between Holguín and Banes, against Máximo Gómez troops. Juan Bautista Osorio [306] was apprehended on June 30 in Camagüey and executed. The *Real Audiencia de Santiago de Cuba* was closed. Guantánamo fell under siege by rebel forces. Juan Clemente Zenea was executed in Havana on August 25 and the eight medical students accused of desecrating the grave of Gonzalo Castañon were shot in Havana on November 27.

On October 8 General Julio Sanguily was captured by Spanish cavalry troops on the road to Puerto Príncipe; he was miraculously rescued by troops under Ignacio Agramonte in one of the most daring, gallant and well publicized actions of the Ten Year War.

In 1872 General Serrano formed a new government in Spain replacing Práxedes Mateo Sagasta; Valmaseda returned to Spain and Calixto García's troops took the town of Holguín. In Havana, work commenced on the Colón Cemetery and the Church of *El Carmelo* in *El Vedado*.

After a long disease Gertrudis Gómez de Avellaneda died on February 1, 1873, in Madrid from complications due to diabetes, leaving behind twenty plays and novels and many po-

---

[305] A February 28, 1869 article in *La Voz de Cuba* stated: «The liberal reforms that have been adopted in Cataluña can not be applied in Cuba. There, those new liberties were considered as generous; here they are interpreted as weakness. It is time to stop the *libertades intespestivas en mala hora concedidas a Cuba* (the improvised and ill-timed freedoms granted to Cuba).»

[306] Juan Bautista Osorio (1847-1871) had been contracted by *the Junta Cubana de New York* to bring expeditions to Cuba. He had turned a merchant ship into the first Cuban Navy ship, the *Yara*. Céspedes gave him the title of Capitán de Fragata. On a mission in Cuba he was captured.

ems. Her novel *Sab* was compared by the world literary press to Harriet Beecher's *Uncle Tom's Cabin*. On May 11, General Ignacio Agramonte died at an encounter in Jimaguayú, Camagüey, as he was hit in the head by a stray bullet.

On February 11, 1873, Amadeo I of Spain abdicated, opening the country to its first short lived republican form of government with Pi y Margall as president. He was soon replaced in 1873 by Emilio Castelar, [307] who was in turn made to resign by the Cortes before they were dissolved by a *pronunciamiento* by generals of the Spanish army Sagunto and Primo de Rivera.

On a parallel disruptive and turbulent action, the Chamber of Deputies of the Republic of Cuba in Arms, on October 28, 1873, deposed Carlos Manuel de Céspedes as president of the Republic in Arms. He was replaced by his nemesis Salvador Cisneros Betancourt. Four days later the *Virginius*, a fast American steamer hired by the *Junta Cubana de New York* to take expeditions and weapons to Cuba, was captured by the Spanish cruiser *Tornado*. All 165 crew members were condemned to death in Santiago de Cuba.[308]

Salvador Cisneros, concerned about the personal safety of the deposed Carlos Manuel de Céspedes, asked the Chamber of Deputies to reinforce his escort. The Chamber did not take any

---

[307] Castelar was pro-American, pro-Catholic Church, anti-Carlist and a political enemy of the Serrano-Topete-Prim trio. The famous *Virginius* incident took place during his presidency and almost caused a rupture in US-Spain relations. He was deposed in 1874 with Serrano back as president and the monarchy restored in the figure of Alfonso XII, son of Isabel II. In the Cuban issue, Castelar was a firm believer in *Cuba Española*, i.e., keeping Cuba in the hands of Spain.

[308] The *Virginius* was a small, high-speed steamer that had served, under the name *Virgin*, as a blockade runner for the Confederacy during the American Civil War. The Spanish government knew of its missions from spies in Jamaica. When captured, Spanish authorities in Santiago began to execute its crew as pirates, without trials. The British had to sent the sloop *HMS Niobe* —with instructiosn to bombard Santiago— to stop the carnage. Of the 165 crew members 53 had already been executed (including Pedro de Céspedes, brother of Carlos Manuel, and Herminio de Quesada, son of Manuel de Quesada) by firing squads, their corpses decapitated and their bodies trampled with horses.

action and on 27 February of 1874 Céspedes was ambushed and attacked in San Lorenzo, and killed.

In the winter of 1873 and the spring of 1874 Máximo Gómez won battles at *La Sacra, Palo Seco, El Naranjo, Mojacasabe* and *Las Guásimas*, a battle area comprising the entire territory around Guáimaro and Puerto Príncipe, Camagüey, causing close to 2,000 casualties to the Spanish army.

Before the end of 1874, Victor Hugo wrote several noble proclamations in favor of the Cuban independence and «generously received Cuban exiles who arrived to Paris,» according to the French weekly *La Gazette*. Calixto García was captured in San Antonio de Baja, near Bayamo, and survived an intended suicide.[309] He was replaced in his command by General Vicente García, soon to be called el *León de Santa Rita*.

In the meantime, in Spain, Práxedes Mateo Sagasta formed a new government, Arsenio Martínez Campos brought on a *pronunciamiento* in Sagunto and Cánovas del Castillo became a regent-minister; in Cuba José Gutierrez de la Concha became Captain General for the third time, the *Acueducto de Albear* and the *Plaza del Vapor* began to be built and, on December 27, at a stadium in Palmar del Junco, in what is today known as Pueblo Nuevo, Matanzas, several youngsters played Baseball for the first time in Cuba.

The year 1875 began with Máximo Gómez crossing the *Trocha de Júcaro a Morón*, a line of fortifications built by Spain to prevent the expansion of the war to the western area of Cuba. Gómez was successful in his first battle at *El Jíbaro*, Las Villas.

---

[309] Calixto Garcia, in an attempt to avoid giving the Spanish the satisfaction of his seizure, shot himself with a with a .45 caliber pistol. The bullet went from under his chin out of his forehead, knocking him unconscious. The wound gave him a great forefront scar, causing severe headaches for the rest of his life. He called ther wound "his star." When the Spanish authorities came to Holguín to tell Lucía Iñíguez, Calixto's mother, she said that her son would have never allowed himself to be captured. When the officials explained to her that Calixto tried to commit suicide, she replied «I now believe it was my son, first dead than captured!» He was imprisoned until the Pact of Zanjón. Calixto García was one of several patriots that fought in each of the three wars of independence.

In another instance of disruptive and turbulent action, General Vicente García, refusing to leave his area of birth in Las Tunas to join Máximo Gómez in his plan to invade Las Villas, started a protest later known as the *Sedición de Lagunas de Varona*. He also declared his opposition to the government of Salvador Cisneros Betancourt. After a deadlock lasting two months, General García was given the command of Oriente and Camagüey provinces and Cisneros was replaced by a new president, Juan Bautista Spotorno. The Republic of Cuba in Arms more and more looked like the convulsed and unstable governments in Spain.

In order to ameliorate the moral devastation created by the *Lagunas de Varona* incident, a group of reformist journalist from Havana gave publicity to a document written by Captain General Lersundi as he abandoned the governorship of Cuba.[310]

---

[310] The document read in part «Is sad but necessary to confess the absolute lack of a uniform and consistent policy toward the island of Cuba from the government of the metropolis; it promised concessions and reforms; yet it has repressed and defrauded the hopes that it promised. It has produced a state of distrust, unease and general restlessness, which can now hardly be remedied. The powerful and unshakable organization of our colonies has been replaced, haphazardly, with an spasmodic and bureaucratic system, which is at the same time expensive, ignorant and deceiving, allowing the most scandalous immorality on one hand, and helping to disparage and discredit Spain with the other. There is no future for Spain in the Cuba of today.»

On November 1, 1873, the Spanish cruiser *Tornado* exited Santiago de Cuba and began to search for the rebel ship *Virginius* at 14-knot speed; the following day, at 10:00 AM, it made visual contact. As soon as Captain Fry of the *Virginius* found his ship in peril, he headed for Jamaica.

For three years, the *Virginius* had been traveling from ports in the Caribbean and Central America to the coasts of Cuba bringing men and weapons for the fight for independence. It had been bought in August 1866 by Manuel de Quesada with funds provided by Miguel Aldama. On this day it was headed for Cuba via ports in Kingston, Port au Prince and Dominicana. An informant from New York had given word to the Spanish Navy of the plans of the *Virginius*; otherwise there was no reason for the *Tornado* to be fully equipped in a secluded place inside Santiago de Cuba harbor. On that fateful date, the *Virginius* was as good as dead; it had not been docked and scrapped for fifteen months and its bottom was full of *escaramujos* (barnacles); its supply of coal on board was short and it had to resort to burning petroleum, cooking grease, fats and even foods to keep up a speed of nine-knots. It was not until 9:00 PM that the *Tornado* was at cannon range of the *Virginius*. It happened to be a crystal clear night, where the horizon could be seen plainly under a full moon; it was easy for the *Tornado* to keep track of the *Virginius*, particularly since an oily, dense black smoke was coming out of its two funnels.

Captain Fry, master of the *Virginius*, decided to make the only level-headed decision: to throw everything overboard. A frightful panic and disorder overcame everyone when the crew began to consider it a doomed vessel. Overboard went cannons, horses, food, uniforms, jungle boots, two thousand Remington rifles for which Mr. Aldama of New York had paid a small fortune, seven recoilless *mitrailleuses* donated by French Republican sympathizers, cases and cases of ammunition and almost two tons of smokeless powder. Even Fry's beloved pet *Augustus*, a large old German shepherd that had accompanied him throughout the American Civil War was, in the confusion, thrown in the waters at the Jamaica's coast by orders of an *alférez*.

It was all in vain. The *Tornado* came on the side of the *Virginius* and fired three shells across its bow. A fourth shell burst near its helm and set the American flag on fire. For the first time in his long and distinguished career, Captain Fry surrendered a ship under his command.

(continued)

The Story of the *Virginius*

(continuation)

Captain Granados, master of the *Tornado*, and three crew members boarded the *Virginius* and ran up the Spanish flag where the American flag had been. He seized all maps, charts and documents and took command of the ship. The next day he entered the port of Santiago.

In Santiago de Cuba, Governor Juan Nepomuceno Burriel gave a dazzling get-together the following night aboard the *Virginius*. Six tables full of cheap wine bottles and meats were set on the deck. Three small boats with musical groups circled the *Virginius* playing Spanish patriotic songs. The next morning the officers reassembled on the *Tornado*; this time for court-martials. One hundred and forty four persons were briefly interrogated and sent to prison throughout the day. The decision had been made beforehand that all would be shot to death. The first four were scheduled to die on November 4th: **Bernabe Varona**, Cuban Division General; **Pedro Céspedes**, brother of Carlos Manuel and Commanding General of the Cienfuegos troops; General **Jesús Del Sol** and US Civil War Brigadier **Washington Ryan**. 49 additional men were executed in the presence of the entire Corps of Volunteers. Even Gabriel Meléndez, the man who was in contact with the New York spy and who meddled with the *Virginius* engines to impede its escape, was shot. After finding out his error, Captain Granados declared that it had been «a just award for his treachery.»

E. G. Schmitt, American vice-consul at Santiago, had been turned down in his request to interview the prisoners; he was also denied the use of the marine cable to communicate with the American consul in Kingston. At that point Santiago's Governor Burriel was holding back two important documents: first, an order from **Emilio Castelar** (1832-1899), the famous orator and President of Spain, asking the Spanish authorities in Cuba to stop the massacre; second, a letter from the family of a Cuban magnate, **Ignacio Franchi Alfaro**, offering one million dollars in gold for the release of all the prisoners.

Once the news of the carnage in Santiago reached Kingston, Captain Lampton Lorraine, commander of the British sloop of war *Niobe*, rushed his ship full speed to Santiago. He presented himself to the authorities demanding that the butchery be stopped. He backed his words with threats to bombard Santiago and turn it into ashes. A United States *man-of-war* and a *frigate* had arrived on port at Santiago and had blocked the exit, trapping inside both the *Virginius* and the *Tornado*. It was the only way the carnage stopped. By then 53 men had been butchered and only 91 were left. All US papers denounced the incident, including the *New York Times*, the *New York Tribune*, the *New York Herald* and the *National Republican*. President Grant, however, decided that «war with Spain was not desirable.»

The Story of the *Virginius*

Images, top to bottom:

A 1870 Spanish engraving showing the fight in Cuba, from ***La Ilustración Española***;

a 1872 drawing showing the ***rescue of Julio Sanguily*** by troops under the command of General *Ignacio Agramonte*.

a scene from the 1916 Cuban film ***Rescate del Brigadier Sanguily***, produced and directed by Enrique Díaz Quesada, first shown in Teatro Payret on January 9, 1917.

Images, top to bottom:

Spanish soldiers in Cuba in 1879;

Defensores de la Integridad Española, 1869, from a book by Gil Gelpi y Ferro, journalist and tireless defamer of Cubans with considerable followers in Havana's paper *La Voz de Cuba*;

uniforms of the Spanish troops in the 1800s.

Images, top to bottom, left to right:

The **Chamber of Deputies** in Spain in 1873;

Emilio Castelar y Ripoll (1832-1899), president of the First Spanish Republic in 1873-74, after the resignation of Amadeo I;

José Gutiérrez de la Concha, Marquis of Havana, three times Captain General of Cuba between 1850 and 1875, *Grandee of Spain*;

Young **Alfonso XII** of Spain in 1870, son of Isabel II, husband to María Cristina de Austria, preceded by Amadeus I, succeeded by his son Alfonso XIII. He reigned from 1874 to 1885, after a *Coup d'état* restored the monarchy and ended the efemeral Spanish First Republic.

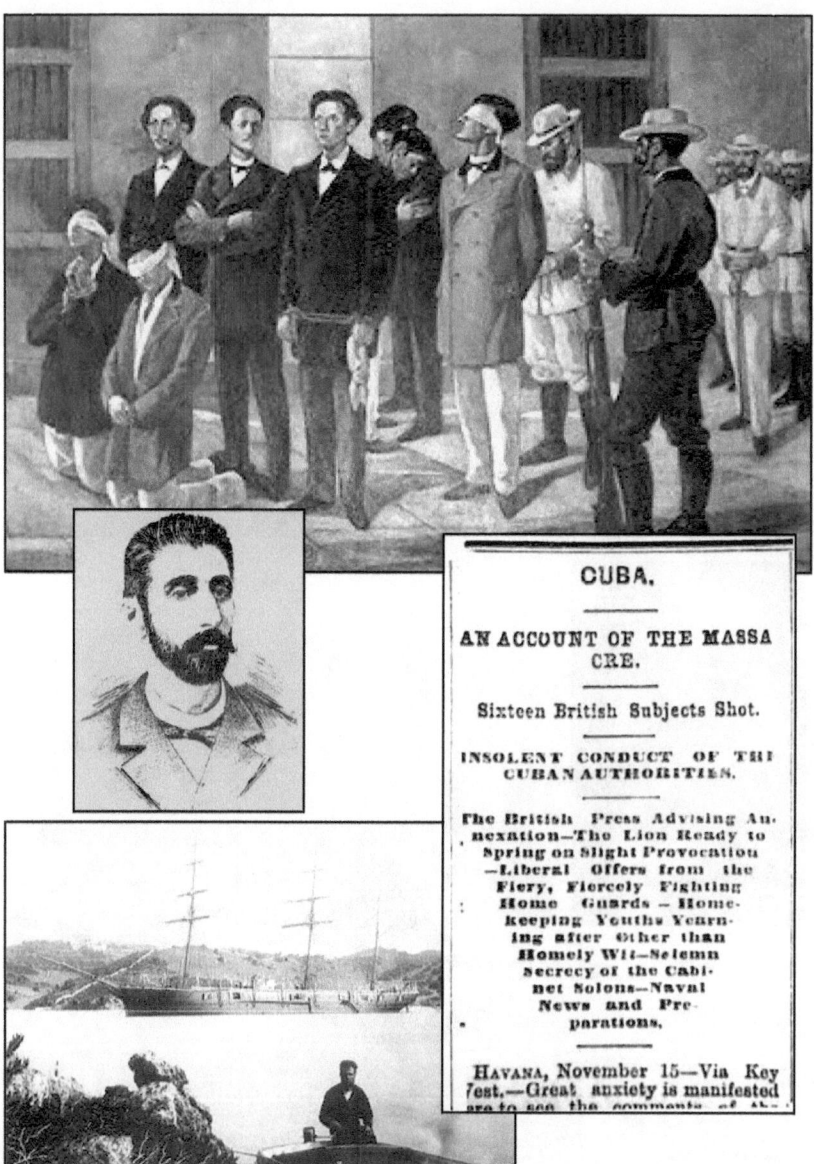

Images, top to bottom, left to right:

The **eigth students of medicine** shot by the Spanish colonial government under Blas Villate, *Conde de Valmaseda*;

Federico Capdevila, the conscientious military man who defended the medical students shot in 1871, even under threats by angry mobs;

an account of the massacre of the prisoners of the **Virginius**;

the Spanish warship **Tornado** in Santiago de Cuba harbor.

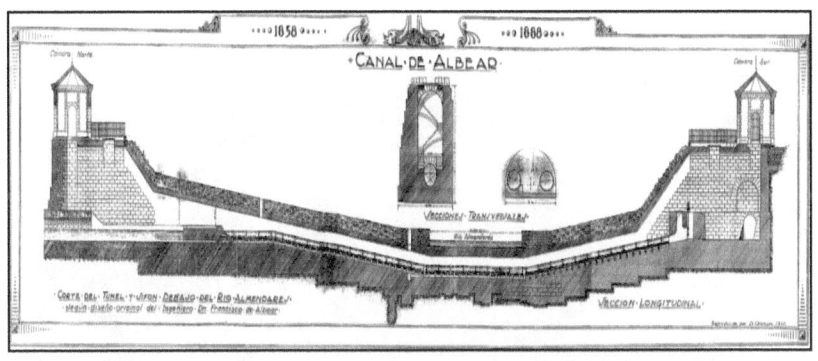

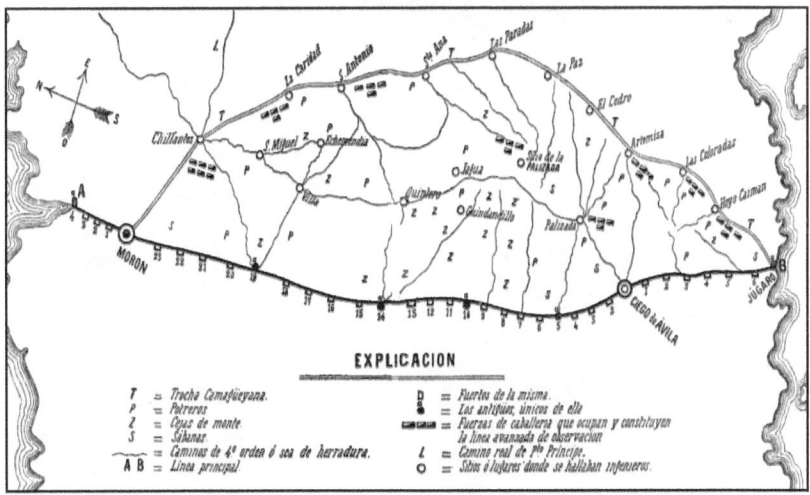

Images, top to bottom:

Two views of the **Albear Aqueduct**, started in 1861 and concluded in 1893. *Top*: the plan to go under the Almendares River; *Bottom*: the main building and the grand reservoir;

A diagram of the 68 Km long **Trocha de Júcaro-Morón**, built between 1869 and 1872 to impede the pass of rebel forces from east to west during the *Ten Year War* of Cuban Independence. It was the largest Spanish fortification in the colonies during the XIX century.

Images, top to bottom, left to right:

The **Junta Cubana de New York**, presided by Miguel de Aldama during the Ten Year War of Independence, 1868-1878;

the 1869 issue of **Harpers Weekly** dedicated to the 1868 campaign of the Cubans to gain their independence.

two photos of **Calixto García**, as a 27 year old young man and, after the war of 1895, as emissary to the US government before his death in 1898;

a photo of **Juan Bautista Spotorno** (seated) with **Serafín Sánchez** (left) and **Carlos Roloff**;

the 1869 **merit medallion** presented to the Voluntarios in 1869.

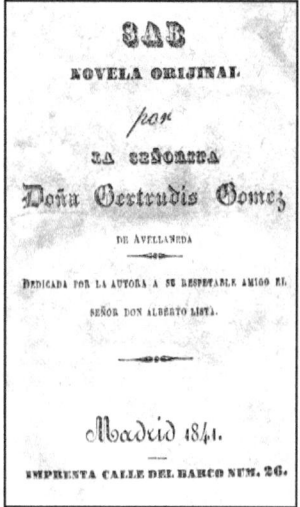

Images, top to bottom, left to right:

A **stamp of La Avellaneda** printed inCuba in 1914;

1841 front page of the first edition of **Sab**, Avellaneda's anti-slavery novel that could not be published in Cuba until 1914;

the brothers **Manuel (left)** and **Julio Sanguily**;

A plaque commemorating the **1871 execution** of Juan Clemente Zenea at the *Patio de los Laureles* in the fortress of *La Cabaña* in Havana;

the last image of **Juan Clemente Zenea**. Zenea reintroduced *romanticism* in Cuban literarture. He was shot as he was returning to the US after having entered Cuba surreptitiously in support of independence.

Images, top to bottom, left to right:

Four books published in Spain in support of the colonial status.
Historia de la Insurrección y Guerra de la Isla de Cuba by Eleuterio Lofriu y Sagrera, published in Madrid in 1870;
Insurrección en Cuba, published in Barcelona, 1869;
Cuba Siempre Española by Gelpi y Ferro, 1869;
a 1923 **Historia de los Voluntarios Cubanos** by Jose Joaquín Ribó.

Images, top to bottom, left to right:

A cartoon showing US Secretary of State William Steward asking President Lincoln to "**pluck (take) the pear of Cuba**;"

an allegory of **Havana** as Spain's "*always loyal*" city;

a cartoon presenting **Cuba-Spain commerce** in the 1880s.

On October 24, 1868, four days after the rebel forces of Carlos Manuel de Céspedes had taken Bayamo in eastern Cuba, two Spanish columns under Colonel Demetrio Quirós Weyler took the town of Baire, positioning themselves to attack the newly occupied Cuban plaza. Four days latter, in response to that move, Céspedes ordered General Donato Mármol to establish a strong defensive position in the region of Jiguaní in order to hinder the advance of the enemy column. Mármol immediately ordered Máximo Gómez to take command of two hundred men and attack the Spanish forces before they could reach Bayamo.

Gomez took positions in *Lomas de Yarey*, but on hearing that the column remained stationed in Baire decided to run a deceitful maneuver to ambush the Spaniards. On November 4, Colonel Quirós prepared his forces to advance on Bayamo, selecting two companies, totaling two hundred men, to march to the forefront; he made the mistake, however, of not providing them with advance vanguard scouts or flankers.

Early in the morning of that day, Gómez had deployed thirty or forty infantry men near the town of Baire, in the area known as *Tienda del Pino*. It was his plan to attack Quirós' men with a combination of firearms and *machetes*. Around noon, when the enemy vanguard was approaching the area of the ambush, Gómez gave the order to charge the advancing columns with *machetes*; after a few shots from both sides of the road, the rebels fell upon the two Spanish columns. The Spaniards, terrified by the unexpected *machete* charge, could not organize a defense and were annihilated. They had about two hundred casualties; very few survivors were able to retreat to Baire.

Taking advantage of the surprise at *Tienda del Pino*, Gómez took positions at *Loma del Sitio*, east of town; there he anchored two pieces of artillery taken from the enemy. 50 if his men were also positioned west of town, preventing any escape route for the decimated Quirós column. The Spaniards stayed in Baire until November 8, when they began to retreat back to Santiago de Cuba. They were harassed by Cuban forces all the way there.

On that day at *Tienda del Pino*, and for the next 30 years, the *machete*, a simple farmer's work tool, became the most prized weapon by fighters of the Cuban Army.

***Machetes*, farmer's tools that became weapons**

30
The War of 1868 Comes to an End

THE GATHERING OF VICENTE GARCÍA'S troops on April 30, 1875, in *Lagunas de Varona*, the publication of his demands of May 5 against President Betancourt Cisneros and his manifesto of June 11 against the presidency and the legislative branches of the Cuban Republic in Arms, severely affected the moral of the rebel forces.

On May 1, President Salvador Cisneros and General Bartolomé Masó, both without escort, showed up at Vicente García's headquarters trying to persuade him to drop his challenge to the constitutionally established authorities. García received them cordially but reiterated his reasons for his protest, alleging his men would not agree to fight to liberate other territories but Las Tunas.

As soon as Antonio Maceo received the manifesto he wrote a scolding letter to General García rejecting his points of view and asking for discipline and a public retraction. Máximo Gómez, at great personal peril, took a brief detachment to *Loma de Sevilla* and had a meeting on June 24 with Vicente García to politely but forcefully suggest García he had to choose between discipline or banishment and dismissal from the independence forces. President Salvador Cisneros Betancourt, hurt but willing to accommodate to the situation, resigned his position and Juan Bautista Spotorno temporarily assumed the presidency.

It was the most serious constitutional crisis the Cuban forces had encountered, second and very close in time and scope to the dismissal of Céspedes. Spotorno tried to conciliate all sides and probably made the worst possible decision. He promoted Vicente García to chief military authority in both Camagüey and Oriente, with García's promise to assume the command of the Camagüey troops at once. After almost a month trying to mediate in the crisis, Máximo Gómez returned in mid-July to Las Villas; he found there the same malaise and discomfort among his men that he had left behind in Oriente. On two letters to Miguel Aldama in New York and Antonio Maceo in Oriente he expressed his doubts that the independence forces could recover from this sedition episode. It was a desperate situation at a time when Madrid had returned a man so heartless and ruthless as Count of Valmaseda to the Captaincy General of Cuba.

The consequences of the attempted sedition began to be felt very soon across the lines of the Cuban independence army. In March of 1876 Julio Sanguily resigned from his assigned post in command of the Las Villas territory. He truthfully gave as his reason that his men, empowered by the *Lagunas de Varona* example, were rejecting his right to give orders far from his Camagüey native soil. He was replaced by General Carlos Roloff.[311]

On March 29, at a meeting in *La Matilde*, Camagüey, a farm owned by Ignacio Agramonte's family, the Cuban Chamber of Deputies elected Tomás Estrada Palma as President of the Republic in Arms. The war was slowly coming to an end. The men were tired and confused. Many were questioning the possibility of success. Most had lost faith in the leadership. A few actions, although potentially dramatic in impact, were not sufficient to once again elevate their combative spirit. Other important events took place before the final day of hostilities:

In Spain, the Third Carlist War ended and the Bourbons abandoned Spain. Only the Spanish troops in Fort San Hilario in Nuevitas had joined the *Carlistas* in Cuba. In Ciego de Avila,

---

[311] Carlos Roloff (Karol Rolow-Mialofski, a Poland native, 1842-1907) served in the Union Army during the American Civil War in the 9th Ohio Infantry regiment; by the time the war was over he had the rank of officer. After the war, he moved to Cuba and worked as a clerk in the sugar business. He was an active member of the *El Progreso* Club and other local community organizations, including the masonic lodge *San Juan;* soon he became a popular and successful accountant and a social VIP. In 1868, Máximo Gómez offered him the rank of general in the Cuban forces.

José González Guerra, head of the Cuban army in Cienfuegos, was wounded and, because of lack of treatment, died of tetanus as the result of wounds received on a battle in Baraguá; he was replaced by Brigadier General Henry Reeve, (*el Inglesito* 1850-1876), [312] who would die on August 4, 1876.

A new Captain General, Joaquín Jovellar Soler, appointed for the second time by Madrid in January of 1876, disposed as one of his first decrees, the prohibition of *ñañiguismo* in the island. [313]

General Vicente García, still in Oriente, took Las Tunas after a fierce fight, on September 22, 1876. He burned the town to the ground.

General Arsenio Martínez Campos arrived in Cuba on November 3; he brought with him 28,000 men ready to repress the insurrection in the eastern part of Cuba. He was placed hierarchically on top of the Captain General of the island

Máximo Gómez, in an attempt to raise spirits, left Roloff on his own in Las Villas and moved to Camagüey, fully expecting an aggressive and forceful campaign by Martínez Campos. He was offered the title of General in Chief by President Estrada Palma but declined it, alleging it should be given to a Cuban-born general.

---

[312] Reeve had arrived in Cuba aboard the vessel Perrit. The expedition was ambushed by the Spanish Army and he was taken prisoner. A firing squad shot the entire group leaving them unburied and presumed dead. Reeve was not; he crawled away and was found by a Cuban patrol; Agramonte baptized him *Enrique el Americano.* He baptized Agramonte as *El Mayor.* He participated in the *rescate de Sanguily*. Died at age 27 by his own hand rather than surrender at *Yaguaramas*, one of the oldest Cuban towns near Cienfuegos.

[313] *Ñañiguismo* or *Abakuá* was a mysterious cult of African origin which settled in Cuba during the 1700s; it was mostly professed by slaves from Cameroon. Legend has that Princess Sikán, daughter of King Efor, accidentally killed the sacred fish Tanze. As punishment, she was sacrificed and her skin was used to cover the sacred drum Ekwe. Abbasid, a supreme deity, began to speak through this drum. She had to be fed with blood obtained from human sacrifices.

President Estrada Palma, testing the change of heart and transformation of General Vicente García, appointed him Military Chief of Las Villas on February 21, 1877.

The Chamber of Deputies, also testing García's reformed posture, declared Las Tunas to be part of the command area of Oriente and no longer part of Camagüey's. García sent an ill-mannered and disrespectful message to the Chamber; troops in Las Tunas, mutinying in Santa Rita, refused to accept any orders from anyone but García. The riotous soldiers in Santa Rita demanded the destitution of Estrada Palma and the dissolution of the Cuban Chamber of Deputies. Vicente García made no effort to set them straight; on the contrary, he made a *pronunciamiento* and directed his troops towards Las Tunas instead of Las Villas.

Maceo received a letter from García on June 3, asking him to join forces to take by themselves the entire territory of Oriente. Maceo refused and sent him a letter reminding him that Las Tunas was no longer his territory to defend or conquer. A sad and now pessimistic Máximo Gómez reinforced his views that the war was irretrievably lost. Antonio Maceo disagreed but could not explain why.

At a combat in *Los Mangos de Mejía*, Oriente, Antonio Maceo was gravely wounded. [314] The medic in charge cleaned his wounds and extracted six of eight bullets he received from .44 Remington rifles. General Manuel de Jesús (Tita) Calvar y Odoardo (1832-1895) replaced him temporarily. Maceo's men refused to accept the command of Calvar and expressed their protest to Maceo while in his own sickbed.

On October 4, 1877, Máximo Gómez arrested Cuban high officials Antonio Bello, Jaime Santiesteban, Esteban de Varona

---

[314] Maceo was saved by José María (Mayía) Rodríguez, a young student who in 1868 joined the revolutionary troops of Donato Marmol, whom he replaced after his death. Mayía was a recognized authority on logistics and knew well the Cuban countryside. His merits as a tactical expert were praised by both Generals Máximo Gómez and Antonio Maceo. In fact, thanks to his courage and bravery on August 6, 1877, he saved the life of general Maceo in 1877, the day of the "*Los Mangos de Mejía.*"

and José Castellanos; they were guilty of approaching the enemy to enter peace arrangements.[315] Three of them were condemned to death; Santiesteban was spared, probably in attention to his many and old efforts in support of Cuban independence.

On October of 1877, Tomás Estrada Palma fell in the hands of the Spanish army at *Las Tasajeras*, near Holguín. He was deported to Spain, where he remained prisoner in Gerona until the end of the war; he was replaced in the Cuban Republic at Arms by his VP Francisco Javier de Céspedes, brother of Carlos Manuel. General Vicente García was appointed his successor as the new President-elect of Cuba.

On November 18, Vicente García took possession as the new president of the Republic at Arms; the Cuban army was victorious against the Spanish troops at *Nuevas de Jobosí*, near Sancti Spíritus, Las Villas. There were numerous casualties on both sides and members of the Cuban Army, including Máximo Gómez, looked with better eyes at conversations with Spain about a truce. Martínez Campos, on a campaign at Sierra Maestra, Oriente, rushed to the news and took a ship at Santiago towards Santa Cruz del Sur, Camagüey, where he was to meet with Esteban Duque Estrada and Enrique Collazo. Upon reaching Camagüey, Martínez Campos ordered a tactical unilateral cease of hostilities.

At a meeting with the Chamber of Deputies in San Agustín del Brazo, Camagüey, on February 7, 1878, General Vicente García found out about the peace conversations with Martínez Campos. He asked for a meeting with the Spanish General the following day at *El Chorrillo*, Camagüey. Martínez Campos suggested to dissolve the Chamber of Deputies and replace it with a *Comité del Centro*. Vicente García did not agree with

---

[315] In 1875, when Spotorno replaced Salvador Betancourt Cisneros after the *Lagunas de Varona* incident, Spotorno issued the *Principle of Spotorno*: «any one, Cuban or Spaniard, dealing in conversations aimed at ending the war, will be summarily charged, indicted for the crime of high treason, and will be expeditiously executed.»

most of the troops and left the meeting; the *Comité* was formed and given the task to define and follow-up the Spanish peace offer. Esteban Duque Estrada and Enrique Collazo were to act as leaders of the Truce Committee.[316]

Two days later, on February 10, the rebels agreed to have a ceremony at *San Agustín del Brazo* to sign the peace accord. Several couriers were given the task to inform other rebels in Oriente and Camagüey, particularly Máximo Gómez and Antonio Maceo.

A meeting of the Truce Committee with Maceo took place on February 27 in *Piloto Abajo*, near San Luis, Oriente, in the presence of Máximo Gómez. Maceo asked for a meeting with Martínez Campos. Gómez asked for a passport to leave Cuba. The following day all insurgents in Las Villas —with the exception of Ramón Leocadio Bonachea's troops— deposed their arms. Maceo planned to continue the war with the help of Miguel Aldama in New York; a new constitution and a provisional government were set up; the rebel spirit had vanished.

On March 1, 1878, a government decree in Madrid granted Cubans representation in the Spanish Courts. On the very same day Maceo had a resounding victory over the *Batallón de San Quintín*, the elite military unit of the Spanish Army, on the road to San Ulpiano, in Oriente, Cuba. It had been the unit that surrounded and killed Carlos Manuel de Céspedes in 1873. Maceo knew it and it inspired him to avenge his slain president. The Battle of San Ulpiano took place at a time when Martínez Campos was trying to discourage Cubans with a policy of pacification and generosity. Most of the fight had ended across the is-

---

[316] Esteban Duque Estrada was an engineering graduate from Stevens Politechnic Institute in New Jersey; he would later serve with Cosme de la Torriente, José Ramón Villalón, Perfecto Lacoste, Enrique José Varona, Emilio Nuñez, José Miguel Gómez, Miguel Gener, Leopoldo Cancio and others in the government of US General Leonard Wood after the end of the 1895 war and the US intervention in Cuba in 1898. Enrique Collazo was a graduate of the Segovia Military School. In 1892 he had helped José Martí and Mayía Rodríguez to formulate the strategy of the 1895 War of Independence. In 1898, he was the man who accompanied Andrew S. Roman in his quest to find Calixto García in the mountains of Cuba to give him a message from President William McKinley, the now famous *Mensaje a García*.

land, with the exception of Manzanillo, Bayamo and Holguín. Only 80 Spanish soldiers survived from San Ulpiano, out of 325 that faced Maceo. The Chief Spanish leader was Commandant Alonso de Santocildes.

Antonio Maceo finally had his meeting with Martínez Campos at a location known as *Mangos de Baraguá* on March 15, 1878. The meeting did not go well and Maceo summarized the result as: «We started this war to liberate the slaves and turn Cuba into a free and independent republic. The slaves are still slaves and Cuba is not free. The war has not ended.»

On the 19th Martínez Campos informed Cánovas del Castillo of the failure to convince Maceo. On the 23rd Maceo renewed the hostilities and continued the war under a new Cuban Government in Arms presided by Major General Tita Calvar.

On the 16th of August governor Martínez Campos signed a decree granting Cubans the right to freely assemble. Two parties were born on that day: the *Liberal Autonomista*, uniting Cubans wishing a higher degree of freedom from Spain, led by Leopoldo Cancio Luna, and the *Unión Constitucional*, the party of those favoring a *Cuba Española*.

Most rebels had deposed their arms and embraced the *Pacto del Zanjón* by the end of September. Bonachea, without surrendering, buried his weapons and went home on April of 1879. Calixto García was also an exception. In October he blasted those that had acquiesced to the «siren songs of Martínez Campos.» A new military chief was appointed in Cuba, Ramón Blanco y Erenas (Marquis of Peña Plata (1833-1906). He would have to deal with a new war of independence: la *Guerra Chiquita* of 1879-1880. The 10 Year War was definitely ended.

Calixto García was freed from his prison in Alicante, Spain on May 29, 1878. Antonio Maceo was allowed to leave Cuba on May 10, under pressure from his fellow rebels. José Martí returned to Cuba on August 31, 1878. He was deported a year later on September 17th. José Antonio Saco died in Barcelona on September 26th. Martínez Campos left Cuba on February 5, 1879.

May 15, 1878 was the day chosen for the meeting between Martínez Campos and Antonio Maceo. The Spaniard had chosen the date and time, barely a month after *Zanjón*, and the Cuban had the last word on the place and the number of delegates on each side. The general expectation on the Cuban side was that Maceo had resolved not to surrender. Maceo, wanting to make a collegiate and not a personal decision, had asked the Cuban officials of the troops of Holguín, Guantánamo, Jiguaní and Tunas to come to Baraguá. By the 15th he had received at his camp most of the leaders and commanders of the troops that remained in the *manigua*: Manuel Calvar, Donato Mármol, Flor Crombet, Pedro Martínez Freire, Ríus Rivera, José Lacret, Fernando Figueredo Socarrás, Belisario Grave de Peralta, José Maceo, Vicente García and Payito León. Early in the morning, they began to move silently on horse to the agreed meeting place, a thick and almost impenetrable grove of tall Mango trees, densely packed with yellow flowers or full grown fruit. Maceo, Calvar, Figueredo and Ríus set up their hammocks at a small clearance in the forest and readied an equal number of hammocks for the Spaniards. They all fixed their eyes on the western side of the clearance, where they expected the Spanish cortege to show up. Within twenty minutes the scouts announced the presence of Martínez Campos, who was received with all honors by the Cuban troops. Side by side with the current leadership of the Cubans were several older and retired Cuban chiefs of the 1868-1878 war, like Prendergast, Morales de los Ríos and Cassola, who had requested from Maceo the honor of accompanying him during the difficult negotiations. On the entourage of Martínez Campos all officers were Brigadiers and Lieutenant Generals. Martínez Campos came riding a Moorish horse, so black that it seemed to have tinges of shimmering dark blue. The first thing he said after dismounting was «Who among you is Antonio Maceo?» Maceo identified himself and introduced all officers from his entourage. After a similar treatment by Martínez Campos, both men sat on their hammocks.

Martínez Campos started the talks by showing Maceo an anonymous letter he had received the day before; it stated: «Do not have the interview with Maceo. You will be assassinated.» Maceo responded: «Although we both agreed to come with no more that 15 associates, I find it difficult to believe you would feel insecure, having deployed, as you have, a Spanish cavalry squadron less

(continued)

The Protest of Baraguá

(continuation)

than 300 meters from here.» Upon realizing that Maceo's scouts had tracked him and knew of all his whereabouts since he left the town of San Luis, north of Santiago de Cuba, Martínez Campos smiled and sat at his hammock; General Polavieja, Spanish military chief of the area, sat next to him. Martínez Campos was of middle height, with myopically alert eyes. His face was tanned, cut horizontally by an overgrown white mustache that complemented his pleasant and very dignified face. Polavieja, on the other hand, had a vulgar aspect, overwhelmed by a dusty beard that covered a sordid round face that tried to hide his displeasure in the presence of the Cuban troops and its Mayor General. As the conversation got started Martínez Campos was making an effort to be polite. He tried to please Maceo by indicating he did not know that his adversary was so young. Maceo was not impressed, particularly when he realized Martínez Campos was not referring to him as "General" or to his troops as the "Cuban Army."

The meeting was polite but with each side firm in its viewpoints. Martínez Campos began a speech announcing that Vicente García had accepted the Pact of *Zanjón* and surrendered. Maceo informed him that, just like the Spaniards had stationed a cavalry squadron 300 meters from the meeting place, such squadron and the meeting place itself were surrounded by troops under the command of Vicente García. Martínez Campos attempted to appeal to peace and prosperity for all Cubans by saying: «Enough of fights and sacrifices; you have impressed everyone with your determination and tenacity; the time has come to join Spain marching through the road to prosperity and civilized behavior.» Maceo riposted by saying that «nothing short of independence was acceptable. Please spare us your explanations.» Martínez Campos tried to convince Maceo that he did not know in full what the *Pacto del Zanjón* included, and asked Polavieja to bring him a copy. Maceo's answer was to tell Martínez Campos: «Don't bother to read what we already know. We do not want any of this. We are determined to reject it.» Martínez Campos asked: «Then, we do not understand each other.» «Exactly,» responded Maceo. «We do not understand each other.» Martínez Campos, in his last effort to save the conversations asked Maceo if he would allow him to address the Cuban troops and explain the terms of the *Pacto del Zanjón*. Maceo responded that he would agree to that if Martínez Campos allowed him to address the Spanish troops to seek their desertion.

After this suggestion Martínez Campos became very upset.

«How much time do you need to return to your positions?» asked Martínez Campos.

«*Ocho Días,*» answered Maceo. «We will resume hostilities on March 23rd.»

That said, Maceo adjourned the meeting. Martínez Campos furiously mounted his horse and raced away from the area, leaving Polavieja behind, all by himself.

The Protest of Baraguá

Images above:

An issue of Harper's Weekly in 1869, with a drawing of **Miguel Aldama**, President of the *Junta Cubana de New York*, describing the situation in Cuba;

A drawing of the **Trocha de Júcaro a Morón**, with images about its construction and design, from a 1874 issue of *Harper's Weekly*.

Images above: top to bottom, left to right:

All through the 50 years of Republican Cuba, the Ministry of Communications honored Cuban patriots from the 10 Year War with postal stamps.

Carlos Manuel de Céspedes (1819-1874),
Salvador Cisneros Betancourt (1828-1914),
Manuel de Jesús (Tita) Calvar (1827-1895),
Bartolomé Masó (1830-1907),
Juan Bautista Spotorno (1832-1917),
Tomás Estrada Palma (1832-1908),
Francisco Javier de Céspedes (1821-1903),
Vicente García (1833-1886),
Máximo Gómez (1836-1905),
Julio Sanguily (1845-1906) and
Calixto García (1839-1898).

Their average age when the 10 Year War started was 37 years old. The youngest was 23; the oldest was 49. Only six of them got to see the independence of Cuba in 1902.

Images above: top to bottom, left to right:

An engraving by Miehle showing a scene of **Ñañiguismo** or *Abacuá*;

a photo of **Tomás Estrada Palma** the day he assumed the presidency of Cuba in 1902;

a 1878 photo of **Máximo Gómez** (seated) with, left to right, **Rafael Rodríguez Enrique Collazo** and **Enrique Canals** in Kingston, Jamaica.

Images above: top to bottom, left to right:

Henry Reeves (*el Inglesito*, 1850-1876), a *Brigadier General* in the Ten Year War, who gave his life for Cuba's independence at age 26;

Julio Sanguily Garrite in 1875, founder of the Cavalry troops in Camagüey; he had to be helped to his horse after almost loosing his left foot in combat; it never impeded his participation or thwarted his valor;

Jesús (Tita) Calvar, took arms of October 10, 1868, at Gua, Manzanillo, close friend of Céspedes and Calixto García, did not accept the terms of the *Pacto del Zanjón* and stood by Maceo's side;

Vicente García González, *el León de Santa Rita*, in 1878 was elected *General en Jefe* with Antonio Maceo his second in command.

Images above: top to bottom, left to right:

Enrique Collazo, writer and fighter for Cuba's independence. Arrived in Cuba in 1869 at Nipe and became assistant to Máximo Gómez. In 1877 was a member of the *Comité del Centro,* negotiating the terms of the *Pacto del Zanjón*;

Arsenio Martínez Campos, Spanish monarchist, fought well and honorably against Cuban independence and against the Carlistas in Spain. In the 1895 war he refused the order of ethnic cleansing that years later made Weyler famous;

Fidel Alfonso de Santocildes, a graduate of the *Colegio de Infantería de Toledo,* member of the *Batallón de San Quintín,* married a Cuban lady after the Ten Year War; died in July, 1895 at *Peralejo* on a battle led by Antonio Maceo;

Joaquín Jovellar Soler, Prime Minister of Spain in 1875, after having served in Cuba in 1842 and in the last days of the Ten Year War. Made very wrong decisions during the *Virginius* affair almost causing a US-Spain war in 1873.

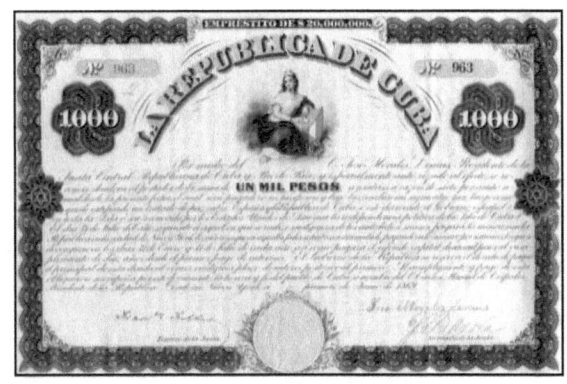

LA GUERRA EN CAMAGÜEY 1868-1873

Images above: top to bottom:

A **1869 Bond** to fund the Ten Year War, issued by the *Junta Cubana de New York* and signed by José Morales Lemus;

The theater of the Ten Year War in **Camagüey**;

Postal Stamps issued by the Government of Cuba in Arms. During the wars of Cuban independence, the rebel postal system was more reliable that Spain's.

«Je remercie Dieu de m'en accorder dès à présent la certitude; le bonheur qui reste au proscrit dans les ténèbres, c'est de voir un lever d'aurore au fond de son âme.»

Lettre Aux femmes de Cuba
signée par Victor Hugo.

Images above: top to bottom, left to right:

A view of **Havana Harbor** in 1869 published in *Harper's Weekly*;

Victor Hugo, on Jan 15, 1870, wrote to Cuban women:
«Women of Cuba, you have eloquently told me so much about anguish and suffering; I kneel before you, and I kiss your aching feet.»

Emilia Casanova, esposa de Cirilo Villaverde, a quien Victor Hugo envió una de las carta dirigidas a las mujeres Cubanas durante la Guerra de los Diez Años.

Images above: top to bottom:

The action at the **Battle of Las Tunas** in 1869, as presented by *Le Monde Illustré* in Paris.

A drawing showing the meeting of Cuban General Antonio Maceo with Spanish General Arsenio Martínez Campos at **Mangos de Baraguá** on March 15, 1878. Maceo rejected on that day the Pact of Zanjón.

Photos of *mambises* (Cuban insurgents) in the Cuban Wars of Independence

From 1895 to 1898

Antonio Maceo's troops in 1895

31

For Cubans, Peace was only a Timely Pause

THE CAPITULATION AGREED ON by the Pact of Zanjón in 1878 was followed by an intended and non-intended exile for many Cubans; about 40,000 found refuge in New York, Key West and Tampa; probably 1,000 or less migrated to the independent countries of the Caribbean and Central America. Many of them were former soldiers like Máximo Gómez, who took refuge in the Dominican Republic, or the brothers José and Antonio Maceo, who ended up in Honduras and Costa Rica. Other surviving leaders of the Ten Year War [317] found refuge in Mexico, Venezuela and other countries of the continent. They felt it was not safe to stay in Cuba or to go to Spain, giving the untrustworthiness of Spain's promises and the abusive intolerance of the empowered and unrestrained *Voluntarios*.

Martí elected to go north, knowing that he spoke English almost fluently [318] and could make an honest living in the US writing and doing translations. He always felt that, even with indifferent or adversarial American governments, the place where most decisively he could influence the destiny of Cuba was in New York, hence his chosen safe haven.

Both in the United States and elsewhere, the Cuban exiles organized Independence Clubs and *Juntas* to raise funds, sustain their national feelings and divulge the plight of Cuba. Thirty such clubs were already organized by 1880. With Martí's help, the number reached one hundred and fifty by the time

---

[317] Ramón Leocadio Bonachea, the last and lonely fighter, did not depose his arms until April 19, 1879.

[318] After a few years, Martí spoke English almost as perfectly as Calixto Garcia and Tomás Estrada Palma, who had lived for several years or had studied in the US.

the Cubans would again fight for their independence. Members of these Clubs were giving ten percent of their earnings to the Cuban cause to buy and temporarily store war materials, with a view to eventually organize expeditions to carry them to Cuban soil. After the *Pacto del Zanjón* Maceo, Calvar, Vicente García, Calixto García and Máximo Gómez had asked the *mambises* to bury their weapons rather than turn them in. It created the false impression that the *mambises* were fighting only with *machetes*, which suited the Spanish government well since they were trying to convince the world they had been fighting against savages. It turned out that hundreds of Remington rifles and the corresponding *cartuchos*, carefully protected with heavy coats of *sebo* (animal fat), were safely concealed all over the *sabanas* of Camagüey and the valleys, mountains and densely wooded districts of Oriente, ready for another confrontation.

In August of 1878 José Martí had returned to Havana after the *Pacto del Zanjón* and began to work on the Law Offices of Nicolás Azcárate. He found that few Cubans were continuing their passion for independence after the promises of change and autonomy by Spain. On the contrary, Arsenio Martínez Campos had become very popular as the man who had peacefully settled the conflict of the War of 1868-1878. In July of 1878, a few weeks before Martí's return, a group of autonomists paid homage to Martínez Campos at a banquet on the premises of the *Teatro Tacón*. The man in charge of the keynote speech was Pedro González Llorente, president of the *Círculo de Abogados de la Habana*, future leader of the Reformist Party and future member of the Constitutional Convention in 1901. His speech concluded stating that

"...*Vuestra obra quedará aquí para siempre como sombra bienhechora... el pacto que habéis promovido nos pone en condiciones normales hacia nuestro destino. Con el pacto ha muerto nuestra calidad de colonos...*"

(... Your work, General Martínez Campos, will always remain as a beneficial presence... the pact that you have secured is placing us with freedom into our true destiny. The pact has been a death blow to our condition as mere colonials...)

In the meantime, in Madrid, the Spanish *Cortes* was referring to the *Pacto del Zanjón* as *la paz maldita* (the damn peace) and *el convenio vergonzoso* (the shameful agreement).

Arsenio Martínez Campos had the misfortune to write a letter to Antonio Cánovas del Castillo in the following terms:

«*Se creía antes que el carácter de estos habitantes no era propio para la guerra; tanto el blanco como el negro han demostrado lo contrario. Las promesas nunca cumplidas, los abusos de todo género, el no haber dedicado nada al desarrollo futuro, la exclusión de los naturales de todos los ramos de la administración, y otra porción de faltas, dieron principio a la insurrección... Deploro ciertas libertades, pero la época las exige, la fuerza no constituye nada estable, la razón y la justicia se abren paso tarde o temprano.*»

(We thought the character of Cubans was not propitious for war and it was. The unfulfilled promises, the abuses of all kinds, our lack of development plans, the exclusion of *criollos* from administrative positions, and many other errors gave birth to the rebellion... I despise certain liberties but these times make them necessary; by force nothing is stable. Reason and justice sooner or later prevail.)

Six months after completion of the pact, in January of 1879, as Martínez Campos kept insisting in those issues, he was replaced by the Council of Ministers and had to leave Cuba. His successors in Cuba were Cayetano Figueroa y Garaondo, for 3 months, and Ramón Blanco Erenas, *Marqués de Peña Plata*, from 1879 to 1881.

By most accounts, Spain counted in 1880 with 20,000 troops and a force of *Voluntarios* that surpassed 60,000. Cuba's past and future rebels, like José Martí, expected that if a state of war were to be reinstated in the island, Spain could and would ship ten thousand fresh regular soldiers a month to respond to any conflagration. Ten to fifteen Spanish gunboats were patrolling Cuban coasts incessantly by 1880; given the 5,746 kilometers of coastal perimeter of the island, 70% of which were occupied by mangroves difficult to patrol, Martí and others were calculating that at least two expeditions per month could safely arrive to the coasts of Cuba.

The New York that Martí moved to in 1880 was not a picturesque metropolis like London, Madrid or Vienna; it had nothing older than 400 years; its people had absolutely no regard for tradition or the ancient, like Parisians had. The lower end of Manhattan, which Martí favored, was full of low buildings with no more than four flights of steps except for the 284 feet steeple of Trinity Church at Wall Street and Broadway. Both Philadelphia and Boston outstripped New York in importance. [319]

One of the first things Martí did in New York was to attended a meeting of the *Comité Revolucionario Cubano*, (CRC), an organization presided by Calixto García that regularly met at García's home on an interior apartment of a building located at 45th Street and 9th Avenue. García was already fighting in Cuba; he had not signed the *Pacto del Zanjón*, and neither had other leaders besides Antonio Maceo, such as Guillermón Moncada, from Santiago de Cuba, aged 39, and Emilio Núñez, born in Sagua la Grande, aged 24. They were all looking for ways to restart the war in the island. The only man with war leadership experience, however, was Calixto García. They had a dreadful lack of weaponry and shells. [320] With Calixto García in the mountains of Cuba, in what later became known as *la Guerra Chiquita*, were Guillermón Moncada, Serafín Sánchez, Emilio Núñez, José Maceo, Belisario Peralta, Limbano Sánchez, Francisco Varona, Jesús Rabí, Gregorio Benítez and Emiliano Crombet, among others; they were expecting to be backed by some six thousand men ready to fight for the cause of independence. A common opinion among them was that Spain had squandered an entire continent and now was tenaciously and irra-

---

[319] Madison Avenue between 40th Street and Columbia College on 49th Street, for instance, was a rough and tattered trail full of potholes, goats, pigs and *apple angel's trumpets* and *zombie cucumbers*, two types of weeds with strong hallucinogenic alkaloid contents that New Yorkers had fortunately not yet discovered as *recreational delirants*, as they used to call them in those times.

[320] In their enthusiasm they were counting on armaments from the Ten Year War that they had buried all over the island, as well as weapons they could wrestle from the Spanish troops.

tionally clinging to Cuba; [321] they also thought that all the presumed respect of the American government for the rights of Spain could be interpreted as nothing but a subterfuge by the American government to wait until the time was ripe to annex Cuba.

The news that Martí and the New York exiles received from the war front a few weeks after Martí had joined the *Comité Revolucionario Cubano* were distressing and demoralizing. The war had been moderately successful only in the territories from Holguín to Gibara; most of the other armed encounters were won by the Spanish forces; there was a scant support from outside Cuba and little or no training for the new Cuban *mambises*. The absence of Martí, Maceo and Máximo Gómez in *la Guerra Chiquita* was decisive for the upset the Cubans experienced in September of 1880, barely 12 months after the war started. Cubans in the field were running, surrendering, captured or dying.

Francisco Carrillo, tightly surrounded by Spanish troops to the point where he could not receive supplies or recruit reinforcements, was forced on October 4th to accept safe-conducts for him and his men to leave the island via the port of Cienfuegos. José Maceo, Quintín Banderas and Guillermón Moncada were captured on September 17th and sent to prisons in the Af-

---

[321] Interestingly, Martí had once discussed that issue with Martínez Campos when they both coincided in Madrid. Martí was a young man about to be deported to Ceuta; Martínez Campos was a *Grandeé* of Spain and a very influential man in the government of Spain. One day, around November 5, 1871, the concierge of Martí's humble residence at Tetuán No. 20, near the *Puerta del Sol*, handed him an envelope with instructions to present himself in front of Martínez Campos, which he did the following day. He was received cordially and told that Spain would not tolerate any revolutionary actions on his part; on the contrary, Martínez Campos said, if Martí remained quiet and settled down he could get an appointment as instructor at the University of Madrid and much better living quarters. He even knew Martí had only one room with a sink in his house and had to use the shower and toilet at the end of the hall. Martínez Campos told Martí he was rescinding the order of deportation to Ceuta, for which Martí thanked him. They shook hands politely and, without making any promises or commitments, Martí left the meeting; he immediately began to make plans to escape to Paris.»

rican colonies of Spain. Calixto García, leading barely fifty remaining men, spent several months in the *manigua* looking for other rebels and finally gave up late in October of 1880. The *Guerra Chiquita* was irretrievably lost. Upon knowing this news, Martí's reaction was far from desperate.

«The war has been a positive experience for us. It has consolidated our resolve, gave us a sense for what Spain's strategies would be in the future and has been a test of the strength of our relations *exilio-manigua*. It was also a warning to Spain that the *Pacto del Zanjón*, far from being the grave of the independence ideals was simply a parenthesis in the struggle. The errors of the War of 1868 and the Guerra Chiquita would not be repeated the next time.»

Surprisingly, in spite of its brevity and the limited Cuban territory involved, Martí thought the war had been the best organized military effort in half a century of struggles for the independence of Cuba. In Holguín, Remedios, Sancti Spíritus and the area of *Ciénaga de Zapata*, the insurgents had over 6,000 men in the field. Spain brought 50,000 additional troops to Cuba, charging that Cubans were trying to establish a black republic. They won the psychological and the manpower war; Spain, once more, deployed her recurrent policy of building up the fears of whites about the presumed ambition of blacks to create a republic similar to L'Overture's in Haiti. During the *Guerra Chiquita*, Martí knew that the man chosen by Spain to perpetuate this despicable myth was Camilo García de Polavieja y del Castillo, *Marqués de Polavieja* (1838-1914), Governor of Oriente in 1879 and 1881 and Captain General of Cuba between 1890 and 1892. Polavieja, Martí would say...

«Considers all blacks abject individuals, with an intellectual level that does not transcend the sphere of instinct. He believes the blacks are dangerous because in the ultimate analysis they are the only ones that can endure the rigors of war. He understands the tensions within the Cubans and knows a credible black menace will weaken the Cuban troops and rally the autonomists to the side of Spain. He has been sending Cuban white fighters to Fernando Póo and Guinea and blacks combatants to suffer relative mild prison in Havana. He has been pardoning blacks ahead of whites; he announces a policy of interning black deportees in Spanish penitentiaries in Africa but is only for propaganda purposes. He wants to see our white soldiers fearing the blacks as untrustworthy and dangerous soldiers that deserve close observation in the island of Cuba»

In the end, Martí told Cubans of all classes that *la Guerra Chiquita* was an event that united several important figures that had signed the *Pacto del Zanjón* with others that had denounced it. It was a time when Cubans in the island and in the peninsula felt that the ideals of independence had lost steam.

Several months later, on July 20, 1882, Martí began to recruit Maceo for the Big War.

«*No conozco yo, General Maceo, soldado más bravo ni cubano más tenaz que usted. Ni comprendería yo que se tratase de hacer —como ahora trato y tratan tantos otros— obra alguna seria en las cosas de Cuba, en que no figurase usted de la especial y prominente manera a que le dan derecho sus merecimientos.*» (I do not know General Maceo a finer soldier or a more unwavering Cuban than you; neither would I understand that anyone would try to do something serious in Cuba without counting with you in the special and prominent position that you have earned and deserve.)

Life in Cuba and among Cubans everywhere did not stop, of course, after the end of the Ten Year War.

José Antonio Saco died in Barcelona on September 26, 1879. Three months later Spain abolished slavery and replaced it with the *patronato* (tutelage), an eight year period of transition for all new *libertos*.

On September 17, 1880, one of the last Cuban insurgent troops, under the command of General Emilio Núñez, deposed their arms. Camilo García de Polavieja, governor of Santiago de Cuba, got 5,000 rebels to surrender and was promoted to Lieutenant General.

In March of 1881, James Abraham Garfield was elected president of the US, defeating Ulysses Grant; he was assassinated in September of that year. He had appointed Stewart L. Woodford as Attorney of the United States for the Southern District of New York, «*una disposición infame*» according to Martí. Confirming Martí's insight, Woodford would later be Minister to

Spain —and very unfavorable to Cuba— on the day Spain severed ties with the US, hours before the 1895 War.

In 1882 Cirilo Villaverde published the full version of *Cecilia Valdés* in New York. The following year *La Habana Elegante* was published in Havana. Three years later, in 1885, Enrique José Varona began publishing *La Revista Cubana* and the autonomists began to publish the newspaper *El País*. In July of 1885 the magazine *El Fígaro* began publication in Havana. In 1886, the weekly *La Fraternidad* had its first issue in Sancti Spíritus.

At the end of 1883, the last fighter of the Ten Year War, Ramón Locadio Bonachea, made an attempt to enter Cuba at Manzanillo. He was captured and executed with several of his men on March of 1884 at the Morro Castle in Santiago de Cuba. A similar expedition was organized by Maceo and Gómez but failed to approach the Cuban coasts. At Varadero, however, Brigadier Carlos Agüero succeeded and disembarked in Cuba. He failed to gain support and left in less than a year.

On October 2, 1884, Martí, Maceo and Máximo Gómez met at *Hotel Madame Griffon*, on Ninth Ave in New York City. They found more differences than common interests and the meeting failed to produce any good results. They departed frustrated and not in good terms with each other.

In Havana, in June of 1884, a Basque proprietor, Ricardo Irijoa, opened *Teatro Irijoa* at the corner of Zulueta and Dragones streets; its first presentation was Puccini's *La Bohéme*. Years later it would be called *Teatro Edén* and finally, in 1900, would be renamed *Teatro Martí*. In 1885, as José Antonio Echeverría was dying in New York, on March 11, his best friend Limbano Sánchez (1845-1885), *el León Holguinero*, landed in *Playa Caleta*, Baracoa, with a small rebel expedition on May 18. He had been next to Maceo in Baraguá, in 1868. In 1885 he was poisoned by a traitor who covered his tracks by taking his cadaver and placing it near a Spanish camp in Mayarí, Oriente, to simulate he had been killed in action.

Starting in 1885, Sagasta and Cánovas del Castillo established the *turnismo* (both political enemies alternating in control of the Madrid government) with the enthusiastic approval of the crown.[322]

Also in 1886, Rafael Montoro became the spokesperson of the autonomismo in Cuba. In Matanzas, the future *Poeta Nacional de Cuba*, Agustín Acosta, was born; in Havana Rafael María de Mendive died; he had been José Martí's mentor. In Madrid, the future Alfonso XIII was born on May 17. Early the next year, Martí's father, Don Mariano Martí Navarro, died in Havana. Martí was doing well in New York as Consul of the Republic of Uruguay.

On the literary and artistic fronts, Enrique Roig published in 1887 the first issue of *El Productor* magazine; Sarah Bernardt was hired for a short season by *Teatro Tacón*; Raimundo Cabrera published *Cuba y sus Jueces*; Fermín Valdés Domínguez published *El 27 de Noviembre de 1871* and Martí became press representative of Argentina across Canada and the US.

In 1888, Valeriano Weyler y Nicolau began to be noteworthy in the Spanish press. As captain general of the Philippines he was already known as *el carnicero* (the butcher). In 1889 Antonio Bachiller y Morales (1812-1888), prominent Cuban-born historian and journalist, exiled since the *Teatro Villanueva* events in 1869, died in New York. On that year Emeterio Santovenia, Moisés Simons and Emilio Roig de Leuchsenring were born in Mantua and in Havana.

In 1890 Antonio Maceo returned to Cuba as a recruiter for a future war. He met and worked with his old friend Flor Crombet in Oriente. Camilo García de Polavieja, as Captain General, ended their headhunting mission and forced both into a new exile. Polavieja was replaced as Cuba's Captain General

---

[322] At that point, Don Alfonso XII had died and his second wife, Doña María Cristina de Hapsburgo (1858-1929), was acting as Regent. Alfonso XII, son of deposed Isabel II, married María Cristina when his first wife died of typhus. He commented with his friends and his sister that «*a mí esta mujer no me parece muy guapa. La que está bomba es mi suegra.*» (I don't like this woman; her mother is the one I would like to seduce). The tempting mother-in-law was Elisabeth Franciska Archduchess of Austria (1831–1903), 54 years old at the time. Her daughter María Cristina was 28.

in 1892 by Alejandro Rodríguez Arias, who in turn was replaced by Emilio Calleja Isasi in September of 1893. Manuel Sanguily published his biography of *José de la Luz y Caballero* in Havana while José Martí was publishing the first of four issues of *La Edad de Oro* in New York. Martí continued his consular activities there and accepted consular appointments from Argentina and Paraguay. Before the end of 1890 two important theaters were opened in Cuba: Alhambra in Havana and Terry in Cienfuegos.

By 1891 the US was buying 95% of Cuba's sugar production, which constituted 87% of all Cuban exports.[323] Commerce with Spain only amounted to 4% of Cuban business. Spain would put an end to this by canceling all US-Cuba commercial business in 1894. In New York, Martí published *Nuestra America* in the January 1891 issue of *Revista Ilustrada de Nueva York*. He travelled to Tampa to deliver there two famous speeches: *Para Cuba Que Sufre* and *Los Pinos Nuevos*.

In 1892 Martí launched *the Partido Revolucionario Cubano* in Key West and the newspaper *Patria* in New York. In September he visited Máximo Gómez at his home in Bani, Santo Domingo and made plans to visit Antonio Maceo in Costa Rica. He made contact with Rubén Darío, set up a meeting for the following year in New York and arranged for a meeting in Mexico with Porfirio Díaz.[324] Before the end of the year Juan Gualberto Gómez, Martí's closest friend and colleague, published his newspaper *La Igualdad*.

In Cuba members of the *Partido Unión Constitucional* boycotted an 1893 plan by Antonio Maura, Spain's Minister of Overseas, to grant special concessions and autonomy to Cuba. It had been the last hope of Spain's *reformistas* to prevent a war

---

[323] In 1890 the US had threatened to discontinue all its sugar purchases from Cuba.

[324] Not yet a renowned dictator, Porfirio Díaz opened all Mexican ports to Cuban rebels but did not contribute any funds to support the forthcoming war of 1895. Martí got his interview with Díaz through the efforts of his close Mexican friend Manuel Mercado.

of independence in Cuba. In October of that year, Julián del Casal (1863-1893), poet and forerunner of *Modernismo* in Cuba, died after a cerebral aneurism.

As 1894 came to a close, Cirilo Villaverde died in New York; the Cuban *autonomistas* gathered in Jagüey Grande, Matanzas, in their last and more tumultuous concentration of forces; Antonio Maceo was the target of an unsuccessful attack by pro-Spain fanatics in Costa Rica; José Martí conveyed an order of starting the war to Juan Gualberto Gómez in Havana; the Hotel St. Denis in New York became the headquarters for the Fernandina Plan.[325]

Image above:
A view of Havana harbor in 1881, published in *La Ilustración Española*.

---

[325] A plan to send three ships with personeel and armaments to the port of Fernandina in Florida, to launch from there an armed revolt in Cuba. The plan would be denounced by Spanish infiltrates in New York and fail. All provisions, included the ships, were confiscated at the last minute by the US government.

Images, top to bottom:

An 1879 photo of **Fermín Valdés Dominguez, Panchito Gómez Toro** and **José Martí** in New York;

a book dedication of *Cecilia Valdés* by **Cirilo Villaverde** to his friend Benito Pérez Galdós;

an equestrian photo of **Máximo Gómez** in 1880.

Images, top to bottom, left to right:

Young **Juan Gualberto Gómez Ferrer** (1854-1933), close friend and collaborator of Martí, son of slaves, Cuban congressman after independence;

Rafael Montoro Valdés (1852-1933), liberal autonomista, founder of the Cuban Academy of Arts and Leters and member of the Royal Academy of the Language in Spain;

Major General **Francisco Carrillo Morales** (1851-1826),combatant on all three Cuban wars of independence. Main organizer of the 1895 war;

Major General **Serafín Sánchez Valdivia**, (1846-1896), combatant who fought on all three Cuban wars of independence. Died in combat;

José Marcelino Maceo Grajales (1849-1896), brother of Antonio Maceo, combatant on all three Cuban wars of independence. Died in combat;

Francisco Adolfo (Flor) Crombet Tejera (1851-1895), combatant on all three Cuban wars of independence, was with Maceo at Mangos de Baraguá. Died in combat.

Images, top to bottom, left to right:

Enrique José Varona (1848-1933), Cuban author, journalist and scholar. founder of *La Revista Cubana* in 1885;

General **José Quintín Banderas Betancourt** (1846-1906), hero of the Cuban War of Independence, known for his fearlessness and bravery;

Major General **José María (Mayía) Rodríguez** (1849-1903), friend and loyal companion of Antonio Maceo, suffered 3 years of prison in Spain in 1879;

Major General **Limbano Sánchez Rodríguez** (1845-1885), fought in the area of Oriente under Máximo Gómez and Calixto García.

Images above:

La Habana Elegante magazine, **La Revista Ilustrada**
And **El Figaro** magazines, three popular papers published
in Havana in the late 1800s;

Alhambra Theater in Havana. This pioneer theater founded in 1890, staged *zarzuelas, juguetes, revistas* and *comedias* for all tastes for over 40 years. It developed its own vernacular genre known as *Alambresco* (Alhambra-like), which was based on the *Bufo* theater of the Villanueva era. The Alhambra was demolished in 1935 and the genre continued at the *Teatro Martí*.

Images, top to bottom, left to right:

A 1880 document dealing with the **patrocinios** of former slaves, granting a former slave owner (a man called Francisco Ortega) an authorization to move the *patrocinado* to the town of Macuriges in Matanzas;

Martí receiving an embrace from Máximo Gómez during his visit to Santo Domingo on 25 March, 1895;

Teatro Irijoa, inaugurated on 8 June, 1884, at the corner of Dragones and Zulueta streets in Havana. In 1900 its name was changed to *Teatro Martí*;

Young **Valeriano Weyler y Nicolau** (1838-1939), first to use the concept of concentration camp. It was later known as *internment*, and was used by the United Kingdom (in Transvaal), the United States (General William Tecumseh Sherman's campaign), Germany (Jews, Gypsies and political opponents), and Russia (the Japanese).

Images, top to bottom, left to right:

Antonio Bachiller y Morales (1812-1889), historian, educator, journalist. He had to leave Cuba after the Villanueva Theater affair in 1869 and went to New York as an exile;

Stewart L. Woodford (1835-1913), served as the U.S. Ambassador to Spain in the months leading up to the 1895 war;

Guillermón Moncada (1841-1895), combatant on all three Cuban wars of independence. Died of Tuberculosis, contracted in the Spanish prisons;

Major General **Juan Emilio de la Caridad Núñez y Rodriguez** (1855-1922), soldier, dentist and politician; participated in the Ten Year War and the 1895 War of Independence and was a member of the Cuban Constitutional Assembly in 1901.

Images, top to bottom, left to right:

Antonio Maura y Montaner (1853-1925), Conservative Prime Minister of Spain on five separate occasions. In 1895 he presented to the Cortes a proposal to grant Cuba ample autonomy, but failed to get it approved;

General **Camilo García de Polavieja** (1838-1914), as Field Marshall assigned to Cuba in 1876, he was considered as brutal as Weyler;

a group of 1868 Spain's **Voluntarios** in their uniforms;

Ramón Leocadio Bonachea (1845-1885), the last rebel of the Ten Year War, commander of the last 100 men to depose their weapons after the Pact of Zanjón. In 1884, about to fight once more in Cuba, he was captured and executed in Oriente on April 7, 1885.

Images, top to bottom, left to right:

Julián del Casal (1863-1893), extraordinary Cuban poet who had a marked influence on José Martí's and Rubén Darío's poetry. He was the first man who was declared *Poeta Nacional de Cuba*;

Agustín Acosta y Bello (1886-1979), one of the best and most popular Cuban writers of the XX century, Senator of the Republic, designated *Poeta Nacional de Cuba* in 1955, forerunner of social poetry in America;

Maria Cristina de Habsburgo (1858-1929), second wife of Alfonso XII of Spain, Regent during the minority of her son Alfonso XIII, who was born after his father had died. She signed for Spain the Treaty of Paris that ended the Hispano-Cuban-American War of 1895.

Archduchess **Elisabeth of Austria** (1831-1903), widow of Archduke Ferdinand of Austria, who died from typhus at age 28, mother of Maria Cristina de Habsburgo and hence mother-in-law of Alfonso XII of Spain.

Cartoons from El Moro Muza in 1869, top to bottom:

May 2, 1869, Emilia Casanova, Villaverde's wife, letting Quesada know she would not organize any more Cuban rallies in New York;

May 30, 1869, making fun of Emilia Casanova, Cirilo Villaverde's wife, who was the person that sew Cuban flags for demonstrations;

May 29, 1870, Quesada and Jordan get presents and toys from Cuba ladies.

32
A New War of Independence Became Inevitable

IN THE AFTERMATH of the Ten Year War, there was no longer any place to hide; you were either Cuban or Spaniard. Halfway positions like *autonomismo* and *reformismo* became insolvent after 1879. It seemed at first like a regional phenomenon that only touched a few educated intellectuals in their ivory towers and the children of the wealthy that were taught by them at the *Seminario San Carlos*, the *University of Habana*, the *Colegio Carraguao*, the *Colegio Salvador* in Havana, the *Colegio La Empresa* in Matanzas, and others. Yet nowhere in the Americas was there a group of graduates from so few schools with the opportunity to change society in the way these men, educated in these learning centers, were ready to alter the destinies of Cuba.

By 1750 it was difficult in Havana to find a paved street. Most people lived along the coast and freely enjoyed the many opportunities for contraband. One hundred years later the population had increased to 1,400,000 inhabitants, the streets in Havana had been named and paved and the houses numbered. Cuba's economy had evolved from that of many small agricultural settlers to a corporate plantation society, a growth not caused by new immigrants but due to the efforts and sacrifices of patrician families whose ancestry preceded the adventures of creating a new society. Close to 80% of Cuba's 500 most genuinely Cuban families had immigrated into Cuba before the year 1800. They were overwhelmingly Catholic, without any trace of Arab or Jewish blood for at least 100 years before disembarking. They became a Cuban aristocracy that almost from the start was at odds with the metropolis. The Spanish response to these developments was the Royal Order of April 19, 1837 which segregated the province of Cuba from the Spanish kingdom and turned it into a mere colony to be gov-

The *Colegio de San Cristóbal de La Habana* or *Carraguao* (the name of a Havana neighborhood) was established at the corner of Infanta and Estévez streets in July of 1829; it stayed there until 1842 when it was moved to the area of Castillo del Príncipe, near *el Cerro*. There the school opened on 33 acres of outdoor grounds and a superb building. At the time, *el Cerro* had become the zone where wealthy Havana families lived. Bishop Espada granted *Carraguao's* founder, Don Antonio Remon Homes, the license to open *Carraguao*; years earlier he had founded the *Academia Calasancia* in Havana.

Among the first teachers of *Colegio Carraguao* was the notable educator José de la Luz y Caballero, who became director of the school a year after settling in it. It was in recognition to his experience and training in education, gained at several European countries. Luz y Caballero had a deserved reputation, particularly for his exceptional universal philosophical thinking skills. His main pedagogical innovations at *Carraguao* were:

- Total elimination of physical abuse and humiliation of students.
- Advanced teaching techniques, based on affection and respect.
- Intransigence with clutter and/or vices.
- Quarterly reports of intellectual and physical condition of students.
- Separate curricula for primary and secondary education.
- Guardianship system with students remaining enough time at school.
- Exercises outdoors and hiking around the College.
- Use of the explanatory method in all subjects.
- Dictation practice to improve spelling and pronunciation.
- Study of geography of Cuba, Spain, and the rest of the world.

Within two years, on February 1831, the Spanish crown, granted the school the title of *Real Colegio de San Cristóbal de La Habana*. Four years later, the *Havana Journal* stated «*Carraguao* is the triumph of zeal, method and constancy; its good results have shaped the educational philosophy of our times. The most famous men of Cuba in literature, politics and philosophy have been through the *Colegio de Carraguao*»

Teachers of the School: José Luis Casaseca, chemist froml Salamanca. Translated and printed in Havana a compendium of Gay Lusac's Chemistry; Pedro Barbastre, renowned French writer, taught French, Latin and Greek grammar; Carlos Roca, geologist and mineralogist. Professor of Geology; with his students formed a superb collection of Cuban minerals; José de la Luz y Caballero; Felipe Poey, eminent naturalist who also taught Latin and French; Jose Silverio Jorrín, both student and teacher at Carraguao, taught linear algebra, geometry, differential and integral calculus; José Fornaris, renown poet; Francisco Ruiz, professor of philosohy; Álvaro Reynoso: remarkable chemist and agronomist, author of *An Essay on the Cultivation of the Sugar Cane*.

Students of the School: Pedro (Perucho) Figueredo, author of Cuba's national anthem; Francisco Vicente Aguilera, one the top entrepreneurs in Cuba, organizer of the uprising of October 10, 1868; brothers Guiteras (Matanzas), brothers Aldama, brothers Zayas (José María, Francisco and Juan Bruno), José Gener, among others.

The Extraordinary *Colegio Carragauao*

erned by the arbitrary will and fancy of crown-appointed *Capitanes Generales*. That decree, more than anything else, fostered in the minds of the *criollos* a resentment towards Spain that did not diminished in half a century.

The descendants of the immigrants, not too sure of what their loyalties were or ought to be, identified themselves with a certain portion of the land. They called themselves Santiagueros, Camagüeyanos, Villareños, Habaneros, etc., showing the importance of the territory in the development of their identity. The realization that they had more in common with each other than just sharing a territory had not yet emerged; they had a similarity of values, interests, ambitions and ways to look and respond to the challenges of life. The Santiagueros, so to speak, realized they were musical, the Camagüeyanos took pride in their love for the outdoors, the Habaneros delighted in their awareness of current events, the Matanceros valued cultural matters and the Pinareños liked their self-sufficiency. In spite of those preferences, and after sensing similarity of values and interests in many other areas, the breath of the national feeling was tested and slowly clarified. In Cuba, like almost everywhere else, a broader island-wide identity was ready to coalesce when the *criollos* realized that their values, dreams, fantasies, deceptions, sufferings and sense of brotherhood were shared beyond the limited confines of the province or region. They would begin to sense their territory was the entire island. The *criollos* of Matanzas had indeed more substantial and existential common interests with the *criollos* of Santiago than just a mere enthusiasm for dances or the love for literature. They were about to discover a community of interests that would bond Santiagueros with Habaneros, Villareños and Camagüeyanos; interests that would be different and at times in conflict with those of the Madrileños, the Catalanes or the Asturianos.

There wasn't a Cuban Nation during the uprisings of Aponte and the two Agüeros, Francisco and Joaquín, early in the XIX century; neither was there one during the times of the conspiracies of *La Escalera* and *Rayos y Soles de Bolívar*. By 1850 all Cubans had only jointly experienced some forceful expressions of opposition to slavery, in other words, slave revolts. They contributed to form a stronger public opinion with regard to the injustices of slavery but those feelings were shared by many Spaniards and were not an exclusive and bonding Cuban national sentiment. During the filibuster expeditions of Narciso López and others, a very fragmented and incipient Cuban soul, immature but rational, could not understand how a bunch of foreigners landing here or there could spark the flames of independence. Narciso López could not wake up and seduce the Cubans in exile and ended up landing with the wrong people at the right places. No support was forthcoming from inside the island because the invaders did not share the interests of the *criollos*. They did not even share a common language.

In spite of the sacrifices and the glorious and generous sagas of the war of 1868, the Cuban Nation was too immature, too embryonic and underdeveloped to support an independence war. The nation of Cuba was practically non-existing at that point. The people from Bayamo were ready to fight but not necessarily side by side with those from Las Tunas; the occidentals –*Pinareños, Habaneros* and *Matanceros*– did not trust the insurgents from Oriente and Camagüey and paid practically no attention to their quest; Vicente García, the *León de Santa Rita*, did not want to fight in Las Villas and the Holguineros proclaimed their own republic, a few square miles as it was, and would only fight to defend their *terruño*. The *cubanismo* had not yet cast aside the *regionalismo*. Under those conditions it was easy to predict the debacle that resulted in *Zanjón* and *Loma Pelada*.[326] Máximo Gómez, Calixto García and many others were disenchanted and disillusioned and laid down their arms; Antonio Maceo, Ramón Leocadio Bonachea and very few others fought until the end but sooner or later were defeated by *regionalismo*. Bonachea, by the way, was the last to quit and the

---

[326] It was at *Loma Pelada*, north of Santa Clara, that the Cuban rebel army gave up fighting on May 21, 1878.

first to die when he continued to fight back with Calixto during the *little war* and was captured and shot in 1885. When Bonachea quit in 1878 he simply vanished with his men in the jungle. He buried his weapons and began to walk. No one in the Spanish army can ever say that Bonachea and his men surrendered. They decided to temporarily suspend operations and that was all.

By all accounts, however, the issue of Cuba as a colony had already become critical to Spain by the end of the 1880s. Cuba was its only important remaining possession and control of the island was imperative not only for economic reasons but also for the prestige and honor of Spain. In the mind of many *peninsulares* in Cuba, the important thing was to *"mantener la bandera Española en alto"* (keep the Spanish flag waiving). Conservative Prime Minister Antonio Cánovas del Castillo (1828-1897), who had been alternating the prime ministership with the progressive Práxedes Mateo Sagasta (1825-1903), feared that a final loss of the empire would generate such a severe shock in Spain that it would bring down the government and even the Bourbon dynasty.

According to the terms of the *Pacto del Zanjón* in Cuba, slavery had been ended in 1886 but the promised autonomy had not been instituted. After a blatant deception in the Spanish *Cortes*, Cuban delegates had returned to the island in disenchantment and disgust. Cuba's natural market was more and more the United States. Spain could neither absorb and pay for Cuban exports nor supply to Cuba, at the right prices, the goods and wares that Cuba needed. The three most virulent complaints in Cuba, even for members of the *Partido Unión Constitucional* (committed to keeping Cuba in the hands of Spain) were taxes, tariffs and corruption. When the turn came for Sagasta to be prime minister in 1892, his colonial *Charge d'Affairs*, Antonio Maura y Montaner (1853-1925) proposed reforms that even Máximo Gómez confessed he was tempted to accept. Sagasta could not find support in the *Cortes* and Maura resigned at once. It was probably the last chance that Spain had to maintain its Cuban colony. The war in Cuba had become not only possible but inevitable.

The situation in Cuba was ripe for war in the early and mid 1890s. Cuba had remained a colony much longer than other possessions of Spain in the continent; African slavery had been abolished much later than in the rest of the continent; the people in Cuba did not develop the close ties that other colonies had with the Catholic Church, hence her support was meaningless; instead of a small self-sufficient peasantry, Cuba had evolved into a society of landless farming workers and absentee land owners. The first were destitute, the second were insecure; other than descendants of slaves and some Orientals, all white classes in Cuba were of Spanish origin –the indigenous population had been totally extinguished by the fevers and infections of the XVI century. Yet, whites in Cuba were by and large discontented. There was too much corruption, favoritism, exploitation and restrictions to trade, too many limitations to express opinions, to seek opportunities and to have access to riches in what evidently was a wealthy territory.

During the XVI to the XVIII centuries Cuba had become important to Spain only for its geographical location, *la llave del golfo* (the key to the Golf of Mexico), rather than for its mineral assets, which for many years had been the driving force for Spanish imperialism. By 1880, however, supported by the importation of slaves in the XIX century and strengthened by the revolution in Haiti, Cuba had become the supplier of one third of all sugar produced in the world. American investors dived into its sugar-based economy and the welfare of the island began to depend more on the ups-and-downs of the American sugar market and less on the will or the indulgence of Spain. In 1894, a year before the approaching third War of Independence, the US Congress, did away with all trade agreements with Spain, reinstating non-favorable tariffs for Cuban sugar. The economic trauma and injury to the Cuban economy was massive and instantaneous. It set the stage for the fund-raising successes found abroad by Martí among the exiles, and the equally successful efforts that Maceo and Máximo Gómez would find recruiting insurgents in the *manigua* of Cuba. The shrewd American politicians and investors knew how to *tickle* the politics of the island so that *"the ripe fruit would gravitate to the United States as predicted by the laws of nature,"* [327] By 1895 Spain had lost all hope to be in control of the fate of Cuba.

Very aware of these favorable conditions to reinitiate the war of independence in Cuba, José Martí, Antonio Maceo and Máximo Gómez knew they had to resolve their many mutual differences before anyone was sent into Cuba to risk his life.

Martí, very generously, took the initiative. He was in fairly good position economically. His monthly income reached $185 some months and every now and then he would be paid $100 for an article, the largest fee received by any Spanish speaking journalist in New York. At the time, a skilled worker's wages were $52 for a 48 hour week. He nevertheless lived very frugally at a small suite on 361 West 58th Street, saving all the money he could for the Cuban cause. Long gone was his passion to buy books at the *Ponce de León's* and *Brentano's* bookstores. He was now using more and more the *Lenox Library* at 5th Avenue and 70th Street. Gone were the white wine and the fried *parguitos* (small snappers) at the restaurant of *Madam Laurel* on Broadway and 21st Street, and the delicacies of *Delmonico's* at 5th Avenue and 14th Street. He was now eating *Arroz a la Vizcaina* at the *Fonda Polegre* on Pearl Street and celebrating occasionally with a glass of *Vin Mariani*, the inexpensive wine favored by Queen Victoria, Pope Leo XIII and Thomas Edison.

In May of 1893 Martí decided to start the process or reconciliation by visiting Máximo Gómez in the Dominican Republic. His course: by sea to Santo Domingo via Kingston, by land to *Santiago de los Caballeros*, then *Laguna Salada* and finally *Montecristi*. In memory of one of his frequent encampments in

---

[327] As repeatedly stated by John Quincy Adams (1767-1848) in 1823.

Cuba, where his son Panchito had been born, Máximo Gómez baptized his new habitat as *La Reforma*. There, inside a farm fenced by rows of banana trees, surrounded by corn, tobacco, *boniato* and orange trees, the compact of two generations was signed: the men of 1868 joined arms with the men of 1895. [328]

Martí spent three days in conversations with Máximo Gómez and departed on June 7th, early in the morning, after sleeping only four hours. [329] After having signed a pact with Máximo Gómez, Martí took the road to Haiti, Panama and finally, on June 29th, *Nicoya*, Costa Rica. He still had to make amends with Antonio Maceo and restore confidence in the unification of all leaders of the coming insurrection. Maceo was, deservedly, the bravest of all men fighting for Cuban independence. He had founded a self sustaining agricultural community in an isolated peninsula facing Costa Rica's Pacific Ocean. He had created a modern Coop, with a sugar mill, warehouses, shops, housing for everyone, telegraph and mail, stores and all the necessities of a small town. Close to one hundred families were making their living there, including some of

---

[328] Martí described the occasion to Gonzalo de Quesada when he saw him again in New York. «After crossing the fence in front of his property I respectfully stepped down from my horse and walked by its side about fifty yards until the entrance to the farmhouse. The General was waiting for me at his porch; I could see his eyes from 20 feet away. They were holding an affectionate but scrutinizing glance. We embraced and he separated no more than one foot, in silence, without letting go of our arms in each other's shoulders. He initiated a second embrace, grateful for the visitor that had traveled so many miles just to talk to him. I told him I was bringing greetings from all the Cubans to which he had given hope. He could not contain his tears and raised his right hand to gently cover my mouth with his old and trembling fingers. Those present, about ten relatives and friends, began to applaud and the General took his hat to make signals for them to stop. "*Bienvenido a mi casa, José Martí,*" he pronounced with emotion. *Bienvenido a mi casa.*»

[329] Years later Gonzalo de Quesada would say that Martí departed *La Reforma* feeling like Alfonso Quijano (Don Quijote) when he left the *Venta* (Inn) after being initiated *caballero*: «... *el gozo le reventaba por las cinchas del caballo...* » (his ecstasy was spilling over the straps of his horse).

the men that he had led in the Cuban War of 1868: Flor Crombet, José y Tomás Elizardo, Juan Rojas, and his own brother José Maceo.[330]

Maceo and Martí had their meeting at the *Gran Hotel* in the capital of Costa Rica. Flor Crombet and José Maceo came for the meeting from Punta Arenas. It did not take long for Maceo and Martí to clinch their hands, hug and embrace, surrounded by patriotic Cubans that were anticipating a successful reencounter and a forbearance of all previous disagreements. On July 8th Martí left Costa Rica. Maceo began immediately to start preparations for disengaging himself orderly from his responsibilities in Nicoya.

Martí would be back in Costa Rica on June of 1894; earlier in the year, he obtained the moral support for the war from very illustrious writers in New York: José María Vargas Vila (1860-1933), a Colombian writer who had a fight with Rubén Dario in which Martí intervened and saved the friendship; Patricio Jimeno (1865-1912), a Peruvian artist, the man who introduced Martí to Hermann Norman, the author of the only oil portrait of Martí; Juan Antonio Pérez Bonalde (1846-1892), a Venezuelan poet, close friend of José Martí; José Asunción Silva and Rubén Darío, all precursors of *modernismo* in literature; José Eloy Alfaro Delgado (1842-1912), an Ecuadorian, future President of Ecuador in 1895-1901 and 1906-1911, who Martí invited to help him on the *Plan de Fernandina*, and Fermín Valdés Domínguez, who traveled from Havana to New York to visit Martí on his 42nd birthday. Martí confidentially revealed to this group of friends that up to that moment he counted with

---

[330] In 1878 General Martínez Campos had tried to convince him in Baraguá to depose his arms, man to man, soldier to soldier, General to General. Not impressed by the honor granted to him by the visit of the top Spanish General in Cuba, nor tempted by the sums offered by Martínez Campos, he vigorously refused any pacts or agreements and reiterated his decision to continue the war. According to legend, Martínez Campos' Galician cook, witnessing the meeting between Maceo and his boss, told his fellow soldiers: "*Seu corpo enteiro está cheo de coraxe.*" (His entire body [Maceo's] is full of courage.) Maceo was adored by all Cubans, Black and White, rich and poor, civilians and soldiers, for his audacity, gallantry and fearless leadership.

$30,000 collected from fees for his speeches, his fund raising trips to Cuban Clubs and his own savings.

During the days before the planned expedition to Cuba, Martí would receive bad news from time to time, but continued to work indefatigably in spite of the setbacks. On April 3rd of 1894, for instance, a large expedition organized by Enrique Loynaz del Castillo was captured in Camagüey and 200 Remington rifles and 48,000 bullets, with a cost of $2,500, were seized by the Spaniards. Bad as the news was, the exiles that had contributed all the funds and all the preparation time did not blink an eye.

On April 8, 1895, Máximo Gómez arrived in New York and on the 14th he accompanied Martí, Máximo's son Panchito Gómez Toro and other patriots to Central Valley, New York, to visit Tomás Estrada Palma. He was now exiled in the US, and had established a school for Latin American Children at Central Valley, a typical Quaker and German town on a basin situated some fifty miles north of New York, close to the United States Military Academy in West Point. The man who had been selected president of the Republic in arms in 1875, had not seen his mother for years and only knew she had died of starvation after being imprisoned by the Spaniards early in the war of 1868. Máximo Gómez brought news about her final days. Tomás had inherited a vast amount of real estate in Cuba, which the Spanish government confiscated before the death of his mother. [331] He received Martí, Gómez and Panchito the way well educated and meticulous people did: a large Cuban flag in a pole was carried by the oldest child during a parade from the train station to the school grounds; the *Himno de Bayamo* was sung *a cappella* by the school choir.

---

[331] Once in New York he Martí and his group reached Central Valley after a three hour trek in a train heading north along the Hudson River. There, according to Martí, «between lime, apple and pine trees, Estrada Palma, a teacher by vocation if there was one, had fashioned an outstanding private school.» Don Tomás belonged to the old school, *los Pinos Viejos*, in the language of Martí.

Don Tomás, cautious and conservative as always, told Martí and his party that the time was now ripe for the Americans, the Cubans and even the Spaniards to get engaged to finish the current Cuban status:

«Cuban courage and resolve will not disappoint you; those who procrastinate and would rather wait are the most effective weapons of our enemies. Victory will not make us wait for another century. Victory is within our grasp. Treat the Spanish enemy humanly but firmly. No one should see them as a people of destitute vagrants, immoral dwarfs, or petty talkers, incapable of action and hostile to hard work. Neither should anyone see our northern neighbors as hungry beasts ready to have us for food. The United States is a nation impregnated in a century of freedom by the best blood of liberty-loving men. It will not employ its power depriving its closest neighbor of the dignity they so proudly have earned.»

Image above:
José Martí with Cuban leaders in Key West in 1892.

Images, top to bottom, left to right:

Seminario San Carlos y San Ambrosio, inaugurated in 1767, where Félix Varela and José Antonio Saco studied in the early 1800s;

the 1885 **University of Havana** at the Convent of *San Juan de Letrán* in Havana;

Colegio Carraguao (also called *Colegio San Cristobal*), Havana, founded at the corner of Infanta and Estévez streets, directed by José de la Luz y Caballero.

Images, top to bottom, left to right:

Brentano bookstore, a favorite of José Martí in New York, headquartered at 586 Fifth Avenue since its founding by August Brentano in 1853;

young **Juan Gualberto Gómez**, loyal friend and associate of José Martí;

presentation card of **Antonio Maceo** in the 1870s.

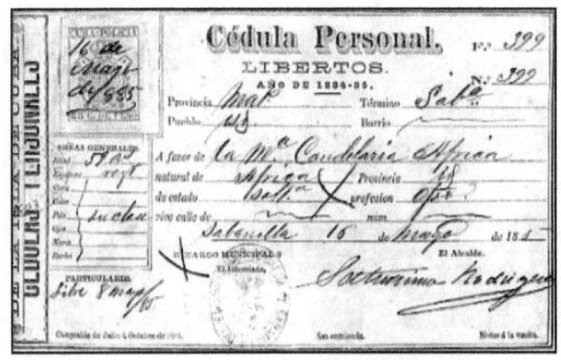

Images, top to bottom, left to right:
Cédula (personal documentation) of a *liberto* in 1885;
Lenox Library, NY City, in 1880, Martí's favorite place of study and research;
Alfonso XIII and his mother, Spain's Queen Regent María Cristina in 1895;
Flor Crombet, dear lifetime friend and associate of Antonio Maceo.

Images above:

Two photos of **José Martí** visiting people in Cuba during his recuiting trips on behalf of the 1895 war of independence.

Images, top to bottom, left to right:

José Marti as a young man with his son José Francisco (Ismaelillo) in New York in 1880;

a **1895 cartoon** showing the US punishing Spain for her sins;

a **1890 cartoon** about Spanish misrule on Cuba leading to anarchy.

Images, top to bottom, left to right:

Cartoon showing US **President McKinley** trying to hold back the US Congress pressure to act on the issue of Cuban independence;

a cartoon showing **Uncle Sam** protecting Cuba from European ambitions (The crocodile is sheding *lágrimas de cocodrilo*);

a caricature of **José Martí** as a writer.

33

Cuban Independence War was Renewed with Brio

AFTER THE 1895 CONVERSATIONS with Tomás Estrada Palma, Martí traveled to Panamá to collect funds for the war; after Panamá, he traveled to Jamaica and Kingston and wrote to Gómez about the details of a planned triple expedition, an event prepared as an extraordinary and surprising start of the insurrection in Cuba. On June 26, he departed again for Central America and on July 13 to Mexico. Upon returning to New York, he received Colonel Mayía Rodríguez, who brought news from Máximo Gómez and Maceo.

Up until 1895, for more than 50 years, Cubans had acquired weapons and ammunitions in uncoordinated ways; in their fervor and enthusiasm for the Cuban cause they had acted openly, arousing suspicions; they had talked explicitly about plans that should have remained confidential. It had been very easy for the Spaniards to detect these efforts and call the American authorities to stop their illegal expeditions. It had also been easy for the Spanish spies to notify the authorities in Cuba to wait at the right place and time for their expeditions to wipe them out. [332] This state of things had to cease immediately, and the men who put an end to it were José Martí and Gonzalo de Quesada. After almost fifteen years promoting and organizing a return of hostilities, Martí's everyday activities were so overwhelming and unremitting that he began to trust more and more on his friend and disciple Gonzalo de Quesada y Aróstegui (1868-1915). In the words of Quesada:

«History some day will remember José Martí as a great poet, journalist, exquisite literary genius and precursor, and the man who put

---

[332] The Spaniards had characterized the expeditionary forces as brigands that were feared in Cuba. To residents in the island, they had been described as bandits persecuted by the American government.

together this coming war with his speech-making and untiring dedication. But eventually one more facet will be discovered by future generations: Martí is a great strategist and a very skilled organizer.»

In Martí's mind, Cuban fighters needed leaders with three specific skills among their ranks: First were persons versed on the law. The purchase of arms and war material was legal in the United States but not the exportation to countries like Spain that were not at war the US. Every time weapons of any kind were moved in 1895, Martí arranged for Horatio Rubens to be ready to intervene if there were blockades, confiscations, detentions or disputes on the high seas.

The second needed skills were those of military experts that would know where and which weapons were the best to procure and purchase. Since they were counting on taking arms from the Spanish soldiers, a good source of ammunition was needed for the *Mausers* used by the Spaniards. Martí asked General Emilio Nuñez to be the weapons expert needed for the war. General Nuñez bought *Mausers'* ammunition but also *Remingtons*, a rifle that performed better than the *Mausers* and with which Cubans were familiar. At the end of the Ten Year War, Cubans had buried hundreds in Cuba.

The third needed skills were those of managing the effort, which included setting up targets for personal weapons contributions from the independence clubs, scheduling how to collect those arms, how to get them into transports by land and sea and how and where to get them to the *mambises*.

In early December 1894, the war launching project was baptized *El Plan de Fernandina*.

Weapons and munitions were purchased to equip a thousand men above the level at which the Spanish troops were outfitted. They were sent to *Fernandina Beach*, on Amelia Island in Florida in wooden boxes and barrels labeled as farm instruments, nails, and shovels and picks for a manganese mine in eastern Cuba.

The best possible ships were leased for the expeditions to Cuba. [333] Two large ships, the *Amadis*, the *La Gonda* and a large and fast fruit steamer, the *Baracoa*; their speed was superior to any Spanish vessel around Cuba. The port papers indicated they were going to Central America. In fact one of them, *La Gonda*, was to stop somewhere on the eastern coast of Florida and bring on board Carlos Roloff and Serafín Sánchez with 800 fighters. They were to go to the northern coast of Santa Clara. The second ship, the *Amadis*, was to move as fast as possible to Costa Rica to pick up Antonio Maceo, Flor Crombet and about 200 men. They would disembark in Camagüey. The third ship, the *Baracoa*, with Martí, Enrique Collazo and Mayía Rodríguez was to land first in Santo Domingo to retrieve Máximo Gómez's group and then depart for Oriente. All men were to dress like *campesinos*; tools and implements would be on board, on the open air, while boxes and crates with weapons, which included 600,000 rounds of ammunition, would be stored on the bilges. When at sea, fully loaded with men and officers, the ships would change course for Cuban destinations that only one assigned man on each ship would know. In Cuba three men would know the landing points and would verify the security and availability of troops to protect the landing destinations. They were all veterans of the 1868 war and, as a precaution, would not know each others' names. Three groups of above 100 infantry men and 15 cavalry each would wait near the landing areas. The men would not know until the last mi-

---

[333] Fernandina was a beach on *Amelia Island*, actually a 14 mile long key nestled between Georgia and the Florida mainland. The island has been under nine flags over the years: discovered by a Frenchman in 1562 it has been in the hands of Spain twice, the British once, the Florida patriots of 1812 once, the rebels of Gregor McGregor, a Bolivar relative of Scottish origin once, a Mexican-French alliance of adventurers in 1817 once, the U.S. twice and under the Confederate flag once. *Fort Clinch* was built by the Union Army; named in 1861 after the hero of the 1830 Seminole wars. The island has been populated by vacationing New Yorkers, including the Rockefellers and the Carnegies. «We have rented as our headquarters a large cottage in the *Florida House Inn*, a secluded small hostel near the end of town,» Martí wrote to Gonzalo de Quesada.

nute the point to which they had to race when the ships were half a day off the coast.

The entire operation would cost, after three years of preparation, $58,000 from the exiles' war chest.

Very trustworthy men under the direction and coordination of Juan Gualberto Gómez would be taking arms in Cuba on February 24, the day of the landings: Saturnino Lora in *Baire*; Juan Gualberto Gómez at *Ibarra*, near the city of Matanzas; Rafael Casallas Monteagudo and Leoncio Vidal Caro at *Camajuaní*, Las Villas, near Caibarién; Juan Bruno Zayas in *Vega Alta*, north east of Santa Clara; Guillermón Moncada, Quintín Banderas, the brothers Sartorius, the brothers Rabí and Rafael Portuondo Tamayo at *Santiago de Cuba*; Bartolomé Masó at *Bayate*, northwest of Guantánamo; Pedro Agustín Pérez at *Guantánamo*; Julio Sanguily near *Havana* and Joaquín Pedroso at *Aguada de Pasajeros*. Six fast ships would be ready to disembark in Cuba before the Spanish army could regroup after the Fernandina expeditions; they had been rented by Gonzalo de Quesada in the eastern coast of the United States and would be under the direction of Emilio Nuñez; they would be sailing from Fernandina, Key West, Kingston and Cabo Haitiano, each equipped, at the tune of $30,000, with one canon, 1000 guns, 500,000 cartridges and no less than 500 men; each under a veteran Cuban officer from the war of 1868.

In spite of the superb planning, the dedication of the men in charge, the adequate supply of funds, the top secret way in which the weapons were handled and moved, and the concealed care with which men discretely moved by the thousands to their positions, a last minute treachery brought to failure the *Plan de Fernandina*. The delator was Fernando López de Queralta. To settle old grievances with expeditionary members, Queralta, who still had some expedition weapons under his control in New York, asked his common-law wife to send them by train to Jacksonville under a declaration of *"military articles."* The weapons were immediately confiscated in New York and a day later, on January 14, 1895, the federal government detained the three ships and confiscated all the war materials of the *Plan de Fernandina*.

Martí was devastated. Aside from the obvious expenditure of time and money, he though it also implied a terrible loss of prestige and confidence in him and every other revolutionary leader. Gonzalo de Quesada, the only person who dared to approach him in his gloom and disparagement, reassured him by saying:

«Horacio Rubens has managed to exercise his law privileges with Colonel James Buchanan Anderson, inspector general of the United States Army in Florida and he has agreed not to confiscate the rifles and ammunitions since there is no firm physical evidence that they were intended to be smuggled into Cuba, only hearsay. I am sure one day soon the entire consignment will make its way to Cuba. We now need to rent a warehouse to protect the shipments from the outdoors since the captains of the three ships are more than eager to leave Fernandina.»

Martí, being a good lawyer as he was, more than knew these facts, yet he smiled as Quesada, another lawyer, was seeking words to please and entertain him.

This apparent catastrophe had the opposite effect of what Martí lamented. Cubans everywhere, including those in the United States and inside Cuba, were startled by the scope of this project after it was revealed. Both insurgents and exiles were pleasantly surprised as they confirmed there was a serious and capable leadership of the war. They found out the expeditionaries were not a band of adventurers or empowered bandits. Fernandina was the action of a professional army, under a competent and inspired civilian leadership, capable of carrying a war and later lead a new country. The fiasco was also a confirmation that they are surrounded by spies and traitors and that all cautions were not enough. Spain had flooded the areas around exiles with spies, snitches, stoolpigeons and squealers.

Word soon came from Antonio Maceo, Máximo Gómez and all military and civilian commands assuring Martí and Gonzalo de Quesada that they were ready to embark towards Cuba by whatever means might be secured. It pleased Martí and Gonzalo that the effort to launch a war for independence was alive and ready to be continued. It was now the time to retake their cause while waiting for news from the island.

Things became very hectic in Cuba and Spain after the failure of *Fernandina*:

In 1895, Spain almost got into a war with Germany when the German governor of the Marshall Islands declared the Providence Islands to be their territory. In accordance to an 1885 treaty, Spain secured the recognition of the islands as part of the Carolinas.[334]

On February 13, Spain's Minister of Ultramar, Buenaventura Abarzuza, [335] presented the Spanish Cortes a project to grant certain degree of autonomy to Cuba; it was supported by Rafael Montoro, the *autonomista* leader. The project was killed ten days later.

Prime Minister Sagasta declared on March 8: «Spain, in order to defend its rights and territories, will spend its last *peseta* and the last drop of its children's blood if necessary.» On the 23rd, the conservative party took its turn as leaders of government and Cánovas del Castillo became again Prime Minister.

On March 14, Juan Gualberto Gómez was taken prisoner in Havana. Most communications between Havana and New York supporters were interrupted.

---

[334] The Caroline Islands (*Islas Carolinas* in Spanish, *Karolinen* in German) are a widely scattered archipelago of tiny islands in the western Pacific Ocean, to the north of New Guinea. Spain had first asserted her rights on the archipelago in the 17th century. Germany disputed the Spanish claim in 1880, and the matter went to the arbitration of Pope Leo XIII in 1885. He decided in favor of Spain based on earlier claims and discovery. In 1899, as a consequence of the Spanish-Cuban-American War of 1895, Spain sold the islands to Germany for 17 million goldmarks (1,000,000 pounds sterling), which rebaptized them as *Karolinen*.

[335] Buenaventura de Abarzuza y Ferrer (1843–1910) was a
Spanish diplomat born in Havana, Cuba. He was ambassador in London in 1873 and Minister of Ultramar under Sagasta. He unsuccessfully promoted several reforms to ease life in Cuba and try to attract moderate Cubans.

José Martí and Máximo Gómez signed the *Manifiesto de Montecristi* on March 25. Both left Dominicana aboard the steam ship *Adirondack* and disembarked in *Playitas de Cahobabo*, near Baracoa, on April 11; soon Martí became the 8th President of the Cuban Republic at Arms and Mayor General of the Cuban Army.

Facing increasing struggles in Cuba, on April 17th Spain sent General Arsenio Martínez Campos to the island for a third time, replacing Emilio Calleja as Captain General.

Antonio Maceo disembarked in Cuba at Duaba, Baracoa, on April 1st. He was accompanied by Flor Crombet, who died ten days later at a combat in *Altos de Palmarito*, near Guantánamo. Maceo was greeted with joy by cries of *"Maceo is Here! Viva Cuba Libre!"*

Maceo met Martí and Gómez on May 5th at the ruins of *Ingenio La Mejorana*, near the small town of Dos Caminos, in San Luis, Oriente. Once more Martí and Maceo disagreed as to how the war should be managed.[336]

On April 4th, Cuban autonomists launched a proclamation opposing the aims of the expeditionaries to liberate Cuba.

Another important loss for the *insurrectos* in early April: on the 5th, Guillermón Moncada died in Oriente, adding to the misfortune of having lost Flor Crombet on the 10th. Of 23 Cubans that disembarked with Maceo on April 1st, only 13 were still alive by the 15th.

---

[336] Months later, on November 21st, Maceo wrote a letter to Manuel Sanguily expressing: «We have not been very fortunate in the make-up of the new government. Again we have been the victims of the vain effort of trying to give it the democratic forms of a republic already constituted when we have the enemy in front of us, and we are not the masters of the land we walk on. As you will understand, while the war lasts, there must only be soldiers and swords in Cuba, or at least men who know how to prosecute the war and how to achieve the final redemption of our people. When this is achieved, which is the objective to which our efforts are directed, the time will then be ripe for the forming of a civil government. Such a civil government should be eminently democratic and be capable of managing the public affairs with prudence and moderation, attentive to our own peculiar political and social requirements.»

On April 21st, Maceo ordered all rebel officers to «hang every emissary of the Spanish government, peninsular or Cuban, whatever may be his rank, who presents himself in our camps with propositions of peace. This order must be carried out without hesitation of any kind or without attention to any contrary indications.» It was a continuation of the 1868 *Principio de Spotorno*.

On May 19th, barely 5 weeks after entering Cuba, José Martí died in a battle at Dos Rios, Oriente. He was 42 years old. Upon learning the news, Antonio Maceo retired to his tent in the woods near Holguín and cried inconsolably all night; Máximo Gómez felt a sharp anguish and thought the Cuban army could never recover from the loss of Martí; all across the manigua Cuban soldiers withdrew to the forests in silence; in the cities many belligerents gathered in small groups to simply seek support from each other; all rebel newspapers ceased publication for a few days, not knowing how to deal with their disastrous news; *guajiros* found no strength to till their lands and at the University of Havana the classrooms remained empty without explanations. Nothing seemed to move in Cuba for a while; the impasse was only broken when Antonio Maceo began to move his troops again.

José Martí was replaced as president of Cuba by Tomás Estrada Palma, who also became the new delegate of the *Partido Revolucionario Cubano* and the new director of New York's newspaper *Patria*.

Maceo won the battle of *el Jobito*, near Guantánamo, against the Spanish *Regimiento de Simancas*; he won the battle of *Peralejo*,[337] where he almost captured Arsenio Martínez Campos

---

[337] At Peralejo, General Fidel Vidal Santociles died in combat. He was married to a Cuban lady, Doña Dolores Miyares y Hernández. After being shot twice at Peralejo he continued fighting until a third bullet ended his life. The fight at Peralejo lasted six hours. Antonio Maceo, who had known Santociles at the end of the Ten Year War, had very heartfelt words about his opponent when told of his death: «only the heroic defense of Santocildes, who gave his life to protect General Martínez Campos, Spain's greatest soldier, saved the day for Spain.»

on July 13th. On October 22nd he started from *Mangos de Baraguá* his campaign to carry the war to the entire island. His brother José Maceo was appointed to replace him in the position of Chief of Operations in Oriente.

Máximo Gómez, in the meantime, ran a successful campaign in Camagüey, where in June and July he captured lots of ammunition in *El Mulato*, near Florida, Camagüey; he routed and caused multiple casualties to a Spanish column of 1,550 men near Guáimaro.

On July 24, Carlos Roloff disembarked in Tayabacoa, near Trinidad, as chief of the 4th Cuban Army. In September he would be selected as Cuba's Minister of War.

On July 25 Arsenio Martínez Campos sent his resignation to Spanish Prime Minister Cánovas after refusing to create concentration camps in the outskirts of Cuban towns and cities. He would be replaced by Valeriano Weyler.

At Jimaguayú, Camagüey, on September 13th, representatives of Cuba elected Salvador Cisneros Betancourt as their president in arms and proclaimed a new Cuban Constitution. Bartolomé Masó was elected VP and Máximo Gómez confirmed as General in Chief of the Armies. Manuel Santander, Bishop of Havana, wrote a Pastoral Letter opposing the independence of Cuba and the War of 1895.

On October 30 Máximo Gómez crossed over the *Trocha de Júcaro a Morón*[338] and started the fight in Las Villas. Máximo Gómez issued a proclamation asking for the inhabilitation of sugar mills and railroad lines and the burning of all sugar fields, to weaken and deprive Spain of its profits in Cuba. On

---

[338] Spanish General Arsenio Martinez Campos tried the same strategy he had employed in the Ten Years' War and constructed a broad barren band across the island, called a *trocha*; it was 80 km in length and 200 m wide. This defense line was to impede rebel activities to cross into the eastern provinces of the island. All along the *trocha*, a railroad ran back and forth in the center, from Jucaro in the south coast to Morón in the north. There were fortifications at several points and on strategic places, several walls made with posts and 400 meters of barbed wire. Booby traps were placed at open spaces intended to lure insurgents to cross. The *Trochas* were safely breached on many occasions by Cubans forces using guerilla tactiques.

the 29th of November Maceo also crossed the *Trocha*, taking reinforcements to Máximo Gómez in Las Villas.

The troops of Maceo and Gómez got together on November 30th. Gómez addressed the combined forces:

«Soldiers! The war begins now, the tough unmerciful war. The weak will fall by the wayside; only the strong and the intrepid will be able to stand the ordeal. In the full ranks which I see before me, death will open great gaps. The strong among us do not expect rewards, but only suffering and work.»

On December 3rd, the combined forces crossed the Jatibonico River into Las Villas. Their first action was the *Battle of Iguará*, where Gómez attempted to capture a large convoy of Spanish goods. He succeeded at the cost of heavy casualties on both sides.

On December 15, at a place near Cruces, Cienfuegos, Máximo Gómez and Antonio Maceo won the *Battle of Mal Tiempo*, defeating a Spanish battalion of 2,500 soldiers and causing over 200 casualties.

On December 20th, Maceo crossed the Hanabanilla River into Matanzas and took the town of Coliseo, where he suffered heavy losses and his horse was shot from under him. The last day of the year he entered Havana province and began to move in the direction of the capital.

Meanwhile, near Mantua, Pinar del Rio, a hurricane destroyed the Spanish cruiser *Cristobal Colón*, equipped with 12 high power cannons and 2 torpedo launchers.

It all happened on December 15, 1895. The Cuban invasion column had left behind the mountains of Las Villas province and were heading south towards Cienfuegos at 7:00 AM. They knew the Spanish army had fortified the city and positioned many soldiers in its surroundings. They also knew they had to control de area if they ever wanted to get to Havana. The troops under General Antonio Maceo took the front positions, followed by 3,000 men under Generals Máximo Gómez and Serafín Sánchez. Covering their left flank were 1,000 men under General Quintín Bandera. They could not find Spanish troops anywhere, although a black boy had told them there was a 1,500 men cavalry force in the area of **Mal Tiempo**. Gómez had a brief meeting with Maceo to set an ambush. When they found the Spanish cavalry, Gómez would make a frontal attack while Maceo would slow down his column and assault the enemy from its left bank.

But things in war are often unpredictable. Gómez' advance scouts were found and had to respond fire and alert the Spanish column of their presence. The element of surprise was gone. Fortunately the Spanish cavalry had concentrated on a *guardarraya* and had a very limited view of the sugar cane field around them. Gómez charged headlong into the enemy; Maceo arrived ten minutes later and wreaked havoc on the Spanish cavalry, cutting them to pieces with a fast charge of *machetes*. The Spanish cavalry lost its discipline; some ran, others dropped their weapons and hid inside the cane field.

Soon a salvo of trumpets announced the presence of a second Spanish batallion, this time infantry. They took defensive positions to protect the decimated cavalry but did not confront the troops of Maceo and Gómez. Soon they were driven out from their positions by General Bandera's men. They were chased into the fortifications of the city of Cienfuegos where they had to stay for several days nursing their wounds. By then more than two hundred Spanish soldiers lied on the grounds, half of them dead. Maceo's troops captured 300 *mausers* and 10,000 rounds of ammunition. Gómez took the archives of the Spanish force, showing up-to-date maps of the entire province.

Five days later General Martínez Campos showed up with a 1,200 men force composed of cavalry and men on foot. He tried to encircle Maceo near the town of **Coliseo** but failed. He fell into a deep depression and despair and cabled his superiors in Madrid: «My failure cannot be more complete. Gómez and Maceo have broken through all my defense lines; communications are cut; my men are in disarray, obsessed with the horrible sounds of machetes when they fall upon our troops. At this point there are no Spanish forces between the enemy and the city of Havana.» His brillant military career had ended in disgrace.

The Battle of Mal Tiempo

Images, top to bottom, left to right:

A view of **Havana harbor** in 1881, published in La Ilustración Española;

a **New York Times** report on the appointment of Valeriano Weyler as a replacement of Martinez Campos in Cuba;

Valeriano Weyler after receiving the honorable award of the **Toisón de Oro** from Alfonso XIII on June 13, 1913.

Images, top to bottom, left to right:

The **Hotel of Madame Griffon** on Ninth Avenue, New York, where Martí, Maceo and Máximo Gómez met on October 1, 1884;

Tomás Estrada Palma school in Central Valley, NY, 1893;

a stamp honoring **Gonzalo de Quesada**, Martí's inseparable collaborator during the 1895 War organizational effort.

Images, top to bottom:

José Martí in the cigar factory **Vicente Martinez-Ybor & Co.**, Tampa, 1893;

The home of Máximo Gómez in Montecristi, where the **Pacto de Montecristi** was signed on March 25, 1895.

Florida House in **Fernandina Beach** in 2013, a hundred and eighteen years after José Martí stayed there during his work on the Fernandina Plan to invade Cuba.

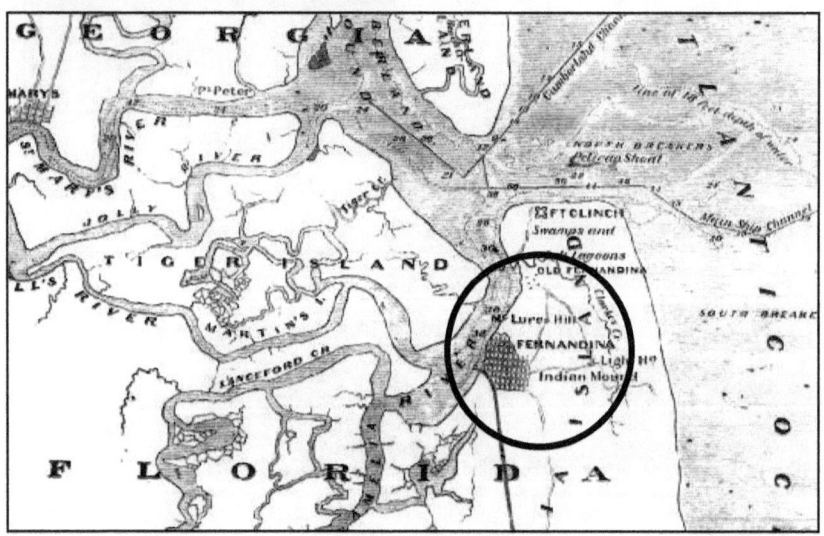

Images, top to bottom, left to right:

Patria, the newspaper founded by José Martí in New York on March 14, 1892. A month later he founded the *Partido Revolucionario Cubano*;

the headquarters of **Patria** and the **Partido Revolucionario Cubano** in New York;

a map of the territory in Florida, US, around **Fernandina Beach**;

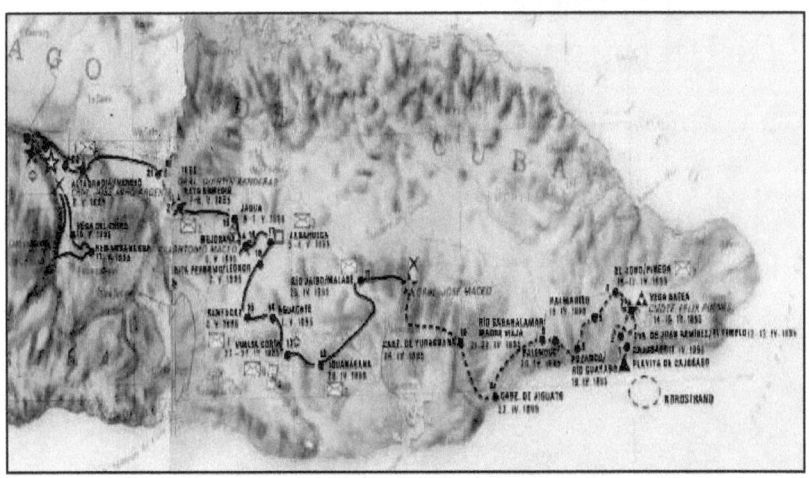

Images, top to bottom:

Playitas de Cahobabo, the area where José Martí disembarked in Cuba on April 11, 1895;

the **monument** dedicated to Gómez and Martí at *Playitas*;

A map showing the route Martí followed in Oriente from **Playitas** to **Dos Rios**.

Images, top to bottom:
A contemporary drawing showing Martí at the time of his **disembarkment in Playitas**;
a view of **Dos Rios**, Jiguaní, Oriente, where José Martí was killed;
a Spanish newspaper showing evidence of the **death of José Martí**.

Image above:
The initial steps of the **1895 War** as shown in a New York newspaper.

Images, top to bottom:

Two scenes from the **Cuban Independence Army** across the island in 1895;

a **Spanish fortification** and the crew defending it in 1897;

the **Cuban Army** ready to depart for a campaign in 1898.

Images, top to bottom:

A cartoon published in Madrid showing the **Spanish lion** in Cuba, ready to receive **the American pig** from the US shores;

a cartoon showing Spain's Prime Minister **Sagasta kicking Uncle Sam** out of Cuba;

José Martí reflecting on one of his poems... «*yo soy un hombre sincero*...»

During Cuban Independence Wars, four constitutions were drafted, to govern the rights and duties of people during their armed struggle against Spain:

Guáimaro Constitution

The first was the Guáimaro Constitution, adopted on April 10, 1869; it ruled 10 years up to February 8, 1878. By its revolutionary origin, it was a document with only 29 Articles that fixed the essential organs of government. It established a single Camera as the lead entity of the government, responsible for appointing and deposing the executive, the Commander in Chief of the Army and the President of its sessions. The executive power was limited to such an extent that it needed the approval of the House for all appointment of Secretaries. Its essential value was that it enshrined the right of all Cubans to freedom and proclaimed the total and final abolition of slavery, which was included in Article 24 which read: «All inhabitants of the Republic are forever free.»

Baraguá Constitution

On March 15, 1878, at the end of the Ten Years War, Cubans enacted the Baraguá Constitution, which resulted from the protest by Major General Antonio Maceo Grajales. It consisted of 6 Articles from which a Provisional Government composed of four citizens was established. The powers of conducting the war were given to a commanding general. Two Articles of the Baraguá Constitution legally endorsed the aims of the Baraguá Protest. Articles 3: «The Government is empowered to make peace only on the basis of independence.» Article 4: «No peace could be made with the Spanish government under any other basis without the knowledge and consent of the people.»

(Continued)

The Constitutions of the Republic of Cuba in Arms

(Contiuation)

Jimaguayú Constitution

The Jimaguayú Constitution went into effect on September 16, 1895, also during wartime. It purposely went into effect for only two years. This Constitution was more complete than previous ones, and it tried to avoid the mistakes that were committed in Guáimaro's. In the elected Constitutional Assembly there were veterans of the war of 1868 who recalled the drawbacks of having placed the direction of the war in the hands of a House of Representatives; therefore, it prescribed a different form of government, giving the supreme direction of the nation to a Government Council composed of a President, a Vice-President and four Secretaries of State. The preamble of the Constitution of Jimaguayú expressed that the war objective was to obtain the independence of Cuba and the creation a Democratic Republic after the separation of Cuba from the Spanish monarchy, i.e., its constitution as a free and independent state with its own government.

Yaya Constitution

Two years after the proclamation of the Jimaguayú Constitution, on October 29, 1897, it ceased -as prescribed- to be in effect and it was replaced by the last of the Cuban at War constitutions: the Yaya Constitution. It was a much more extensive and complete instrument than previous one, with 48 Articles. It was memorable by the inclusion of a statement of principles in the text, defining individual and political rights for the nation and its citizens. The position of General of the Army was omitted, its duties were assumed by a Governing Council, which gave the nation a collegial civilian power. It was a constitution drafted with greater technical expertise, where a positive influence from concepts only summarily outlined in the Guáimaro Constitution could be perceived. This constitution was in effect only a year, due to the participation of the United States into the war, which led to the military defeat of Spain and its withdrawal from Cuba.

The Constitutions of the Republic of Cuba in Arms

34

Lots of Progress in the War Front at the Start

THE DEATH OF MARTÍ was a severe blow to Cubans in the island and in exile; yet it helped to inspire a greater activity and commitment rather than disparagement of the war. Instead of discouraging the patriots, it served to strengthen them. In New York, Gonzalo de Quesada received the news from Bartolomé Masó in a letter that read in part

«Blinded by his courage he hurried to within a few feet of the enemy's lines. His slim body rolled from the saddle never to stand up again. His inspiring face had been destroyed by a bullet than took with it the hopes of the Cubans and the patriotic and sublime poetry of the best of our sons. His eyes, full of melancholy until a few moments before, were no longer dreaming; his lips were sealed forever; for carrying a rifle, his arms would no longer carry a pen. I could not sleep for days when I found out that José Martí was dead!»

The impetus given to the war by the death of Martí was not poetic but real. Within weeks Antonio Maceo, the victor of Peralejo,[339] who was feeling contrite for not having mended his last disagreements with Martí, had control of the entire province of Oriente with the exception of a few fortified coastal cities and encampments. His army was well organized and observed all the rules of civilized warfare; it maintained a high degree of mobility, avoiding large engagements, wearing out

---

[339] «At Peralejo,» Maceo would say, «General Martínez Campos was not caught because he took advantage of our respect for the wounded and had himself placed on a stretcher covered by surgical blood-stained sheets, and was allowed to cross the lines in the direction of Bayamo, only accompanied by two colored medical handlers.» On the last hours of the battle Maceo allowed close to a thousand Spaniards, the shattered remains of Martínez Campos' army, to take refuge in Bayamo. They were surrounded and immobilized there for a week, until Maceo decided to retire and take his troops elsewhere.

the morale of the Spaniards with forced marches, surprise attacks and very innovative and unexpected moves.

To Maceo's successes the Cuban troops could now add others. Jesús Rabí occupied Victoria de las Tunas and decimated a Spanish battalion at Jiguaní; the *autonomistas* in Camagüey turned around and began to sympathize with the *independentistas*; a large Spanish force was virtually destroyed by José Maceo in Guantánamo; Quintín Banderas surprised a newly landed convoy of Spanish supplies and captured numerous weapons and ammunitions, uniforms, boots and dried foods; railroads were being destroyed to fracture Spanish communications; Máximo Gómez broke through the Júcaro-Morón *trocha* and started the war in Camagüey and Santa Clara; Carlos Roloff took the north and west of Santa Clara while General Alfredo Zayas took the south.

The war was not circumscribed to land. A brand new gunboat which Spain had just purchased in the United States was boarded, seized, stripped of all armaments, disabled, scuttled and sank by the Cuban army at the mouth of the Cauto river.

General Martínez Campos began to feel panicky. He asked and obtained 30,000 additional troops from Madrid. He began to recruit soldiers in Brazil, Argentina and Uruguay, thinking that they would be hardier and could best endure the hot climate of Cuba. He became delirious thinking he was been defeated by the weather and not by the Cuban troops.

On December 15th, 1895 one notable action that completed the demoralization of General Martínez Campos took place at *Mal Tiempo*, near the town of *Las Cruces*, thirty miles north of Cienfuegos. Campos was living at the *Union Hotel* in Cienfuegos and his troops were stationed inside the city; 20,000 men, including the battalions of Bailén and Islas Canarias. A 63 year old colored farmer-turned-General fighting in the region, Quintín Banderas, began to raid the Spanish lines that were protecting the city; he succeeded to draw a large contingent of Spanish troops to chase his troops. The battle became one of the most significant of the war although it only involved 2,000 men from each side. It was the first battle in which the Cuban forces used only machetes to fight a well armed enemy: steel *vs* rifles. The heroes of the day were Gómez, Maceo, Eugenio Sánchez, Banderas and Enrique Loynaz del Castillo. They completely annihilated the Spanish troops: 200 dead, 180 wounded, 80 men taken prisoner; 150 deserters from the Spanish regiments; 150 Remington rifles captured, 16 ammunition boxes, documents with up-to-date maps of the western region and the Spanish strategies to defend them, medical equipment, plus several dozen horses and mules and three Spanish flags. On the Cuban side 4 dead and 23 wounded, including Maceo's *aide-de-camp*.

Soon enough, the time came for Martínez Campos to go back to Spain defeated and without the luster with which he had arrived in Cuba. On January 6, 1896, 65 years old General Arsenio Martínez Campos, received a letter from María Cristina, the Spanish Queen Regent stating

«Please receive the appreciation of the government for your activities, the zeal and ability with which you have directed military operations. Extend this gratitude to the army, the navy and the *Voluntarios*, for the bravery and devotion displayed by them.»

That very day the Spanish Minister of War, Marcelo de Azcárraga, was writing in his dairy «The recall of Martínez Campos is the first great victory of the Cubans.»

Martínez Campos had been the only man in 1895 with the correct credentials to keep Cuba in the hands of Spain. He had decisively defeated the *Carlists*, [340] once and for all. Together with Prime Minister Cánovas del Castillo, he had restored Alfonso XII to the throne of Spain in 1876; in 1878 he had pacified Cuba with political and military acumen and skills. He was now facing the government request to pacify Cuba with a sort of ethnic cleansing and was glad to tender the requested resignation and be replaced by Spanish General Valeriano Weyler.

---

[340] Followers of Carlos, uncle to Isabel II, the infant daughter of Fernando VII, whose succession Carlos challenged in 1833, giving rise to a prolonged civil war and disputes that are still under the political surface in Spain.

Valeriano Weyler Nicolau, *Marqués de Tenerife*, was 58 years old at the time. He had been *Capitan General* of the Philippines, where he had first tried the genocidal tactic of *hamleting* or *reconcentration*, and earned the moniker of *el carnicero* (the butcher). He had been in Cuba before, as lieutenant for the ferocious *Conde de Valmaseda* during the Ten Year War. He represented a shift in Spanish policy: from a regular war to a cruel and brutal conflict. Martínez Campos had commented, after knowing of his appointment, that

«Even the dead will rise against Weyler. He is a *Torquemada*, the most blood-thirsty hyena of Spain; anyone who knows of his deeds will prefer to designate him as the butcher, as most Cubans do.»

Contrary to what the Spanish press was publishing, there was a real discomfort in the Queen Regent's *Palacio de Oriente* for the state of things in Cuba. The day Martínez Campos was replaced by Valeriano Weyler, the new Captain General was promised $2,000,000 in additional funds to press on with the war. Ships were chartered; the calling to service of the men in *quintas* [341] was accelerated. Horses were gathered all over Spain, including those that had been trained for *corridas de toros*. Ladies were asked to donate their jewels. All bronze adornments in the buildings of the great cities were removed from the façades; all bronze statues were modeled in clay for future replication and the originals melted for cannons. This included 6 of the 27 statues made in 1591 by Leoni for the *Capilla Mayor del Escorial*, the statue of Philip II in the *Plaza Mayor de Madrid* and most bronze statues at the *Parque del Retiro*, among other statuary jewels erected or collected during the days of Spanish grandeur.

Weyler saw his mission in Cuba in very concrete terms. In a personally flattering and pompous, arrogant and disdainful letter to Antonio Cánovas del Castillo, he promised:

---

[341] A draft lottery consisting of calling to service every fifth man of those available on a list of citizens. For $500 US Dollars your name was permanently and legally deleted from the list and your turn served by the recipient of the $500.

«I will clean out of rebels the province of Occidente (Pinar del Río, Havana and Matanzas) by March 15th; I will have all sugar planters grinding by April 1st; I will make sure all decrees by Máximo Gómez are impeded from implementation; I will prevent the landing of any more supplies to the insurgents; I will end the war in two years; I will work with my friend Dupuy de Lôme, Spanish Minister to Washington, to prevent all expressions of sympathy to the Cuban cause by the US House and Senate.»

Weyler arrived in Cuba on January 20, 1896; on February 10 he took command of Cuba's Captaincy General. Martínez Campos, still the highest honored military man in Spain, immediately began to conspire for the recall of his successor.

For a while, in Cuba, the war continued its successful trend for the rebel armies:

On January 5, 1896, Maceo entered in the town of Alquizar, and on January 6, on Hoyo Colorado and Caimito del Guayabal, all in Havana province.

Between January 5, 1896 and the end of June, Antonio Maceo won many encounters and took several towns in the western part of Cuba: Alquizar, Hoyo Colorado, San Antonio de las Vegas, Santa Cruz del Norte, Batabanó, Bauta and Caimito del Guayabal in Havana province; Cabañas, Las Taironas, Guane, Mantua, Artemisa in Pinar del Rio province. His most notable victory took place on April 14, when he defeated a large contingent of Spanish troops under the command of Valeriano Weyler in *Peladero de Tapia*, on the mountains of Pinar del Rio.

On July 5, Maceo's brother José, [342] died at a combat in *Loma del Gato*, near Santiago de Cuba. He had complained about the appointment of Calixto García as head of the insurgent operations in Orient;, his dissatisfaction was ignored and rebuked by Máximo Gómez.

---

[342] José Marcelino Maceo Grajales (1849-1896) was the third of the Maceo brothers; he had joined the Ten Year War when he was 19 and reached the rank of Colonel. He was corageous but very short-tempered and impatient. He participated in the three Cuban wars of independence. It was said he had fought in 800 combats by the time he died.

On July 16, Habana Bishop Manuel Santander exhorted the Spanish Army to «continue its struggle of civilization against barbarity.» On November 30 he would ask all parishioners to donate money and jewels to help Spain on its war expenses.

Cuban patriots continued to receive expeditions from the US. On August 13, the steamer *Dauntless* left Charleston and landed in *El Macío*, Near Santiago de Cuba, on August 22.

On September 26, 3,000 insurgents led by Máximo Gómez and Calixto García surrounded Cascorro, Camagüey. A volunteer Spanish soldier, Eloy Gonzalo, managed to burn a Cuban offensive position at the risk of his life, becoming a Spanish national hero. He died a year later, still in Cuba, victim of a fever.

On October 21, Valeriano Weyler proclaimed his *Edicto de Reconcentración*. Within six months over 50,000 people died in Havana. All crops began to fail; sugar mills and tobacco plantations became idle. The island was sunk into generalized poverty. Militarily, however, the reconcentration began to pay good dividends. Weyler assigned 40 battalions to seek and engage Maceo in Pinar del Rio. Maceo had laid siege to the headquarters of the Mariel-to-Majana *trocha* in Artemisa, Pinar del Rio.

On November 18, Major General Serafín Sánchez died at an encounter in *Paso de las Damas*, a cross point of Rio Zaza, Sancti Spíritus.

On December 4, Maceo and 20 of his men bypassed the Mariel –to-Majana *trocha* by sea and entered Havana province.

On December 7, at San Pedro, Punta Brava in the province of Havana, Maceo died at a skirmish with the Spanish army. With him died Francisco (Panchito) Gómez Toro, son of Máximo Gómez.

Spain found itself involved in another war in the Philippines, where Governor Ramón Blanco was replaced on December 13 by General Polavieja, both being well known figures in Cuba. The change in governorship coincides with a change in the operations of the Philippine rebels: Andrés Bonifacio was replaced by Emilio Aguinaldo as chief military leader. Very few people in Cuba were familiar with what was happening in the Pacific.

US President Grover Cleveland, on a message to Congress, deplored the inability of Spain to control the Cuban insurrection: [343]

«The insurrection in Cuba still continues with all its perplexities. No progress has thus far been made toward the pacification of the island; no evidence that the situation has in the least improved. If Spain still holds Havana and the seaports and all the large towns, the insurgents still roam at will over at least two-thirds of the inland country. The determination of Spain to put down the insurrection seems limited to increasing military and naval forces; there is much reason to believe that the insurgents have gained in point of numbers, character and resources; they are inflexible in their resolve not to succumb without securing the great object for which they took up arms. Spain has not established her authority; the insurgents have not made good their title as an independent state. The pretense that civil government exists on the island has been practically abandoned. Spain controls large towns and their suburbs. But, the entire country seems to be given over to anarchy or is subject to insurgent military occupation.»

US President Grover Cleveland and a cartoon showing an unattentive US.

---

[343] The message, according to the US Department of State, *Papers Relating to Foreign Affairs*, 1896, ended thus:

« I have deemed it not amiss to remind the Congress that a time may arrive when a correct policy and care for our interests, as well as a regard for the interests of other nations and their citizens, joined by considerations of humanity and a desire to see a rich and fertile country, intimately related to us, saved from complete devastation, will constrain our government to such action as will subserve the interests thus involved and at the same time promise to Cuba and its inhabitants an opportunity to enjoy the blessings of peace.»

The year 1896 began with very unpleasant news for the Spanish army in Cuba. Antonio Maceo, head of the *Ejercito Invasor de Cuba* (Cuba's invading army), was furiously advancing through the southern agricultural lands of Havana province. It had occupied  *Melena del Sur* and *San Antonio de las Vegas* and had burned to the ground the fertile sugar platations of *Quivicán*. Panic and hysteria had invaded the residents of the city of Havana. General Martínez Campos had declared a state of war for the entire provinces of Havana and Pinar del Rio; newspapers were forbidden to publish any information about the war that was not personally approved by Martínez Campos. On the streets of *Havana, Marianao, Guanabacoa, Puentes Grandes, Güines, Bejucal* and many small towns, fully armed Spanish troops had taken strategic locations in preparation for assaults by the invading forces. The hills of *Jesús del Monte* and *Atarés* were covered with heavy artillery. Rumors started to circulate that an army of over 10,000 men were already in the province, trying to surround the city of Havana and strike a final blow to the defending Spanish troops. A warning attributed to Martínez Campos advised all citizens not to panic but gather their most precious belongings and their families for a possible massive evacuation towards the ports of *Bahia Honda, Mariel* and *Cabañas* where the Spanish Army would make a last stand and the Spanish Navy would be ready to rescue thousands of loyal Spanish citizens. The *Diario de la Marina* informed that «packs of vandals are destroying everything on their path.»

Only six days since they had arrived to the territory in early January, the invading army had taken control of the entire province. Máximo Gómez was writing in his diary:

«On the 7th of January, we entered in *Hoyo Colorado*, on the boundary between Havana and Pinar del Rio. Maceo and I split our troops in two columns, each over two thousand men. General Maceo will begin a march to invade the province of Pinar del Río and I will countermarch to defend his rearguard and hold and take Havana. Our armies are as ill-equipped as the rest of the Cuban forces. Our armament consists of some Mauser rifles and Remington carbines, most of them old and shabby. We have no artillery. Total supplies are reduced to about 15 thousand or 16 thousand rounds; each man has 10 or 12 cartridges. They have been told to think twice before firing a single shot with their Remingtons; our constant interest is to economize and not burn our provisions in a few minutes.»

(continued)

The 1896 Cuban Invading Army

(continuation)

«Maceo and his troops, after evading a strong column that tried to stop them at Playa Baracoa on January 8, had to overcome a strong enemy resistance in the Palomino and Lucia sugar mills, when they attempted to block their path into Pinar del Río. Two Cuban squads fought against the Spanish vanguard at Guanajay; the Spanish command believed that Maceo was heading towards the Pinillos fort and sent formidable reinforcements. General Antonio, however, led his forces into Cabañas, assaulted the fort and forced the garrison to surrender on January 9, during a torrential downpour. We took 200 rifles, 13,000 ammunition cartridges and abundant supplies. They proceeded to take Bahia Honda and burned the Gerardo sugar mill, capturing 100 rifles. They then destroyed the *Rio Blanco*, *La Mulata* and *Verraco embarcaderos* (piers), moved south to *Las Taironas*, an area about six kilometers south of Pinar del Rio's capital, beating over a thousand Spanish troops. On our part, we faced victoriously an enemy column in *Ceiba del Agua*. Five days later Maceo was capturing a railroad train west between El Gabriel and La Salud. Less than 24 hours later, on January 13, he took La Salud in the morning and Bejucal in the afternoon, following small actions in Nazareno, Santa Amelia, Moralitos, Tapaste and Guines. By the 23rd he was around Quivicán, following the trail after Spanish general Iberian Suarez Valdes.»

Meanwhile, Maceo and his troops reached Guane on January 20. For two days they took care of their horses and gave maintenance to their weapons. At four in the afternoon of January 22, 1896, the *Cuban Invading Army* entered Mantua, to the applause and cheers of the population. As they sang the National Anthem, the Cuban flag was hoisted. It was the flag that some ladies in Camagüey had embroidered for the Invading Army and had delivered to Maceo during its passage through the province. In 92 days, since leaving *Mangos de Baraguá* on October 22, 1895, Maceo's invading column had traveled over two thousand miles in the midst of strongly fortified enemy armies. At its peak, it had not exceed five thousand troops and had fought a formidably equipped Spanish army counting with 42 generals and more than 160 thousand soldiers, aside from irregulars and Spanish paramilitary forces, for a total of about 60 thousand individuals.

The 1896 Cuban Invading Army

Images, top to bottom, left to right:

The three top heroes of Cuban Independence.

José Martí (1853-1895), died on the battlefield at *Dos Rios* at the age of 42;

Antonio Maceo (1845-1896), died in action at *Punta Brava* Cuba at the age of 51.

Máximo Gómez (1836-1905), survived the War of 1895 and died in Havana at the age of 69.

Images, top to bottom:

A painting illustrating the **death of José Martí** in Dos Rios, Oriente, on May 19, 1895, barely six weeks after entering Cuba to join the Independence Army.

A drawing showing the **death of Antonio Maceo** in the vicinity of Punta Brava, Havana, on December 7, 1896.

SUPLEMENTO
AL
DIARIO DE LA MARINA

HABANA, 21 DE MAYO DE 1895

IMPORTANTE TELEGRAMA.

MUERTE DE MARTI.

En la Capitanía General se ha recibido el siguiente importantísimo telegrama que trasmite en esta fecha el General Salcedo, desde Santiago de Cuba:

Santiago de Cuba, 21 de mayo.

General en Jefe:

Ayer combate cconsidero resultado político gran trascendencia. Por confidencias supe gruesa partida se hallaba entre Palma y Remanganaguas, y dispuse salida columna Coronel Sandoval en su busca, encontrándola entre Bijas y Dos Ríos, orilla derecha Contramaestre, en número 700 hombres, con Martí, Máximo Gómez, Massó y Borrero. Marchaban, según se asegura, á pasar Cauto para seguir Tunas y Príncipe.

Combate duró hora y media, siendo enemigo desalojado sus posiciones y rechazado, huyendo subdividido tres fracciones, siendo perseguido, muerto titulado presidente república cubana, José Martí, cuyo cadáver ha sido recogido é identificado, á pesar empeño retirarlo. Enemigo tuvo, además, 14 muertos vistos y muchos heridos, cogiéndosele las armas y correspondencia de Martí, del titulado comandante de estado mayor, 37 caballos muertos y once útiles con monturas. Por nuestra parte cinco muertos y siete heridos. Aseguran prisioneros que Máximo Gómez y Estrada han sido muertos ó heridos, faltando comprobación de ésto, que procuraré obtener por medios posibles.—*Salcedo.*

Image above:

A transcription of a telegram received at the **Diario de la Marina** two days after the death of José Martí; it was immediately published in the newspaper.

MUERTE DE MACEO

ANTONIO MACEO

A las doce del día empezó á cundir por Madrid la noticia de que Antonio Maceo había muerto en un combate próximo á la Habana.

Al principio la gente se mostraba incrédula: ¡Se ha repetido tantas veces el mismo rumor!

Después se supo que había telegramas oficiales que confirmaban la noticia.

En varios departamentos ministeriales existían cablegramas de los que resultaba que el cadáver del célebre mulato había sido encontrado.

Entonces empezaron á prevalecer impresiones satisfactorias y á cundir en todas partes el entusiasmo.

El instinto popular se ha adelantado y sobrepuesto á todos los juicios y reflexiones sobre la trascendencia de esa catástrofe de la insurrección.

Así sus parciales como sus enemigos, habían condensado en la figura del cabecilla la representación entera de la rebeldía. No sólo se ve en su muerte un fracaso inmenso para la causa de los traidores á España, sino poco menos que el fin de la guerra.

Pertenece Maceo á una raza cuyas cadenas hemos roto los españoles emancipándolos y enalteciéndolos. Su ingratitud odiosa, unida á su arrojo casi salvaje, había hecho de él la figura saliente de esta guerra sangrienta, oscureciendo por completo el renombre de todos los otros jefes de la insurrección.

De él y solo de él se hablaba, contra él se acumulaban poderosos ejércitos y cuando esta misma mañana se recibía la penosa noticia de que había pasado la trocha para llevar el horror de sus devastaciones é incendios á la provincia de la Habana, se supo que un puñado de valientes, cerca de Punta Brava, luchando en la desproporción, heróica para nosotros, de uno contra seis, le había hecho morder el polvo y había dejado tendido su cadáver en medio del campo.

Hé aquí los telegramas primeramente recibidos y que acreditan este hecho, en el cual la Providencia y la divina justicia, por medio de la bravura é intrepidez de nuestros valientes soldados ha castigado duramente al feroz partidario que he-

muerte de Maceo, recibíamos el siguiente de nuestro corresponsal en Barcelona, confirmando el anterior:

Barcelona 9. 11'41 m.

Acaba de recibirse un cablegrama de Cuba por la vía Inglesa, anunciando la muerte del cabecilla Antonio Maceo.

El cablegrama lo ha recibido la casa Nell, la cual tiene un individuo en la trocha en calidad de voluntario.

FIGUEROLA.

***

En la Presidencia del Consejo se ha facilitado á las cuatro de la tarde á la prensa el siguiente cablegrama:

HABANA.

(Sin fecha y sin hora).

El segundo jefe del apostadero al ministro de Marina:

El almirante salió ayer en el *Legazpi* á revistar la costa de Pinar del Río.

La columna Cirujeda, después de varios encuentros con Maceo, pasada la trocha, en esta provincia, y según pruebas, prendas, ropa, armas y documentos que se hallan en poder del general Ahumada, resultó comprobada su muerte, y por suicidio la del hijo de Máximo Gómez por no abandonar el cadáver de Maceo, según escrito que dejó con el suyo.

GOMEZ IMAZ.

***

LA PRIMERA NOTICIA

Recepción del cablegrama oficial en la Central.

el suelto que en nuestros *Ecos políticos* publicamos en la edición de la mañana, en cuyo suelto acogíamos la probabilidad de que en el Consejo de hoy se adoptara algún acuerdo de importancia, relacionado con tan grave cuestión, y que ya entre el jefe del gobierno y algunos consejeros se habían celebrado conferencias preliminares de la conversación que con carácter oficial habrían de sostener los ministros en su reunión de hoy.

No nos limitamos á decir sólo eso cuando redactamos dicho suelto; fuimos aún más allá, é hicimos constar á continuación que á nuestra noticia habían llegado rumores relacionados con algunos cablegramas que se dice se han cruzado entre el general don Sabas Marín, gobernador general de Puerto Rico, y el ministro de la Guerra y con algún otro despacho de carácter confidencial que se suponía obraba ya en poder del general Ahumada.

Después de la noticia que el cable ha trasmitido, es posible, según las impresiones que esta mañana hemos recogido, que en los propósitos del gobierno se opere algún cambio radical, ó por lo menos, según los mejor informados, algo parecido á un aplazamiento.

El comandante general del apostadero de la Habana, contraalmirante Navarro, está cruzando por la costa Norte y Sur de Pinar del Río por orden telegráfica del general Beranger, quien lo había dispuesto así para que fuese mayor la vigilancia del litoral y Maceo no se fugase por mar de dicha provincia antillana.

Marianao está á ocho kilómetros de la Habana. Sin duda el cabecilla mulato al pasar la trocha, pensaba ir sobre la capital.

***

Coincidencia singular.

Uno de los funcionarios que se hallaban de guardia en la sala de aparatos, se llama como el hijo del *generalísimo*, Francisco Gómez.

Naturalmente que los telegrafistas dieron algunas bromas, de buen género, al homónimo del hijo del jefe insurrecto, que por otra parte es uno de los mejores linguistas españoles y una persona muy digna y muy querida entre todo el personal de la Central y del cuerpo de Telégrafos.

En la plana segunda y edición de la noche van la biografía del mulato, la hoja de servicios del comandante Cirujeda y otras noticias importantes, con los últimos telegramas recibidos.

POLAVIEJA TIENE LA PALABRA.

La cuestión que tanto ha preocupado estos días al país y á la prensa, sobre los antagonismos posibles entre los generales Blanco y Polavieja y la actitud del gobierno de la metrópoli al decidirse por una de las dos direcciones encarnadas en cada uno de los ilustres caudillos, ha tenido una rápida y definitiva solución; prevista, sin duda, tiempo há por quien envió al general Polavieja, é inesperada para cuantos estos días hemos venido discutiendo.

En la acción militar hemos creído que ambos eran compatibles y aun que se completaban; en lo concerniente á la política, veníamos sosteniendo que el último de los dos generales allí enviados llevaba las instrucciones más inmediatas del ministerio y sería el designado para implan-

Image above:

An account of the **death of Antonio Maceo** published on
La Correspondencia de España, Madrid, December 9, 1896.

Images, top to bottom:

A 1883 chart describing the characteristics and component parts of **Mauser rifles**, the preferred long weapon of the Spanish Army.

A 1896 photo taken aboard the steamship **Three Friends**, showing Juan Rius Rivera, Demetrio Castillo Duany, Henry Reeve (*el Inglesito*) and José Ramón Villalón, hours before they disembarked in Cuba.

Images, top to bottom:
Two goups of soldiers from the competing armies:
of the **1895 Cuban War of Independence**.

The **Cuban rebel army** in 1895.

The **Spanish colonial army** in 1896.

Images, top to bottom:

Two important battles of the 1895 war won by Cuban troops.

Scene from the **Battle of Peralejo**, near Bayamo, July 13, 1895, where Maceo almost made prisoner his Spanish rival, Spanish Captain General Arsenio Martínez Campos.

The **Battle of Mal Tiempo**, near Cienfuegos, December 15, 1895, won by troops under the command of Cuban General Máximo Gómez.

Images above:

Reportage about the **Battle of Mal Tiempo** published in the *Diario de la Marina*, Havana, on December 21, 1895.

A **1933 Cuban postage stamp** commemorating the *Battle of Mal Tiempo*.

Images, top to bottom:

Four successive statues placed in the same spot at **Central Park** in Havana: *Isabel II of Spain* (1850-1869), *Christopher Columbus* (1870-1875), *Liberty* (1902-1903), *José Martí* (1905-Present);

a 1895 leaflet published by the newspaper **Cuba en Tampa**;

a **1895 coin** with the image of young Alfonso XIII;

a **1898 cartoon** depicting *Yankee Imperialism* in Cuba.

LO QUE HA COSTADO LA GUERRA A LOS CUBANOS

La Liga Cubano-Americana pide cuentas al señor Estrada Palma de las siguientes cantidades, inferiores á las realmente recaudadas, según parece:

De los cubanos en los Estados Unidos, pesos 100.000 mensuales, durante cuatro años, 4.800.000.

Arístides Agüero, desde Sur América, 100.000.

Emilio Terry, 80.000.

Señora Marta Abreu, 50.000.

Mr. Rockefort, 100.000.

Hacendados cubanos, 250.000 pesos anuales, durante cuatro años, 1.000.000.

De los cubanos en Paris, pesos 100.000 al año, durante cuatro años 400.000

Donativos particulares de americanos y cubanos en los Estados Unidos, 250.000.

Total 5.780.000.

Images, top to bottom:

An account of the **cost of the 1898 war** presented on the pro-Spain newspaper *Noticiero Salmantino*, Salamanca, on July 6, 1899;

General **Arsenio Martínez Campos** at the time of the 1895 *Peralejo Battle*;

A commemorative plaque at the site where Martí and Máximo Gómez signed the **Pacto de Montecristi** in 1895.

APRES LA MORT DE MACEO

Le général Weyler (présentant la tête de Maceo).
La reine régente. — Ne t'effraye pas, mon fils! Canovas dit que c'est le commencement de la fin.

Caricature de Johann Braakensiek (*Weekblad voor Nederland*. d'Amsterdam, 1896).
Canovas est debout derrière le fauteuil de la reine régente.

La campanya de Cuba continúa avansant ab una rapidés extraordinaria.

Images, top to bottom:

A **1910 cartoon** in the French magazine *Jeune Premier de l'Europe*, showing Valeriano Weyler bringing the head of Maceo to Spanish Regent Maria Cristina while Prime Minister Cánovas watches from behind her seat.

An August 15, 1896 cartoon published in *La Campana de Gracia*, Barcelona, finding fault with the slowness of **Weyler's campaign** to pacify Cuba.

35

A Strong Succession of Victories for the Cubans

«**THE MIDNIGHT SKIES** of Cuba are glowing red everywhere our troops operate,» Fermín Valdés Domínguez wrote Gonzalo de Quesada after the battle of *Mal Tiempo*.

«Cane fields, sugar mills, Spanish-owned haciendas, small government buildings in unprotected towns, railroads, coffee plantations, storage buildings, tobacco curing barns, everything is being set on fire by our troops. Our advancing armies are leaving behind a broad swath of charred waste and destitution, the result of our inescapable patriotic scythe. Tall darkened chimneys are the only thing left standing as mute witnesses of our resolve to be free. Day after day this infernal and fiendish hallway of destruction is approaching Havana. We are close to Marianao and can see caravans of residents escaping westward. We help them as best as we can and even offer them places to stay overnight. They are stoic and understanding. This is more than anything else their own war. Many men leave their families to continue their ghostly procession to the west, turning around by themselves and joining our columns. The women and children take turns sleeping under the protection of twisted and blackened machinery and blackened tin roofs that still stand upright shielding desolated factory floors. Havana is isolated on all sides. All railroads have stopped operations. All roads in and out have been taken by our troops. Quintín Banderas and Antonio Maceo are holding Martínez Campos on check in Havana while Máximo Gómez has broken through the Spanish lines and has marched his entire army into Pinar del Rio.»

A few days later Gonzalo received another letter, this time from Bartolomé Masó:

«This is the end of the road for Martínez Campos. In spite of his martial law, the entire island is now in flames. Pinar del Rio is pledging all its sons to Gómez, who has no time to train these many insurgents; they are joining and training as they go. All the tobacco plantations of *Vuelta Abajo*, formerly in the hands of Spanish farmers, are now empty fields. Cuba no longer has an export economy. Since

Peralejo, Oriente is ours and now supports the war in other parts of the island.»

The situation inside the Cuban army, however, was not as glowing for the Cubans as those letters and communiqués would indicate. The eternal conflict of civil-military authority in the Cuban command was still unresolved. It had already caused three mayor misfortunes: the deposition of Carlos Manuel de Céspedes at Bijagual in 1873, his probable demise at San Lorenzo in 1874 and the conflict between Martí and Maceo at Madame Griffon's Hotel in 1884. As late as November 21st, 1895, with Martí already dead, a man of unquestionable patriotism and generosity as Antonio Maceo had written to Manuel Sanguily:

«We have not been very fortunate in the make-up of the new government; we are the victims of the vain effort of some who are trying to give a democratic form of government to a republic not already constituted. They ignore we have the enemy in front of us, and we are not the masters of the land we walk on.»

Meanwhile, the exiles in New York had turned more and more optimistic about the outcome of the war. Sugar and tobacco in Cuba were at their lowest prices in years since they could not be reliably exported. Taxes in Cuba were at their highest. Even the loyal Spaniards in Cuba were favoring a change in government or status.

Weyler was so discouraged by these news that he took refuge in the Captain General's palace in Havana and did not show up in public for almost a week. Rumor was that he was most of the time in his bathroom, submerged in the luxurious Roman-style marble bathtub that every other Captain General had enjoyed as one of the perks that Spain granted its noblemen for being so far from the Spanish shores. He was obsessed by the knowledge that his opponents were nothing but agile free-lancers who practiced hit-and-run tactics and lived off the land, blending in with the non-combatant population. He had come to the conclusion that to defeat the Cuban army and pacify the island, Spain would have to separate the insurgents from the non-combatant civilians. He could only accomplish that by emptying the rural towns and setting safe havens where the later would be *"protected"* by loyal Spanish troops. Moreover, this would prevent civilians from giving any kind of help to the enemy soldiers. And that, rather than any humanitarian concern, soon became the top item in his strategies and agenda: a concentration of all civilians into towns or fenced-in camps across the entire island. This Weyler solution was to be a novel Spanish invention that would be forever condemned by the civilized world: *the concentration camp.*

Days later, a letter from Bartolomé Masó was in Gonzalo de Quesada's hands:

«We have moved our revolutionary government from the southern part of the *Sierra Maestra*, in the area between Santiago and Manzanillo, first to Las Tunas and now to the Sierra de Cubitas, in the province of Camagüey, halfway between the city of Camagüey and the north coast. We are now manufacturing dynamite, machetes, uniforms and boots and we have just sent to our troops an experimental dynamite gun. We have our own printing facilities and equipment; we continue to pack dry meat and baked *galletas*; our operations have all the appearance and looks of an industrial camp or a self-sufficient Coop. Our island-wide mail system gets letters faster to their destinations that the Spanish mails, for almost the same price; we are training rural guards to get rid of contraband and illegal profiteering everywhere. The only insecure, dishonest and deceitful operations left in Cuba are those under the control of the Spanish government.»

Gonzalo de Quesada made sure a copy of this letter was posted on the front door of the offices of *Patria* in Manhattan.

Inspired by Martí's and the Maceos' sacrifice, Máximo Gómez, Serafín Sánchez, Mayía Rodríguez, José Lacret, Bartolomé Masó and others joined their forces to score against Spain a final blow. They counted with 20,000 men who were gathered in southern Las Villas. Gómez remained in Santa Clara where Spain had only a faint hold in Cienfuegos; two columns under Lacret were assigned to take Remedios. A general movement towards the west was initiated, following the path once taken by José Maceo. Enrique Collazo and Calixto García were called from Oriente and Camagüey to contribute to the assault on the west with 25,000 troops.

Calixto García in particular was already 57 years old but he was as sharp as the day he had joined Donato Mármol at Santa Rita and Baire during the Ten Year War. He was still inspired by the same sentiments that he had at San Antonio de Baja, in Oriente, during 1871, at age 32, when after swearing never to fall in the hands of Spain he found himself surrounded and placed the muzzle of his pistol beneath his chin and fired. A scar in the centre of his forehead marked in his face the path of the bullet: across the tongue, through the roof of his mouth, behind his nose, up the frontal sinuses and out his forefront. Mockingly he would always tell his friends «*so much trouble to end up exiled in 1881 in Madrid working as a bank clerk.*» By 1896 he was landing at Baracoa, his soul consumed by a third attempt to free Cuba from its colonial chains.

Across the world, people were reading about events that were impacting the struggles in Cuba.

During January of 1897, Carlos García Vélez, son of Calixto, blew up the Spanish gunboat *Relámpago* out of the Cauto River, as reported by The New York Times on January 18, 1897; in Guanabacoa a train full of Spanish troops was derailed by a Cuban guerrilla; the *Dauntless* continued to disembark troops and war materials in Cuba, this time in Pinar del Rio.

On February 20, General Valeriano Weyler moved 20,000 troops to Las Villas in an attempt to bring to an end the threat of Máximo Gómez. Gómez eluded Weyler's battalion, leading Weyler to conclude there were no Cuban troops in the area.

On March 18, the steamer *Laurada* completed its 4th successful trip to Cuba with men and supplies, landing in *El Esterón de Júcaro*, in Banes. Carlos Roloff and Joaquín Castillo Duany were part of the expedition.

On March 28, General Juan Rius Rivera, Maceo's successor as Commander in Chief of western Cuba, was made prisoner at a combat in *Cabezadas*, Pinar del Rio, with 250 of his men. He was gravely injured and interned at hospital *San Ambrosio* in Havana. Later, he was deported to the Montjuïc Prison in Barcelona, Spain, where he remained until the end of the war

General Weyler notified Madrid on April 29 that only 1,100 rebels were left in Cuba and he did not need additional reinforcements.

In June, former General Steward Lyndon Woodford became the new US ambassador to Spain. President McKinley notified Spanish ambassador Dupuy de Lôme that US patience had reached its end, warning Madrid to replace Weyler and grant independence to Cuba. Weyler's troops began a policy of total destruction in Oriente. In Havana a military train was destroyed as the bridge over the San Miguel River was dynamited under it by troops led by Colonel Néstor Aranguren. Santa María del Rosario, in El Cotorro, Havana, fell in the hands of the rebels. The Spanish offensive had lost its momentum.

On August 8, Spanish President Cánovas del Castillo was murdered by an anarchist in Guipúzcoa, Spain. Práxedes Mateo Sagasta replaced him on October 4, 1897.

On August 28, Calixto Garcia's troops took the city of Las Tunas in Oriente. The city had been taken five times in two wars by Cuban troops; it had been baptized *Victoria de las Tunas* in 1869 when the Spanish army recovered it after one of these occupations by the Cuban armies.

On October 29, Cuban delegates met in Guáimaro, Camagüey, and adopted the new Constitution of *La Yaya*, two years after the Constitution de Jimaguayú, as prescribed by law. Bartolomé Masó was elected head of the government; Domingo Méndez Capote as Vice-President.

Spain replaced Weyler with Ramón Blanco Erenas on October 31, 1897, and sent 300,000 additional troops and a promise of autonomy for Cuba and Puerto Rico. Blanco Erenas abolished Weyler's concentration order. Máximo Gómez respondió on November 13th, with a *Bando* promulgating the death penalty to any official from the Cuban army trying to accept the offer of autonomy.

In the last days of 1897, Calixto García took the town of Guisa in Oriente; Estrada Palma and Bartolomé Masó, recognizing that the war had reached an impasse, discussed the possibility of making an offer of US 150 million to Spain for the independence of Cuba; Fitzhugh Lee, US consul in Havana, rendered a report to US President McKinley stating that over 50,000 civilians had died of starvation during Weyler's concentration; the report prompted a gathering of *Voluntarios* in front of *Diario de la Marina*, in Havana, defending Weyler and accusing the newspaper of betraying Spain. Máximo Gómez received several conciliatory visits at his headquarters.

On December 31, 1897, the New York newspaper *The World* published an account of Máximo Gómez applying the *Principio de Spotorno*: [344]

«General Headquarters of the Army of Cuba. The chiefs, officials and soldiers of the Cuban Army, to Spanish public opinion and to the Spanish press: a decision of ours has recently stirred very profoundly the people of Spain. An officer of the Spanish Army, Lieutenant Colonel Joaquín Ruiz, attired in military uniform, and ostentatiously wearing the insignia of Field Adjutant to the General-in-Chief of the Spanish Army, penetrated our lines intending to induce a colonel of the Cuban Army, Nestor Aranguren, to commit treason. He was shot in accordance with a sentence pronounced in strict compliance with orders expressly promulgated for such cases. He had forgotten his duties as a soldier and assumed the sad and shameful mission of persuading another soldier to betray his country and his flag.»

---

[344] Decree approved during the Ten Year War, punishing any person, Spanish or Cuban, making overtures of peace, not based on the independence of Cuba and the abolition of slavery, to be sentenced to death.

Images, top to bottom, left to right:

Dr. Joaquín Castillo Duany (1858-1902), physician, graduate of the University of Pennsylvania, fought in Cuba under Antonio Maceo;

Domingo Méndez Capote (1863-1934), lawyer and professor of law, fought under Máximo Gómez, member of ther 1901 Constitutional Convention;

General **Carlos Roloff** (1842-1907), fought in the 3 wars of independence;

a medal commemorating the birth of General **Bartolomé Masó**;

General **José Lacret Morlot** (1848-1904), fought all 3 wars of independence;

General **Nestor Aranguren** (1873-1898), head of the Havana Cavalry Regiment;

Horatio Rubens (1869-1941), US-born lawyer of the Cuban Independence Army;

Brigadier General **Carlos García Vélez** (1867-1963), son of Calixto García.

Images, top to bottom, left to right:

A rare photo of young General **Calixto García** during the Ten Year War of 1868-1878, before his capture and attempted suicide;

Brigadier **Juan Rius Rivera** (1848-1924), seated and Colonel **Bartolomé Masó** in a 1878 picture at an encampment in Oriente;

the US newspaper *The World* with an account of the **Principio de Spotorno** applied by General Máximo Gómez in 1897 in the case of Spanish Army Lieutenant Colonel Joaquín Ruiz.

Images, top to bottom, left to right:

The city of **Cienfuegos** during the 1895 Cuban War of Independence;
a 1896 contemporary map of the theater of war in the province of **Las Villas**;
a 1897 view of **Havana** from the hills around La Cabaña fortress.

Images, top to bottom, left to right:

a 1898 US newspaper account of the **concentration camps** in Cuba;

a contemporary drawing of **Spanish troops leading Cuban peasants** into concentration camps;

the account of the **recall of Valeriano Weyler** by Madrid, as presented on July 2, 1897 by the newspaper *Ann Arbor Argus* in Michigan.

Images, top to bottom, left to right:

General **Arsenio Martínez Campos** (1831-1900), refused to set ethnic cleansing in Cuba and could not repeat in 1895 his pacification process of 1878. He was replaced by Valeriano Weyler in 1896;

Fermín Valdés Domínguez (1852-1910), José Martí's best friend. He was a surgeon and served as a Colonel in the 1895 War;

Enrique Dupuy de Lôme (1816-1885), Spanish diplomat, best known for his letter criticizing US President McKinley, published by the *New York Journal* on February 9, 1898;

Gonzalo de Quesada (center, 1868-1915), disciple of José Martí and a key architect of Cuba's independence;

General Stewart Woodford (1835-1913), appointed by President McKinley ambassador to Spain during the war of 1898;

Ramón Blanco Erenas, (Marqués de Peña Plata, 1833-1906), Captain General of Cuba during the 1879 Little War.

THE THREE FRIENDS READY

TO TAKE ANOTHER FILIBUSTER-ING EXPEDITION TO CUBA.

Bonds Have Been Given in the Libel Proceeding, So that She May Sail at Any Time—Her Previous Trips.

JACKSONVILLE, Fla., Dec. 5.—The Three Friends and three revenue cutters are lying in the river. An evaporator has been put into the little steamer so that fresh water may be made at sea. She has thirty-days' coal capacity, and when equipped with the evaporator can stay in the open sea or lie among the Florida reefs for a month at a time.

The crew of twenty-two men, most of whom are ashore, rendezvous nightly at Bettilini's, an all-night restaurant and barroom, within a block of the river front. They wait there for word to go aboard. Charles Silver, pilot, of Key West, who knows the reefs that for a hundred miles by forty are sown off the southern tip of Florida, and Santos, pilot, of Havana, who knows the Cuban coast, both of whom are members of the crew, lodge in the neighborhood. John Daly, an Irishman, who is the engineer, sleeps aboard.

The libel proceeding brought by the Collector of Customs on behalf of the United States, will, it is understood, not interfere with The Three Friends sailing at the proper time, as bonds have been given. The owners, Napoleon Bonaparte Broward, Montcalm Broward, and Amanda Barrs, have contracted with the Cuban Junta in New York to land three more cargoes of fighting material, and then they propose to go out of the perilous business.

The Skipper of the Steamer.

Images, top to bottom, left to right:

The Three Friends, famous tugboat built in 1896. It made several expeditionary trips to Cuba with men and war materials;

the **staff of Bartolomé Masó** during the 1895 war;

a Spanish small fort along the **Trocha Júcaro-Morón**;

The Three Friends in 1897 at its regular base in **Jacksonville**.

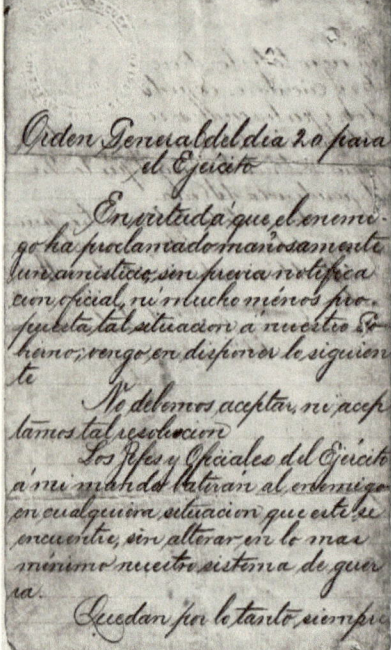

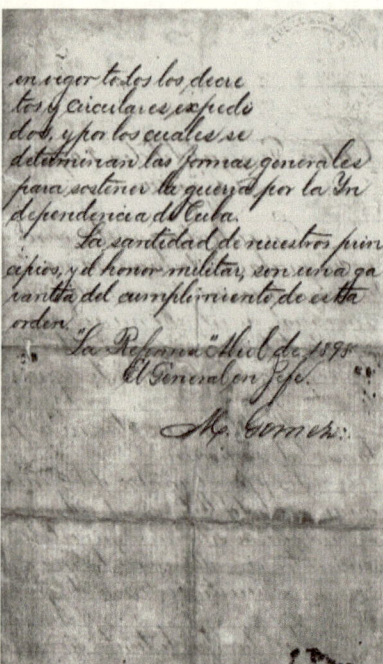

Images above:

The document emitted, signed and sealed by Máximo Gómez alerting Cubans in the Independence Army not to accept recent **offers of amnesty** issued by the Spanish government in April of 1898.

THE BLIND LEADING THE BLIND

Images above:
Three popular contemporary cartoons during the War of 1895:

Published in the US, Uncle Sam watching developments in Europe to ensure no interference with the war in Cuba;

Published in Spain, a view of the true intentions of the US with respect to Cuba;

Published in the US, Weyler, one of the harshest Spanish Captain Generals in Cuba, leading a blind Spain into the abyss;

On Sunday, January 24, 1897, side by side with the news from the war of independence and current events in the city, Havana newspapers commented on an incredible invention: **movie films**. No one imagined then that a new art had been born that day.

The previous day, Saturday January 23, 1897, French photographer Gabriel Veyre had shared an evening with a group of journalists and artists in the *Lumiere Cinematograph*, a venue presenting a photographic device that captured and reproduced movements.

The next day *Havana News* reported the event in these terms: «Last night the *Lumiere Cinematograph* opened in Central Park, next to the *Teatro Tacon*. The Director of this wonderful device has been kind enough to devote the opening night to the press, sending invitations to different newspapers published in the city. Last night the *Lumiere* people exhibited beautiful views in motion to a privileged group of 35 city journalists. Together we saw *The Parade of a Squadron of Cavalrymen*, *The Tempest at Sea*, *A Runaway Train*, *La Puerta del Sol de Madrid* and *The arrival of the Czar to Paris*. These functions were presented in batches of half hour from 6:30 pm to 11:30 pm.»

The *Diario de la Marina* wrote: «In the vicinity of Central Park the public have been able to see at the *Lumiere Cinematograph*, the wonders of the *Kinetoscope*, presenting an extraordinary fashion show. Gabriel Veyre came here from Mexico with the famous and universally acclaimed *Cinematographer*. There it won applause and earned good money. The *Cinematographer* was a favorite show at the Mexican Capital, and it will also be successful among us. It won prizes at the *Imperial Exhibition*; it is a remarkable invention that produces all the charms of an illusion that is felt or a chimera that happens in front of your eyes. The *Kinetoscope* was invented by Thomas A. Edison a few years before, but could only be seen individually and through binoculars; this is a general public spectacle.»

Cuban *empresarios* could not wait to make films of their own. On Friday February 12th, 1897, a mere two weeks later, *Lumiere Cinematograph* released the first Cuban film called *Simulacro de Incendio* (Fire Drill) to an amazed and applauding public.

The film studio was located on *Paseo del Prado*, southeast of Central Park, in the corner of *Prado* and *San José* streets, next to the San Jose Fire Department; there, Veyre photographed this first Cuban film, inside a building marked with the number 126. It was designed, produced, processed and released by Cuban aficionados. Actress *Maria Tubau*, a star at the Tacón, had proposed the theme to Veyre. There were no other places in the world where, in less than 15 days, artists and cinematographers had contributed to the emergence of an international film industry.

1897 *Simulacro de Incendio*, the First Cuban-Made Film

36

The Impasse in the War Cannot be Resolved

THE SITUATION IN CUBA at the end of 1897 was clear: east of the *trocha Júcaro-Morón*, all through Camagüey and Oriente, Cuba was free. It took Calixto García a minimal effort to keep the Spanish troops inside the cities and out of open spaces. No convoys bringing relief to the Spanish troops were allowed to get close to any city. Cuban troops had captured gunboats three times on the *Cauto River* and sunk them with torpedoes. Gómez was keeping Weyler former troops close to Santa Clara, with no will to come into the open. According to the *London Times*,

«Spain would need £100,000,000 over the next year and would have to bring their own food from the peninsula. Madrid has had to sell to a British firm their monopoly rights to tobacco and salt from Cuba. It was the only way to pay for their war expenses in the island. Once these moneys are gone they would not know what else they will have to sell.»

The *London Times* predicted a Cuban republican government in Havana in about eighteen months.

The New York Times was equally pessimistic about the future of a Spanish Cuba:

«The only Spanish military operations these days are the forwarding of weekly convoys between Bayamo, Jiguaní, Santiago, Las Tunas and Holguín. Each day these tasks become more and more difficult for Spain, in spite of the heavy guards. The convoys carry ammunitions, clothing and *"herméticas."* [345] Almost every convoy in the last two months has been captured by Cuban troops; right now they have almost no shortages of food or weapons. Many homesteads are de-

---

[345] Literally "air-tights," the containers preserving all sorts of canned foods like evaporated milk, sausages, fish, sweetened fruits, grains and soups.

serted in the country side; the families that owned them, rich and poor, have fled to the towns. The doors are almost always wide open and tall flowers bloom against their chalk-white walls. It seems the buildings are respected and not vandalized.»

For almost a year now, General Emilio Núñez and Horatio S. Rubens had sat down periodically to coordinate their operations to keep supplies reaching Cuba regularly, minimizing legal problems and losses due to interceptions. They often felt Cuba was collapsing into chaos and with the land having been laid to waste, an American involvement was almost inevitable. Nuñez in particular felt that all the efforts of Martí to keep the war exclusively Cuban were collapsing. He felt they were running the risk of never being able to recover the control of their destiny, in spite of the Spanish enemy being crushed and in total retreat.

Until early in 1898, however, it seemed that the war would not last more than a few more months. Máximo Gómez, who never liked to put a time table on things, was often talking of reaching victory by the end of the year. He used to say that summer months were his best generals, meaning they were his most successful times to fight. On a letter to Nuñez he had written:

«June is almost here and the Spanish troops are hiding in their barracks. Yet the savagery of Weyler has turned into an obsessive smoldering issue for the American public opinion. The Americans are demanding intervention and we cannot finish out the Spanish troops because they would not take to the open to fight us. We cannot take each city separately either; it would be a long, protracted and very expensive war in men and funds.»

The Cubans' worst fears would soon be confirmed.

On the early morning hours of February 15, 1898, the United States battleship *Maine* was wandering lazily around its mooring in the bay of Havana. It was a cool and moonless night and occasional lights were coming from her open portholes and the bridge lazily reflected on the water surface. At his desk in the Captain's quarters, Charles D. Sigsbee was entering items in his personal diary and record book:

«General Ramón Blanco, the new Captain General of the island seems to have things under control. He looks like a well behaved gentleman and I got along fine with him and his wife. For the last three weeks I have not received any worthy news about the rebels. Last night I entertained several Spanish officers aboard to reciprocate the invitation I got to attend a bullfighting session. We had a good time until the first bullfighter was about to strike the bull dead, at which point I stood up with my men to leave the somewhat barbaric function. Several men on my left side stood up too and began to scream to us: *"No se vayan Maricones,"* at which point my hosts began to apologize for the crude remarks of these men. I just spoke in the afternoon with Fitzhugh Lee, the American consul, and he also seems optimistic. I did not know he was the nephew of our Robert E. Lee and he had fought us under him as commander of a cavalry division. I have just heard taps five minutes ago. In the quietness of the night this beautiful and crisp sound must have traveled very far into the city, which a few minutes ago ended officially the day with the grave sounding blast of the *cañonazo de las nueve*....» [346]

The note-taking by Sigsbee ended cruelly with this last sentence. An unexpected and devastating explosion made the *Maine* tremble from stern to bow, weaving a threat of desolation and a deafening roar of immense volume into the hearts of every navy man on board. No one was expecting that in such a quiet night, this metallic shriek from the battleship was to awake and ravage most of its crew and startle every citizen of the Cuban capital. Sigsbee knew it immediately: the *Maine* had been blown out of the water and was sinking fast. He took to the aft section and quickly assessed the seriousness of the situation. The front of the ship, where most of his men had their quarters, was already under water. Within minutes some lifeboats from the *Alfonso XII*, the largest Spanish ship inside the harbor, were in the waters near the *Maine* trying to rescue survivors. Captain Sigsbee could not but recognize their gallantry and heroism. The initial explosion was being followed by many small ones during the entire night and the whole city seemed to be under a spot light of flames and conflagration. In the morning, a twisted wreckage of rails, masts, glass windows, plates,

---

[346] The *cañonazo* was a traditional XVIII century warning that the gates on the city walls were about to close, leaving all those who had not entered the city at the mercy of pirates and criminals outside the protection of the walls.

floor, bridge and chimney sections, funnels, portholes, cannons and human bodies was all that was left of the largest ship that had ever entered the port of Havana.[347] Over the next few days, the Spanish authorities spared no effort to help the survivors and determined that an internal accident had caused the disaster. On 25 February, Assistant Secretary of State Theodore Roosevelt issued orders placing the navy on full alert. If the US could not permit Spain to transfer sovereignty over Cuba to another power, neither could they allow Spain to cede sovereignty to Cubans.

Days later, in New York, William Randolph Hearst's *New York Journal* had no doubts about who sank the *Maine*. It even showed a sketch of a Spanish saboteur fastening an underwater mine to the bottom of the *Maine* with a wire leading to shore where a man was ready to activate a detonator. Assistant Secretary of the Navy Theodore Roosevelt declared:

«I cannot understand how the bulk of our people can be asked to tolerate the hideous infamy that has attended the two last years of Spanish rule in Cuba, as well as the treacherous destruction of the *Maine* and the murder of over 200 of our men; I feel so deeply that it is with great effort that I can refrain myself.»

After the Maine incident, there was no power on earth that could have prevented the United States to go to war with Spain. The entire country was thrilling with war fever. Over 250,000 soldiers began to rush enthusiastically into service in the US Army. Soldiers began to gather in Florida waiting for supplies and transportation. Large and small towns were organizing and outfitting regiments of their own. Some politicians, like Teddy Roosevelt, Assistant Secretary of the Navy, were resigning their post and forming volunteer regiments of cavalry. Everyone was ready for a punishing war.

---

[347] The explosion of the warship *Maine* took the life of 2 officers and 266 US Marines. On February 17, two days after the incident, the Spanish warship *Vizcaya* arrived in New York harbor, as part of the protocol for which the Maine had gone to the port of Havana. There were no incidents in New York.

President McKinley began to feel pressure from all fronts. William Randolph Hearst, who had converted his father's respectable San Francisco paper into a sleazy but profitable tabloid, the *New York Journal*, was joined on the Maine affair by Joseph Pulitzer's *New York World*. Both papers were now dominated by sensationalism, weaving in and out of the gray area between truth and fantasy. They wanted a war and were determined to get it in Cuba. There would be no low to which they would not stoop. Senator George Norris of Nebraska, the best speaker in Congress these days, went on record saying that the style of the Hearst and Pulitzer newspapers was spreading

«like a venomous web all across the US. They've become the sewer system of American journalism.»

To further complicate things, Enrique Dupuy de Lôme, the Spanish minister to Washington, wrote a scandalous letter to José Canalejas, Spain's Foreign Minister.[348] It was printed in the *New York Journal* on Feb 9th. It had a sentence that made McKinley furious and resulted in Dupuy losing his job:

«McKinley is a weak man and a bidder for the admiration of the crowds, besides being a pandering politician (*politicastro*) who tried to leave the door open behind himself while keeping on good terms with the jingoes of his party.»

A further pressure on McKinley were the *jingoes*, those advocates of the Manifest Destiny, dressed up in the language of Social Darwinism; they were led by two powerful leaders, Theodore Roosevelt, McKinley's assistant secretary of the Navy and Massachusetts Senator Henry Cabot Lodge, always a seeker of a more aggressive belligerent foreign policy. They had become the defenders of the US virility, believing that superior civilizations had to keep their inferiors under control, thereby

---

[348] The letter was intercepted by a Cuban expatriate working in the Spanish mission in New York, who mailed it to Gonzalo de Quesada, who in turn made it available to Hearst's *New York Journal*.

improving the human race.³⁴⁹

On July 1, 1989, 15,000 American soldiers were ready at Tampa, Florida to embark towards Cuba. Much faster and eager than the official American troops, Theodore Roosevelt's volunteers, the *Rough Riders*, all dressed in custom-made Brooks Brothers uniforms, were ready to fight Spanish troops in Cuba. The American army war strategies were designed by Calixto García, a Cuban General that knew and controlled the entire region of Oriente and was hoping the American troops would fight alongside his men.

As a Spanish-Cuban-American war was closing in, other news were making the papers.

During the last days in February of 1898, the Cuban expeditionary ship *Dauntless* landed in Matanzas and Nuevitas, Camagüey, with weapons and soldiers. In New York, the newspaper *Patria* reported they were trips numbers 33 and 34 since 1895. In Havana pro-Spanish elements launched violent demonstrations against General Blanco and Cuban autonomy. Holding undisputed control over the Cuban countryside, the insurgent army command began to prepare for the final phase of the insurrection: the assault on the cities.

On March 4, the Spanish government began to assemble a transatlantic fleet that would sail to Cuba with reinforcements. Spain asked the US government to replace consul general Fitzhugh Lee because of his bellicose attitude towards Spain. The US government ignored the petition and approved a $50 million credit towards defense.

On March 14th, President McKinley offered Spain to purchase Cuba for US$ 300 million. Spain rejected the offer. US

---

[349] The term *jingoes*, meaning chauvinistic patriots, was applied to Americans who immoderately supported their country, right or wrong, even in belligerent terms. Originally, it was used as an exclamation, *By Jingo!* It originated in Britain during the war of 1870 against Russia. Presumably it was used to avoid saying *By Jesus!*, which was considered a profanity. The term became popular during the Spanish-Cuban-American War on 1898.

ambassador to Spain Stewart Woodford was declared *persona non grata* and expelled from Spain.,

On March 20, Captain General Ramón Blanco contacted General Máximo Gómez asking him to join forces with Spain to fight an invading American army trying to occupy the island. Máximo Gómez rejected the proposal as an insolent pretension on the part of Spain.

Before the end of March, the US sent a report on the Maine incident to the Madrid government, accusing it of blowing up the warship. Washington recalled consul Fitzhugh Lee. The Spanish government ordered the naval force in Cádiz to set sail towards Cuba.

On April 15, Admiral Manuel Cervera, commander of the Spanish fleet that had been assembled at Cádiz, arrived surreptitiously at San Vicente, Cabo Verde to load coal and continue towards Cuba.

General Calixto García, on April 18th, accepted to be liaison with the soon-to-disembark American troops, asking all Cuban insurgents to support the Americans. The following day the US Congress proclaimed a Joint Resolution: "*Cuba es y de hecho debe ser libre e independiente,*" adding that the US did not have the intention or the desire to exert dominion or sovereignty in Cuba.[350] President McKinley issued a proclamation calling for 200,000 volunteers to join the US armed forces.

On April 22nd, a US fleet left Key West to establish a blockade to the ports of Matanzas, Havana and Cienfuegos in Cuba. In the war front, Calixto García took Bayamo and the Spanish government firmed up its positions in Santiago de Cuba. On 23 April the Spanish light gunboat *Ligera* successfully attacked and immobilized the US warship *Foote* in Cárdenas, the first engagement of the war. Admiral William Thomas Sampson,

---

[350] On 21 April the US presented an ultimatum to Spain. Spain declared war against the US on 23 April. The US declared war on Spain, retroactive to 21 April. The existence of a Cuban rebel government was totally ignored by both powers.

commander of the US naval operations in Cuba, ordered his ships blockading Matanzas and Cienfuegos to open fire on the defenses of the cities.

A week later Admiral Cervera departed from Cabo Verde towards Cuba. He told his officers: *"Vamos a un sacrificio tan estéril como inútil."*

On May 1st, Lieutenant Andrew S. Rowan, following orders from President McKinley, arrived in Cuba to meet Calixto García.[351] García responded to McKinley's message sending General Enrique Collazo to visit the president in Washington. A second visit went on May 17th, this time presided by Domingo Méndez Capote and with instructions to coordinate war details.

US troops twice tried unsuccessfully to disembark in Pinar del Rio on April 30 and May 4. American ships bombarded Matanzas on April 27 and Cárdenas on May 11. On May 13th, Spanish warships in Havana exited the harbor, trying to penetrate the US blockade. They had to retreat back to port. On May 18th the Spanish batteries of *El Morro* and *La Socapa* in Santiago de Cuba exchanged fire with US ships blockading the port. On June 10, US marines landed in Guantánamo and made camp.

Days earlier, on May 19th, the Spanish fleet of Admiral Cervera had entered the port of Santiago de Cuba. It consisted of battleships *Infanta María Teresa* (with Cervera on board), *Admirante Oquendo*, *Cristobal Colón* and *Vizcaya*, with destroyers *Furor*, *Terror* and *Plutón*. None of the ships were in top shape.

---

[351] The meeting was immortalized in the worldwide known bestseller *"A Message to García."*

Images, top to bottom, left to right:

The arrival of **Captain General Blanco** (circled) to Havana in 1896;

The expedition steamboats **Dauntess** (left) and **Three Friends** (right), carriers of countless trips to take soldiers and armaments to the rebels in Cuba.

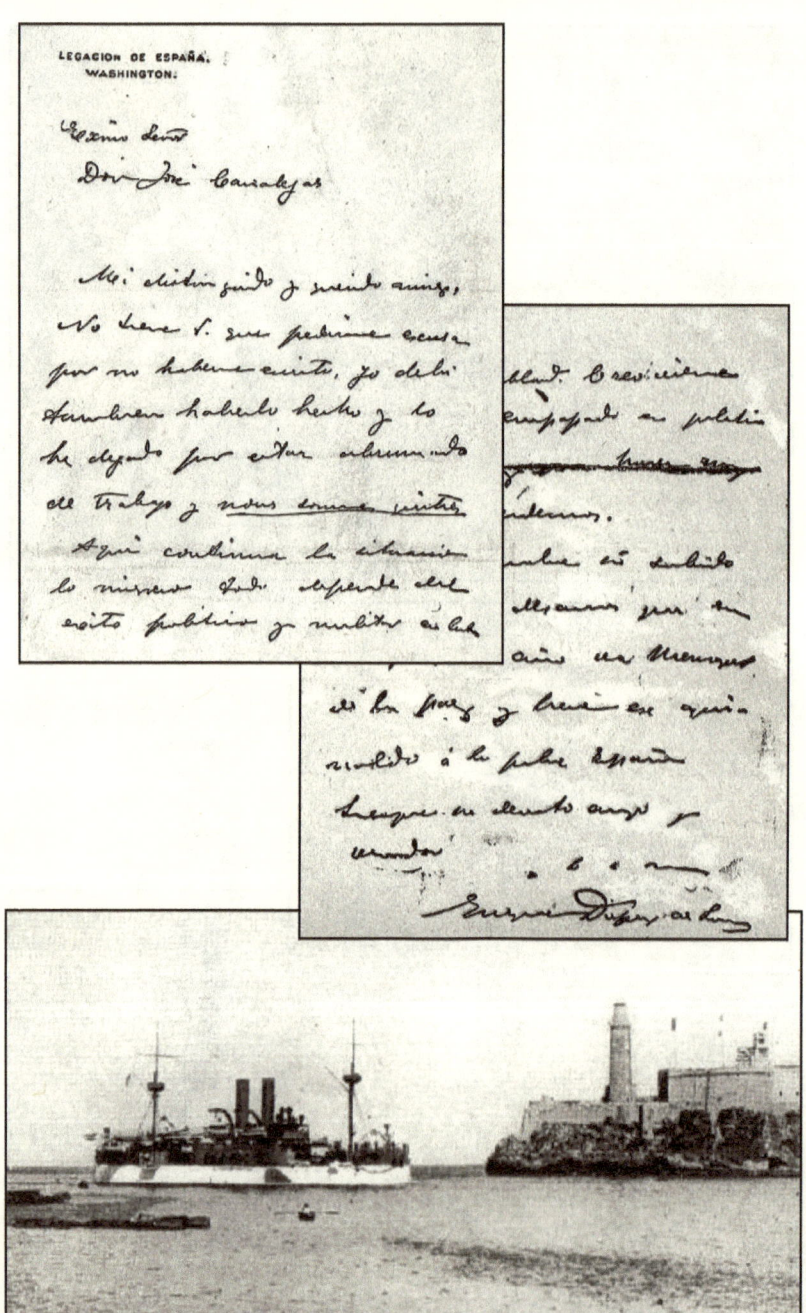

Images, top to bottom:

First and last pages of the **Dupuy de Lôme letter** to Madrid in 1898;
The **Battleship Maine** entering the port of Havana in February 1898.

Images, top to bottom, left to right:

Crew men abord the **Maine battleship** before it was blown in the port of Havana in 1898;

Pulitzer's **New York World** and Hearst's **New York Journal** front pages reporting the Maine incident;

the 1898 **burial procession** of the US Maine casualties in Havana.

Images, top to bottom:

The **New York Journal** account of having sent journalists to Cuba in 1898;

the **El Morro** fortress, at the eastern side of Santiago de Cuba's bay entrance;

the **12 Apostles battery** at La Cabaña, the main defense of Havana bay in 1898.

Images, top to bottom:
US troops ready to embark in the **port of Tampa** in March of 1898;
a Spanish convoy crossing **River Cauto** in Oriente;
the **Cervera squadron** leaving Cabo Verde for Cuba on April 30, 1898.

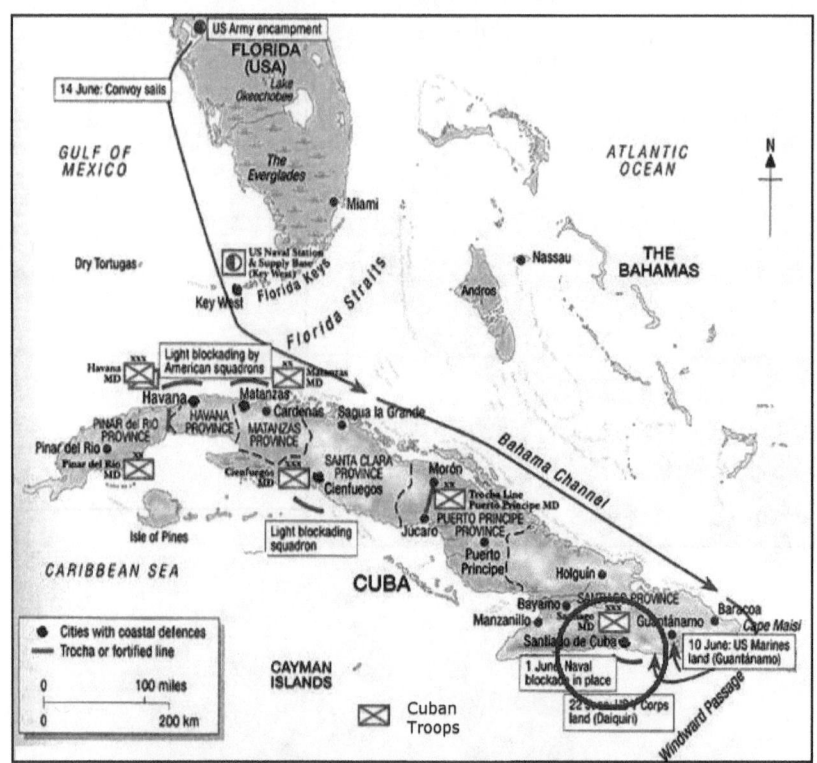

Images, top to bottom:

The **path of the US fleet** under Admiral Sampson as it approached Cuba in 1898;

Spanish soldiers in eastern Cuba in 1898.

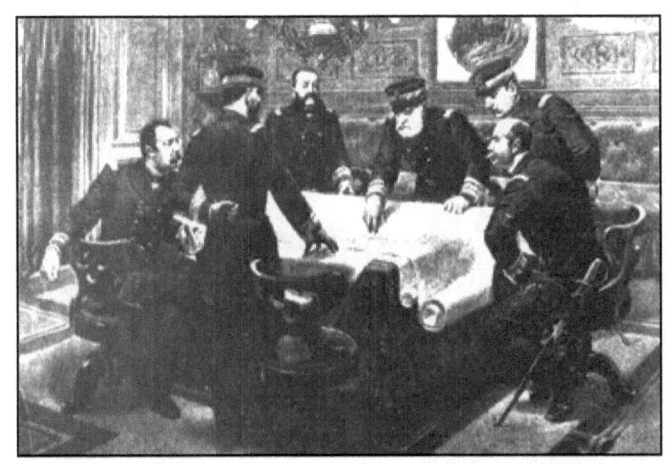

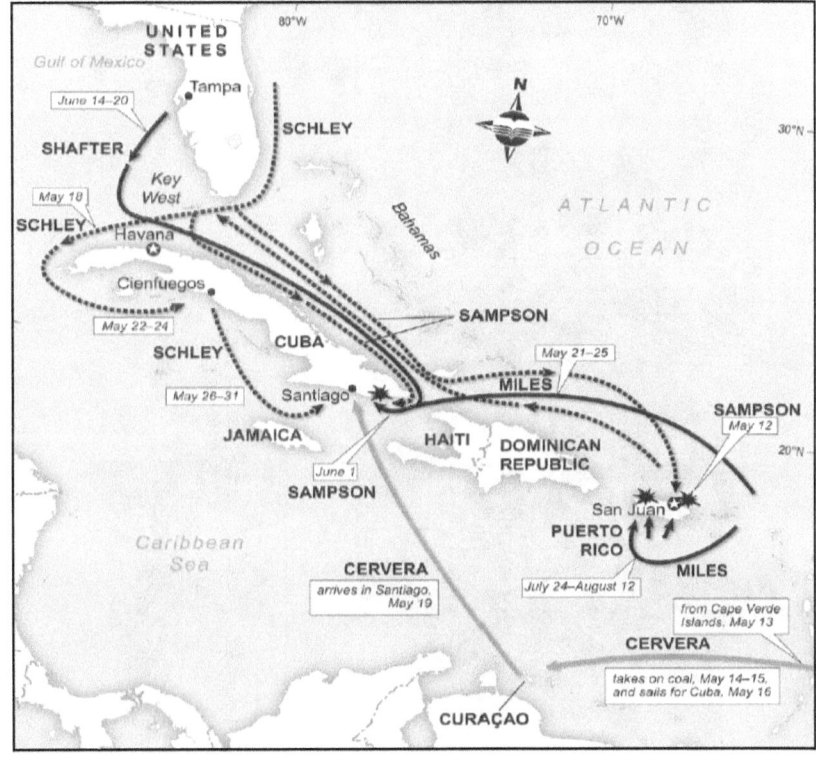

Images, top to bottom:

Spanish Admiral Cervera meeting with his staff aboard the battleship *Infanta Maria Teresa* a few days before entering Santiago de Cuba's harbor;

the movements of **US Admiral Sampson's fleet** and **Spain Admiral Cervera** as they approached each other for the main naval battle of the the 1898 Hispano-Cuban-American War at Santiago de Cuba.

Images, top to bottom, left to right:
a cartoon showing the **European view of the US Monroe Doctrine**;
anti-Spanish propaganda in the US in 1898;
a cartoon showing **US Admiral Sampson waiting for Cervera's fleet** outside Santiago de Cuba harbor.

Ricardo del Monte, pioneer of the press in Cuba.

At the time of the 1895 War of Independence there were more than 100 newspapers in Cuba; some dailies, others weeklies. Most of the papers in the provinces based their news and articles on the Havana newspapers, of which there were about a dozen important ones:

El Triunfo was the official organ of the autonomist party. It was edited by Ricardo del Monte, Domingo del Monte's nephew, and published articles and essays by notable intellectuals like Rafael Montoro, Antonio Govin and Enrique José Varona.

El Diario de la Marina was the paper of the Spanish liberals, mostly inspired by law and order principles. Its founder was Nicolás Rivero; its roots went back to 1813 with *El Lucero de la Habana* and *El Noticioso Mercantil*. It had the highest circulation in Cuba.

La Lucha, an evening liberal paper, was the best source of important news and had a large daily section published in English. Its circulation was undisclosed and its articles generaly supported the principles of Cuban independence.

La Discusión was a more radical pro-independence newspaper. It had many articles by Julio Sanguily and Juan Gualberto Gómez. Its editor was Manuel Coronado.

La Nación was published by Enrique Collazo and was the official paper of the *Union Democratic Party*; Rafael Montoro, Mayía Rodríguez and Calixto García Velez where frequent writers. The paper presented a conservative viewpoint and its readership included some of the wealthiest and best educated men in Cuba, most former Cuban *autonomistas* and *anexionistas* turned pro-independence, as well as many Spaniards in the island.

El Figaro was a weekly illustrated newspaper, edited by Manuel Pichardo.

The Havana Post was the English newspaper, powerfully pro-American, of course.

The Cuban Financeer and Havana Advertiser was a paper tailored to the needs of tourists and newcomers; a companion to *The Cuba Immigrant*, published by the same owners.

Other specialized papers of smaller circulation included *La Patria*, *El Cubano*, *The Commercial Journal*, *El Comercio* and *Avisador Comercial*.

The Press in Colonial Cuba

37
At the End, Credit to Win the War Went to the US

THE DAY AFTER CERVERA entered the bay of Santiago de Cuba, Spain's Queen Regent María Cristina de Austria dressed up the boy-King, Alfonso XIII (Alfonso León Fernando María Jaime Isidro Pascual Antonio de Borbón y Austria-Lorena) in the uniform of Infantry Cadets and showed up at the Senate Chamber door, where they were received by spectators, deputies and senators with feverish enthusiasm. The Queen Regent addressed the crowd with these words:

«The loyalty of our people in Cuba will frustrate forever the hopes of those who, from neighboring shores, have been supplying the rebels with material resources and kept alive the fires of insurrection.»

As these declarations were made, Bartolomé Masó, Calixto García and Máximo Gómez in Cuba had received from Gonzalo de Quesada a long report describing what was then called *The Concert of Europe*, the alliances existing between European powers at the end of the XIX century.

«The great powers of Europe, through extraordinary balancing maneuvers and political acrobatics have set aside their differences and, for the last few years, have been peaceful with each other. Spain, however, has remained in isolation since Europe, for most Europeans, ended at the Pyrenees. Germany, Austria-Hungary and Italy have formed a sort of Triple Alliance, while France and Russia are accommodated in a counterpart, the Dual Alliance. Spain is now appealing to both alliances to pressure the United States to force the Cubans and pro-Cuban Americans to accept Spain's sovereignty and drop all aid and war offensives against Spain in Cuba.»

All along the US east coast, particularly in New York, there were unconfirmed rumors that Cervera's intention was to attack New York instead of sailing towards Cuba. The *Heraldo de Madrid*, on the other hand, repeatedly reported in the first week of May that Cervera's squadron was sailing towards the Philippines to protect the islands from an imminent threat from the American navy. On Oriente's countryside, everyone knew the whereabouts, if not of his mission, of 41-year-old-gringo Andrew Summers Rowan, the man who had met with Calixto García. The *guajiros* had protected him step by step throughout his difficult trek, only knowing that he was "*el delegado Americano.*" In Washington, President McKinley had to turn down a proposal from John D. Long, his impulsive Secretary of the Navy, who wanted to attack and sink the Spanish Squadron in the middle of the Atlantic. In Lisbon, the American fleet deployed there received orders to proceed to Liverpool to escort the brand-new US battleship New Orleans to Santiago de Cuba. In Santiago de Chile, the US battleship *Oregon* had left harbor for a rough passage around Patagonia to meet a US squadron under Commodore Winfield S. Schley. Between the *Flying Squadron* of Schley and the *North Atlantic Squadron* of Sampson, the US was deploying four battleships, four armored cruisers and three gunboats around Santiago de Cuba. The battleships *Massachusetts* and *New York* were blockading any Spanish ships from entering the gulf of Mexico.

Calixto García, a man well versed in the arts of war, very skilled in the use of mobile artillery, controlled the interior of Oriente Province, and prepared the landing places for the U.S. Army near Santiago. Cuban insurgents would attack from the west, northwest and east of Santiago, and the American army would disembark at *Daiquirí*, 18 miles east of Santiago, and from there, move to *Siboney*, 8 miles west, and then proceed towards Santiago. The American army, he foresaw, had to work hard to resolve or compensate for three problems: first, they had no experience or equipment to bring safely so many men and horses to solid ground; they had to disembark 12,000 men, 3,000 animals, artillery and supplies from thirty two transports. It would take 12 hours or more for the landing at a cost of perhaps 100 men killed and some 300 wounded. Second, no one had anticipated that General Shafter weighted over 300 pounds and there was not a winch on board. Third, there were no maps or any knowledge whatsoever of the terrain and vegetation in the areas of *El Caney, Daiquirí, Santiago* or *San Juan*. They would have to depend on ten or more scouts from the Cuban army. [352]

For more than a week Admiral Cervera had been quiet at the end of Santiago harbor, right in front of the city; the entire harbor was planted with submarine mines. The entrance was defended by the Morro Castle, with a commanding position of about 180 feet above sea level. On the same side of the Morro was the *Estrella* battery having a straight field of fire down the harbor. A quarter of a mile north was the *Santa Catalina* battery and 1000 yards north of it, the *Punta Gorda* battery. West of the entrance was the battery of *La Socapa* and two miles further west the *Cabañas* battery. The American warships would not be able to reach Cervera's ships at the end of the harbor if he took the option to defend the city of Santiago from the water front. It was quite common in war conflicts to have the navy assisting an army by bombarding the opposite army's positions. The battle of Santiago, however, would be the first instance in history in which a fleet had to call the army to destroy another fleet.

Cubans had to join forces with the Americans to guarantee a speedy access to the hills surrounding Santiago to neutralize the fire power from the *Morro, Estrella, Santa Catalina, Punta Gorda* and *Cabañas* batteries. At that point Cervera's fleet would have two choices: either remain on site and be decimated by the American and Cuban artillery from the hills or leave the harbor and be decimated by the American ships waiting for them at the harbor entrance. The entire war plan had been con-

---

[352] Cuban Captain Escalante Beatón, an aide-de-camp of General Jesús Rabí, recorded in his memoires:

«One had to have compassion for the poor mules carrying General Shafter around upon listening to their profound anguishing *mujidos* (groans) during their trip downhill because of the cargo with which they were been punished.»

Rabí was a 53 year old black officer, a veteran of the 1868 War who had joined the 1895 war with his black classmate Guillermón Moncada.

ceived by Calixto García and approved by General Shafter for the Army and Admiral Sampson for the Navy.

As US troops were moving towards Santiago, they ran against unexpected problems. At *Las Guásimas* the First United States Volunteer Cavalry of Leonard Wood, Theodore Roosevelt's Rough Riders, and the First and Tenth United States Regular Cavalry, unprepared, faced Spanish troops [353] and were losing heavily. A contingency of Cubans came in to reinforce them. Together, Americans and Cubans, numbering 1,000 men, repelled a 2,000 strong battalion of Spanish soldiers, who then retreated towards Santiago in a westerly direction. It was a not very promising first encounter with Spanish troops.

After the battle, as they would do many times later, the *New York Times* reported:

«The Rough Riders, that extraordinary regiment of college kids, cowboys, amateur athletes, New York policemen, Boston architects, artists, actors, native Americans and impoverished noblemen, has behaved magnificently at *Las Guásimas*, under the direction of our former Vice Secretary of the Navy, who directed his troops by screaming *"Stop swearing and advance!; No vulgar insults, just shoot! Damn it! You bunch of sissies, move faster and shoot the SOBs!"*»

From there on, the war proceeded smoothly. On July 1, 1898, the US troops won the battles of *San Juan* and *El Caney*. [354] General Shafter was unable to direct the course of the battle as any commanding general was expected to do; he had taken his position on a high hill near Santiago to get a good view of the battle fields but, due to fatigue and heat he had to retire to his quarters. On July 2, hundreds of Spanish soldiers began to retreat in panic to Santiago de Cuba. To the dismay of Calixto García, General Shafter ordered a temporary retreat to the east

---

[353] The Spanish troops were hiding inside what Roosevelt —but no one else— called a *chaparral de guásimas (*presumably a *jungle of Guásima Trees; chaparral is* a voice of Mexican lingo not understood by any Cuban).

[354] At the *El Viso* fort in *El Caney*, near Santiago, 520 Spanish soldiers without artillery lost to the invading American troops. The defending Spanish General, Joaquín Vara del Rey (1840-1898), died in the action on 30 June with 350 of his men.

to provide a rest to the American troops. They moved in the direction from which they had come, retiring from the territory they had conquered and moving away from Santiago, the target they had so valiantly approached. Worst of all, Rear Admiral William Sampson, the senior American naval commander in Oriente, had not heard from American Infantry General Shafter after the agreement with Calixto García at *Aserradero*.[355] As things stood, Sampson had to wait until Shafter destroyed the Spanish ships with his land artillery or until Cervera left the harbor to face him at high seas. [356]

Surprisingly, on July 3, Admiral Sampson intercepted a message from Captain General Blanco to Admiral Cervera.

«The glorious Spanish Armada has been designed to fight, not to hide cowardly on a safe port. Get your ships going and come to defend Havana.»

From that moment, General Sampson knew the Spanish ships were going to make a run outside the harbor within the next six hours or so. Indeed, Sampson's lookouts inside Santiago reported that the Spanish fleet was lining up to leave port in a desperate attempt to break through Sampson's blockade and fight their way to Havana through three thousand miles of treacherous waters.

At 11:00 AM, the *María Teresa*, the *Vizcaya*, the *Colón* and the *Oquendo*, accompanied by torpedo boats *Plutón* and *Terror* proceeded at full throttle towards the harbor entrance, each ship like a bull entering a bull-fighting *ruedo* hoping to be spared

---

[355] General Shafter had agreed on 20 June to attack Santiago's fortifications from land, silence the guns and cut the cables that activated the harbor mines, allowing them to be removed. That, according to Calixto García's commentaries to his men, «*le quita las plumas a la gallina para poderle apuntar bien a la pechuga*» (would remove the feathers of the hen to allow a better shoot to its breast.) Shafter's men had fought many bloody battles in *Siboney, Daiquirí, El Caney, San Juan, Kettle Hill* and *El Pozo*.

[356] Shafter did not feel like complying with the agreed plan of his army destroying the forts in Santiago Harbor; it would mean that Sampson would immediately enter the harbor and destroy the Spanish navy, taking the credit for the conquest of Santiago; a credit Shafter felt belonged to his men.

from the matador's spade.[357] Within the next hours, over fifty miles along the eastern side of the southern coast of Oriente was polluted with the debris of Spain's once proud Atlantic fleet; every Spanish ship was bombed, burned and destroyed, with one third of its crew killed. [358] Only Admiral Cervera and 1,200 of his marines survived the suicidal massacre. The Spaniards in the town of Santiago de Cuba now knew they were doomed. On July 4th their armed forces tried to block the entrance to the victorious American vessels but failed. [359]

In Havana Captain General Blanco issued a manifesto stating:

«Fortune does not always favor the brave. Our Spanish squadron under Admiral Cervera has just performed the greatest deed of heroism in the annals of the navy in the present century. It succumbed gloriously. It is a hard blow but it would be unworthy of Spanish hearts to despair...»

On July 12th, after a few days of sketchy fire and an ultimatum from General Shafter, Spanish General Toral, commander of the Spanish army in Santiago, began conversations with American Generals Miles and Wheeler. He had decided to ignore a deal that Calixto García was ready to negotiate with him. In the words of Toral:

---

[357] At the time Cervera's fleet was attempting to exit the harbor, a Spanish Infantry Regiment of 3,750 men under Colonel Federico Escario García had left Manzanillo and Bayamo and was arriving in Santiago to reinforce the troops in the city. They had spent close to 30,000 Mauser cartridges in 38 actions in a futile effort to reach Santiago de Cuba.

[358] Spanish battleships destroyed outside Santiago de Cuba's harbor: *Infanta Maria Teresa* (insignia ship for Cervera, 20 cannons, 10 machine guns and eight torpedo tubes); *Almirante Oquendo* and *Vizcaya* (each with 28 cannons, 2 machine guns and eight torpedo tubes); *Cristobal Colón* (with 38 guns, 2 machine guns and 4 torpedo tubes). Destroyers *Furor* and *Pluton*. Casualties: Spain had 326 dead, 215 wounded and 1,720 Spanish prisoners; the US had only one soldier dead.

[359] The fleet of Comodore Winfred Scott Schley blockading Santiago de Cuba had consisted of battleships *Iowa*, *Indiana*, *Oreon*, *Texas* and cruisers *Brooklyn* (insignia ship for Schley), *New York* (insignia ship for Sampson), *Gloucester* and *Vixen*, and others reaching 19 ships in total.

«Spain was willing to surrender its 22,000 men from the entire province of Oriente, provided the Cuban Army and particularly General Calixto García, were kept away from the negotiations and the surrender ceremony.»

With the surrender of the Spanish navy and army, the war was over; not so the independence of Cuba. The United States conceded sidelining Calixto García but requested that Spain would relinquish all claims of sovereignty and title to Cuba and evacuate the island before year end. Upon an insistence by the United States that the Cuban army would be recognized as a victorious contender, Spain had a counter-offer: It declared its willingness to cede its rights to the island of Puerto Rico rather than establish negotiations with any Cuban insurgent, officer, soldier, advisor or even chaplain. The Spanish proposal was accepted the US on August 12th, much to the consternation of Máximo Gómez, Calixto García and all other *mambí* leaders. [360] Before December 31, 1898, 130,000 Spanish officers and soldiers evacuated the island, with 15,000 military and civilian employees and their families. It became the end of Colonial Cuba. Disregarding four hundred years of calling Cuba "*the ever faithful island,*" Spain began to act like a scheming mother that does not let her children grow and be on their own and would rather see them humiliated or dead.

To the exile community in the United States, from New York, all along the east coast of the United States down to Key West, the years of *nostalgia* and the torments of expatriation had apparently come to an end. Many began to prepare themselves to return to Cuba and eagerly began to finish their studies, sell their businesses and pack their belongings. The *raison-d'être* of the exile organizations began to disappear. Contribu-

---

[360] As had occurred in 1868 during the Ten Year War, Cubans had numerous internal discordances during and after the Hispano-Cuban-American war of 1898. On August 13, 1898, the Cuban Government in Arms deposed Calixto García as Chief of the army in Oriente due to internal frictions. On September 24, 1898, Máximo Gómez resigned his position as General-in-Chief of the Army due to disagreements with the civilian authorities of the Republic in Arms.

tions to Martí's PRC began to decline. The party organizations began to dissolve. General Emilio Núñez, with good cause, cancelled all pending expeditions and began to *sell*, instead of buying weapons.

Images, top to bottom, left to right:

a 1898 issue of **Scientific American** showing young Alfonso XIII and his mother Queen Regent Maria Cristina de Austria;

General Calixto García with Lieutenant Andrew Summers Rowan, the man who brought to Cuba the **message to García**;

Major General **Calixto García Iñiguez** (1839-1898) was a prosperous landowner in Holguín, Cuba, dedicated to agribusiness. At the beginning of the 1868-1878 War of Cuban Independence, he joined the conflict on October 13, 1868, taking part in the battles of *Jiguaní, Santa Rita, Manzanillo, Baire* and *Boquerón*. He was surprised by Spanish troops in 1874 as he was left alone after the death of his escort; knowing he was defenseless, he fired a shot to his chin with his .45 caliber pistol to avoid be-
ing taken prisoner. The bullet went out his forefront without affecting the brain. When his mother Lucía Iñiguez was told her son was a prisoner of the Spaniards, he did not believe it; when told he had chosen to forgo life rather than be captured, she said: «That's indeed my son Calixto.»

Calixto was imprisoned until the *Pacto del Zanjón* at the end of the war. He went into voluntary exile in Paris and New York and in 1879 organized the *Guerra Chiquita* (Little War). With three of his sons he escaped to Spain after Spain's victory in 1880 and returned to Cuba with a well supplied expedition in March 25,1896. He had a long string of victories in the *1895 Hispano-Cuban-American War*, including the capture of *Tunas* and *Guisa*, the emotionally significant re-occupation of *Bayamo* and the battles of *Guáimaro* and *Yerba de Guinea*.

In May of 1898, on the world famous **Message to García**, he received a request for help from U.S. troops who were preparing to intervene in Cuba. García designed the US strategy to organize several US army columns and ensured the consent of Cuban Generalissimo Máximo Gómez, who authorized to cooperate as much as possible with the U.S. Army. On June 19, 1898, he reached the *Aserradero* (Sawmill) camp and had a meeting with the high command of the US troops, which fully approved his plan to encircle and capture Santiago de Cuba. The Cuban army under his command, with skillful use of mobile artillery, shared the weight of the fighting with the US Army and secured the capitulation of Santiago. He was denied a victorious entrance into the city when the Spaniards surrendered; it was one of the most distressing events of the war.

Calixto died of pneumonia in Washington DC on December 11, 1898, at the age of 59 while on a diplomatic mission and was buried temporarily at Arlington. At Washington's *Raleigh Hotel*, the place of his death, there is a plaque with a line from *Horace's Odes* placed in his honor. It reads:

«*Dulce et decorum est propatria mori.*»
(It is sweet and fitting to die for your country).

The Awe Inspiring Major General Calixto García Iñiguez

Images, top to bottom, left to right:

Cuban troops near Santiago de Cuba during the 1898 War.

A trail detachment showing **General Shafter** carried by a mule on his way to the front lines;

President McKinley with Generals Shafter, Wheeler, Lawton and Kieffer confering in Tampa in 1898.

Images, top to bottom, left to right:

The Spanish cruiser **Infanta Maria Teresa**, insignia ship for Admiral Cervera in 1898;

Cuban cavalry during the attack on Santiago in 1898;

Admiral **Pascual Cervera y Topete** (1839-1909), chief Spanish naval officer at the Battle of Santiago;

General **Emilio Nuñez** (1855-1922), commander in chief of the Cuban expeditionary forces, appointed by Martí in 1895;

Former Superintendent of the Naval Academy Admiral **William Thomas Sampson** in 1898.

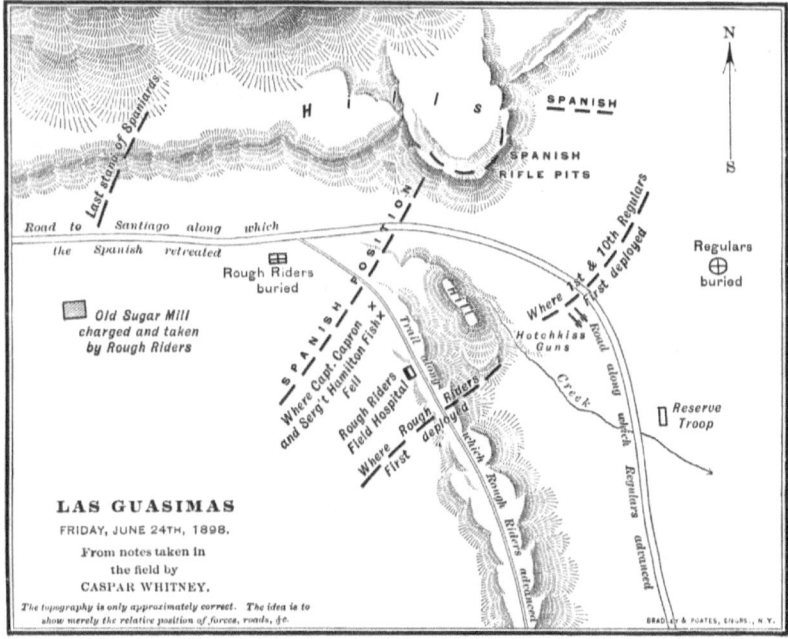

Images, top to bottom, left to right:

a meeting of (left to right) Generals Castillo, Shafter, Wheeler, Kent, Miles and García **planning the land battle** in Santiago de Cuba;
a map showing the positions of the US and Spanish armies during the Battle of **Las Guásimas**.

Images, top to bottom, left to right:

a drawing of the 10th USCavalry at **Las Guásimas** in 1898;
a drawing presenting the battle at **Fort El Viso** in *El Caney*;
a map showing the battles of **San Juan** and **El Caney** in 1898.

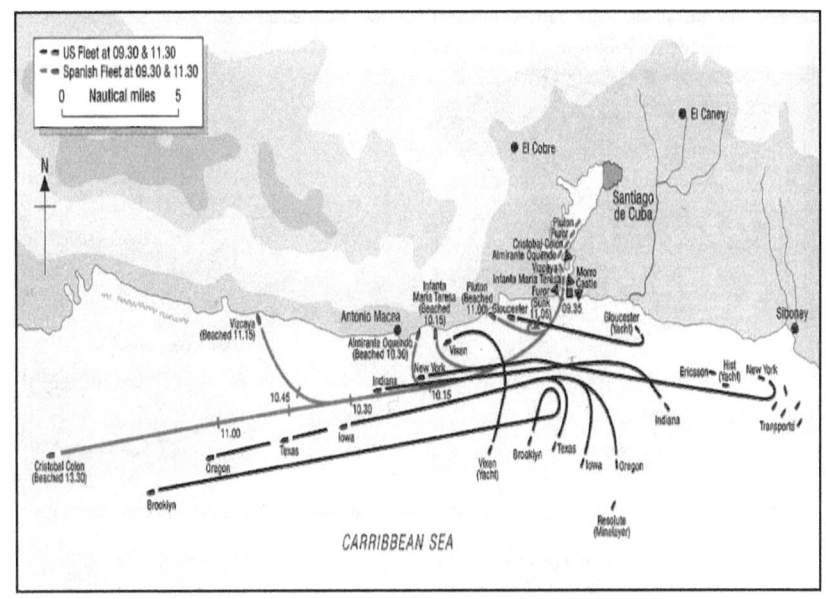

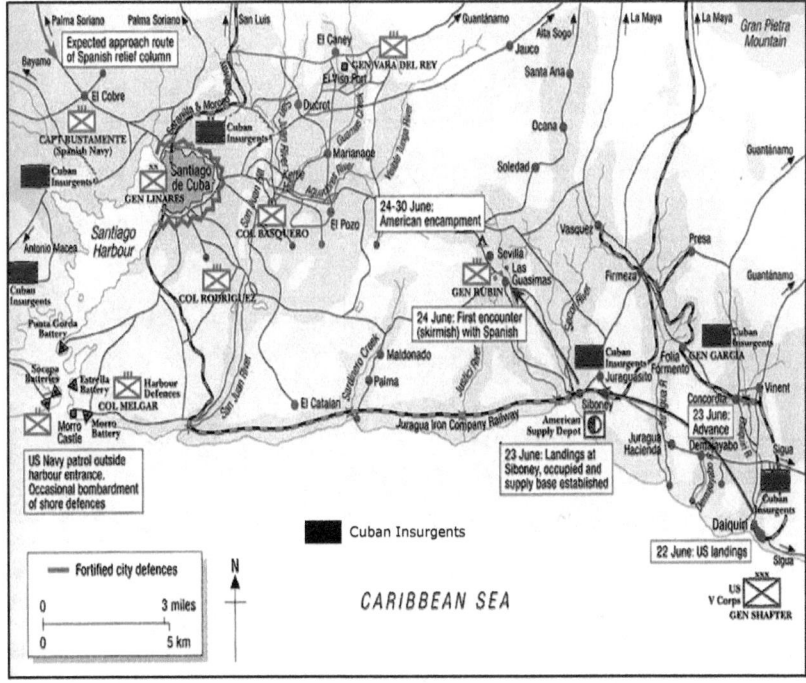

Images, top to bottom:

Two maps of the **US-Spain maneuvers** around Santiago de Cuba: at sea and on land.

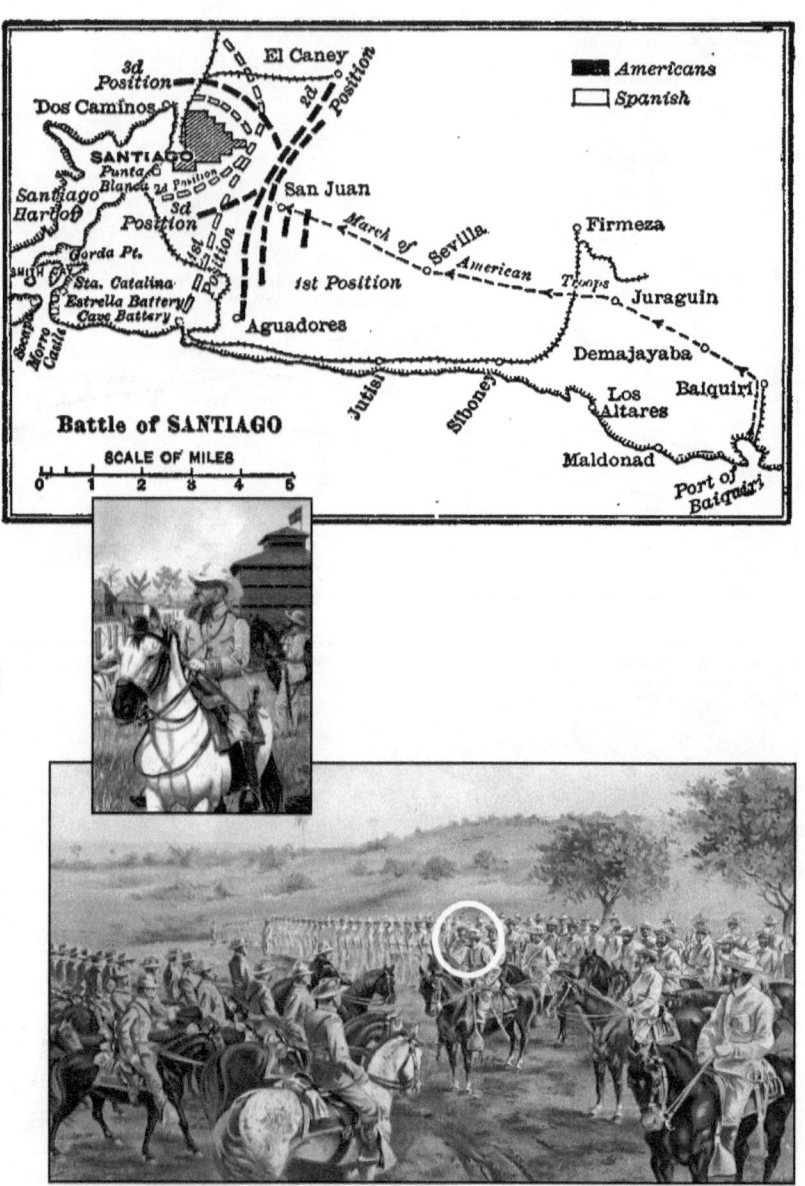

Images, top to bottom, left to right:

The positions of the Spanish and US troops during the **Battle of Santiago**;

Spanish General **Joaquín Vara del Rey** (1840-1898). With only 550 men and no artillery heroically defended *El Caney* for ten hours against 12,000 US soldiers.

The **surrender of the city of Santiago de Cuba** by Spanish General José Toral (1832-1904) on July 17, 1898.

Images, top to bottom:

Top two photos, the Spanish battleship ***Almirante Oquendo*** before and after the Naval Battle of Santiago de Cuba; bottom two photos, the Spanish Cruiser ***Vizcaya*** before and after the battle.

Images, top to bottom, left to right:

Three photos of Spanish troops embarking out of Cuba in 1898;

The *Philadelphia Evening* paper reporting on **General Toral's surrender** of the city of Santiago de Cuba;

Images, top to bottom:

Uncle Sam wodering if Cuba can play on its own after 1898;

a cartoon showing the **deceiving stance of France** with respect to the Spain-Cuba-US War in 1898;

A cartoon in the US press warning of the **false politeness** of Spain in 1898.

COLONIAL CUBA - 553

Epilogue

THE SPANISH 400 YEAR DOMINATION that ended in 1898 was followed by four years of US occupation that offered Cubans their first lessons on how to govern a country. The enlightened European civilization that Spain had brought to Cuba had been blighted by selfish economic and political impositions. After 1898, the constructive years of American government control were marred by the burden of the unwelcomed Platt amendment. Cubans in the island, unfortunately, replicated the undeserved *Black Legend* that the British had created against Spain with a mantra of *American Imperialism*. Cubans that for most of the XIX century had sought refuge in the US began to return to an independent Cuba, energized by the values and opportunities they witnessed in the American political and economic model. Over the first 50 years of republican life, however, they could never cast aside the resentment that their compatriots felt for the encroachment of US interests in Cuban affairs.

All great figures of the Wars of Independence had died when Cubans, in 1902, had to fly solo in their own governance: José Martí, Antonio and José Maceo, Calixto García, Ignacio Agramonte and most major generals of the wars were no longer on hand to lead Cuba in the task of shaping a new state. By default, the political alternatives to run the country were secondary military figures that, regardless of their best merits and intentions, had already clashed repeatedly among themselves during the wars. Witness the three Cuban requests to the US to bring order to Cuba invoking the Platt amendment; they brought US military interventions in Cuba in 1906, 1912 and 1917.

In the first years of the republic, no civilians disputed the pre-eminence of former Cuban militariy men to try their hands at ruling Cuba. A very well educated elite, men like Manuel Sanguily, Ramiro Guerra, Rafael Montoro, Enrique José Varona, Herminio Portell Vilá, Fernando Ortiz, Enrique Collazo, young Manuel Márquez Sterling, young Jorge Mañach and others, dedicated their energies to study and try to resolve the ineffectiveness and deficits of civil institutions, while remaining absent from the political sphere.

Soon, however, the recurrent instabilities of Cuba's economy, its commercial and trade dependency on the American markets and capital, the notion by American politicians that they had bestowed the gift of independence to the Cubans, and the suicidal failure of the 1933 revolution, poised a dilemma to Cuban intellectuals. Many of them and their successors began to trace all of Cuba's misfortunes to the policies of the US. Eventually, what ensued was a fatal disruption of Cuba's young democracy with a revolution that in 1959 sold itself as a final emancipation from US imperialism. It was a myth that clear-thinking Cubans in the island and in exile were not able to unmask. Neither could they debunk the folk tale that the Cuban landed and urban aristocracy had sold the country to foreign interests.

Thus the fervent hopes of Cuba to be free continued and continues to be discounted and snubbed by both the US and Spain. Cuba, in the hands of a wrong, malignant and incompetent crew, floats now like a rudderless ship in the Caribbean, unsure about what destiny will bring to its uncertain future. It is a sad legacy of 400 years of Spanish Colonial rule.

RAÚL EDUARDO CHAO
CORAL GABLES, FLORIDA
MAY 2014

Appendices

I Governors of Colonial Cuba
   1535 to 1898

II Dupuy de Lôme's Letter

III Weyler's Reconcentration
    Policy

IV Chronology of the Slave Trade
   in the Americas

 V October 10, 1868. The Ten Year
War Manifesto

I Governors of Colonial Cuba 1535 to 1898

TENURE	INCUMBENT	NOTES
SPANISH COLONIZATION		
1535 TO 1538	GONZALO DE GUZMÁN	
1538 TO 1542	HERNANDO DE SOTO	
1544 TO 1546	JUAN DE ÁVILA	
1546 TO 1548	ANTONIO DE CHÁVES	
1549 TO 1555	GONZALO PÉREZ DE ANGULO	
1556 TO 1565	DIEGO DE MAZARIEGOS	
1565 TO 1567	FRANCISCO GARCÍA OSORIO	
1567	FRANCISCO DE ZAYAS	
1567 TO 1574	PEDRO MENÉNDEZ DE AVILÉS	
1572 TO 1574	SANCHO PARDO DONLEBÚN	
1574 TO 1577	GABRIEL DE MONTALVO	
1577 TO 1579	FRANCISCO CARREÑO	
1579 TO 1584	GASPAR DE TORRES	
1584 TO 1589	GABRIEL DE LUJÁN	
1589 TO 1593	JUAN DE TEJEDA	
1593 TO 1602	JUAN MALDONALDO BARNUEVO	
1602 TO 1608	PEDRO VADÉS	
1608 TO 1616	GASPAR RUÍZ DE PEREDA	
1616 TO 1619	SANCHO DE ALQUIZA	
1620 TO 1624	FRANCISCO DE VENEGAS	
1624 TO 1626	DAMIÁN VELÁSQUEZ DE CONTRERAS	
1626 TO 1630	LORENZO DE CABRERA Y CORBERA	
1630 TO 1634	JUAN BITRIÁN DE VIAMONTE Y NAVARRA	
1634 TO 1639	FRANCISCO RIAÑO Y GAMBOA	
1639 TO 1647	ÁLVARO DE LUNA Y SARMIENTO	
1647 TO 1653	**DIEGO DE VILLALBA Y TOLEDO**, MARQUES DE CAMPO MARQUÉS DE CAMPO	
1653 TO 1654	FRANCISCO XELDER	

1654 TO 1656	JUAN DE MONTANOS BLÁZQUEZ	
1656 TO 1658	DIEGO RANGEL	
1658 TO 1663	JUAN DE SALAMANCA	
1663 TO 1664	RODRIGO DE FLORES Y ALDANA	
1664 TO 1670	FRANCISCO OREGÓN Y GASCÓN	
1670 TO 1680	FRANCISCO RODRÍGUEZ DE LEDESMA	
1680 TO 1685	JOSÉ FERNANDEZ CÓRDOBA PONCE DE LEÓN	
1685 TO 1687	MANUEL DE MURGUIA Y MENA	REMOVED FROM OFFICE
1687 TO 1689	DIEGO ANTONIO DE VIANA Y HINOJOSA	
1689 TO 1697	SEVERINO DE MANZANEDA SALINAS Y ROZAS	
1697 TO 1702	DIEGO DE CÓRDOBA LASSO, MARQUÉS DEL VADO	PROMOTED OUT CAPTAIN-GENERAL OF NEW
1702	PEDRO NICOLÁS BENÍTEZ DE LUGO	DIED SHORTLY AFTER ASSUMING OFFICE
1702 TO 1706	LUIS CHACÓN AND NICOLÁS CHIRINO VANDEVAL	INTERIM GOVERNORS
1706 TO JANUARY 1708	PEDRO ÁLVAREZ DE VILLARÍN	
18 JANUARY 1708 TO 18 FEBRUARY 1711	LAUREANO JOSÉ DE TORRES MARQUÉS DE CASA TORRES	FORMER GOVERNOR OF FLORIDA
26 MAY 1711 TO 1718	VICENTE DE RAJA	
23 JUNE 1718 TO 1724	GREGORIO GUAZO Y CALDERÓN FERNÁNDEZ DE LA VEGA	
29 SEPTEMBER 1724 TO 1734	DIONISIO MARTÍNEZ DE LA VEGA	
1734 TO 1746	FRANCISCO GÜEMES SÁENZ CONDE DE REVILLAGIGEDO	
1746	JUAN ANTONIO TINEO Y FUERTES	
1746 TO 1747	DIEGO PEÑALOSA	
1747 TO 1760	FRANCISCO ANTONIO CAGIGAL DE LA VEGA	
1760 TO 1761	PEDRO ALONSO	
1761 TO 1762	JUAN DE PRADO MAYERA PORTOCARRERO Y LUNA	

BRITISH OCCUPATION

12 AUGUST 1762 TO 1 JANUARY 1763	GEORGE KEPPEL, EARL OF ALBEMARLE	
1 JANUARY 1763 TO JULY 1763	WILLIAM KEPPEL	

SPANISH RESTORATION

1763 TO 1765	AMBROSIO DE FUNES VILLALPANDO, CONDE DE RICLA	
1765 TO 1766	DIEGO MANRIQUE	
1766 TO 1771	ANTONIO MARÍA DE BUCARELI Y URSÚA HINOSTROSA LASSO DE LA VEGA	
1771 TO 1777	FELIPE DE FONDESVIELA Y ONDEANO, MARQUÉS DE LA TORRE	
1777 TO 1780	DIEGO JOSÉ NAVARRO GARCÍA DE VALLADARES	

1781 TO 1782	**JUAN MANUEL DE CAGIGAL Y MONSERRAT**	
1782 TO 1785	**LUIS DE UNZAGA Y AMEZAGA**	
5 APRIL 1785 TO NOVEMBER 1785	**BERNARDO TRONCOSO MARTÍNEZ DEL RINCÓN**	
1 DECEMBER 1785 TO 1789	**JOSÉ MANUEL DE EZPELETA**	
18 APRIL 1789 TO 1790	**DOMINGO CABELLO Y ROBLES**	
1790 TO 1796	**LUIS DE LAS CASAS Y ARAGORRI**	
1796 TO 1799	**JUAN PROCOPIO BASSECOURT Y BRYAS**, CONDE DE SANTA CLARA	
1799 TO 1812	**SALVADOR DE MURO Y SALAZAR**, MARQUÉS DE SOMERUELOS	
1812 TO 1816	**JUAN RUÍZ DE APODACA**	
1816 TO 1819	**JOSÉ CIENFUEGOS**	
1819 TO 1819	**JUAN MARÍA ECHEVERRI**	
1819 TO 1821	**JUAN MANUEL DE CAGIGAL Y NIÑO**	
1821 TO 1822	**NICOLÁS DE MAHY Y ROMO**	
1822 TO 1823	**SEBASTIÁN KINDELÁN Y OREGÓN**, PROVISIONAL GOVERNOR	
1823 TO 1832	**FRANCISCO DIONISIO VIVES**	
1832 TO 1834	**MARIANO RICAFORT PALACÍN Y ABARCA**	
1834 TO 1838	**MIGUEL TACÓN**	
1838 TO JANUARY 1840	**JOAQUÍN DE EZPELETA**	
JANUARY 1840 TO 1841	**PEDRO TÉLLEZ GIRÓN**	
1841 TO SEPTEMBER 1843	**JERÓNIMO VALDÉS**	
SEPTEMBER 1843 TO OCTOBER 1843	**FRANCISCO JAVIER DE ULLOA**, PROVISIONAL GOVERNOR	
OCTOBER 1843 TO 1848	**LEOPOLDO O'DONNELL**, DUKE OF TETUAN	
1848 TO 1850	**FEDERICO RONCALI**	
1850 TO 1852	**JOSÉ GUTIÉRREZ DE LA CONCHA**	1ST TERM
1852 TO 1853	**VALENTÍN CAÑEDO**	
DECEMBER 1853 TO 1854	**JUAN GONZÁLEZ DE LA PEZUELA**	
1854 TO 1859	**JOSÉ GUTIÉRREZ DE LA CONCHA**	2ND TERM
1859 TO 1862	**FRANCISCO SERRANO Y DOMÍNGUEZ**, DUKE DE LA TORRE	
1862 TO MAY 1866	**DOMINGO DULCE**	1ST TERM
MAY 1866 TO NOVEMBER 1866	**FRANCISCO DE LERSUNDI Y ORMAECHEA**	1ST TERM
NOVEMBER 1866 TO SEPTEMBER 1867	**JOAQUÍN DEL MANZANO**	
SEPTEMBER 1867 TO DECEMBER 1867	**BLAS VILLATE**	1ST TERM
DECEMBER 1867 TO JANUARY 1869	**FRANCISCO DE LERSUNDI Y ORMAECHEA**	2ND TERM

JANUARY 1869 TO 2 JUNE 1869	**DOMINGO DULCE**	2ND TERM
2 JUNE 1868 TO 28 JUNE 1869	**FELIPE GINOVÉS DEL ESPINAR**, PROVISIONAL GOVERNOR	
28 JUNE 1869 TO 1870	**ANTONIO CABALLERO Y FERNÁNDEZ DE RODAS**	
1870 TO 1872	**BLAS VILLATE**	2ND TERM
1872 TO APRIL 1873	**FRANCISCO CEBALLOS Y VARGAS**	
APRIL 1873 TO NOVEMBER 1873	**CÁNDIDO PIELTAÍN**	
NOVEMBER 1873 TO 1874	**JOAQUÍN JOVELLAR Y SOLER**	1ST TERM
1874 TO MAY 1875	**JOSÉ GUTIÉRREZ DE LA CONCHA**	3RD TERM
MAY 1875 TO JUNE 1875	**BUENAVENTURA CARBÓ**, PROVISIONAL GOVERNOR	
JUNE 1875 TO JANUARY 1876	**BLAS VILLATE**	3RD TERM
JANUARY 1876 TO OCTOBER 1876	**JOAQUÍN JOVELLAR Y SOLER**	2ND TERM
OCTOBER 1876 TO FEBRUARY 1879	**ARSENIO MARTÍNEZ CAMPOS**	1ST TERM
FEBRUARY 1879 TO APRIL 1879	**CAETANO FIGUEROA**, PROVISIONAL GOVERNOR	
APRIL 1879 TO 1881	**RAMÓN BLANCO Y ERENAS**, MARQUÉS DE PEÑA PLATA	1ST TERM
1881 TO AUGUST 1883	**LUIS PRENDERGAST Y GORDON**, MARQUÉS DE VICTORIA DE LAS TUNAS	
AUGUST 1883 TO SEPTEMBER 1883	**TOMÁS Y REGNA**, PROVISIONAL GOVERNOR	
SEPTEMBER 1883 TO 1884	**IGNACIO MARÍA DEL CASTILLO**	
1884 TO 1886	**RAMÓN FAJARDO**	
1886 TO 1887	**EMILIO CALLEJA**	1ST TERM
1887 TO 1889	**SABAS MARÍN**	1ST TERM
13 MARCH 1889 TO 6 FEBRUARY 1890	**MANUEL SALAMANCA Y NEGRETE**	
FEBRUARY 1890 TO APRIL 1890	**JOSÉ SÁNCHEZ Y GÓMEZ**, PROVISIONAL GOVERNOR	
APRIL 1890 TO AUGUST 1890	**JOSÉ CHINCHILLA**	
AUGUST 1890 TO 1892	**CAMILO DE POLAVIEJA**	
1892 TO JULY 1893	**ALEJANDRO RODRÍGUEZ ARIAS**	
JULY 1893 TO SEPTEMBER 1893	**JOSÉ ARDERIUS**, PROVISIONAL GOVERNOR	
SEPTEMBER 1893 TO 1895	**EMILIO CALLEJA**	2ND TERM
1895 TO JANUARY 1896	**ARSENIO MARTÍNEZ CAMPOS**	2ND TERM
JANUARY 1896	**SABAS MARÍN**, PROVISIONAL GOVERNOR	2ND TERM
17 JANUARY 1896 TO OCTOBER 1897	**VALERIANO WEYLER**, 1ST DUKE OF RUBÍ	
OCTOBER 1897 TO 1898	**RAMÓN BLANCO Y ERENAS**, MARQUÉS DE PEÑA PLATA	2ND TERM
26 NOVEMBER 1898 ANUARY 1899	**ADOLFO JIMÉNEZ CASTELLANOS**	LAST SPANISH GOVERNOR

II Dupuy de Lôme's Letter to Canalejas

LEGACION DE ESPAÑA. WASHINGTON.

December 16, 1897

His Excellency Don José Canalejas.

My distinguished and dear friend:

You have no reason to ask my excuses for not having written to me, I ought also to have written to you but I have put off doing so because overwhelmed with work and nous sommes quittes.

The situation here remains the same. Everything depends on the political and military outcome in Cuba. The prologue of all this, in this second stage (phase) of the war, will end the day when the colonial cabinet shall be appointed and we shall be relieved in the eyes of this country of a part of the responsibility for what is happening in Cuba while the Cubans, whom these people think so immaculate, will have to assume it.

Until then, nothing can be clearly seen, and I regard it as a waste of time and progress, by a wrong road, to be sending emissaries to the rebel camp, or to negotiate with the autonomists who have as yet no legal standing, or to try to ascertain the intentions and plans of this government. The (Cuban) refugees will keep on returning one by one and as they do so will make their way into the sheep-fold, while the leaders in the field will gradually come back. Neither the one nor the other class had the courage to leave in a body and they will not be brave enough to return in a body.

The Message has been a disillusionment to the insurgents who expected something different; but I regard it as bad (for us).

Besides the ingrained and inevitable bluntness (grosería) about Weyler which is repeated by the press and public opinion in Spain, it shows what McKinley is a weak and a bidder for the admiration of the crowd besides being a would-be politician (politicastro) who tries to leave a door open behind himself while keeping on good terms with the jingoes of his party.

Nevertheless, whether the practical results of it (the Message) are to be injurious and adverse depends only upon ourselves.

I am entirely of your opinion; without a military end of the matter nothing will be accomplished in Cuba, and without a military and political settlement there will always be the danger of encouragement being given to the insurgents, by a part of the public opinion if not by the government.

I do not think sufficient attention has been paid to the part England is playing.

Nearly all the newspaper rabble that swarms in your hotels are Englishmen, and while writing for the Journal they are also correspondents of the most influential journals and reviews of London. It has been so ever since this thing began.

As I look at it, England's only object is that the Americans should amuse themselves with us and leave her alone, and if there should be a war, it would better stave off the conflict which she dreads but which will never come about.

It would be very advantageous to take up, even if only for effect, the question of commercial relations and to have a man of some prominence sent here, in order that I may make use him here to carry on a propaganda among the senators and others in opposition to the Junta and to try to win over the refugees.

So, Amblard is coming. I think he devotes himself too much to petty politics, and we have got to do something very big or we shall fail.

Adela returns your greeting, and we all trust that next year you may be a messenger of peace and take it as a Christmas gift to poor Spain.

Ever your attached friend and servant,

ENRIQUE DUPUY de LÔME.

III Weyler's Reconcentration Policy

On February 10, 1896 General Valeriano Weyler was appointed Captain General of the Island of Cuba by the Spanish Prime Minister Antonio Cánovas del Castillo. On arrival at the island, the General undertook to reorganize the army, reinforce the *trocha* (bloqued transit zone) Júcaro- Moron and create a new *trocha* Majana-Mariel, thus isolating the provinces of Havana and Pinar del Rio, where the Cuban army was operating under orders of *Mambí* Major General Antonio Maceo.

Weyler then ordered a reconcentration of country side residents to the cities, in order to stop the success of the liberation army, which depended on the support they received from the inhabitants of the villages near the zones where they operated. The measure was to relocate civilians in camps set up for this purpose in the major towns and cities; this led to the abandonment of crops and therefore a great famine that decimated the population of the island. It also resulted in the concentration of large numbers of people in camps lacking essential conditions and led to the spread of disease and the death of the most vulnerable individuals.

The proclamation giving the order of reconcentration read as follows:

> **Proclamation**
>
> ONE. All the inhabitants of rural areas or areas outside the fortified city line, will be concentrated in cities occupied by Spanish troops within eight days. Anyone who disobeys this order or is found outside the prescribed areas will be considered a rebel and tried as such.
>
> TWO. Is strictly prohibited without permits of the military authorities of the original residence of each individual, to remove food from the cities and move them anywhere, by sea or by land. Violators of these rules will be tried and sentenced as rebel collaborators.
>
> THREE. It is ordered to all cattle owners to take their animals to the nearest city or its surroundings, where they can receive adequate protection.

The irregular way of life in barracks, warehouses and abandoned shelters, with people sleeping without the slightest protection from the elements, created a situation particularly severe to the elderly, women and children. There was no separation between men and women, and there were no toilets, or beds. Disease among these families increased by the day. Spanish troops occupied so many buildings that there was none left with suitable and decent accommodation for the rest of the population. The reconcentrados lived in little more than pigsties without clean air. That, coupled with food shortages, resulted in hundreds of deaths.

On November 8, 1897, after the mandate of Weyler had ceased following the assassination of Canovas del Castillo, it took a month before the privations and sufferings of the population found relief. It was estimated that by December 1896, four hundred thousand Cubans non-combatants had been *reconcentrados* in different sites; Weyler's was a policy of genocide and extermination. Before Cubans began to fall dead in the fields of battle, the amount of dead persons by disease an hunger amounted to approximately one-third of the rural population of Cuba.

IV Chronology of the Slave Trade in the Americas

1442	Anthony Gonsalves introduces in Portugal ten blacks, obtained in the Rio de Oro, in exchange for Moor prisoners.
1502	Nicolas de Ovando gets a permit to move blacks from southern Spain to Hispaniola.
1517	Bartolomé de las Casas asks Carlos V to replace native indians with blacks for the work in mines.
1562	John Hawkins transports to the West Indies the first shipment of African slaves under the British flag.
1619	The British introduce the first slaves in Virginia.
1642	France begins to introduce African slaves in Martinique.
1663	The Italians Grillo and Lomelin contract with Spain to transport 24,000 slaves to America.
1695	The Cachu Company (Franco-Portuguese) contracts with Spain the annual sale of 4,000 slaves.
1711	The French Company of the Indies contracts with Spain to transport blacks to Cuba for an unknown number of years.
1713	England obtains from Spain (by the Peace of Utrecht), the monopoly of introducing African slaves in its colonies.
1715	Ricardo O'Farrill establishes in Havana the first factory for the importation and sale of slaves.
1773	The Marquis of Casa Erile gets a license to bring slaves to Cuba.
1777	Spain acquires Fernando Poo to establish a slave trade.
1789	A Spanish Royal Statute authorizes foreigners and Spaniards the importation of African slaves in Spanish colonies.
1791	Spaniards are authorized to purchase slaves anywhere.
1801	Toussaint Louverture takes of Santo Domingo and slavery ceases.
1807	England prohibits slave ships to be repaired in its dominions.
1808	England prohibits the entry of slaves inall of its dominions.
1808	The United States prohibits admission of slaves into its territory.
1819	France abolishes the slaving of men and women.
1820	Spain abolishes slaving south of Ecuador.
1821	William Wilberforce (1759-1833) founds and presides *The American Colonization Society* (founding of Liberia).
1825	Slavery is abolished in the south of South America.
1826	Brazil abolishes the slave trade north of Ecuador.
1829	Mexico abolishes slavery.
1831	England and France signed a treaty abolishing of the slave trade.
1838	Slavery ceases in the British dominions.
1845	Slavery ceases in Colombia, Venezuela and Ecuador.
1847	All Spanish slaving factories on Sierra Leone and Liberia destroyed.
1848	The French established Libreville, a colony of free blacks.
1849	Slavery is abolished in France.
1863	Holland abolishes slavery.
1865	Slavery completely ceases in the United States.
1886	Slavery is abolished in Cuba.

V October 10, 1868. The Ten Year War Manifesto

Speaking from the steps of his sugar mill, and calling upon men of all races and walks of life to join the uprising, Carlos Manuel de Cespedes gave the following speech, during which he unfurled and raised the new flag of an independent Cuba, and rang the bell tower of his sugar mill in celebration of the proclamation:

> In rebelling against Spanish tyranny, we want the world to know the reasons for our action.
>
> Spain governs us with blood and iron; she imposes on us levies and taxes as she pleases; she has deprived us of political, civil, and religious freedoms; we are subjected to martial law in times of peace; without due process, and in defiance of Spanish law, we are arrested, exiled and even executed. We are prohibited free assembly, and if allowed to assemble, it is only under the watchful eyes of government agents and military officers; and if anyone clamors for a remedy to these abuses, or for any of the many other evils, Spain declares them a traitor.
>
> Spain burdens us with rapacious bureaucrats who exploit our national treasure and consume the product of our noble labor. So that we may not know our rights, it maintains our people ignorant of those rights, and to ensure that the people are kept ignorant, she prevents the people from participating in responsible public administration.
>
> Without impending military danger, and without any reason or justification, Spain imposes on us an unnecessary and costly military presence, whose sole purpose is to terrorize and humiliate us.
>
> Spain's system of customs is so perverse that we have already perished from its misery and she exploits the fertility of our land while raising the price of its fruits. She imposes every imaginable obstacle to prevent the advancement of our *criollo* population. Spain limits our free speech and the written word, and she prevents us from participating in the intellectual progress of other nations.
>
> Several times Spain has promised to improve our condition and she has deceived us time and time again. We are now left no other recourse than to bear arms against her tyranny, and by doing this, to save our honor, our lives, and our property.
>
> We appeal now to Almighty God, and to the faith and good will of civilized nations. Our aspirations are to attain our sovereignty and universal suffrage.
>
> (continued)

(continuation)

Our aim is to enjoy the benefits of freedom, for whose use, God created man. We sincerely profess a policy of brotherhood, tolerance, and justice, and to consider all men equal, and to not exclude anyone from these benefits, not even Spaniards, if they choose to remain and live peacefully among us.

Our aim is that the people participate in the creation of laws, and in the distribution and investment of the contributions.

Our aim is to abolish slavery and to compensate those deserving compensation. We seek freedom of assembly, freedom of the press and the freedom to bring back honest governance; and to honor and practice the inalienable rights of men, which is the foundations of the independence and the greatness of a people.

Our aim is to throw off the Spanish yoke, and to establish a free and independent nation.

If Spain recognizes our rights, it will have in Cuba an affectionate daughter; if she persists in subjugating us, we are resolved to die before remaining subject to her brutal domination.

We have chosen a commander to whom will be given the mission of fighting this war. We have authorized a provisional administrator to collect contributions and to manage the needs of a new administration.

When Cuba is free, it will have a constitutional government created in an enlightened manner.

signed:

Carlos Manuel de Cespedes,
Jaime M. Santiesteban,
Bartolomé Masó,
Juan Hall,
Francisco J. Céspedes,
Pedro Céspedes,
Manuel Calvar,
Isaías Masó,
Eduardo Suástegui,
Miguel Suástegui,
Rafael Tornés,
Manuel Santiesteban,
Manuel Socarrás,
Agustín Valerino,
Rafael Masó,
Eligio Izaguirre.

Alphabetical Index

Acera del Louvre, 340
Adelantado, 76, 116, 130, 133, 145
Al-Andalus, 29, 30, 31
Alejandro Ramirez, 254
Alfaro, 453
Alfonso XII, 330, 332, 354, 390, 433, 486, 521
Alfonso XIII, 433, 536
Amadeo I of Savoy, 331
Antonio Maceo, 146, 301, 340, 376, 405, 406, 408, 410, 411, 412, 428, 433, 434, 435, 468, 469, 470, 471, 482, 488, 491, 505, 562
Aserradero, 540
Astillero, 214
Atahualpa, 78, 79, 80, 81, 108, 109
Autonomists, 485
Azcárate, 426
Baire, 465, 507
Baraguá, 2, 407, 411, 412, 413, 432, 453, 470, 482, 492
Bartolomé Masó, 405, 465, 470, 484, 504, 506, 508, 536, 565
Bayamo, 15, 58, 117, 121, 129, 146, 147, 160, 161, 162, 170, 227, 242, 253, 256, 279, 280, 283, 284, 294, 316, 318, 355, 357, 358, 375, 376, 391, 404, 410, 448, 454, 484, 519, 525, 541, 544
Bishop Diego Evelino de Compostela, 182, 183
Bishop Fray Jerónimo Valdés, 194
Bishop Juan de las Cabezas Altamirano, 159
Bishop Juan José Díaz de Espada, 241, 244, 263, 281

Bishop Morell de Santa Cruz, 152
Blanco, 520
Bonachea, 410, 411, 425, 432, 448
Buccaneers, 91, 92, 101, 169, 170, 172, 173, 179, 197, 198, 199
Cabeza de Vaca, 83, 107, 130
Calixto García, 284, 389, 391, 410, 411, 426, 428, 430, 448, 488, 489, 506, 507, 508, 519, 524, 525, 526, 535, 536, 537, 539, 540, 541, 542, 544, 554
Camagüey, 15, 77, 117, 147, 301, 304, 353, 356, 358, 370, 373, 375, 376, 387, 388, 389, 390, 391, 392, 405, 406, 407, 408, 409, 410, 426, 448, 454, 464, 470, 485, 489, 492, 506, 508, 519, 524
Cánovas del Castillo, 338, 354, 359, 391, 411, 427, 432, 449, 467, 486, 487, 508, 562
Capitol, 6
Carlos Manuel de Céspedes, 256, 356, 357, 369, 372, 376, 390, 391, 394, 404, 410, 505
Cassava, 22
Castillo, 427, 430, 449, 454, 486, 487
Cervera, 525, 526, 536, 538, 540, 541
Charles II, 185, 186, 197
Charles V, 66, 77, 128, 130, 133, 134
Christopher Myngs, 198
Ciego de Avila, 299, 406

Cienfuegos, 56, 64, 254, 264, 292, 294, 394, 407, 429, 434, 471, 472, 485, 506, 525, 559
Cimarrones, 132, 147
Cirilo Villaverde, 240, 269, 301, 321, 322, 353, 432, 435
Claudio Martínez de Pinillos, 267, 269, 279, 282, 309
Colegio Carraguao, 445, 446
Colonial Cuba, 2, 7, 8, 10, 89, 152, 292, 293, 535, 542, 556, 557
Columbus, 7, 9, 13, 14, 15, 37, 38, 39, 40, 43, 44, 45, 46, 47, 48, 55, 56, 57, 63, 64, 65, 76, 89, 90, 105, 106, 107, 116, 128, 129, 130, 149, 226, 292
Conde de O'Reilly, 211
Conde de Pozos Dulces, 240, 335, 337
Conde de Ricla, 211, 224
Conquistadores, 7, 16, 20, 73, 75, 76, 78, 79, 80, 81, 82, 83, 89, 106, 107, 110, 116, 118, 134, 145, 169
Constitution of 1812, 238
Count of Albemarle, 211, 215
Countess of Merlin, 228, 253
Dauntless, 489, 507, 524
Diario de la Marina, 300, 388, 491, 509, 518, 535
Diego Columbus, 107, 128
Diego Velázquez, 57, 58, 76, 106, 107, 116, 117, 128, 161
Domingo del Monte, 162, 240, 282, 314, 333, 352, 371, 535

Domingo Dulce, 338, 339, 355, 359, 371, 559, 560
Dupuy de Lôme, 8, 488, 508, 523, 556, 561
Eduardo Facciolo, 322
El Cobre, 149, 168, 201, 301
El Faro Industrial, 321, 338
El Fígaro, 432
El Moro Muza, 337
El Morro, 144, 163, 169, 180, 212, 215, 300, 526
El Principe, 212, 225
Emilio Nuñez, 428, 463, 465, 543
Encomiendas, 58, 63, 64, 65, 122, 129, 144
Enrique Collazo, 464, 506
Espejo de Paciencia, 152, 161, 162
Estrada Palma, 407, 408, 425, 454, 462, 508
Felipe II, 66, 91, 93, 145, 147, 148, 149, 159, 161, 163, 171, 242, 329
Félix Varela, 183, 226, 227, 253, 255, 256, 267, 269, 283, 321, 333
Ferdinand, 30, 37, 38, 39, 47, 56, 57, 64, 65, 121, 133, 142, 144, 184, 239, 303
Fermín Valdés Domínguez, 194, 433, 453, 504
Fernandina, 64, 254, 279, 435, 453, 463, 464, 465, 466, 467
Fernando VII, 181, 242, 250, 252, 253, 256, 266, 267, 269, 270, 278, 279, 281, 294, 295, 298, 486
Figueredo Socarrás, 412
Flor Crombet, 412, 453, 464
Francisco de Arango y Parreño, 224, 228, 240, 255, 267, 285

Francisco Dionisio Vives, 264, 265, 278, 559
Francisco Pizarro, 55, 76, 78, 79, 81, 82, 106, 108, 109
Francisco Vicente Aguilera, 268, 355, 356, 374, 446
François L'Olonnais, 172
Frédéric Miahle, 242
Gabriel de la Concepción Valdés, 240, 301, 322
General Donato Mármol, 375
General Francisco Serrano, 331, 338, 359
General Juan Prim, 331, 359
Ge-neral Vicente García, 392
Gertrudis Gómez de Avellaneda, 253, 284, 321, 337, 390
Gilberto Girón, 161, 162, 163
Gonzalo de Guzmán, 128, 129, 131, 143, 557
Gonzalo de Quesada, 462, 464, 465, 466, 484, 506, 523
Guáimaro, 2, 358, 373, 391, 470, 482, 483, 508, 544
Guanahatabeyes, 13, 15, 16
Guantánamo, 412
Guerra Chiquita, 430, 431
Guillermón Moncada, 428, 468, 538
Habana, 58, 89, 90, 146, 147, 179, 180, 181, 182, 214, 215, 228, 253, 254, 263, 281, 282, 296, 301, 310, 320, 322, 329, 334, 338, 339, 386, 426, 432, 445, 446, 489, 535
Hatuey, 57, 58, 64, 107, 116, 117, 120, 121
Havana-Güines, 309
Henry Morgan, 169, 173, 199
Hernán Cortés, 37, 55, 57, 76, 77,

106, 107, 108, 128, 174
Hernando de Soto, 80, 81, 109, 133, 141, 143, 226, 557
Hispaniola, 15, 16, 21, 45, 46, 47, 48, 55, 56, 57, 63, 65, 66, 76, 81, 91, 101, 116, 118, 119, 128, 129, 131, 133, 159, 160, 161, 162, 170, 173, 174, 201, 226, 241, 563
Holguín, 58, 122, 147, 179, 183, 184, 253, 284, 316, 357, 389, 391, 409, 411, 412, 429, 430, 469, 519, 544
Ignacio Agramonte, 300, 340, 358, 389, 390, 406, 554
Inés de Bobadilla, 141, 143
Isabel, 30, 37, 38, 39, 44, 47, 55, 65, 66, 121, 133, 142, 143, 200, 267, 278, 279, 281, 294, 301, 330, 331, 332, 339, 340, 354, 356, 369, 390, 433, 486
Jean Baptiste Vermay, 263
Jimaguayú, 2, 390, 470, 483, 508
Joaquín de Agüero, 300, 318, 319, 333
José Agustín Caballero, 227, 253, 283
José Antonio Aponte, 252, 315, 316
José Antonio Saco, 152, 227, 240, 269, 281, 282, 283, 284, 310, 321, 329, 338, 353, 354, 411, 431
José Bonaparte, 242, 251, 252, 254, 270
José Francisco Lemus, 268, 304
José Gutiérrez de la Concha, 302, 559, 560

José María Heredia, 240, 268, 269, 285, 304
Juan Bautista Spotorno, 392, 405
Juan Clemente Zenea, 284, 389
Juan Gualberto, 465
Juan Ríus Rivera, 507
Julián del Casal, 338, 340, 435
Julio Sanguily, 389, 406, 535
Junta de Información, 338, 339, 353, 354, 356
Key West, 425, 465, 542
Kingston, 394
La Cabaña, 212, 215, 222, 225
La Escalera, 448
La Fuerza, 91, 143, 169, 256, 265
La Gloriosa, 331
La Punta, 180, 181, 215
La Voz de Cuba, 388, 389
Lacret, 412, 506
Las Casas, 7, 14, 58, 63, 64, 65, 66, 67, 73, 74, 75, 77, 90, 117, 119, 224, 227
Las Guásimas, 391, 539
Leopoldo O'Donnell, 300, 314, 330, 559
Leyenda Negra, 66, 67
López de Queralta, 465
Louis Moreau Gottschalk, 329
Loynaz, 454, 486
Lucayans, 14
Maceo, 425, 426, 428, 429, 448, 451, 452, 453, 464, 467, 484, 485, 486, 504, 505, 506
Maine, 142, 520, 521, 522, 523, 525
Mal Tiempo, 471, 472, 485, 504
Manigua, 374, 412, 430, 451, 469
Manuel de Jesús Calvar, 376
María Cristina de Austria, 536
Marianao, 504
Mármol, 412

Martínez Campos, 332, 359, 391, 407, 409, 410, 411, 412, 413, 426, 427, 429, 453, 468, 470, 472, 484, 485, 486, 487, 488, 491, 504, 560
Matanzas, 55, 117, 148, 170, 179, 183, 256, 266, 268, 284, 299, 301, 304, 314, 316, 333, 336, 371, 391, 433, 435, 445, 446, 447, 465, 471, 488, 524, 525, 526
Máximo Gómez, 116, 284, 338, 375, 376, 389, 391, 392, 404, 405, 406, 407, 408, 409, 410, 425, 426, 429, 432, 434, 448, 449, 451, 452, 454, 462, 464, 467, 468, 469, 470, 471, 472, 485, 488, 489, 491, 504, 506, 507, 508, 509, 520, 524, 536, 542, 544
Mayía Rodríguez, 410, 462, 464, 506, 535
McKinley, 523, 537
Message to García, 526, 544
Miguel Aldama, 301, 337, 356, 393, 406, 410
Miguel Tacón y Rosique, 279, 294
Miguel Teurbe-Tolón, 256, 304, 336
Moncada, 428, 429, 465
Naboríes, 20
Napoleon Bonaparte, 237, 240, 254
Narciso López, 226, 269, 284, 299, 300, 302, 319, 320, 321, 333, 335, 373, 448
New York Journal, 522, 523
New York Tribune, 573
New York World, 523
Nicolás Azcárate, 268, 354, 355, 356

Nicolás de Ovando, 47, 55, 57, 63, 107
Niobe, 394
Pact of Zanjón, 391
Panchito Gómez Toro, 454
Pánfilo de Narváez, 77, 89, 107, 117, 118, 121, 128, 129, 130
Papel Periódico, 224, 228, 283, 351
Patria, 506
Pedro Menéndez de Avilés, 91, 145, 557
Peralejo, 469, 470, 484, 505
Pinar del Río, 170, 171, 180, 240, 302, 319, 471, 488, 489, 491, 492, 504, 507, 526, 562
Polavieja, 413, 430, 431, 433, 489, 560
Práxedes Mateo Sagasta, 389, 391, 508
Puerto Príncipe, 58, 117, 145, 146, 161, 162, 169, 180, 184, 199, 266, 268, 284, 299, 300, 316, 317, 318, 319, 353, 357, 389, 391
Quesada, 452, 462, 467, 504, 506, 536
Quintín Banderas, 429, 465, 485, 504
Ramón de la Sagra, 255, 269
Reconquista, 30, 58, 121
Reforma, 452
Remedios, 117, 172, 183, 198, 201, 316, 430, 506
Remington, 393
Revista Bimestre Cubana, 227, 281
Roloff, 464, 485
Roosevelt, 522, 523, 524, 539
Rubens, 463, 466, 520
Sagasta, 449
Salvador Cisneros Betancourt, 268, 390, 392, 405, 470
Sampson, 539, 540

Sancti Spíritus, 58, 117, 146, 169, 183, 199, 388, 409, 430, 432, 489
Sanguily, 465, 505
Santiago de Cuba, 58, 77, 92, 108, 128, 129, 131, 132, 141, 145, 146, 147, 148, 149, 152, 168, 169, 170, 171, 172, 179, 184, 198, 199, 201, 228, 239, 253, 280, 284, 292, 300, 301, 338, 376, 389, 390, 393, 394, 404, 413, 428, 431, 432, 465, 488, 489, 525, 526, 536, 537, 539, 541, 544
Santiago de las Vegas, 179, 183, 214, 336
Sebastian de Ocampo, 55, 117
Shafter, 539, 540
Siboneyes, 15, 20, 59
Sir Francis Drake, 93
Sociedad Económica de Amigos del País, 255, 263, 282, 283
Society of Jesus, 134, 200, 233, 254
Suns and Rays of Bolívar, 304
Tainos, 13, 14, 15, 16, 20, 21, 22, 23, 27, 46, 57, 58, 59, 63, 65, 77, 89, 117, 118, 119, 129, 132, 146, 147, 161
Teatro Principal, 292, 297, 303, 329
Teatro Tacón, 293, 298, 337, 426, 433
Templete, 90, 97, 263, 268
Ten Year War, 425, 428, 445, 487, 507
Tenochtitlán, 74, 77, 78
Theodorus de Bry, 67
Tínima, 117, 169
Toison de Oro, 280
Tomás Estrada Palma, 284, 406, 409, 425, 469
Tornado, 393, 394
Tratado de Tordesillas, 46
Trocha, 470, 485, 489, 519, 562
University of Havana, 227, 228, 255, 269, 355, 469
Valeriano Weyler, 358, 359, 376, 433, 470, 487, 488, 489, 507, 560, 562
Varona, 428
Vicente García, 412, 413
Virginius, 390, 393, 394
Voluntarios, 355, 370, 371, 373, 388, 389, 425, 427, 486, 509
Weyler, 486, 487, 505, 519, 520
Ximénez de Cisneros, 65
Yaya, 483, 508
Zanjón, 412, 413, 425, 426, 427, 428, 430, 431, 448, 449
Zayas, 465, 485

Raúl Eduardo Chao *received his PhD from Johns Hopkins University at age 25 and after a brief stint in industry spent 18 years in academe, as full professor and Department Chairman at the* **Universities of Puerto Rico** *and* **Detroit***. In 1986 he founded a very successful management consultancy, assisting companies and government agencies to develop positive work environments and process improvement techniques as the means to secure improvements in productivity and quality.*

The Systema Group *had as clients many Fortune 100 companies and Federal and State organizations, both in the US and abroad. As its Chairman, Chao has written a dozen books and numerous articles in newspapers and reviewed journals. He and his wife Olga live in Coral Gables, Florida and spend long periods of time in Paris.*

This book was printed in the United States.

The font used throughout the text has been **Palatino Linotype**, one of the classic old style serif typefaces inspired by designs of the 16th century Italian calligrapher **Giambattista Palatino**. The font was reissued in 1948 by **Hermann Zapf** for the Linotype Foundy, the company created by Ottmar Mergenthaler, a German immigrant to the U.S. who invented the revolutionary line typesetting machine that was first used in 1890 by the **New York Tribune**.

The font used in the covers, title pages, headings and ornaments is **P22 Franklin Caslon**, a faithful interpretation of the type used by Benjamin Franklin in the 1750's in his printing shop and particularly in his **Poor Richard's Almanac**. This font was developed in 2006 by the International House of Fonts for the Philadelphia Museum of Art to commemorate the 300th birthday of our most remarkable Founding Father.

The font accompanying the photos and illustrations is Verdana; a humanist sans-serif typeface designed by **Matthew Carter** for *Microsoft Corporation*, with hand-hinting done by **Tom Rickner**, then at *Monotype*. Demand for such a clear and easy to read typeface was recognized by **Virginia Howlett** of *Microsoft's* typography group. The name "Verdana" is based on a mix of *verdant* (something green, as in the Seattle area and the Evergreen state of Washington), and *Ana* (the name of Howlett's eldest daughter

www.ingramcontent.com/pod-product-compliance
Lightning Source LLC
Chambersburg PA
CBHW022209090526
44584CB00012BA/355